William Carlos Williams

Poet from Jersey

Reed Whittemore

illustrated with photographs

HOUGHTON MIFFLIN COMPANY BOSTON 1975

To Florence Herman Williams

◄ ◄ ◄ ◄ ◄ ◄ ◄ ◄ ◄ ◄ ◄ ◄ ◄ ◄ ◄

The author is grateful to New Directions Publishing
Corporation for permission to quote from *Collected
Earlier Poems* by William Carlos Williams, copyright
1938 by New Directions Publishing Corporation and
Collected Later Poems by William Carlos Williams,
copyright 1944 by William Carlos Williams. Further
acknowledgments appear on pages v–viii.

Library of Congress Cataloging in Publication Data
Whittemore, Reed, 1919–
    William Carlos Williams, poet from Jersey.
    Bibliography: p.   Includes index.
    1. Williams, William Carlos, 1883–1963
Biography. I. Title.
PS3545.I544Z95   811′.5′2   75-20274
ISBN 0-395-20735-5

Printed in the United States of America

W 10 9 8 7 6 5 4 3 2 1

William Carlos Williams

Poet from Jersey

Also by Reed Whittemore

Heroes and Heroines
An American Takes a Walk
The Self-Made Man
The Boy from Iowa
The Fascination of the Abomination
Poems, New and Selected
From Zero to the Absolute
Fifty Poems Fifty
The Mother's Breast & The Father's House

Acknowledgments

WILLIAM CARLOS WILLIAMS hated to throw anything away. With the help of his wife, Florence, who was more orderly than he, the Williams attic at 9 Ridge Road in Rutherford, New Jersey, filled up slowly over the half century of their marriage with letters and manuscripts. As temptation for future biographers the attic was eventually emptied upon academia, chiefly upon the poetry room of the Lockwood Memorial Library of the State University of New York at Buffalo, and upon the Collection of American Literature, Beinecke Rare Book and Manuscript Library, Yale University. At Buffalo and Yale the WCW scholars have labored hard and produced, in the last ten or fifteen years, a steady flow of books and articles as well as dozens of unpublished school treatises; but oddly these have, up to now, been largely critical rather than biographical.

I say "oddly" both because WCW's life is unusually accessible at these libraries and because WCW himself wrote steadily about his life. He did so not only in his autobiography, which has to be any biographer's bible, but also in his poetry, fiction and drama. His life is thus constantly recorded in his creative work, and if the biographer is at a handicap because WCW has already done much of the work for him, the critic who wishes dutifully to stick to the art is at a handicap because the life keeps illuminating the art. In any event, this book, focusing on the life, is also an effort to contribute something of interest and novelty about the art.

As the selective bibliography in the back indicates I have not tried to be comprehensive in reading and assessing WCW criticism but have concentrated upon the biographical elements in his own published work, and upon the letters and manuscripts in the libraries. I am indebted to the staffs of the libraries, that is, to the imaginative steady help of Karl Gay and his staff at Lockwood and Donald Gallup and his staff at Beinecke. I am also grateful to Neil E. Baldwin and Steven Meyers at Buffalo, for their having produced a most useful bibliography of Lockwood's WCW holdings, as well as personally leading me through a few manuscript thickets; and to Norman Holmes Pearson at Yale who knows my subject better than I do and provided advice and comfort.

Beyond New Haven and Buffalo I acknowledge the assistance of the staff of the Clifton Waller Barrett Library of the University of Virginia where good collections of WCW letters to Kathleen and Clayton Hoaglund, and to Fred Miller, are deposited. I also benefitted from a talk with Mrs. Eckert of the Rutherford Public Library and from looking at the WCW holdings of the New York Public Library, the Fairleigh Dickinson Library in Rutherford and the McKeldin Library of the University of Maryland. At Maryland, where I teach and where most of the writing of the book took place, I found especially useful the Library's good collection of the literary magazines of the early century.

Until 1975 the only extensively biographical study of WCW was Mike Weaver's *William Carlos Williams* (New York: Oxford, 1971), a volume from which I have perhaps derived more information than the footnotes indicate. One useful new work by Robert Coles has entered the biographical arena, *William Carlos Williams: The Knack of Survival in America,* published by Rutgers University Press in 1975, and the author was kind enough to allow me to read it in manuscript; it deals chiefly with WCW's social vision, especially in his thirties stories and in the Stecher trilogy. Among critical works I found myself indebted to Jerome Mazzaro's *William Carlos Williams: The Later Poems* (Ithaca: Cornell, 1973), which seems to me the most suggestive nonbiographical study I have come upon. Then there is Emily Mitchell Wallace's most thorough *Bibliography of William Carlos Williams* (Middletown, Conn.: Wesleyan University Press, 1968), which is second only to WCW's autobiography as a necessary reference book. (I also wish to thank Emily Wallace for giving me a fine tour of the University of Pennsylvania haunts of WCW and Pound, filling me in with lore of their early days, and providing me with a photograph of WCW's self-portrait, which is reproduced in the picture section.)

Others who have been helpful in filling me in with information about WCW's life are Kenneth Burke, David McDowell, Clayton and Kathleen Hoaglund, Fred Martin and, most particularly, James

Laughlin, who as WCW's publisher for many years knows perhaps more about WCW's writing life than anyone else who is not a Williams. Mr. Laughlin was kind enough to read the manuscript and make a number of important suggestions and corrections; he did not wholly agree with my approach to WCW but remained immensely considerate and obliging, as well as being most helpful with details of rights and permissions.

But it is of course to the Williams family that I am most indebted: to Mrs. Florence Williams for sitting with me for long sessions at 9 Ridge Road, telling me of her own rich past and her husband's triumphs and tragedies, and allowing me to read many letters that have been sealed away until now, particularly the letters that WCW wrote to her from Leipzig in 1909–1910 before their marriage; to sons William Eric and Paul for their kindness and warmth as well as their excellent memories (and to William Eric for helping with pictures, letters and dozens of details) ; and to cousin William Wellcome and his son for a pleasant afternoon on the old Williams-Wellcome shore property in West Haven, Connecticut.

The John Simon Guggenheim Foundation granted me a fellowship in 1974–1975 which, combined with a sabbatical from the University of Maryland, made it possible for me to devote full time to finishing the book. And the Graduate School of the University of Maryland backed me with a grant of travel funds in 1973–1974. I thank these institutions and thank also my Maryland students in a 1974 summer graduate seminar devoted to WCW. They were not only imaginative readers of WCW but had an enthusiasm for him that a biographer in midstream badly needs. Also I wish to thank four colleagues at Maryland: Merrill Leffler who helped me in the book's early stages, and Ruthven Todd, Jackson Bryer and Jean Morgan who read the completed work, checked details and told me where I had gone wrong. Jean Morgan not only read the manuscript critically but typed the final clean copy and struggled with the footnotes.

A distant but important debt: to my fellow panelists on a William Carlos Williams program of the English Institute at Columbia in 1966, Dr. William Ober, Muriel Rukeyser and Mark Linenthal who helped stir my interest in WCW. Dr. Ober made an additional contribution, giving me a bottle of Florida Water, the *eau* that WCW's father made his living from.

Finally I thank Helen and Cate and Ned and Jack and Daisy for letting this book interrupt our lives for so long.

For permission to include excerpts from private and in some cases restricted letters in the libraries I thank not only Mrs. Florence Williams but also Allen Ginsberg, Robert Lowell, Allen Tate and John Riordan. The excerpts from letters of H.D. and Robert McAlmon are published with the permission of Norman Holmes Pearson, literary executor for H.D., and the owner of her copyrights as well as the owner of the McAlmon manuscripts. And I thank the libraries themselves; that is, for authorizing me to quote from manuscripts and letters in their possession I thank Donald Gallup, the curator of the Collection of American Literature, Beinecke Rare Book and Manuscript Library of Yale University; Karl Gay, the curator of the poetry collection of the Lockwood Memorial Library of the State University of New York at Buffalo; and Edmund Berkeley, Jr., the curator of manuscripts, William Carlos Williams Collection, Clifton Waller Barrett Library, University of Virginia Library.

For permission to reproduce two pages of a Pound letter in the personal collection of Dr. William Eric Williams I thank Dr. Williams and also James Laughlin acting as agent for the Ezra Pound Literary Property Trust; and for permission to reprint the following poems by WCW I thank Mrs. Florence Williams and James Laughlin: "Dedication for a Plot of Ground," "Hic Jacet," "The Young Housewife," "Danse Russe," "The House," "This Is Just to Say," and "Tract," all of which appeared in *Collected Earlier Poems,* and "The Cure," which appeared in *Collected Later Poems.* For permission to reproduce the self-portrait of William Carlos Williams I thank Mrs. Westlake, curator of the manuscript collection at the University of Pennsylvania Library; and for the other photographs of WCW and of Pound I thank Mrs. William Carlos Williams, New Directions Publishing Corporation, Dr. W. E. Williams, and Irving Wellcome. For the watershed map of the Passaic area I thank *Perspective* magazine, George Zabriskie and Lib Zabriskie.

Contents

Illustrations

CHAPTER ONE

Early Life

THE PASSAIC RIVER, which this book is to be about, shares with the Hackensack River slightly to its east the responsibility for having created the Jersey meadows. Geologically the Hackensack and the Passaic are meandering streams; they are in the old age of stream dynamics and wander lazily through the flat country of their own alluvial deposits before reaching the sea.

Socially the country of these rivers is in its old age too, the old age of nineteenth-century industrial America with a number of twentieth-century warts on top. This biographer is from Connecticut and it may be impolite of him to look down his nose at the sick society of Northern New Jersey, but he does. New Haven is sick too — it even has its own sick meandering stream, Mill River — but not that sick. Northern New Jersey is a nightmare of industrial age and sickness — not the Montclair, rich-suburbanite sections but the industrialized sections along the Passaic and the Hackensack. Come at this world's end country from the south on the Jersey Pike, notice that its six lanes of highway convert, somewhat before Newark airport, to twelve. Then note — it is impossible not to — that the twelve lanes of noise and motion on the ground are mixed with the noise and motion of planes coming in on final. Nothing is stationary except acres of gas tanks and refinery pipe-jungles letting forth poison gases. New Haven can't match this. No place can.

Just north of the airport the highway has a great fork in it, with one tine going off to become the Skyway, a now ancient elevated terror-road across the meadows to the tunnels under the Hudson River, and the other tine shooting north — and slightly east of Newark itself — toward George Washington Bridge. Just about where the fork occurs the poor demented Passaic finds its way into a body of dirty water called Newark Bay. The bay is full of tankers and freighters and it joins Upper Bay and the ocean via the narrow kills that make an island of Staten Island. But none of these waters can properly be called natural; they are leaky plumbing.

Moving upstream along the Passaic as it curves through Newark and north to Kearny, the traveler can see no green at all on its banks for several miles, but on the west bank a double-decker highway and on the east bank factories and oil tanks. The factories are old three- or four-story grim-brick factories, and their air of decay is made richer, just north of Newark, by an old iron drawbridge across the river that is perpetually open. Newark is being reconstructed now — or perhaps reborn? — but the new life being pumped irregularly into it is to be seen mostly in isolated building projects away from the river. On the doors of banks and hotels is plastered the sign "Push for a Greater Newark," but the push, such as it is, hasn't reached the river. Not until north of Kearney does the river take on life. There unexpectedly a few small power boats appear, bravely anchored in brown water, and a children's playground stretches for a hundred yards at riverside. After this comes Rutherford.

Rutherford is a leafy and pleasant square mile — we will return to Rutherford, home of William Carlos Williams. But put it aside for a moment and move further upstream. Above Rutherford are the industrial cities of Passaic, East Paterson and Paterson, every one a river killer. The stench of that river was so great once, claims Williams' widow, that it peeled paint off houses. Now it is better but not much, and it was probably always worst just east of Paterson.

Yet in the middle of Paterson something happens to the de-

mented Passaic River. Geologically there is nothing wrong with a
meandering stream having something going for it besides meandering, but to find the Great Passaic Falls in the middle of Paterson is a surprise. Drive through two miles of urban slum-wilder-
ness, climb a steep, barely paved street that looks as if it dead-ends
in a nineteenth-century dungeon for child labor, take an unlikely,
going-nowhere ninety-degree turn, and arrive for no reason at all
at a small but modern sports stadium. Walk behind that to a little
grassy area with benches and — behold, the falls.

The falls are stashed away behind the benches as if God's cost
accountant had decided there was no money to provide them with
the sort of space that great falls are entitled to. But they are great
falls all the same, having a lot of water and letting it fall perhaps
two hundred feet. The odd thing about the falls is that the water
descends into a sort of slot about thirty feet wide. Pocket Niagara.
Or better, hidden Niagara. The Passaic Falls are probably what
persuaded William Carlos Williams to write his longest poem,
Paterson, about Paterson rather than his original tentative choice,
Newark.

William Carlos Williams was born in Rutherford in 1883.
Allen Ginsberg was born in Paterson in 1926. LeRoi Jones was
born in Newark in 1934. Three prominent modern poets bred
along the banks of one small dirty river. Probably some local
patriot will write in to point to other poets also born along the
Passaic — there is Stephen Crane for example, who was born a few
years before WCW, in Newark — but these three will do. They
have in common the river as an environmental momma.

LeRoi Jones discovered along the river the hopelessness of the
urban black, and grew into a radicalism that made him reject his
own American name (he became Imamu Amiri Baraka), question
the word "poetry" itself because he came to feel that it was whitey's
word, whitey's art, and go overboard into anger:

> The best is yet to come. On how
> we beat you
> and killed you

and tied you up.
And marked this specimen
"Dangerous Germ
Culture." And put you back
in a cold box.

Allen Ginsberg discovered along the river what the twentieth century could do to take the shimmer off Walt Whitman's open road. His contribution to anger was the poem *Howl,* which includes a tirade against the false god Moloch. Ginsberg brings Moloch up to date to look like a blend of Manhattan and northern New Jersey:

Moloch whose eyes are a thousand blind windows! Moloch whose
    skyscrapers stand in the long streets like endless Jehovahs!
    Moloch whose factories dream and croak in the fog!
    Moloch whose smokestacks and antennae crown the cities!

Of these three poets Williams was the only one to pay much attention to the river itself in print. He learned to live with it as the others didn't. He was not without anger, he could see the Jersey landscape as the others did but he could see life in it too, and poetry. In an early poem, *The Wanderer,* he described the river as filthy, muddy, rotten, black, shrunken, degraded — all the unpastoral words he could think of — but then he added that it was hallowed by its own stench, and he thereupon took it unto himself as a sort of pastoral spirit presiding over his destiny.

In other words, the pastoral — and the poetic — were lurking there in the river for WCW, hidden within the industrial shell just as the falls were hidden in the middle of Paterson. It was the hiddenness that appealed, like finding beauty in a weed. In fact, with that weed thought in mind WCW called an early version of his autobiography *Dock: The Autobiography of William Carlos Williams* and put beneath it this elaborate epigraph:

The acanthus is a weed that signified for the Greeks neither fruit
nor flower but was prized for another reason. Because of that they
raised it to the head of their temple column. Dock with us is a
comparable weed growing unheralded about the edges of the dung-

heap. Of its roots the practical (and hungry) Chinese make a delicacy.

When he wrote that he was probably thinking of the weediness of his lineage, which we will get to, but his finding poetry in the dirty Passaic is in the same key. It is a slightly different thought from Allen Ginsberg's in "Sunflower Sutra" where Ginsberg finds that the sunflower he is looking at in a railroad yard is a beautiful sunflowery sunflower *despite* the locomotive grime plastered all over it. WCW wished to include the grime.

But there was another poet from the North Jersey region who liked his beauty straight. He was born in New Brunswick, New Jersey, on the next river system south. He was a contemporary of Williams' but they seem not to have met. He was Joyce Kilmer. He is remembered for saying "I think that I shall never see / A poem lovely as a tree." Millions of Americans who have still never heard of Williams, Ginsberg or LeRoi Jones know Joyce Kilmer and think of poetry as an art practiced by his kind. That is why there is a Camp Kilmer in New Jersey, and why there is a Joyce Kilmer Plaza on the Jersey Pike. America's poets come in different models but it will not do to ignore the Kilmer model. Not only has it been enormously successful, but in different guises it continues to be so. Also its presence has been a prime cause of the anger, the literary rebelliousness in Williams and the others.

Kilmer rhymed, Kilmer iambed. Kilmer did all the things the poets in the old country had done in the name of poesy — he even wrote a learned treatise, while at Columbia University, on the traditionalist English poet Lionel Johnson — and he brought to his verse as well a sort of faith in things American as apple pie that marked him instantly, for the modernists, as the enemy. He did lapse briefly into socialism as a youth but soon mended his ways, became a fierce Catholic (converting from the Episcopals), landed himself several good establishment jobs as a literary journalist in New York, and became a real go-getter. Like Williams he came to live on the Erie Railroad, but further out, in the Ramapo foothills. And like Williams he liked commuting. There the connection stops. Unlike WCW he wrote about the wonders of the conventional; unlike WCW he kept affirming the middle-class proprieties like marriage and the nine-to-five day. He had little time for the "stray dogs of the literary world" who found fault with America's and art's rules. Bored, as his biographer, Robert Cortes Holliday, put it, "by feminism, futurism and free love," he did just fine as an establishment man until World War I. In the early part of the war he was a pacifist of sorts, but upon the sinking of the *Lusitania* he quickly joined the army. He was killed in action in 1918.

In contrast, WCW in 1918 was to be found at home in Rutherford living under a social cloud because his neighbors suspected him of being, like his father-in-law, pro-German. The neighbors were wrong but the contrast between the celebrated dead war-hero poet and the uncelebrated live modernist remains striking. WCW was a patriot but not Kilmer's kind. WCW was a homebody but not Kilmer's kind. And the gulf between them in poetry was greater yet. WCW stood firmly with art's stray dogs including a number of experimentalist painters, an eccentric aesthete named Alfred Kreymborg, a wild Italian dissenter Emanuel Carnevali, a dedicated dropout Robert McAlmon, half the angry little magazine editors in the United States, Maxwell Bodenheim, Ezra Pound, and dozens of other artists who shared with him suspicion and contempt of establishmentarianism wherever found and however defined. The tradition of artistic dissent does not begin with WCW and his many diverse dissenting allies but with them it does become, slowly as the century moves on, the Way, a complete recipe for living and thinking — so completely so that those who now sign on tend to think of dissent and art as synonymous.

For Kilmer modernism in painting was "Incomprehensibilism"; in music it was discord; in poetry a "celebration of the queer and nasty instead of the beautiful." In one of his very last letters, written from the front in France, he remarked bitterly to a fan of his who had asked him questions about the future of poetry that "when we soldiers get back to our homes and have the leisure to read poetry we won't read the works of Amy Lowell and Edgar Lee Masters. We'll read poetry." If he had known WCW he would have added him to his nonpoet list, since WCW stood for everything Kilmer opposed.

How could there be that much difference between Rutherford and New Brunswick? There couldn't be and there isn't. The difference between these poets is not between their towns, though Rutherford is an odd small-town refuge in the industrial jungle as New Brunswick is not. North Jersey presses in on anyone who lives there, even in Rutherford on a quiet shady street with well-spaced old-frame houses. No one can escape hearing, smelling, touching, seeing, tasting it. WCW and Kilmer did all that together but Kilmer, unlike WCW, put aside what he sensed because he didn't want his interior vision messed up, he wanted life and art to be beautiful.

Dissent in American art has taken many forms; the dissenters do not make friendly bedfellows, and some of them are as anxious as Kilmer not to disturb dear Beauty. But if there is any common bond among the dissenters it is probably a recognition that the conventional idealism of the society they live in is pap. They come to the recognition by different routes but if they are like WCW they come to it mostly by hearing, smelling, touching, seeing, tasting.

WCW was a modernist in the root sense in which modernism's most radical early patriots thought of themselves, persons fighting for a full-scale revolution in human consciousness. After seventy-five years the revolution has not yet occurred but the faith in it is not dead yet and the name of WCW is now firmly identified with it. It was not in his early years; his reputation was a late bloomer, perhaps because competing modernists had a better storefront than WCW had, especially T. S. Eliot whom he hated, and Ezra Pound whom he could only like. WCW's particular brand of modernism is hard to describe or catch on to. It is more a mystique than a rational aesthetic — in fact rationality is sometimes its enemy — and it is easy to ignore or overlook when other voices are making loud rational noises. But there is something durable at the heart of it, something, as Karl Shapiro said, authentic, and that authenticity eventually hove into sight. Shapiro's essay "The True Contemporary" is perhaps the best essay yet written on WCW and its key refrain runs like this: "Poetry to him was a daily function of life, a means of seeing . . . He survives as a poet even better than his contemporaries, a consequence, perhaps, of his roots in a pedestrian world. Williams never became an 'exile'; how can an obstetrician become an exile?" The exiles Shapiro was thinking about were those who had flown the American coop, like Pound and Eliot — but one could say that Ginsberg and LeRoi Jones became in a sense exiles too by being dropouts from conventional North Jersey dailiness. WCW did not drop out even in that sense and yet he remains a major dissenting figure. Call him Rutherford modern. The odd mix that is Rutherford did him good.

Quiet staid conservative Republican Rutherford. EP called it a hole in the wall. WCW in his autobiography commented on the changes he had seen in it, from outhouses and unpaved streets to "neon lighted drugstores and real estate offices," but to an outsider he is not convincing. It is an island in the industrial sea; it is surrounded by dirt and fast-moving objects but it seems neat, rural, patient, fixed. What has changed is not Rutherford — though the pressure is on, the high rises are moving in, the soot's on the thorn — but the region around the square mile it takes up. Where the farm community of East Rutherford was, for example, is now a highway system where half the world's macadam has been poured, but Rutherford itself has escaped. So far. Even the Passaic River has a bit of pastoral about it as it passes west of Rutherford, and it is crossed there by a narrow old-fashioned iron bridge that a more "progressive" community would have replaced (as a young man WCW painted the river somewhere along there, making it look like Rousseau's wilderness). The one main street is devoted to modest unmodernized stores and banks, and at the lower end of that street is the nearly defunct Erie Railroad station looking seedy but not slummy. At the upper end of the main street is a fork, and if one bears off to the left on Ridge Road the stores suddenly stop and residences begin. The very first house on the left on Ridge Road — for a long time it faced a funeral parlor — is the Williams house. WCW lived in it for fifty years. His widow still lives in it. His doctor-son still has his office in it. Modernism where art thou?

But even that was not the original Williams house. There were two before it on Passaic Avenue a few blocks away. The first, where WCW was born, is down now. It was very small and had to be abandoned soon after WCW's younger brother, Edgar — born thirteen months later — produced overcrowding. The house moved to, at 131 Passaic, is still there though, and until a few years ago continued to be occupied by Williamses, that is, brother Edgar and family. It is a three-story frame affair with an unscreened front porch and an air of comfortable inelegance. It is across the street from the campus of Fairleigh Dickinson University. WCW's first memory was of that house and how, in the notorious blizzard of '88, "they" put him outdoors right after the snow stopped and he went to "yelling to be taken in again."

Very well, but wait a minute. In another version of the story, hidden away in an early handwritten version of the autobiography, it was not WCW who was outside yelling to get in but his half-cracked Uncle Godwin who had been inadvertently locked out, not after the storm but in the middle of it. In this version WCW is one of "them" inside who didn't hear Uncle Godwin knocking. Poor Godwin had to find refuge next door. Which version should we believe?

History is not graced by such quibbles, but anyway in the following year WCW, now aged six, was still on the bottle. "They," whether putting WCW out or not letting Uncle Godwin in, were not treating him well — reality arrives again like filth in the Passaic. If we are to find out what kept WCW from Kilmerism we need to look at "them" as well as the wasteland around Rutherford. Or so WCW himself says. He says that though he was precocious enough at the age of six to say "son of a bitch" to a young neighbor who tried to lord it over him with "son of a gun," he was seriously kept back in his maturing by "them" — for example, "they" told him nothing about sex with the result that enough curiosity was generated in him to "burn up fifty growing boys." Well, who *were* "they," then?

2

"They" were his grandmother and his mother. They competed for him. There were others in the house — his father, William George Williams, plus his grandmother's other children, Uncles Irving and Godwin (sired not by a Williams but a Wellcome) — but it was the women who had him in charge and both of them wanted to make him into a gentleman. The grandmother was so strong on gentlemanliness that when her indoctrinated son Godwin went mad, attacked members of the family and had to be captured by the police, he cried, "Don't touch me! I'm a gentleman!" The mother also had remote upper-class visions and they were mixed with a nice old-fashionedness about sexual conduct:

> A woman does not need to be a prude to have some sence [sic]; even the savages have a sence of disency [sic] and cover their sexual parts, and they get all the sun and air a human is possible to afford . . . Of course the idealistic and romantic age has vanished — we have realism in full now. Before the young man marries he is well acquainted with his future wife's body if not with her character and that is a mistake.

So the women were the ones who put him out in the snow. He alternately speaks gently and fiercely of them. They continually appear in his writings but the fierce grandmother comes off best, since two of his very best and fiercest poems describe her directly. Here is one, doing in 232 words what a biographer can't do in a thousand.

Dedication for a Plot of Ground

This plot of ground
facing the waters of this inlet
is dedicated to the living presence of
Emily Dickinson Wellcome

who was born in England, married,
lost her husband and with
her five year old son
sailed for New York in a two-master,
was driven to the Azores;
ran adrift on Fire Island shoal,
met her second husband
in a Brooklyn boarding house,
went with him to Puerto Rico,
bore three more children, lost
her second husband, lived hard
for eight years in St. Thomas,
Puerto Rico, San Domingo, followed
the oldest son to New York,
lost her daughter, lost her "baby,"
seized the two boys of
the oldest son by the second marriage
mothered them — they being
motherless — fought for them
against the other grandmother
and the aunts, brought them here
summer after summer, defended
herself here against thieves,
storm, sun, fire,
against flies, against girls
that came smelling about, against
drought, against weeds, storm-tides,
neighbors, weasels that stole her chickens,
against the weakness of her own hands,
against the growing strength of
the boys, against wind, against
the stones, against trespassers,
against rent, against her own mind.

She grubbed the earth with her own hands,
domineered over this grass plot,
blackguarded her oldest son
into buying it, lived here fifteen years,
attained a final loneliness and —

If you can bring nothing to this place
but your carcass, keep out.

Tough old Emily. What the poem omits is how, when she followed her oldest son, William George Williams, to New York, she,
with her older children, lived with him for some years in Rutherford and even presided at the birth of WCW:

> Her [mother Elena's] labor and delivery were a nightmare. In
> silence, without intimate unassisted by proper medical advice. The
> Doctor Howard or Williams or whatever his name was of the place
> didn't show up until the next day. Emily took charge of things
> after what fashion heaven only knows . . . Anyhow it was a boy.

The poem also fails to question whether the first husband — the
husband in England who fathered William George Williams —
was ever in fact a husband or even named Williams. If he was not
named Williams there is glory in the deception since William
George Williams fathered William Carlos Williams who fathered
William Eric Williams who once roomed in Williams Hall of Williams College in Williamstown, Massachusetts. He — the original
one — probably *was* named Williams but in the autobiography
there is interesting fuzz on the subject: Williams is described as
"the son of an Episcopal minister, or an iron worker," unlikely
alternatives. Then there is Ezra Pound's unannotated assertion
that Williams was "in fact half English and half Danish." And in
one of WCW's manuscripts at Yale the mystery of Williams' identity is made much of; there it is claimed that only once did Emily
talk with her son William George Williams about his father's
identity, and having done so made him swear that he would not
pass the secret on: "the legend is that Gramma . . . took Pop to
the cemetery where Rosita [an epileptic child by Wellcome] was
buried, made him kneel by her grave and promise her that he
would never reveal the truth. He never did." The unrevealable
truth may have been — it is suggested in passing in the autobiography — that the original Williams was in fact named Godwin. Or
the truth may have been — WCW seems to have believed this at
the end of his life — that Williams was simply a traveling man. In
any event the Godwin clan was important to the grandmother.

Godwin? "Now the Godwins," says WCW, "were a well-known
family in London. William Godwin's wife was Mary Wollstone-

craft, the intimate of Percy Bysshe Shelley, and the whole lot of them supporters of the principle of free love." Grandmother would not have liked him to say that, which is probably why he said it, and was wrong in saying it. Mary Wollstonecraft died forty years before the English grandmother was born, so if there was a connection between *her* Godwin and the free-lovers it was a connection separated by two generations. But it makes a good story, especially since there *were* Godwins that Grandmother admitted to, even was proud of. She allowed as how she had been born an orphan but had been brought up as the "ward" of a high-class family named Godwin. That is where she learned about gentlemanliness. She "dropped her aiches like any cockney" and was tough as nails, but preached gentility. She could be surly, sullen, impossible; then she would turn around and, playing the actress she had always wanted to be, gush:

DEAR WILLY
Yes I do love you . . . I could throw my heart right open to you . . . My heart is calling out now, this moment, are you thinking of me tonight November 6 and is my spirit vibrant with yours . . .

As the poem says, she spent her life struggling with everything from people to weasels, and she struggled hardest of all with WCW's mother, Elena. When WCW was born, Elena from the beginning did not nurse him so that the bottle became, in WCW's word, Grandma's weapon. And with the birth of the younger brother, Edgar, the grandma simply took over WCW — "or tried to." Thereafter she floated through the lives of WCW and brother Edgar for years, either as part of the Rutherford household or within tyrannizing distance. She was tough, she was big, she was hard to handle, and when one hundred-pound Elena once "laid" her out with a "smack in the puss" that was brave of Elena. The grandma was hateable but admirable, but always a loner, hard to get close to. She mellowed a bit in age; in 1911 WCW describes having a rare "delightful talk" with her "on the subject of the worthlessness of all striving except for the expression of one's individuality, and the pettiness and degradation involved in envy of other people's lots." She had spent much of her life envying other people's lots; WCW remarks that her affairs had mostly led her "in a direction entirely opposite from her now opinion." Delighted with her "now opinion," he concludes that "she speaks from rich experience with a vivacity which shows the joy she finds in her new, late conviction." But she was to be fierce again many times before her death in 1920.

WCW liked her so much when he didn't hate her that he made her his muse in *The Wanderer,* parts of which may have been written in 1910 or 1911. There she walked "imperious in beggary," she was "ominous, old, painted — with bright lips and learned Jew's eyes / Her might strapped in by a corset," but she brought him the wisdom of his trade, taught him to respect the earth he stood on, taught him especially to respect the "filthy Passaic." WCW's curious aesthetic of the ugly begins here and Grandma is an important instrument in it. "At her throat is loose gold, a single chain / From among many, on her bent fingers / Are rings from which the stones are fallen."

And then there was Elena, the mother, Elena Hoheb, partly "French out of Martinique" and partly Dutch-Spanish-Jewish out of Amsterdam. She was tiny, she was romantic, and when she was young she went to Paris and that made it worse. She went to Paris as an art student and never got over it, never stopped being a child in hope. She hoped for the culture of the grand old families of the islands, she hoped for her painting, for her music — but she got shunted away from it all in Rutherford, the end of hope.

Not that her Paris had been the Paris of lords and ladies and famous early impressionists. The art school she went to there had the proletarian name *L'Ecole des Arts Industrielles,* and while she was in it she felt herself to be merely "an obscure art student from Puerto Rico," knowing nothing of the great names and movements in modern painting. But three years in Paris are three years in Paris:

> She returned from Paris unscathed, certainly unpenetrable. A good deal the snob. Saving it for what? Bitterly resenting the necessity for her defeat.

Something new began to be born out of her.
She did not nurse her babies.

But how did she get to Rutherford? There was a surgeon in St. Thomas or Puerto Rico named Carlos Hoheb who played the flute. Young William George Williams played the flute too, and they met, and soon Carlos Hoheb said of his friend, "Williams is a fine young man. I like him very much. He is no musician." (WCW would later find satisfaction in describing EP as a fine young man who was no musician.) Carlos introduced Williams to his sister Elena who had not only just returned from Paris but had had an affair with a Spaniard that had ended when the Spaniard revealed to her that in her honor he had jilted another girl. She married Williams "on the rebound" and they sailed for America.

Or rather they sailed for America and then were married — at the home of a Hoheb friend. In Jersey City! This would be 1882. Williams *père* had been in "the rum trade" in the islands but he came to New York to work for the company of Lanman and Kemp, which produced "Florida Water," a sort of cologne. Jersey City was temporary. Williams soon took Elena to live in a little town on the Erie RR. Rutherford.

WCW thinks it was the unfulfilled affair with the Spanish lover that "ended it and ended her life dream of happy love . . . How mad to have thrown him over. How many times have I heard her say it." But if it was not the Spaniard it was Rutherford. Williams *père* became one of the early commuters on the Erie Railroad — to Jersey City, thence by ferry to Manhattan — but Elena stayed home. She imagined briefly a career for herself and had a business card printed up "inscribed with the legend, teacher of French and Spanish," but never had a pupil. She gave herself over instead to childbearing. "She became pregnant at once. She couldn't speak the language. Her husband began commuting to the city while she, not even knowing how a baby was to be born, not the physiology of the thing, was left home — to cook! To care for the house."

On top of that, along came Grandma:

. . . God help us all, Mr. Wellcome had died in Puerto Rico and Emily and her three children were about to follow Willie to the states.

Poor girl. She didn't know what she was in for. Rutherford Park, New Jersey. What can that have meant to her after her upbringing.

WCW wouldn't let it go, her Parisian-art-school, Spanish-caballero debacle. Seeing the results in himself? She could be serene and joyous, as he could, and then she would play the piano and sing — she was a good musician — and would paint (her work was representational, but deft and delicate — children's portraits, still lifes) and be warm and outgoing; but then she would turn moody, morose, melancholy, also as he could, and then she was an alien in a remote land. Her English was poor, her heart was elsewhere, she moped, fell into trances, frightened the children with her strangeness. WCW felt the same tug in himself; it shows in his pictures where at one moment he may look outgoing, naive, WASPish with the hair boyishly out of kilter (see his self-portrait, p. 4 of insert 1) and at another dark, saturnine, brooding (see p. 5 of insert 2). And since the mother was physically strong and lived to a great age he had his heritage with him for much of his adult life. It was not, he tells us, until the 1930s when she was slowly sinking that he could talk easily with her. Then she, like the grandmother in old age, calmed down and WCW would spend long hours with her and she would talk and talk about her island past: she remembered "when she could still sing her arias from *La Traviata* and her teacher would encourage her, *Allez, allez! ma petite!*" She remembered crazy little old anecdotes:

> You heard about the little French old lady? They were talking about machines and they were saying they were going to make a machine to make the babies. And she said, No, I don't think so, I think the best way is the old natural way!

And she remembered dreams, childhood tragedies, dozens of other pastnesses, including the times she hated Grandmother Emily — "sometimes I could have taken her by the neck and strangled

her" — so many that WCW finally sat down and wrote a book
about her which was not, as he said, a book *about* her but a book
that was simply herself, being a collection of her remarks that he
wrote down as she made them.

What are you writing there, she would say accusingly.
Oh, just something I want to remember.
Are you writing down what I say, because if you are . . .
Well, Mother, after all. I like to remember those proverbs you tell
   me. I think they are worth preserving. She wasn't fooled.
I don't want you to write my biography, she said. My life is too
   mixed up.
So much the more reason, my dear, I answered her. For here you
   are.
Very unhappy . . .
Very happily, my mother! I made a bow. She smiled.

And then there was Pop. He did play at being a good father.
He took the kids on long hikes, flew kites with them, taught them
to handle tools and equipment (he had a fine machine shop in the
cellar) , read good books to them, and twisted their arms to read
on their own (he once offered WCW a dollar to read *On the
Origin of Species* and *The Descent of Man:* "I took him up. It was
well-earned cash") . He was also a good storyteller, full of tales out
of the islands in *his* youth, how he had eaten *"pâtés* of black ants"
when starving in the mountains of Costa Rica and how a monstrous tidal wave once hit St. Thomas and nearly drowned him.
But he was "curiously mild"; WCW remembers him being angry
only once, when he tried to force WCW to eat a detestable tomato.
He was liberal and a socialist, he was a hardworking breadwinner,
he helped found the Unitarian Society of Rutherford — but
primarily he was a gentleman and his gentlemanliness did not
compete with the two "determined women" of his household.
The determined women determined WCW's fate, thought the
victim.

Ezra Pound disagreed. He liked Pop. He told WCW that
gentlemanly Pop with his English ways had been an influence on
the "form" of life WCW lived. WCW replied that Pound over-

rated Pop's Englishness since Pop had been brought up in the tropics; but then he himself reported on his Englishness, how they would go on long hikes and the Englishness, though slightly warmed by the southern sun, would drive them smartly along for twenty or thirty miles a day, saying nothing to each other, fifty or sixty feet apart. Yes, Pop was "at heart a northerner" and "a stickler for fundamentals" — and if he was an influence on WCW it was probably with those fundamentals, fundamentals WCW came to want to reject.

He was also a stronger-willed and more sociable person than the children could see. The house bottled him up; Elena particularly bottled him up; his best and fullest living was out of the house so that the children remained ignorant of his fullness. They did look up to him, and in general they obeyed him, but their respect for him was patronizing; the women were in charge. He was reserved, remote, shy — and a genuine traveling man. He worked for the Florida Water Company for thirty-five years, commuting to New York City daily when he was in this country but going off on long sales trips to South America, once for a whole year. Sometimes he seemed to be an important figure in the company, wandering through foreign lands with the secret formula for the water in his pocket, setting up factories, but sometimes he seemed more like a British Willy Loman. WCW remembers him in his last year, as he was dying of cancer, still struggling down the street to the Erie Railroad station to make the 8:12.

Then there was the Christmas morning when, having dwindled to nothing, he failed to waken. WCW entered his room and after looking at him said to his mother who had come in with him, "He's gone." But Pop wasn't gone. "He shook his head slowly from side to side. It was the last thing I could ever say in my father's presence and it was disastrous." That was 1918.

So "they" who put him out in the snow, and Pop, were a lovely odd family who did and did not get on, who were and were not close, who did and did not talk ("We must have been an uncommunicative tribe though we could talk, plenty, when we were spurred to it"). Pop was the most literary one — he would read Shakespeare to the assembled family in the parlor, and read forbidden works to Elena in the bedroom (with WCW listening behind the door) — but they were all interested in theatrics, culture, the higher things that Rutherford did not have much of, and they were all eccentric in that interest. Together they were a private melting pot of their own culturally, racially. WCW was the first of their tribe to be born in the U.S., and when to expatriate Ezra Pound he wrote in his twenties to say that he had discovered that he was an American writer, a local writer, a writer who would not benefit — just as Pound was not benefiting — by living away from his American roots, Pound replied, "What the h——l do you a blooming foreigner know about the place." Pound had a point. He had been born in Idaho to a clan that claimed ties to Henry Wadsworth Longfellow and a lieutenant governor of Wisconsin, so he said kindly to WCW, "my dear boy you have never felt the swoop of the PEEraries." Not that there were many in Rutherford who had; most of the population was new, didn't believe they belonged there: "To call them Americans is like calling them Martians they were so ill-assorted, disassociated with the land and each other." But there they all were anyway in the newness together, and some of them dug in quick and easy and some didn't. The Williamses did and didn't. They settled in but not to be Rotarians, Elks, not to blend. They kept their distance so that when WCW had reached forty in that town and was plotting a book he called *In the American Grain,* he could still feel the islandness in him, his separateness. If that was a bad feeling because it made him insecure in his profession and sometimes angry that the community did not in good grace accept him as he was, it was also good because, as Pound said, "None of his immediate forebears burned witches in Salem . . . he could not by any possibility resemble any member of the Concord School." Pound had more opinions than he needed and he was especially full of opinions when it came to WCW, but on the strength of the frailty of WCW's Americanness he was on sure ground (all this in an essay called "Dr. Williams' Position," first printed in *The Dial* in 1928). He said that WCW had a European's attitude toward America, started "where a European would start if a European were about to write about America: sic: America is a subject of interest, one must inspect it, analyze it, treat it as a subject." Which was more than Pound the native could do; from across the sea he had to save it.

When the American goes into his hole to write the American novel, play or poem he may well be the better American if he has not been one long or strong. WCW may have benefited from his familial aliens while Pound suffered from having so much Longfellow in him, as well as so much American else to react to. Even so they were not without likeness in their Americanness, the one in Rutherford, the other in London and Rapallo. For both of them man was a wanderer mostly, a nonpolitical, noninstitutional tramp.

Pound would regurgitate the wisdom of Chinese sages while WCW described proletarian females seen through the windshield of his car; EP would play at being Odysseus or Sextus Propertius while WCW stayed home with WCW; but for both of them writing was a loner's trade. "A plane over Wyoming at night," said Auden, describing American poetry. Nothing down there. Great empty places. Eliot and the traditionalists bemoaned the emptiness but there were those who liked it — like Pound's wild English friend Wyndham Lewis who should have been a traditionalist but spoke lovingly of America's most excellent vacuum (in *America and Cosmic Man*), and like D. H. Lawrence who admired the American capacity to slough off the old, make new starts. And like Pound and WCW. Detached observers exercising their freedoms, trying to look with their own eyes, write with their own guts. The world hadn't seen much of that before. In that was the revolution, if it could happen.

Rutherford is a small town and small towns have been a locus for the other kind of vision, where A proposes to B and there are ripples, and where C betrays D and there are ripples. Man influences man, life is a run of contacts and connections that serve as cause. The loner view denies that; the loner view would have it that we buy and sell, we meet and say goodbye but the sources of change in our lives are inside us: B goes on with his life no matter what A says or does to him. Ships in the night.

Not quite. A loner who does not believe that God or the President runs *his* life may still dream steadily of a tiny poem changing the lives of others. That is imagism and vorticism. It is not that the loner is so egotistical as to believe that he is God or the President, but that, rejecting the culture's developed reverbatory systems, he comes to believe mystically in interaction between man and man at a root level. Or between man and thing.

Put an image in front of us. Don't say what it is *like* — that is the conventionalized reverbatory system — but let it sit there and do its work, its own work. Or tell us of a casual street encounter but don't let anything *happen* as a result — that again would be the old way. Just let the encounterers meet, have their say and depart. Now a writer who chooses to write in this new mode does so in part *because* he is a loner; the mystique of it is bred out of his feeling that beyond his social being, his political being, there is always a residue of experience unaccounted for, undealt with, and that residue makes life unplumbed, unfulfilled until it *has* been dealt with. Such a writing premise is absurd to the Marxist or Tolstoyan, or maybe the Rotarian or the Kilmerite, but it lies at the heart of Pound's and WCW's work. As for WCW himself — who can speak for EP? — could it not be that the premise came to him first from "them," the ones who put him out in the snow? They knew of the private residue too, being loners standing on street corners. Their resort was to the private sensing since in the end that was mostly what they had.

3

WCW's boy-days were spent on Passaic Avenue in Rutherford, with sojourns on a farm in East Rutherford that the Williams family tried to make a go of. His younger brother, Edgar, caught up with him in school when they were both small, and from then on they moved through school together in the same grades, first in the Rutherford schools, then abroad for a year, then at Horace Mann in New York City. Edgar was bigger than WCW, and by the time they reached college WCW sometimes called himself little brother — but they got on. Also present at the family table were Grandmother Wellcome, Uncle Irving (who was good with an air gun) and retarded Uncle Godwin (who once saved Ed and WCW from falling in a well). For some years Pop was saddled with supporting two families.

In the autobiography WCW spends more words on the farm than on town life. The farm, with a house on it called Bagellon House, was a place for running and running, and for fooling with firecrackers (at nine WCW came near to losing an eye). It was a place for rabbits and kites, for looking at the moon through a telescope mounted in a cupola, and for crazy Uncle Godwin to try growing vegetables. It was a place that was squirrels and barns, eggs and apples and horses. When Pop had to give up the farm the return to town was a great sadness.

But not for Mother Elena. She never liked Bagellon House. She felt more lonely there than in Rutherford and "if she painted at all it was no more than an occasional flower." And she was more boxed in with Grandma Wellcome at the farm than in town. Grandma was "the restless and resistless Emily" who "under the pretext of dividing the work divided the children" — that is, left Ed to Momma and took WCW as her own. There is a strange WCW story, written in the twenties, that has the young hero of the story regularly spending summers with his English grandmother at a summer shack on Long Island Sound following the *death* of the mother. The father is "a real gentleman right enough and of the old school, charming but useless," so the grandmother has a clear field for rearing the boy. That is the real English grandmother right enough, and the summer place is her place in West Haven ("a one-room summer shack" with the water "not twenty feet from her front door," where she could breathe again and was her own mistress) , but the "charming but useless" gentlemanly Pop is not, from available evidence, WCW's pop but Uncle Irving, and the hero of the story is Irving's son, Billy Wellcome. In other words the weak-daddy scene was to be found on the other side of the family too.

Certainly Elena had her troubles with Pop as well as with resistless Emily. WCW tried to be generous and praise their marriage — "she enjoyed the love of her husband, I am sure. She gave him love. I am sure of that" — but sometimes his guard went down: "a house built out of disappointed hopes" and "What of the love between this man and woman? She developed a cold front, whether she would or no." The house moved between sweet and sour. When sweet the family would be gathered in the parlor and Pop would be presiding, old patriarch, and reading good literature to them (the main books were Shakespeare, Dante, the Bible — especially Isaiah) . When sour they would sulk or argue, or perhaps Pop would be in South America on a business trip and Elena would be upstairs wishing she were in Paris. "It was a good, tragic, enervating, challenging atmosphere for a child to grow up in," said WCW and, thinking of Elena's cooking, added, "especially on the days of her cooking of beans and overdone meat."

At least WCW learned more about words and literature at home than at school. School gave him a different kind of learning that had "nothing to do with classwork":

> Lizzie, Lilah, Janet, Mable, Mary, Susan and Vera — these are the magic names to say to any boy who spent his winter days in the sixth and seventh grade those days — John, Nelville, Charlie, and Fred! Fabulous names, a mythology that nothing that came after could ever rival . . . The classwork was a mere fringe to those mysteries.

WCW took pot shots at schoolbook learning all his life, and kept finding the true wisdom elsewhere, as from watching the bad boys of Rutherford:

Charlie and Fred . . . surely went to hell, jumping out of a back window to escape the police, getting this girl pregnant, dying of tuberculosis. These are the boys who, naked, would hop a slow freight over the meadows, climb to the top of a boxcar and as the train went over the bridge at Berry's Creek dive from it into the stream. They were aloof, in a class by themselves, while the rest of us looked on in wonder and envy but not with entire approval.

To hear him talk, WCW would have been the Huck Finn of Northern New Jersey but for the two "determined women."

But he also talked of the little voice inside him, his own little conscience voice telling him to be good or be damned. There are odd passages where he regrets his early wildness and wonders how he managed to survive his lack of discipline and "the lust that burned me to a cinder." There are also passages where he shows fear about what would have happened to him as a professional man if he had let himself go. With his English-French-Spanish-Jewish blood and past he was a puritan on odd days, a libertine on even, but the puritanism was always strong enough in him to make him think he could not afford to be *too* happy.

Freud might have said that his writing served him, later on, as a substitute for diving with the bad boys into Berry's Creek, but WCW would not have liked that. When he was sixty he went out of his way to take a crack at Freud's sublimation theory for literature, and long before that in the bulk of his mature work he had shown that he thought of himself as a writer of the real, a confronter, not an escape artist. Nor was he an escape artist, at least not an escape artist in the Walter Mitty mode. Freud's account of sublimation, particularly in "The Poet in Relation to Daydreaming," is simplistic and does suggest that all writers are Walter Mittys, but they are not and WCW was not. WCW was — or became — a strong practicing unbeliever in fantasy literature except when he was with his children. The children he did like to tell tall tales. (A story the children remember is of a dragon that lived in a copper mine in the Jersey meadows, and of a heroic Indian boy who lived on the hill in East Rutherford overlooking the copper mine. One day the Indian boy whizzed down the hill and disposed of the dragon with bow and arrow, an event that both Paul Williams and Bill Jr. still find satisfying.)

And yet he did take ego trips, his own kind. He rejected early the rusty mythology of heroes, great leaders, triumphant justice but he did not reject the bad boys of Berry's Creek. They appear later in many forms, notably in the form of the Allen Ginsberg of *Howl*, of whom WCW said admiringly that the man had been through hell. WCW remained envious of those who *could* go through hell, chuck the puritanism he could not himself chuck, the radicals, the expatriates, the indulgent ones who were always off somewhere living somehow better — better even if worse — than he. And though a part of his mind always knew that in fact they were not living better, the other part did build fine illusions of a betterness out beyond Rutherford and doctoring. The illusions were not his alone — they were shared by the bad-boy rebels themselves of whom he was envious — but they were illusions. They were illusions about art largely, art and the artist's life and the role of art in the culture. They were illusions about artistic freedom and the capacity of the artist to revolutionize human thought. They were grand illusions with great staying power for good minds, not passing Mittyish fancies, and WCW shared them with the best and worst of those we have come to call modernists. The difference between WCW and the bad boys was that WCW could only afford to indulge the illusions part time, being Rutherford-bound, Rutherford-modern. Yet the restrictions upon him may have just made the illusions grander — and they did *remain* illusions, in the sense of being finally unrealizable. Hence a source of discouragement.

But we should begin more simply with illusions, the illusions of childhood, and note that WCW was, from early on, in the unfashionable phrase, inner-directed. Though he had his full quota of fishing and fighting and playing "hare and hounds," he was also a young Hamlet. Pound has a story of the Hamlet side of WCW when very young:

The young William Carlos . . . arose in the morning, dressed and put on his shoes. Both shoes buttoned on the left side. He regarded this untoward phenomenon for a few moments and then carefully removed the shoes, placed shoe *a* that had been on his right foot on his left foot, and shoe *b* that had been on his left foot, on the right foot; both sets of buttons again appeared on the left side of the shoes.

This stumped him. With the shoes so buttoned he went to school but . . . and here is the significant part of the story, he spent the day in careful consideration of the matter.

Beyond his inner life with shoes there was sex, dreams of which he realized through keyholes. He reports on the inspiration he received from servant girls of the family — Irish, Finnish, and "especially Georgie, from Georgia, who could peg a rock left-handed over the top of the chestnut tree two doors down from where we lived," and whom WCW secretly watched take a bath.

And beyond sex there was a larger dream of love — later WCW would call a play of his *Dream of Love* — that was to be dreamed about Grandmother Emily or Mother Elena or perhaps the whole big world and the love therein, but especially dreamed of Mother, dreamed and then undreamed, the waking being a waking to the unpleasantness of the parental marriage and the mother's deep darkness.

She had Dostoevskian attacks. She attended spiritualist meetings at which she would go "out of her head." She would be "possessed at such times . . . her face would flush, and she'd reach out her hand and grasp the hand of one of us . . . Her face would be red, contorted, she couldn't talk . . . A name would be offered. No. Then another . . . Finally Pop might say, 'Is it Carlos?' meaning her brother, and she'd grasp the hand offered in both hers, and the presence would leave her . . . How Ed and I dreaded these occasions!" Dreaded because the dream of love wouldn't stick but kept being replaced by an ugliness. But WCW would dream the dreams anyway, chiefly when he was away from the family. His letters home from college in Philadelphia, and then from New York City when he was an intern, and then from Leipzig when he took medical courses there, were steadily letters of passionate declaration. The letters to Mother Elena were the gushiest; sometimes he seemed not to be writing to her at all but to an ideal image of Ma.

Another great dream, the dream of literature, did not begin for him until he went to the Horace Mann School. Until then he simply shared the familial dream of culture — Pop with his Shakespeare, Emily with her actress hopes, Elena with her music and painting, and all of them with their nostalgia for gentility. In Rutherford the dream of culture was a strong dream because the culture there was not strong, and as a child WCW, still not distinguishable in taste and preference from his elders, dreamed of culture as they did. His early poetry aspired to Beauty and was a clumsy parody of conventional prosodic graces. Even when he was thirty he dreamed of cultural uplift and composed a long list, for the benefit of his new wife and himself, of activities that would improve them, such as going to the opera. He would then suddenly turn against that dream and set up shop as a bad boy, but he could not have done so without first having had the dream, nor would he be consistent in the bad-boy role. All his life he continued to respect his family's cultural legacy even as he lashed out elsewhere at cultural pretensions.

The family's cultural legacy was in the parlor with the reading of books, the painting of paintings, and the music; but it was also in church with the Unitarians. The Unitarians were important for the Williamses in the early Rutherford years. The Unitarians were not so much religious as cultural, and Pop liked that in them and led his family to their fold within a few years after his marrying mystical, fallen-Catholic Elena. Grandmother Emily, though converting to Christian Science, was willing to tag along because the Unitarians had social events and put on amateur plays, and Elena was willing to tag along because there she could play the piano. WCW and Edgar tagged along because they were children; they sang in the choir and Mother Elena played. As for Pop, Pop was a leader in that tiny and poor church for eighteen years, though the WCW account (in the autobiography) does not tell us what he did when he led, except direct plays. That he loved.

So there they all were, in a church that was not a church, practicing family solidarity and indulging, with what seems at this distance a fine innocence, the dream of culture. The organist even brought the two children to Kant in Sunday school — though there were lapses, such as the time that a child asked teacher the nature of circumcision. Answer: "Circumcision is a formal rite of mutilation practiced by the Jews."

Then as an additional boost to culture and light came the year of the trip abroad. Pop sent Elena with the two children to Geneva while he sailed for a business year in Argentina, bringing Florida Water to the great unwashed. "That at least is what he must have told Mother," says WCW in the autobiography. Ed and WCW then went through eighth grade at the *Chateau de Lancy,* where WCW would later send his own children. There they felt "a hundred years younger than most of the sixty-two other boys," who were from twelve nations, but they played soccer, swam in freezing Lake Geneva, collected postage stamps — Pop had begun to make a business of buying and selling stamps — and, while practicing "General deviltry of all sorts," picked up culture too in the form of the Alps, flowers (WCW would be a greatly knowledgeable flower nut) , and the assassination of the Empress of Austria. Elena got culture too; she was delighted to be back in civilization, away from Rutherford and Pop. She had a good year and at the end of the year persuaded Pop to extend it into the next. Then she took the children to her lovely Paris and stuffed them in school *there.* The school did not work but they learned much from Paris itself and from a splendid aging relative who taught them how to drink wine and crack walnuts and sing risque French songs. The dream of culture entered them so deeply that when they returned to the States in 1899 the schools in Rutherford looked as bad as they probably were.

WCW was going on sixteen, Ed fifteen. Pop's money was low but he agreed anyway that Horace Mann School at 120th Street in Morningside Heights was the place for such advanced children.

One paper written by WCW at Horace Mann has been passed down and is about Switzerland, but it does not seem advanced. It describes castles in Switzerland and particularly a "feudle castle" near where "Joan of Arch" was captured:

> On waking from our sleep at the hotel or bording house where you are staying you will see if your room be on the right side of the house the immense castle, the first thing that is noted is its immense size.

The height of the castle is then mentioned, and the moat "which has partly falled apart," plus gateways and towers and passageways leading inward to the impressive prisons where "the walls are from 15 to 20 feet thick and in some there are no windows and the bottom of the tower is a pit in which are thrown the prisoners who are doomed."

To remedy some of the faults in that paper it was necessary to get up at 6:00 A.M., dress, have breakfast, and walk down through Rutherford to the station to catch the 7:16 to Jersey City. Then came the ferry to lower Manhattan, then the trip uptown on either the 6th or 9th Avenue el. Was it worth it? The class in history was not good because there was a Miss Butler — Nicholas Murray Butler's* sister — who taught it and whose services to "general culture" WCW doubted. Latin was better but for some reason he was able to take it for only one term, which was not enough and was all the classical training WCW ever had and made him open to jibes from classicist Pound. Then there was manual training, which was not good, and a sports program, which was not good. From the evidence, Horace Mann and all the commuting might have been written off as a loss if it had not been for "Uncle Billy" Abbott.

In his old age WCW dedicated his *Selected Essays* to the memory of Uncle Billy, "the first English teacher who ever gave me an A." The dedication does not say what other English teachers gave him A's later and there is no record in the autobiography of his having *had* other English teachers, but perhaps if one has Uncle Billy one English teacher is enough. Uncle Billy began "simply enough with El Penserosa [sic] Comus and Robert Louis Steven-

* Butler became the President of Columbia University and a favorite academic puritan for Pound to take pot shots at.

son," and WCW loved it and got an A. Uncle Billy was a "gentleman in the mild sense of my father" and his "lounging way" made
WCW feel at home. It was Uncle Billy who brought him the
dream of literature.

It may be that there is always an Uncle Billy. There was even
an Uncle Billy, and at about the same time, in the life of wholly
self-sufficient Pound, who was born with all knowledge in his
head; Pound's Uncle Billy was named Spencer and was his instructor at Cheltenham Military Academy and recited a part of
The Iliad to him after a game of tennis. But if there is always an
Uncle Billy it may be that Uncle Billy is not as big a part of the
enlightening process as those who are enlightened later come to
think. Good Uncle Billys know this. Anyway WCW's Uncle Billy
played his role and WCW was taken a step further down the road
than Pop had taken him, being introduced not only to Milton and
Stevenson but Coleridge and Whitman, and also being encouraged
to write. The paper that he wrote for Uncle Billy that provoked
the great A was not a story of his own but a retelling of an uplifting Stevenson story about a canoer who lost his paddle:

> at one point the canoe had upset, the man was spilled into the
> water, but in spite of everything he had not lost his paddle . . . I
> stuck to that, driving the point home: he had not lost his paddle!

From the paddle story he went on to poetry, and records in the
autobiography what he believes to be his first poem:

> A black, black cloud
> flew over the sun
> driven by fierce flying
> rain.

He does not tell us what Uncle Billy thought of it but ridicules it
himself for saying that clouds were driven by rain. He might well
have complained about the two "blacks" too, since later he would
not try to win the world over with attributives; but what he
should have said about the poem in its favor is that it is a poem
with an image. No other early WCW poem that survives has an
image, which is perhaps a reason to doubt WCW's memory that

this was in fact his first poem. Not until ten or twelve years later would the imagist movement seize him; as late as 1909 he was dedicated to Love, Beauty and other capitalized abstractions.

Whatever mode of poetry he may have been capable of at Horace Mann, he discovered there that he wanted to write, and aside from writing poems themselves he began keeping a note-book, which he tells us expanded, by the time he got to college, to twenty-three notebooks "before disappearing." "They had stiff board covers of a black and tawny water-wave design" and they were full of his "Whitmanesque 'thoughts,' a sort of purgation and confessional, to clear my head and my heart from turgid obses-sions." Beside the Whitmanesque notebooks he took with him to college a copy of *Leaves of Grass,* but the notebooks are gone and the poems, if there were any that show Whitman's influence, are gone too. At college he switched his allegiance from Whitman to Keats. So what happened to him intellectually at Horace Mann we know only at secondhand, except for odd documents like the unpromising essay on "feudle castles" and the perhaps wrongly dated black-cloud poem. What he tells us in the autobiography is chiefly of Billy Abbott and of an early sexual experience — maybe his first — with certain white legs in a small lake near Esopus, New York — and of running too hard and long in training for the 300-yard dash. He collapsed and was taken to a doctor who said that he had "adolescent heart strain" and would have to give up ath-letics forever. The doctor was wrong, WCW was able to continue to play strenuous games like tennis and soccer, to become a varsity fencer at Penn, and to be for the whole of his active life a tireless walker, all without further heart trouble; but the doctor's an-nouncement had its effect, encouraging further the dream of lit-erature. A quiet life, literature.

4

Forty years later the literary life was not a quiet life for WCW but a dirty war. By then he had been in the war long enough to know that it was truly a war, and dirty, but he had not reconciled himself to it. At odd intervals he continued to be bitter about the war right to the end, and would complain of the neglect of his work, of the too great attention paid others' work, the rotten economics of literature and the rottener entrepreneuring. When he was bitter he was no more pleasant a person than any other writer nursing his occupational sadness, but at least WCW was lucky and had much of the opposite in him too. He could be generous, modest, selfless. He could praise.

What is curious about his bitterness is that in the autobiography he tells us that it was part of him even as he was just starting to write, and that the bitterness he felt then contributed as much as Uncle Billy or the misfortune on the track to his writing urge. In a comic passage he describes how he ran through the óther arts and rejected them one by one — painting, which was all right but messy; music because he didn't "qualify"; sculpture because he couldn't stay in one place that long; and the dance because his lègs were too crooked — and settled at last on writing because he "wanted to tell people, to tell 'em off, plenty." He adds that he felt this would give him "bitter pleasure" because he "instinctively knew that no one much would listen." How could he have known even instinctively, at the age of seventeen or eighteen, that most of the world's words went out to gather dust and rejection slips? He could not have known; in the autobiography he must have been speaking wisdom after the fact. But at least in his vagueness about the nature and object of his bitterness he was making a point about himself beyond the writing point, which was that he was unsure of himself, had no confidence that he could get along with people, was a loner. All the more reason to dream the dream of literature.

Of course he could have had a specific grudge toward his parents at the time, and been resentful of their imposing upon him *their* dreams for him, pushing him into doctoring. Mother Elena was the chief one; she had dreamed of him in medicine since his infancy because her dear brother, Carlos, was a successful surgeon and Elena needed success, needed images of her brother around her. As for Pop it is not recorded that he was pushy about medicine, but after his children's expensive year abroad and their expensive years at Horace Mann he was anxious to get them a practical education and a start in life, and he did pull WCW out of Horace Mann before he had finished all the requirements. Maybe the parents were the people WCW chiefly wanted to tell off.

He went off to the University of Pennsylvania Medical School in 1902 while at the same time brother Edgar went off to M.I.T. Superficially all was sweetness and light, the parents had been generous, the schools were fine schools — but underneath something darker was stirring. In the first place WCW was a poet now, scribbling in his black and tawny notebooks — and to be at the same time studying embryology, histology, anatomy and neurology was hard on the dream of literature. In the second place his medical commitment — he started in dentistry but soon switched — kept him from college proper. He lived on campus with the undergraduates but had no ties with the liberal arts faculty and took none of the ordinary undergraduate courses. The one English teacher he mentions during his university years was a Professor Bates at Ed's M.I.T. He once brought Bates an offering of poems.

WCW managed to persuade himself that the omission of college was a good thing, making him "a better writer at least a more liberal thinker" than he would have been if he had continued his "course of formal instruction"; but whether ordinary college courses would have helped or hindered him intellectually, their omission made stronger his aloneness. He was not one of the boys and he would have liked to have been. He compensated by seeking out the extracurricular in the form of fiddle playing, soccer, fencing, singing, acting, and even editing (art) the medical school yearbook. He needed such diversion, since the bitter pleasure of being alone, of writing to an empty house, of picking up culture on weekends had its sadistic side. He could say to himself that he was going to make a living out of doctoring and a life out of writing, and then turn around and batter away at himself for having neither the talent nor the stamina to do either:

> I was going to work for it, with my hands, which I had been told (I knew it anyhow) were stone-mason's hands. I also looked at my more or less stumpy fingers and smiled. An esthete, huh? Some esthete.

Thus, the belligerent Dr. Williams. But he was mild and shy mostly, saving his ferocity for his writing, or if displaying it to others doing so half humorously, as a put-on. His granddaughter Emily, who called him Poppops and felt close to him, remembers that he would pull her up on his lap as if he were going to be kind and loving, then would bite her ear till it hurt, and would stare fiercely at her with pop eyes, and then g-r-o-w-l. There is also a story of a friend's visit, and how WCW went to his own front door, opened it, stepped out, peered up and down the street, returned, shut the door, returned to the friend, leaned over and whispered, "There are lots of sons of bitches out there."

Similarly in a late poem, "The Controversy," he can be seen taking on "the sons of bitches out there" in the form of an Executive and an Architect, and doing so with the same mix of comedy and real anger. The Executive and the Architect ridicule him for his impracticality and poor business sense; he tries to defend himself but they keep at him until finally

> I can
> still read and collate experiences
> you never dreamed, I
>
> answered them. Nuts! they said. Very well. Nuts!
> and decorated nuts and nuts again,
> I said, to you, gentlemen.

What he said to the gentlemen leads directly and with hardly a breath-pause to Ezra Pound.

Pound's biographer Hugh Kenner may have been suffering from biographers' paranoia when he named his most recent book about him, *The Pound Era,* but the title has merit and if the era was in fact Pound's, or part Pound's, it must have been his because of his temperament as much as because of his poetry or critical views. He had a temperament that liked to say nuts and decorated nuts and nuts again to almost anyone, and that was the correct temperament for the era, maybe its chief mark. Pound and WCW shared that temperament, and though they had no monopoly on it each knew that the other was like that and the knowledge comforted them in their differences. Sometimes it seemed as if all they had was differences; Pound said that their friendship was one "of literary differences and never one difference concealed," and he might have added that the differences went beyond literature; but they could live in friendship for sixty years anyway — and when WCW died Pound could cable his widow that he would never find another poet-friend like him — because of their temperamental communion. The two of them reinforced each other as loners by passing back and forth between themselves images of an enemy to whom one *could* say, tirelessly, nuts and decorated nuts again. It was a coincidence of a high order that these two strangers with little in common but the temperament, sharing only their common mixture of private ambition and worldly unease, should have found themselves living across from each other on the same quad.

Pound had come from Hailey, Idaho, with its one street of wooden houses and forty-seven saloons, but he was not the hick that Hailey would have liked to make him. He had culture in his veins, being related to early New England settlers and none other — he didn't brag about the connection — than Henry Wadsworth Longfellow. Unlike WCW he was old America, and so could call WCW dago and furriner but not ungently. Old America didn't interest Pound. Besides, some of his ancestors had not been New England Brahmins but horse thieves: "They were horse thieves, very good horse thieves, charming people, in fact the 'nicest' people in the country, but horse thieves, very good horse thieves, never, I think, brought to book."

Hailey was momentary. Pound's father just happened to have been there when Pound was born because the grandfather had owned silver land there and had landed the father a government job there. At the age of eighteen months Pound steamed east in the blizzard of '87 — WCW's blizzard was the blizzard of '88 — to New York and then Philadelphia. In Philadelphia the father came to rest at a desk in the U.S. Mint. He and his family settled in a Philadelphia suburb, Wyncote, where they were surrounded not by the poor and by industrial waste but by "publishing executives and other Philadelphia *nouveaux riches* — Widener, Elkins, Stetson, Wanamaker" who "filled the surrounding countryside with Renaissance palaces."

Pound was precocious and agedly learned when at sixteen he entered the University of Pennsylvania. He was also shy, had trouble getting on with people, and made up for that with great pretendings. Richard Aldington said of him later that he was "one of the gentlest, most modest, bashful, kind creatures who ever walked this earth," adding that since he was a kind creature it was "wearisome" of him always to be adopting a pose of "arrogance and petulance and fierceness."

This mild and arrogant, bashful and fierce person walked in on WCW in the fall of 1902 or early 1903, and when he did it was (said WCW) the difference between B.C. and A.D. EP lived alone in a ground floor room of the Memorial Tower. WCW lived alone across the way on the second floor of Phillips Brooks Hall. They met through a third party named Van Cleve who later would help WCW with shirt studs and neckties, and who was struck that he should suddenly have had the acquaintance of two live poets. Pound had a head of blond hair that WCW described as leonine. WCW had a short bourgeois haircut and was disgusted with his round, moon face. Pound was two years younger and unqualifiedly in charge.

Pound became not only WCW's best literary friend but also one of his pet subjects — the autobiography is full of him. WCW liked to dwell on the contradictions in him. Pound the great classicist told WCW to read Longinus on the sublime and other vast works but Pound the sometimes honest scholar confided to WCW that one didn't need to *read* all the works one *talked* about. Pound the authority on sex told WCW about sex, but in fact neither of them knew about sex and they "were both too refined to enjoy a woman if they could get her . . . and too timid to dare." And Pound the great musician played all the classical composers and "everything, you might say, resulted, except music." Pound was the "livest, most intelligent and unexplainable thing" WCW had run into, but he was also vicious, catty and an ass. He was fascinating but "one did not want to see him often or for any length of time."

One critic has said of Pound that he was a poet of many voices but nobody could ever figure out which voice was his. Pound himself once described a mixed-up English lady in the same way; she was "ideas, old gossip, oddments of all things" and full of great riches, but not hers — and the "not hers" was what she was:

> No! there is nothing! In the whole and all,
> Nothing that's quite your own,
> Yet this is you.

Kenner thinks that Pound's central identity was a problem for him in his youth only — "all his early work asks, 'Who am I?' " — but then describes a sort of certainty in Pound's old age that may have been worse than the early doubt: Pound achieved a "mystical conviction . . . that one might actually be possessed, beyond role, by the actual virtu of the great dead whom one has much pondered" — or in other words came to believe that he could be Homer or Dante or Shakespeare.

At the university WCW was not contending with a Pound with megalomania. Pound needed some years for that; he was searching out himself and wanted to have his own way in the searching. He was determined that it would be he who would choose the courses he would take and the books and subjects he would study; and when the University of Pennsylvania was not cooperative he went off to Hamilton College to finish his B.A. on his own terms. Hamilton let him take "21 units of French, 9 of Italian, 9 of Old English, 9 of Spanish, 1 of Provençal and 8 of German"; he also was able to spend a summer abroad during his undergraduate years in libraries in Spain and France, so that when he returned to the university as a graduate student in 1905 he could be even more agedly knowledgeable than when he left — and began to cultivate canes and silk cravats. But he was human, no megalomaniac, and he and WCW sat around talking more low talk about sex than high talk about Longinus.

Pound would go on to write poems in the modes of many bards of many ages and countries. He would study Greek and Chinese and become an advocate of a sort of universalist, panhistorical approach to literature. He would also discover a certain Major Douglas and the dark Douglas view of usury, which would make him march forth to fight the moneymen with one hand as he fought his academic and literary enemies with the other. He would perform these duties while WCW, except for an occasional glance at Longinus and Keats and Shakespeare, stayed home with medicine and his homey writing. It was homey because anti- and unliterary, and anti- and unhistorical, at least as soon as he got over Whitman and Keats. And before he got onto Cortez and the Paterson archives.

Pound made several appearances in Rutherford in the college years and after, and he was not liked by the Rutherfordites except Pop. Pop liked to talk with him and did not mind his pretendings. Pop once caught him up on an unnecessary obscurity in a poem and WCW was delighted to be able to report on it — but later WCW would himself come to have a reputation in Rutherford, which he enjoyed, for being literary and obscure. Bill Jr. remembers his father being kidded by a local boor for writing "those shitty verses" that nobody could understand. Writing the "shitty verses" gave him social searoom, made him brainy and unfathomable like Pound.

Pound was like the bad boys at Berry's Creek for WCW; WCW admired but did not, except on paper, join the bad boys or Pound. He did not bury himself in Greek or Chinese or Provençal poetry, he did not elect to live abroad, he did not (quite) give up on capitalism and the American Way. At college WCW, whatever he may have been thinking, was a conformer while Pound was out antagonizing his peers and teachers. The peers ridiculed Pound and once threw him in the pond in the Botanical Gardens behind WCW's dormitory (the same small pond in which after an all-night party, WCW's son Paul would catch an enormous catfish). His teachers thought of him as a poseur and one of them even flunked him in a subject, literary criticism, that by the time of graduate school he probably knew more about than the professor.

WCW was never a showman like Pound, and at college though he was two years older he felt inferior to him just as he did to his own younger brother, Edgar. When WCW said nuts to the gentlemen he had to say it softly so they wouldn't hear. Later he rationalized his early timidity in a letter to his son in college:

> Don't think I don't realize that college is an extremely limited field of effort. It is a stronghold of privilege, of dyed in the wool conservatism, even of bought and paid for conservatism, but all you have to do is *realize* that, then work for what you can get out of it. Sure there are bastards among your very teachers but give them the best you have.

Pound would not have said that, and might have been better off if he had; yet WCW was better off for having been close to a man who would not have said that. WCW was so naive and good-hearted at school that he did need toughening. He wrote home and to brother Ed about girls and parties and athletics as if he were the original Joe College. The university had a "crackerjack team" that was going to put it all over Columbia; the art-school girls were "all to the mustard"; and Philadelphia, "talk about Philadelphia being slow well I can't see it." He was serious when he told Ed that "there is nothing better to put a fellow in condition than pure cod liver oil," but he could try for comedy and that would be good too:

> . . . quite a swell affair. Gee! but I had a job to get ready. I started to dress at five o'clock. When I got my dress suit on I found I didn't have any collar, so off I went to a dry-goods store. I bought a collar,

then I went up to my room and found it was too large. About this time I didn't have a necktie so I went up to Van Cleve's to borrow one. He of course was out so I had to buy a new collar and tie. I couldn't get the darn tie straight, so at last I started off for Wilson's at six-thirty about half dressed . . . This was Dot's first dance and of course she was scared pea green. Well we got there anyway and after about a year the party was over.

Brother Ed was more worldly but not much. He came to visit WCW in the fast town of Philadelphia and they were "both puritanical — shocked, dreaming through Philadelphia, talking to servant girls, trying for a whore." WCW confided in him about a French girl into whose eyes he had looked and forgotten everything. Feeling "sort of funny" he returned home and wrote a sonnet to her brown eyes. The letter to Ed ends, "Isn't that fierce?"

His innocence about girls, tuxedos, and sonnets was matched by his passionate earnestness in letters to Mother Elena. He would complain bitterly to her that he was not receiving the love and backing of his family, then would turn around and by special delivery eat crow. When *she* was morose with *him* he would be fatherly and tell her how to live:

> . . . You must be more merry . . . really, mama, you seem to think that all your happiness is past. That is not right. You have two sons that would die to make you happy . . . You never talk of your plans and ambitions tell them to me I am absolutely sure you often ache to pour your heart out to someone, to lean your head on someone's shoulder and cry yourself to sleep. Let me be your son and brother. Let me here [sic] your secrets. Wouldn't that be just what you long for. Am I not right. I am a man Mama.

In his poetry life he was vulnerable too, despite Pound. When he gave up on Whitman and zeroed in on Keats, especially *Endymion,* he tried his hand at a couple of long narrative poems full of o'ers and wheree'ers. Also he looked for culture in Palgrave's *Golden Treasury.* He dreamed, and sometimes wrote, of princesses hidden away in primeval forests.

But he was studying anatomy and neurology, and singing his head off at the Mask and Wig. He made the Mask and Wig by singing "Tit Willow" in *The Mikado,* and played in other productions including a *Hamlet* entitled *Mr. Hamlet of Denmark* in which he played Polonius. (There is a story passed on by his children that he liked to vary the Polonius lines, and one night when he thought President Roosevelt in the audience, he said to King Claudius, "Has Your Majesty been moose hunting?") And he fenced on the varsity, and did a lot of walking, and obediently finished his assignments so that his grades were always good and he was not an academic problem — except in a course in prescription writing where he nearly flunked. The University of Pennsylvania was more kind to him than it was to Pound, and when he left Philadelphia and moved on to internship and Life he became nostalgic for the place — as Pound could not; Pound could only be angry about it. For WCW the University of Pennsylvania and Philly were all leafy and the dormitories were new and comfortable and Franklin Field where the crackerjack team played was new and big time. The days were good there, and being broke and having to have a girl pay carfare was good, and being thrown out of a Greek play full of goddesses that he tried to crash was good. Even the food was good when he took his meals out at Mrs. Chain's boarding house and met Charlie Demuth over prunes. All his life WCW liked good food, and he was lucky to marry a woman who would cook well for him and take care of him so that he wouldn't have to cook himself or put up with his mother's overdone meat — and in Philly he was taken care of too. The University was in retrospect fine except that it did not help him with his writing at all. It just introduced him to a handful of persons who would help — like Pound, and Demuth, and a man named Wilson, and H.D.

Charles Demuth whom he met over prunes was a painter but also a writer, and he was a sickly man — he would die young of diabetes — and a warm thoughtful man with a chin, WCW said, like Robert Louis Stevenson's and fingers that were long and slender; and when during internship WCW felt like chucking medicine it was to Demuth he wrote and Demuth was very happy for him and welcomed him to the freedom of art. Demuth later went to live in New York and WCW would sometimes care for him in his sickness. Demuth did a painting of one of WCW's poems. Demuth was an important part of the artists' circle in which WCW moved after his marriage. Together they experimented with bringing painting to poetry, poetry to painting.

John Wilson was a painter too but he was important to WCW not because he was a painter but because he was a failure. WCW needed failure the way his mother needed success. Wilson was a failure as a painter and he "used to paint, right out of his head, landscapes with cows, pictures 24 X 36 inches or so, that sold as 'art' for from ten to twenty dollars," and he did not mind being a failure because painting was all he knew and all he wanted to know. When WCW came to Wilson's house Wilson would tell him to join in, would give him some clean brushes and paints and tell him to get to work. That, said WCW, was fun, and when he went back to Rutherford to settle down he would gather up some clean brushes and paints — and paint, because it was fun. But he did not paint his subjects from memory like Wilson. He painted them live, and his favorite subject was the Passaic River where it looked green, leafy, and pastoral.

Hilda Doolittle was fun too when WCW walked with her out at her place "where hepaticas grew so thick the ground was blue with them." He reported to Edgar,

> Oh but she is a fine girl no simple nonsense about her no false modesty and all that. She is absolutely free and innocent. We talked of the finest things: of Shakespeare, trees, books and pictures . . . She said I was Rosalind in *As You Like It* and she was Celia, so I called her that though her real name is Hilda.

Hilda's father was an absent-minded astronomer, and Hilda lived by his observatory in hepatica country that one took a trolley car to. She was tall and "not round but willowy and rather bony, no

that doesn't express it, just a little clumsy but all to the mustard."
He sat down and wrote an acrostic poem to her that began, "Hark
Hilda, heptachordian hymns / Invoke the year's initial ides / Like
liquid," and had her name stretching down on the left, and he
talked flowers and literature with her. They discovered that they
were both writing poems but had been too shy to show them to
each other, and so WCW broke the ice, "relented and brought
forth for her inspection" something that he had "been intent on
instead of the study of pathology."

> It was an ode — after Keats I presume — on of all things the skunk
> cabbage. She listened incredulously and then burst into a guffaw.

Later she made more kindly remarks about his work but she had
her doubts and soon Pound was the prominent poet in her life.
Ezra became "wonderfully in love with her" and WCW had to
make do with thinking of her as "a good guy." She thought of him
as a good guy too so that early in 1908, while he was interning, she
wrote to him to say that she wanted him to be among the first to
know that she was going to marry Ezra. First in the letter she was
deprecatory about the intensity of her own feelings; then she went
on to hope that despite her limitations she could be of use to one
who had been, "beyond all others, torn and lonely." The torn and
lonely Pound would not be on her stage long; soon he would be
rejected by her father as "nothing but a nomad" and have to aim
his sights at a certain Mary Moore of Trenton, New Jersey; but for
the moment H.D. was convinced that she was going to devote her
life to making him less lonely and she was proud of her martyrdom: "all great love is crucifiction of the self." She was also anxious that WCW should not think that she had forgotten him, he
who would always remain "nearer and dearer than many." She
wound up the letter with reference to a letter from WCW:

> And I know that I shall never, as you wrote in your last letter, "feel
> ashamed of you" — I have as do all who know you the greatest con-
> fidence in you and your work — and hope some day to see you
> realize in some way your noble ambitions.

It was a comedown from the day she called him Rosalind. Why he had thought she might have been ashamed of him is not recorded. A few months later she wrote to say, "Ezra and I are not going to marry each other — and I am happy now as I was before — and I know that God is good." The intimacy between them seems to have ended here, though she visited him in Rutherford in 1911. She would go on to be labeled as an imagist, as would he, but she was mannered and would retain in her verse, as he would not after his "Keats" period, a highfalutin air that was more Pound's than his. She was an *imagiste,* WCW was an imagist. He could not have written, in 1913, anything like this poem of hers:

> *Sitalkas*
>
> Thou art come at length
> More beautiful
> Than any cool god
> In a chamber under
> Lydia's far coast
> Than any high god
> Who touches us not
> Here in the seeded grass.
> Aye, than Argestes
> Scattering the broken leaves.

WCW was not for her. Pound, though he liked references to Lydia and the Argestes, was not for her. She would marry Richard Aldington who was tough-minded but capable of such phrases in his own verse as "myrrh-tressed Heliodora," which would stir WCW to say in a review in 1919, "Bah, bah, bah, bah!"

He had good years at the University of Pennsylvania but came out of them unsure of himself as doctor, lover, and poet. And on top of his unsureness he had worries about what to do with Mother Elena. Mother Elena was Pop's problem but Pop was defecting. Pop was asking WCW to be a grown-up and take over. Earlier he had asked WCW to take over brother Ed's problem, which was that Ed was working too hard at M.I.T. and wouldn't listen to Pop, and so Pop asked WCW to write him. In 1907 Ed was all right, the trouble was at home. Pop thereupon set forth on a long business trip, and from the high seas as he headed out he wrote WCW that he was in effect leaving Elena in WCW's hands. He recommended that she be taken to the opera. He talked about home expenses and how to meet them. And then he proposed that if necessary she be taken to a sanatorium in Dansville, New York for three or four weeks:

> This would cost about $100 . . . If you think of this get a catalogue. Keep an eye on her. She wants care.

There is no record that Elena was taken to Dansville, and after his trip to South America Pop came back to 131 Passaic Avenue. But the Elena trouble was hard on a young man who was trying to believe that everything was good, that truth and love would never fail, and who was telling brother Edgar to "remember you are going to live forever." On the envelope that Pop's high-seas letter seems to have been mailed in, WCW scribbled for no one's eyes, "Marriage is a disease. There is no honesty extant the breed is dead."

"WCW was about five feet nine," writes his son Bill, "shoe size 8D, hat size 7¼, shirt size 15½-32, waist 32-34 with an erect stance and a purposeful walk. He grew up in a time when walking was in. He and his father and brother walked hundreds of miles for the fun of it. Penny postcards bearing Edgar's sketches of landmarks along their route to Lake George document their ability as hikers. They walked the 80 miles to the cottage at West Haven. Dad himself between 1900 and 1910 would take a trolley out of town, 6, 8, or ten miles then walk back."

Pound was a good walker too but he walked away and didn't walk back. It was said of him — he denied it — that in 1908 when he went abroad in earnest, having been kicked out of Wabash College, he landed in Gibraltar and walked to Venice carrying the manuscript of his first book *A Lume Spento*. Whether he walked or rode it was the direction that mattered. He said that he "did not walk from Gibl to Woptalia" but he did use the word "escape" to describe his departure from Wabash and America. He had gone to Wabash out of the University of Pennsylvania to teach French and Spanish, had been caught with a woman in a brief midwestern morality play in his boarding house. When fired he was furious but could joke about it: "Nothing like it to stir the blood and give a man a start in life." It had stirred the blood, it did give him a start — but it was a start in walking away for good rather than walking out for an evening stroll.

Another poet who was a good walker but walked back was Wallace Stevens. Like WCW he was specially strong on walking in his youth before he married and had a settled profession. He was in New York then, trying not to starve as a free-lance reporter. Sometimes he would walk up and down Manhattan but New Jersey was his favorite hiking ground. One day he walked forty-two miles. Another day he

> left the house after breakfast and went by ferry and trolley to Hackensack over in Jersey. From H I walked the 5½ miles to the Spring Valley Road, then 4 miles to Ridgewood, then another mile to Hoboken and back towards town seven more miles to Paterson; 17½ in all, a good day's jaunt at this time of year. Came from Paterson to Hoboken by trolley and then home.

And then home. Home wasn't much, a small hole in the city. His real home was Reading, Pennsylvania. He thought of giving up journalism and taking up writing seriously which would have been a way of walking away. He wrote his father, in Reading. His father said no, and so Stevens, not being Pound, turned around and again walked home:

> This morning I heard from him and, of course, found my suggestion torn to pieces. If I only had enough money to support myself I am afraid some of his tearing would be in vain. But he always seems to have reason on his side, confound him.

Pound kept walking away all his life while WCW and Stevens, with occasional sprees, heeded "reason." Stevens, at his father's request, soon went to law school in New York, then joined a law firm. The law decision left him with many discontents, which he recorded in a "book of doubts and fears" and tried to provide an antidote for by concocting fine fanciful stories either for himself in his notebooks or by letter for his prospective wife in Reading. Then came poetry. He stuck to the law for life (he became a lawyer for a Hartford insurance firm) but kept dreaming.

WCW lived a double life too, but he had more sympathy than Stevens did for Pound's intensities, and for walking away. Pound turned out four volumes between 1908 and 1910, and in none of them was it clear who Pound was. He was walking away from his identity as well as his society. His style was a mash of the modern and the archaic, and his subjects were out of books and museums. In the same period Stevens, who was eight years older, turned out no volumes at all but took walks and wrestled with who he was:

> Tonight there was a long twilight and after dinner I took a stroll as I am wont to do in the summertime. I could not realize that it was I that was walking there. The boy self wears as many different costumes as an actor and only midway in the opening act is quite unrecognizable.

WCW was not an identity scholar, and like Stevens and Pound he was always, at least at this stage, wearing different costumes; but unlike Pound he was wearing them at home. He was angry and all the world was bad; he was happy and it was good. He was a lover and the world was flowers; he was an intern and the world was a grotesque sideshow. If it was Palgrave's *Golden Treasury* that started him on Beauty, it was the interning that started him on his later, tough-guy style. The influences on him were many but the strong ones were in his life not his reading. Even before his French Hospital internship in New York the style of his letters to Edgar took a new, medical turn.

> I have just received a postal card telling me to go to the maternity hospital to examine a case. I have to feel around an old bum's belly, a woman of course and see which way the kid is coming. Then in about two weeks I will have to yank the thing out. It will be my first experience in this line of work so I guess I will have lots of fun.

A dozen or so years later the tough-guy manner that had crept into the letters to Edgar slopped over into the literary letters too; he would write Kenneth Burke, "sewage makes gardens grow so one should shit among the beans and do some good in the world . . . a soliloquy on: Shitting among the beans by Moonlight should make Beethoven green with affection." By then his literary style had mellowed to a consistency with the mundane. In the earlier intern years he was stylistically at least two people; he commuted daily from tough guy to Keats because he still thought that poetry was a purer element than the elements that composed French Hospital.

It was WCW rather than Pound or H.D. who first made the big jump and wrote in verse as well as prose about the plain and the ugly, and did so without lo's and wheree'ers; but in the intern years (1907–1909) he had not jumped yet. He would come home from the hospital where he had been fighting with a madman with a temperature of 106° from typhoid, and he would add a few lines to the romantic Keatsian tragedy he was writing about two lovers kept apart by a bad daddy. He had the lovers arrange a secret tryst beside a tree. Then he had them meet there; the boy proposed and she replied:

> Thou ask'st me all I have kind sir
> And yet perchance 'twas thine e'er now
> This night will I consult my heart
> And if I find thou worthy art,
> To be there I do vow.
>
> That thou may'st know how I decide
> A written paper I will place
> Within the oak leaning over the brook
> So there e'er sets the sun thou'lt look
> And read by the light of his face.

Next day he would return to the hospital and deal with a "poor whore" who had been beaten, whose breasts were "especially lacerated and on one could be seen the deeply imbedded marks of teeth." Back, then, to the typewriter "stinking of ether" where he would find that his heroine, after thinking hard, *did* put her written note inside the oak tree that was leaning over (why not o'er?) the brook — but alas, a bird flew the note away to his nest. To the hospital again where he would talk with the tough nurse Miss Diamond, hearing her announce that she was going to string a banner out in front of the hospital that would read BABIES FRESH EVERY HOUR, ANY COLOR DESIRED, 100% ILLE-GITIMATE. And again back to the tragedy, in which he arranged that the hero came too late to the oak, found no note, and in despair vanished.

Luckily at the end of the tragedy he made something happen of medical or at least Freudian interest. The girl came to the oak, discovered what had happened, fell to the ground weeping copiously; and while she was prostrate there the bad daddy entered. Finale: "while kneeling o'er as though he prayed / The father sooth[ed] her throbbing breast." Bad daddy indeed.

In the autobiography WCW lays on thick the ugly of hospital work — the drunks and the maniacs. the maimed and the dead — and tells us how much he liked it. At the end of one chapter he says that as a medical student he fell "in love with the corpse of a young negress." She was "high yaller" and lay "stripped on the dissecting table" in front of him. That was in Philadelphia. In New York in his three-year internship at two different slum hospitals he saw other specimens to fall in love with. He lived with the blood and gore of the emergency room. He met an army of medics and nurses, some of them as ugly as the patients. He came to know the city itself in its sick vigor and filth as he had not known it before. And he came to know himself and his own reactions to flesh, came to know, for example, that although he could tell himself that he loved a corpse he could see his own drawing back from "people's guts" and understand to the last goose pimple that he didn't like "dabbling" in them. " 'One thing I'm not going to do,' I told [the head doctor], 'and that's surgery.' "

It was a time to grow up, and in knowledge of the world he did grow up, leaving behind the pastoral quad at the University of Pennsylvania. He was almost ready to live with the ugly in poetry as well as hospitals, to make for himself a sort of aesthetic of the

ugly, as a way of saying nuts and delectable nuts to the apostles of
Beauty he kept running across. But not quite ready. He was still
himself too much a Beauty apostle. His long tragedy of the lovers
and the bad daddy was just one of a number of similar productions; it was not printed but his first book of short poems followed
hard after it, must have been written entirely in the intern period,
and is strictly a Beauty book.

It is so much Beauty that WCW was later embarrassed by it and
did not want any of the poems in it reprinted. He told his publisher James Laughlin of his wish and the publisher passed — and
continues to pass — the wish on to the biographers and critics of
WCW. To the knowledge of this biographer none of the poems in
the book were until 1975 (when Louis Simpson printed one in
Three On the Tower) printed anywhere in their entirety except
in the original edition, though two copies of that edition are available at Yale to biographers and critics. The restraint that has been
shown is most respectful of WCW and his wish, but there should
be an end to it. The poems are not good but they are naive,
simple, innocent — more innocent than WCW's aged wish to bury
them. To bury them is to suggest there is something to hide, and
there is not. Besides, in their badness they are instructive of how
WCW grew into something better. Here is one:

> *Love*
>
> Love is twain, it is not single,
> Gold and silver mixed in one,
> Passion 'tis and pain which mingle
> Glistering then for aye undone.
>
> Pain it is not, wandering pity
> Dies or e'er the pang is fled;
> Passion 'tis not, foul and gritty,
> Born one instant. instant dead.
>
> Love is twain, it is not single,
> Gold and silver mixed in one,
> Passion 'tis and pain which mingle
> Glistering then for aye undone.

No one should bet too much that the poem has nothing to do with the dividedness of WCW's life at the time, because it does have to do with it. It says so several times, and even throws in the foul and gritty as proof that WCW did not think that Love or Beauty or any of the good things were all beer and skittles. But the jingling of the verses negates what the verses say — there is no dividedness there — and anyway the lines do not say what they want to say because they do not *show* us the foul and the gritty, or the pain and the passion, or show us anything much at all. And they also do not say what they want to say because gold and silver are not twain in the way that mighty opposites are supposed to be twain. A critic should not try to rewrite a poet's poem, but would not gold and lead have been better?

Maybe not. Maybe nothing would have been better. The poem is a mess, and it is so because it makes love simplistic and idyllic when it is trying to do the other. But at least it is an instructive mess because it shows what a heavy load of the conventional — and the bad conventional at that — WCW was lugging along with him. Here is another:

On a Proposed Trip South

They tell me on the morrow I must leave
This winter city [city crossed out, replaced by "eyrie"]
   for a southern flight
And truth to tell I tremble with delight
At thought of such unheralded reprieve.

E'er have I known December in a weave
Of blanched crystal, when, thrice one short night
Packed full with magic, and oh [crossed out] blissful sight!
N'er so warmly doth for April grieve

To in a breath's space wish the winter through
And lo! to see it fading! Where, oh, where
Is caract could endow this princely boon?

Yet I have found it and shall shortly view
The lush high grasses, shortly see in air
Gay birds and hear the bees making heavy droon.

Something about going to Florida? Yes. It is also a poem about the chasm that lies between Jersey and Florida. That is a big chasm and the young poet is anxious to jump the chasm, to get away forever from the bleak north to where the bees make droon. But even with one "oh" crossed out there remain one "oh" and one "lo," not to mention the mysterious caract. The young poet will not get away, truly, on this "flight" by such verbiage. He would do better to stick to his walking.

The book, entitled *Poems* and containing twenty-six poems like those above, was printed by a friend in Rutherford for $32.45. Two hundred copies. The cover design cost nothing because it was done by brother Ed. It was full of misprints, which Pop corrected in a copy on file at Yale. WCW sent Pound a copy and he set out to be kindly in thanking him but had to mention that WCW was out of touch with "the progress of English poetry in the last century." Four copies were sold at Garrison's Stationery Store in Rutherford. Most of the rest were stored in a chicken coop that burned. Fifty years later WCW said that there had been nothing in the book of slightest value except the intent, and the intent was to get the fool things out of his system.

But he thought more highly of it in 1909, and was depressed by its reception. He thought of it as one of his early serious efforts in trying to "show the world something more beautiful than it has ever seen," and he was full of passion about other beauties around him that it was his job as artist to compete with. He went to see a performance of Isadora Duncan's, for example, and was so struck that he wrote a poem about it that began,

> Isadora when I saw you dance the interrupting years
>   fell back,
> It seemed with far intenser leave than lack
> Of your deft step hath e'er conferred no flaw . . .

The poem was not more beautiful than anything the world had seen before, nor was its syntax more understandable — but was Pound doing better in 1909? He had walked away from his homeland with *A Lume Spento* to Venice at *his* own expense there, and carted the copies with him to London. There he began the entrepreneuring that was to make him famous in magazine- and poetry-publishing circles in the next decade (he had his fingers in prose, painting, sculpture, and music too), with the result that *A Lume Spento* did receive more attention than WCW's *Poems*. But whether it was a better book was another matter. It was literarily more sophisticated, its archaisms better digested, but it was all contrivance and no heart that had not been cooked to death. One could not say of it, even Ezra could not say of it, what WCW had said of his own book in a letter to brother Edgar, that "what I express is the best that I honestly feel." Pound's tack was not toward honest feeling — in a poem called "La Fraisne":

> By the still pool of Mar-nan-otha
> Have I found me a bride
> That was a dog-wood tree for some syne . . .
>
> I have put aside all folly and all grief.
> I wrapped my tears in an ellum leaf
> And left them under a stone
> And now men call me mad because I have thrown
> All folly from me, putting it aside
> To leave the old barren ways of men,
> Because my bride
> Is a pool of the wood . . .
>
> Once there was a woman . . .
> . . . but I forget . . . she was . . .
> . . . I hope she will not come again.
>
> . . . I do not remember . . .
>
> I think she hurt me once but . . .
> That was very long ago.
>
> I do not like to remember things any more.
>
> I like one little band of winds that blow
> In the ash trees here:
> For we are quite alone
> Here 'mid the ash trees.

This is poetry "after the manner of," and though Pound does not in this instance specify whose manner (in many poems he did), the reader is expected to understand that the poet is walking around in the guise of one of his probably medieval French personae. He should not look for a biographical connection and say that the girl from very long ago was perhaps H.D.; nor should he say that the present pastoral scene in which the speaker of the poem finds himself was the world of poetry that the speaker had just walked in on as a substitute for Wabash. Those are the familiar rules of personae poetry and could be applied to this poem, which was originally the title poem of the volume, if the volume did not have a preface to tell us that it was intended to be a little more personal than that. It is a most erudite preface. It tells us that when a soul "is exhausted in fire" it returns to "its primal nature" in a wood, where it becomes "kin to the faun and the dryad." It tells us that Mr. Yeats has "treated of such" in his *Celtic Twilight,* and then it says that he is now treating of such because he is in such a mood — "I because in such a mood, feeling myself divided between myself corporal and a self aetherial, 'a dweller by streams and in wood-land.'" He then compares himself to someone in *The Book of the Dead* who has taken his soul with him to the simplicities or essentials of nature, that is, the wood pool of the poem.

WCW did not like *A Lume Spento* because sometimes he mistook the persona of a poem for Pound, and he did not like the persona — to which Pound replied, "Is a painter's heart crooked because he paints hunchbacks?" But WCW also detected personal remarks in the book that he thought bitter — perhaps the sour grapes about the girl from very long ago in "La Fraisne" — and Pound seemed surprised, said, "Send 'em over to me for inspection." He tried hard to be nice to WCW about his criticism — "Good Lord! of course you don't have to like the stuff you like" — but he was shaken or would not have delivered such an extended lecture (a complete aesthetic — one of the important Pound letters). Years later Pound had changed his mind, agreed with

WCW and thought it a dreadful book. He did not try to censor it as WCW had done with *Poems,* but when Pound's publisher brought out a new edition of it\in 1965 Pound wrote an introduction to it in which he said that it was "a collection of stale cream-puffs. 'Chocolate creams, who hath forgotten you?' " He added that he had written the book "at a time when Bill W. was perceiving the 'Coroner's Children.' " (The real title of WCW's poem was perhaps supplied by Pound and was "Hic Jacet.")

Pound was wrong about the timing of the "Coroner's Children." It did not appear in 1909 in *Poems.* It first saw print in 1912 in England in a magazine that Pound put it in. But though he was wrong about the date he was right in seeing that the poem was a breakthrough, a non-creampuff.

> *Hic Jacet*
>
> The coroner's merry little children
>   Have such twinkling brown eyes.
> Their father is not of gay men
>   And their mother jocular in no wise,
> Yet the coroner's merry little children
>   Laugh so easily.
>
> They laugh because they prosper.
>   Fruit for them is upon all the branches.
> Lo! how they jibe at loss, for
>   Kind heaven fills their little paunches!
> It's the coroner's merry merry children
>   Who laugh so easily.

Some of the archaisms in the poem are imitation Pound, and awkward ("of gay men" is the worst), but the poem is a fine poem all the same, a small triumph of social commentary and aimed at those who make dough off the dead and dying. Even the archaisms mostly work, mixing the old and the new, the elevated and the mundane — "kind heaven" is just right, and so is "paunches." It was a poem that WCW could write not only because by then he had met coroners but also because he had discovered — perhaps it was the debacle of *Poems* that helped him discover it — that coroners were something that could be written about in poems. He had not known that before. When he came to know that, all of his daily experience lay before him to be written about. He did not need to walk away even to indulge the dream that had him in his earlier verses stationed remotely in a pastoral wood, or in Florida where the bees did droon. Poetry could stay home with doc.

CHAPTER TWO

Marriage

Home was 9 Ridge Road in Rutherford. WCW lived there with his wife for fifty years, and when he died she continued to live there.

It is 1973.

The visitor enters and Flossie is seated at one end of the old couch. Her lap is covered with a small throw-blanket. She beckons the visitor to sit on her right on the couch, near her good ear. The couch is comfortable and sedate, but cluttered. In front of it is a cluttered small table. The clutter is new editions of WCW's work, requests for information about WCW from graduate students, business notes from *New Directions*.

She has a copy of the *New York Times* in front of her, open to the obituary page. Margaret Anderson of *The Little Review* is dead and there is a picture of her and a lengthy article. A beautiful woman, Flossie says. Both she and WCW had known her well and WCW had been a strong contributor to *The Little Review*. Margaret had been warm and friendly but her lesbian friend Jane Heap "would shut you out of her apartment if you were not on the right side."

Flossie worries briefly about where Margaret was born — she finds in the article that she was born in Indianapolis — and where she met her and when *The Little Review* moved from Chicago to New York. She looks at the obit picture and is led to remark that Margaret was one year younger than herself. A slight smile. The subject of Margaret is over.

The visitor remembers something that Malcolm Cowley said that might be useful, and utters the name Cowley. "That son of a bitch," she says, and the subject of Cowley is over. (But some months later she apologizes for her description, says Malcolm was a good friend, thinks that she must have been referring to what Robert McAlmon thought of him.)

She is brusque about others too. Alfred Stieglitz comes up and she says, "little tin god." Hemingway is mentioned and she exclaims "pshaw," then describes a tennis match between Humbo and Bill that Humbo grew tired of because he couldn't win it — he quit or Bill would have beaten him. Of Alfred Kreymborg, "Krimmie? Oh he was a 'pity me' person. He lost Bill's play *The Apple Tree* and they didn't get on after that." Of Harry Kemp, "You mean the tramp? Oh, he was a nice man, I liked him." Of Marsden Hartley, "He would climb all over you."

She is a tough old girl and her words are crisp, but the head shakes slightly and the hands. She sits erect (once her neck was broken in a car accident), stares ahead mostly, but for the good subject she turns, smiles, is discursive. A good subject is Robert McAlmon, who was a "good guy" and a long-time friend and she went to his wedding and there were orchids, orchids. Ezra is a good subject too, though she didn't like him and her children didn't like him and her own parents didn't like him. He was impossible, he was unmannerly. He jumped on a chair at her parents' house during a formal dinner to swat a mosquito. He ate off other people's plates, he ate like a pig. He would lounge at full length on the couch across the room — she points — and pontificate. The last time she saw him was after St. Elizabeth's and he brought his whole entourage and they stayed a day or two, and he would sit over there on that couch and Bill would sit opposite him and they would have nothing to say to each other. It was lucky that Townley Scott came down because he and Ezra got along.

And WCW, Bill, is himself a very good subject, whose writings she will defend against all the others, and the business side of whose estate she has long been in charge of. She didn't like Gertrude Stein because Stein once told Bill that writing was not his trade. She shares Bill's feelings about T. S. Eliot and the academics and talks of how badly Bill was once treated at Harvard. She complains of the restless ones who moved in and out of their fixed lives, like Maxwell Bodenheim who was filthy and arrogant and spent weeks with them, and afterward she never wanted him in the house; but she warms to those who had troubles and were modest and helpless — to Demuth, to the artist Charles Sheeler (maybe Bill's best friend, she says), to poet Wallace Gould. The old names float out over the couch but it is Bill who is really there, not the names. She is reconstructing Bill's life with poets and artists for the visitor — because she feels that it is that life the visitor wants to hear about — but what she remembers best is not that life but her own life with Bill at 9 Ridge Road.

And on trips. They went to Europe twice, they loved ships, they once took the *Delta Queen* down the Ohio to New Orleans, they sailed to Newfoundland. They loved to walk, they loved to get away, and Bill needed to get away, the doctoring would press in on him. He would be moody, depressed — yes, he was like that — and they would go away for a trip and sometimes he would go by himself or she would go by herself — but always they would come back. Rutherford was their life; 9 Ridge Road was fixed; it was a mail drop for their roving friends.

The moodiness? She nods her head, looks solemn. He had great depressions. He was very bad after his stroke (1952) but there was always some of it. When he was silent and gloomy you could guess that he was going to write and pretty soon, yes, he would go upstairs and you could hear the typewriter. Not that he needed to be upstairs to write. He wrote everywhere and on everything. He wrote in the office and in his car, and he wrote on prescription blanks and on toilet paper. But mostly he typed on ordinary paper upstairs and when he was up there, writing, you knew not to bother him.

But now it is lunchtime. To the kitchen. She is unhappy that her arthritis keeps her from making lunch. The visitor puts clumsy sandwiches together that she is polite about but cause her to mention that Bill never made a meal for himself in his life. When the meal is over she will not let the visitor clean up. Pile the stuff in the sink. Back to the living room. Is she tired? No, a little more. Fetch the photographs in the shoe box.

So the intimacies begin, not great intimacies but family. The yellowing snapshots are held up one by one. She didn't mind Grandma Wellcome but that was perhaps because Grandma Wellcome never lived in Flossie's house but in Philadelphia and West Haven. Grandma Wellcome was all right, she liked the stage like all the Williamses and once she sang as Buttercup in *H.M.S. Pinafore*. But the Spanish mother Elena didn't like that; she was too serious, she loved opera, sang *Traviata* around the house. And the house *was* Flossie's house, not Elena's, Elena didn't like *that* and they didn't get on. The mother kept saying insulting things to Flossie so that Flossie would know that she didn't like being in Flossie's house. When Flossie was away in Switzerland for a year and Bill stayed home with her, it was the "happiest year" in her life. When somebody said to Flossie that Flossie's two children would soon be grown up and married, Elena said, "Then you'll see how *you* like it." And when Flossie came back from the hospital after a hysterectomy Elena said, "I never thought I'd see you again." She wasn't easy to live with, says Flossie.

Then the photographs move on to Flossie's family, the Hermans. Pa Herman was kindly — but tough and scrupulous about money, debts, charge accounts — and Mother Herman was a social climber because her parents had been brought up on a great country estate in Norway. Then there was sister Charlotte who played the piano professionally and married someone they called the affinity man because he had affinity for so many. Charlotte was now living in California. Flossie hated California but Charlotte liked it. Charlotte . . . but now Flossie is tired, the visitor thanks her . . .

Here is the woman whom WCW proposed to in 1909, married in 1912. Her hands are delicate. Her arthritis keeps her from writing and she is dead set against Dictaphones but she loves to talk, and talks well. To bring back the past with her is to sit beside her on her couch next to her good ear, and ask questions but mostly listen, listen to and admire a strong voice and mind in a frail body. Her face is an old face and a child face. A smile shows steadily but the smile is not always smiling. She is the servant of the WCW legend, and the loving widow. She is also her own woman.

2

WCW proposed to Florence Herman just before he left for Leipzig for a year of more medical training. He was twenty-six and she was nineteen. He tells us in his Stecher trilogy, which is three novels that he wrote about the Herman family (*White Mule, In the Money, The Build-Up*), that until the day before he proposed to Flossie he had been casting his eyes at her older sister, Charlotte — and so had his brother, Ed. Flossie's legs were well-shaped while Charlotte's were "like bean-stalks," but Charlotte was worldly and wise and beginning to give public musical recitals; the men were around her in the Herman's Rutherford parlor. Flossie was a young thing and no one noticed her in the parlor until WCW did. He did it on the rebound.

Brother Ed had just won a big architectural prize that would send him to Rome for a year with his expenses paid. Pop was pleased and said that since Ed was going abroad he would help WCW go abroad too, to Leipzig. Big decisions were being made, the times of the ships' departures coming close, and both WCW and Edgar were looking at Charlotte in her parlor. WCW wrote later in *The Build-Up* that he and Edgar plotted together, though they were rivals, and came to agree that Edgar would go alone to Charlotte but would represent both of them, and would say that both of them wanted to marry her. Edgar would then add that it would be desirable if she would choose between them. So Edgar did go to Charlotte and it was Edgar Charlotte chose.

WCW was wounded. He "ground his teeth" and "fought back his unreasoning tears." Then he pulled himself together and sat down and thought up a new plan, plan two, that was his own plan without Edgar. The plan was to go for Flossie. That is what the novel says, and Flossie does not after sixty years disagree, but the letters that WCW would soon write to Flossie from Leipzig in 1909 do not show that Flossie knew of the context of the plan at the time, knew that it was a rebound plan conceived because WCW had been rejected by Charlotte the day before.

But WCW knew. It was his plan. He came to her abruptly with his plan; he made no small talk but said to her right out, "Will you marry me?" Flossie replied — in the novel; in the letters it does not appear that she had known enough to say this — "You don't love me. You love my sister."

That was two propositions to answer. WCW chose the last. He denied that he loved Charlotte but the denial had the effect on Flossie, who was very orderly, that she went on to repeat her *first* proposition, saying, "But you don't love *me*."

He went after that one head-on. He said, "I don't love anyone but I want to marry you. I think we can be happy." In the novel WCW adds that that was "a stumper for a young girl."

One of WCW's biographers, Mike Weaver, blames the stumper on WCW's readings of a German writer, Otto Weininger, who had written that a man could will himself into love. WCW had read Weininger and he was himself to write elsewhere about willing one's self into love; but at the time of his proposal to Flossie he had no time to think back on his Weininger readings. As for Flossie, she had not read Weininger but she went off into a huddle with herself about his proposal for eight hours, not telling her parents or her sister, Charlotte, about it, and decided that it was an honest proposal and that she would say yes, tentatively. She went back to him, told him, and so it was official that they were secretly engaged, although WCW was going off to Leipzig, and then would have to set up in medical practice before they could marry. WCW rewarded her for her decision by giving her a "half kiss" and rushing off.

WCW did not just rush off home. He escaped to Cranberry Lake in the northwest corner of New Jersey for a few days, and from there he wrote her his first letter. The letter was also a stumper. He was worried about what he had done in proposing to her, and he put down in writing confessional things that he could not have said to her face — so that she could back out of the engagement if what he said frightened her:

> And oh Florence you do not know me as yet. Sometimes I will appear childish, sometimes weak and impotent . . . This is I or a part of me at least. The rest, if it is true and faithful, may appear in time. If you can love this strange me I will be very happy but if you cannot why look the fact fairly in the face for the truth always has its way in the end.

Flossie was not supposed to take his "strange me" too seriously, any more than she was supposed to be too upset when at the end of the letter he said that he had just been spooning on a porch overlooking the lake with someone named Kate. Beyond the confessionals he had a reserve. Once in a letter to Ed when he was happy and Ed was not, he summed up their young lives as good and their chances in the world as good and said in summary, "Anyhow Bo we have no reason to be cast down so here's where I go and eat some breakfast." At Cranberry Lake he was down but not really down; he was looking at marriage and himself, not liking either much but working on liking them, meanwhile spooning. Leipzig would be harder.

It is not recorded that Flossie took his "strange me" seriously at the Cranberry Lake moment, or that she was unhappy that he spooned there; but she did write him a letter while he was at Cranberry Lake in which she expressed, as he had, doubts about the depth of their sudden commitment. She said first that he should "kindly speak of nineteen year old people with a little respect next time," then observed, "You don't know me Billie and I don't believe I know you either." She said that her ignorance was brought on by the fact that she had never "had the pleasure" of having him call on her. She thought that she did really love him but she did not know why, and she thought that if their love should change while he was in Leipzig they would manage to survive anyway because they had not overcommitted themselves, and suggested that by letter at least they "pretend" to be "just good friends."

With these ambiguities of romance in mind, WCW sailed for Europe on the S.S. *Marquette,* a "cattle boat" (Pound had sailed on a "cattle boat" six months before), in the company of other young doctors also headed for German science. He said of the doctors that they were obliged like himself to travel second-class because they were poor, and added, "Gee! it's great to be poor." This was in his first shipboard letter. He ended it decorously, "with best regards from Willie," but he was decorous only because of Flossie's good-friends plea; and since he understood that plea to be partly a subterfuge he was not inclined to obey with great fidelity. Flossie had said to him — beyond her remark about how little they knew each other — that she worried about her mother's prying: "Mother has always had a way of asking me to let her see my letters and what would I do if she asked me to see one that I couldn't show her." So WCW dutifully wrote a letter to Flossie that she could show her mother but then, in another shipboard missive written the same day, said, "Now that I have gotten that family letter out of my system I must let off steam or I shall burst," and thereupon grew illegally loving:

> I miss you terribly . . . I love you more every minute . . . and if you don't send me your picture inside of ten minutes after reading this letter I'll take the next flying machine home.

Flossie would send the picture and he wouldn't like it — he would complain that it had been touched up, and fuss her by telling her that he had erased some of the touchings. But that was later. In Leipzig when he arrived he was happy and busy, and he wrote touristy things in the family letters and loving things in the Flossie letters. When he received his first letter from her he was so touched that "two funny little happy tears just naturally sprang up in the corner of each eye." He couldn't understand how it was that the two of them had gotten where they were, but there they were, "just as sure as apples don't grow on plum trees." He had discovered that he believed in her as if she were a "young goddess" though he knew that she was not. He had a million things to say to her that he could not say at the moment, and added, "Here is a sonnet, however."

"Here is a sonnet, however" is a line that all lovers should remember, but the sonnet that came with the letter is in the mode of the 1909 *Poems* and is not as warm as the letter. In the letter he called her a young goddess in his *Poems* mode, but also in the letter he retracted the goddess part. And in the letter he had a number of gentle but unpoetic complaints. In later letters the complaints grew.

They grew because Flossie's mother was a busy mother and it wasn't long before she was into the private letters as well as the family letters. So was Charlotte, who kept looking at Flossie "as if she had caught her stealing her stockings." Flossie wrote to WCW to say that he should be more cautious in both kinds of letters. Soon after that she wrote to complain that his letters were too cold. He was put out, and wrote back that he had been cold because she had told him to be cold. But in the meantime she gave him a new and better reason to be cold, having written him about her dates with a Rutherford competitor of WCW's, one with money. WCW was no longer pleased to be poor. He replied,

> If I only had a car, a boat, a canoe and things I might have a show but now that I am poor there is only one chance left for me and that is to be famous. If I fail here nothing is left but a nasty dis-position . . .

Leipzig. Leipzig. Pound had thought he was crazy to go there. It was where they danced round and round the same way for-ever — "it would break a frenchman's heart" — and where they sat down to drink beer and were just flesh on chairs. It was where they were graceless and "the men wore shoes two feet long," the women "had feet proportionate to the men," and "I must say I don't like to see a girl eighteen years old with a 'corporation' big enough for a baby to sit on."

They were plodders. They lacked spontaneity. The young men were "one lump of vanity." And they were petty. All year he had trouble with rooms, meals, prices. He could praise the medical training, he could speak warmly of individuals, he could be diverted by plays and concerts and books (but his eyes were bothering him), and could have a fine holiday with Edgar in Berlin, but mostly he "didn't have much fun" in Germany.

He was lonely. He sat at his desk in an emptiness. He typed neat medical notes on 4 x 7 cards of ailments from "Abscess" to "Vomiting after Anesthesia," and he tried his hand at a new verse form, having come to "detest" the sonnet within less than a year of the publication of *Poems*. The new form, he says in the autobiography, was *abba, bccb, caac* in iambic pentameter. It was not very radical, nor very different from his "Love is Twain" poem in *Poems,* nor an experiment that he liked later since there is no poem in that form in his collected poems. He sat at his desk in an emptiness writing out to a few spots of light in his life — Pound in London, Edgar in Rome, a relative of his father's in Paris, plus the family at home, and Flossie — and a woman named Viola Baxter that Pound had introduced him to in New York — but otherwise living with nothing but the immediacies of his daily rounds. Rutherford when he returned would be an emptiness too; there he would not be able to perform well as social animal either; but in Leipzig he could imagine that Rutherford would be different for him, especially with his dream of Flossie. So that when Flossie and he began to argue across the ocean it was a big argument for him because the images of Flossie and Rutherford were sharp in his mind, and valuable, and he felt them fading.

Flossie had angered him by writing about her rich Rutherford date, and by complaining of his coolness, and by being cool herself, signing her letters "yours sincerely" or "one of your friends." In turn he troubled her with letters about his "strange me" and his "wild desires," by chopping away at her photograph that she sent him, and by suggesting that he was not after all coming home after the Leipzig year but was to be traveling elsewhere, perhaps to Constantinople. He was going out there, he thought, "to teach some branch of 'stomach ache' or other."

The Constantinople letter was a signal for real indignation; it offended Flossie and stirred her mother to righteousness. The mother could see that WCW was a shiftless poet who would never settle down to doctoring and a family. She thought she and Pa Herman should step in and break up the "silly infatuation" so that Flossie could get on with her life and go to Vassar. Flossie did not want to go to Vassar, refused to go to Vassar, proposed a business career for herself instead of Vassar (this dismayed Pa) and then a nursing career (this made him laugh) ; but though she was strong in holding out against Vassar she was not strong in holding out for WCW. Passions were high in the Herman parlor about Constantinople.

But it was not WCW but Flossie's mother or sister, Charlotte, who broke the news to Flossie that was worse than Constantinople — that WCW had competed with Edgar in proposing to Charlotte. The news sat Flossie down to write a strong how-could-you document to Leipzig. In it she said that aside from Constantinople he was not a good fiancé because he had not been open with her. She said also that he was shiftless and undependable, that he lacked religious conviction, and that his ambition to be a poet was idle. It is possible that this document was written by the mother. WCW composed a long reply that he called the letter of his life.

He began by saying that he had never loved Charlotte and had not misrepresented his relations with her. He was shocked that Flossie could think that he had lied: "Oh if you knew how worthless a thing life is and how great is love you would not think that I would lie to you and sacrifice my peace in eternity for the miserable few petty years of gain in this world." He allowed that his dedication to doctoring was limited by his other loves, "the greatest forces in his life," that is, poetry and drama. He felt that he had stuck to medicine out of "cowardice and some regard for his parents," though poetry was where his heart lay. He found it a cruel blow that Flossie should now be attacking him for his faith in poetry. What she had said to him had brought back to him again the "heart-breaking war" in his mind between his two futures, but he could not, even for her, undertake to give one up. He had decided therefore — in another hundred words — that

> I will be a dramatist but that it would be foolish for me to give up medicine, also that as long as my mother and father are alive I must live by them and help them and return in part the debt I owe them. This makes my course clear, it is this, I will live as a doctor merely to support myself. Meanwhile I shall work and strive to do something worthy in my other field but the battle will be hard and as I may mistake my strength it may end in what men call failure.

He had mentioned failure more than once to Flossie. Now he argued that he had mentioned it to her because he was trying to be honest with her and make sure that she understood that he might well end up as a "poor country doctor." But he did not think that failure should be measured in terms of money and he hoped that Flossie would realize that his other aspirations were high. He said that he was "a strange melancholic creature" who could see the folly of "certain American ideas." It was his dream to combat those ideas and "instill some of the spirit of beauty into our crude forms." He concluded that he could not under any circumstances reform himself according to the prescriptions in her letter:

> I will not yield to please you for I love you too much to believe that you would want me to be less than my highest desires . . . You I love and you I will marry or no one . . . I will promise never to mention my feelings to you in the future but I completely refuse to go half way. Either you give up everything and stand ready to die by me if necessary or else not a word of it ever again.
>
> I have warned you that I am melancholy, I am weak, I am wild further I hate religious creeds and all dead forms and I will never yield to them. Yet I am conscious of my own worth and I tell you my heart is no small thing. If you refuse me I can and will work alone.

That was written in the fall of 1909.

3

The Build-Up is WCW's novel about Flossie and himself, how she left her family's nest and joined him so that he did not, as he thought he might have to do in the letter of his life, live and work alone. But maybe the novel is not so much the story of her leaving the nest as of his coming to live in the nest, the wanderer finding a home — to the extent that a wanderer who is true to his trade can ever find one.

The novel was published in 1952 but he had been writing it for some years. In it, even more than in *White Mule* (1937) and *In the Money* (1940), the biographical matter is put down with no visibly intended fictionalizing, as if the work were in fact a biography, not a novel. The exposition, narrative and dialogue are conventional, of a kind that Joyce and the other prose radicals of the early century, including at one time WCW himself, thought that the world was coming to an end of. In other words the novel is very square, and in the romantic sections it is squarest. Flossie, who is called Flossie, is presented as a sweet young thing (though with a stubborn streak) who has love "shining in her eyes." WCW, who is called Charlie Bishop, is presented as a young doctor-poet whom people point to and label "poet." As for the wicked mother of Flossie, who is named Gurlie, she is not really wicked but practical-minded and physical, a family defender, a social climber, a good heart — but with a sharp tongue that does lash out at the lovers:

> "That boy," she would say in the hearing of her daughter, "he's a selfish one. All *he* wants to do is sit in the house and write poems all day long. He says so himself. He isn't the slightest interested in money. That's what he says. He'll be poor, just a poor doctor — who writes poems. Poo!"

Gurlie goes on complaining about the doctor-poet, but at last resigns herself to him — "He'd never amount to much with his lack of ambition, but she liked him, in a way." As for Pa Herman, who is named Joe, he never interferes with the lovers. He is quiet, honest, hardworking, likes fishing, is a plain man.

And then there is sister Charlotte, who is called Charlotte. She is breathless about music and the arts. WCW supplies a conversation between her and the doctor-poet about his new book of poems, and she says she thought the book was beautiful, he declares that "it stank," and she replies that she loved it.

On the Williams side there is more of the same. When brother Ed, who is called Fred, wins the "highest honors accorded to any architectural student in the United States," the joy in the household at having a Horatio Alger in its midst is unrestrained, and is accompanied by a Horatio Alger sermon:

> By his own long years of effort he had capped the family striving, begun when his parents, saving every free penny that they owned, had sent him to school. And he, because it was what in a man should be expected, had applied himself and worked.

The Build-Up is an honest-facts book in the sense that most of WCW's stories and poems are honest-facts works. The dialogue is dialogue that may be assumed to have (approximately) taken place, and the thoughts of the characters are thoughts that the characters may be assumed to have (approximately) had. Also it may be assumed that Flossie was in fact a sweet young thing with a stubborn streak, her mother was in fact a kind heart with a sharp tongue, and her father was in fact quiet, sensible, a good fisherman. And it may be assumed that the Williamses were also as they are portrayed, hardworking, determined to climb the ladder to success, respectful of good schools that help the hardworking up the ladder, and in general apple-pie American of the kind that did not come over on the Mayflower.

But while *The Build-Up* is an honest book in this sense its placidness is striking for a book written by a long-time literary dissenter. What it is is a book of complacent reflection written from inside the apple-pie America. It has not the flavor of the letters of the real young doctor-poet sitting in his emptiness forty years earlier in Leipzig. Then he wrote from the outside. Then he was not only physically outside by three thousand miles but he was still outside his chosen profession, still outside the writing society he wished to join, and still outside the Rutherford nest. He was outside the nest spiritually as well as physically by being in his own mind just what Mother Herman thought he was — shiftless, unlikely to make a go of it, a poet. Between 1909, then, and the time of the writing of *The Build-Up* WCW was *taken* inside, and found that with reservations he liked it there.

He must have liked it there; he would not have written about his wife and his wife's family if he had not thought he could honestly write that he liked it there. Even so the undertaking was limiting. As insider he knew more, but if he had been outside he would have seen what was to be known differently, and he would have been more curious than he was about the insiders' assumptions about themselves. *The Build-Up* has tough sections but what it says about both the Hermans and the Williamses has, finally, the character of a party line.

When the young doctor-poet was in his emptiness in Leipzig he was naive, and he was still dreaming his Keats dreams, but he was free of the party line. What he said in that year, especially when his "strange me" spoke, had a dimension not in *The Build-Up*. In *The Build-Up* the doctor-poet is acknowledged to be different from the rest of them, the nonpoets, but the difference is not developed. Instead it is made into continuing occasions for mild jokes about the doctor-poet's impracticality and idealism. In Leipzig it was no joke.

Flossie was an insider from the beginning. It was her friends that they settled in with in Rutherford, and her life. New York was the big city across the river that WCW went to, sometimes with Flossie, for the other friends, the poets and painters, and the other life. Son Bill has said that those who came most to 9 Ridge Road when he was growing up were Rutherford married couples whose friendships started with the wives. The wives played bridge. When the husbands entered the friendship the wives did

not play bridge; then the husbands and wives sat around and
drank, ate, gossiped — but it was bridge that put them together
first and they were "the gang." Son Bill remembered the men's
"booming voices" — a couple of businessmen, a salesman, an insurance man and an "ambulance-chasing" doctor — coming up
from the cellar. The men were dull, there was no art in them, but
they were normal. They were ordinary suburban commuters and
lived their lives along the Passaic the way the friends of Flossie's
parents, as described in *The Build-Up,* had lived out theirs. The
booming voices would come up from the cellar during parties
when the cellar was decorated and the steaks were cooked on
charcoal in the furnace. Son Bill upstairs would not hear WCW as
one of the voices. He was there, he was a part of it, but quiet,
withdrawn.

And the booming Rutherford voices do not appear in WCW's
autobiography. In the autobiography the memories of friends are
memories of artist friends. Most of them lived in New York and
the Williamses would see them in New York rather than Rutherford.

Sitting on the couch in 1974 Flossie said that she had always
liked bridge and golf, but WCW did not; he had hated "sub-
urbia." She suddenly wanted to talk about their differences and
said that sometimes they had to get away from each other. She
mentioned 1927 which was the year she spent in Switzerland with
the children, then she backed off and said their differences were
not "serious." It was good of her to bring up the differences at all.
She knew that when WCW was sitting up dark at his typewriter he
was inaccessible, but it is a hard thing to admit to the inaccessible
after fifty years.

Son Bill brought up the differences too. He apologized first.
He described himself as antagonistic to his father — perhaps, he
thought, because he and his father were so much alike — but even
so he thought that he knew his father well enough to say that he
was withdrawn and uncommunicative, with no close friends. The
younger son, Paul, disagreed. He felt he had known his father

well and he remembered long close talks, remembered being told bedtime stories, remembered jokes about sex, remembered warmth.

But both agreed that he was a loner. He was not even close to his neighboring medicos. He was angry at the rich ones. His own patients were mostly among the poor, and sometimes he "turned people off" because he didn't charge enough. He called the rich ones society doctors and "top brass" and he was proud that he was not like them, but he wasn't close to the doctors he liked either. As for the doctors they were respectful of him because "he was a good doctor, he knew his stuff" (son Bill) but they didn't know what to make of him, especially his poetry. Once he gave a poetry reading for the doctors. They were quiet and attentive as if in church, but they couldn't put their minds to the poetry as poetry. At the end of the reading one of them said to him, "Bill, are you a Catholic?" WCW gave him his goggle eyes, shook his head, said "no-o-o-o."

So the difference was there. Between Flossie and WCW. Between son Bill and WCW. Between Rutherford and WCW. But when he wrote his letters from Leipzig in 1909–1910 he had not spent forty years with the difference. He was alone with his dream of literature and his doubts, and to all the points of light out beyond him in the emptiness he reached out in the hope that with at least one — and Flossie was the likely one — the difference would go away. It never did.

When he reached out he played a different role with each correspondent. With his mother he was alternately parental and childish, with brother Edgar alternately down-to-earth and utopian, with Pound literary and tough-minded. Then there was Viola Baxter, Pound's discovery in New York City. With Viola he was urbane and delivered himself of bad imitations of Henry James. (Sample: "A poor little idle word of mind it seems has been at fault, and therefore let the petty offender lie.") He began flirting with Viola in 1907, mostly by mail, and even his marriage to Flossie did not stop him from making occasional trial steps toward her. She was handsome, she was more sophisticated than Flossie, she was a non-Rutherford alternative in his dream life.

To Flossie he was many different persons. Sometimes he called her "dear child," sometimes he was the child, sometimes he was flip and signed off with "Your personal property," sometimes he was passionate and reached for hyperbole. Always he shuttled between his Jekyll and his Hyde. In January of 1910 after his big letter had been received with grace, he had his confidence back and lectured her on marriage, telling her that it should not be a prison for the man or the woman because that was "an old worn out and untrue viewpoint." By February he was down on himself again and said that she should forget him and "find some real man not a mess like I am." Two days later in February he was again high, having had his hair cut and his mustache removed:

> . . . there's nothing left for you to grab but my nose and my ears. Gee how I tremble.

In March he was angry again, defensively, because she had again suggested that she was disappointed in him. He wrote that if she was disappointed it wouldn't bother her "to forget such a person":

> As far as I am concerned I never saw anyone yet that I wasn't disappointed in in one way or another. Oh well it's all in the game I guess I can smile at hell itself when the time comes.

By early spring he had had all he could stand of Leipzig and the emptiness. He set out on a European tour that included France, Switzerland, Italy, and Spain, as well as a week in London with Ezra. The London week he mentioned to Flossie beforehand, but after he had been there he was silent about it with her. Flossie's mother would not have been happy to hear of Pound with his cane and pompadour hairdo living in artist splendor and squalor in Kensington, trying to resuscitate the dead art of poetry. But in the autobiography later he called the week fabulous. He met William Butler Yeats twice, with Yeats reading poetry by candlelight at one meeting, and being put down by Edmund Gosse for defending drunkenness and lechery at the other. Also Pound and WCW toured the town, saw the Elgin marbles at the British Museum, eyed girls (one of them did bumps and grinds in reply) and drank a very special Dutch coffee that Pound filtered through cheesecloth with great labor. Pound gave WCW his full dose of lectures about what to read and how to write so that when WCW left Pound could write his mother and say he thought WCW had *learned* something. He had, but he didn't write Flossie about it.

He wrote about the other countries in detail. In Paris he read Heine to annoy his French hostess, a relative (perhaps) of Pop's. In the Alps he gaped at waterfalls. In Italy he joined Edgar and the two of them became very cultural in the southern part, visiting Paestum, Amalfi, Sorrento, Pompeii, Capri, Naples. But as it came time for him to sail home he was erratic — as Flossie seems to have been on the other end — and in his letters he would leave off describing his trip and sulk — "the best thing we can do is call the game on account of darkness" — or he would giggle nervously that she had only a few weeks to escape from him and if she wanted to escape she had best write a letter to be delivered at the dock in Hoboken. Just before he sailed from Naples to Gibraltar he complained that she had not been writing enough; if he did not find a letter waiting for him in Gibraltar he wouldn't bother to look her up when he returned. Then there was a letter waiting in Gibraltar and he was happy again. He took a quick Spanish tour on a train, Spain was lovely, she was lovely and he had a fine argument with a Spanish conductor:

> You should have heard me sling my choice Rutherford Spanish at him with that peculiar Hackensack accent which you know so well.

He even included a heavy poem to women in that letter. He thought they were "wonderful creatures," threw a poetic curse at the "idle mockery" in names women were called, and went on very Poundlike, remembering his London lessons.

In his last letter from abroad he meditated for a page on what would happen at the dock when he landed, wondering if she would be there to meet him, and if she were there if she would kiss him, or wait for him to kiss her, or just shake his hand. Then he looked further ahead and asked how they would conduct themselves *after* the meeting:

> Shall I follow her wishes whatever she means them to be and do her pleasure or shall I do what she really wishes and have my own way?

He concluded that whatever happened he would be looking for her the moment land was sighted.

Landing in Hoboken after all the fuss he found the dock empty.

4

It didn't matter. Maybe Flossie decided, or maybe Flossie's mother decided, that Flossie shouldn't go to the dock; but it didn't matter. The lovers found each other in Rutherford, it wasn't hard, and they put aside letter writing for two months and actually talked. They talked, and actually came to know each other, and out of knowing each other they came to be pleased with each other. With great good faith they settled in for the last two years of their three-year engagement.

Too long, said WCW. The first months at home for him went fast. He was readying for doctoring and was courting Flossie, and Flossie was bringing him a "degree of blessedness" he couldn't estimate. But then the tedium settled in, and trouble with parents. Also WCW resumed correspondence with Viola Baxter in New York, and though the letters were decorously distant there was fire there. All through 1911 and 1912 the marital train stood still and the forces lined themselves up, duty and moneymaking on one side, poetry on the other — poetry and sundry dark unruly things in a mash. Too long an engagement. Too much of the nesting business.

But Flossie performed well, survived. Once she angered him by complaining that he had been paying too much attention to the woman next door, and at no time did she let down on her Flossiness; she was his ball and chain, his anchor. But she was what she was in a way that he liked. He was grateful for her Flossiness. He would tell her that he hated work and responsibility, but then compliment her for keeping him on the straight and narrow. He would say that he "despised morality" but then agree to be virtuous — for her sake only. He would cry out against marriage, one of his favorite cries, but then he would add that to be married to Flossie was a different matter. He allowed that many times he wanted to "shun success and all the silly things" that were important "at all times" to her, but he said he didn't mind working for the silly things so long as he was doing so for her sake. He lived in the "glory" of her love, and sometimes he was soppy about it, sometimes comic:

> He kissed her under the mistletoe,
> He kissed her under the rose,
> He kissed her under the holly and
> He kissed her under the nose.

He even tried his hand at being Bobby Burns:

> She's a winsome wee thing,
> She's a handsome wee thing,
> This sweet wee wife o' mine, etc.

When in August of 1910 he was getting his first office ready — it was to be in the family front hall — Flossie went off to the mountains with her own family and he became a correspondent again, writing her about wading deep in plaster, ordering a telephone, choosing green wallpaper, and preparing to put up his doctor's shingle. Then in a couple of weeks came his first patient and he wrote to say that he wished the patient had been Flossie. He wished she could have been there as his patient so that he could have given her "the latest and most peculiar treatment" — though he would not have wanted to cure her because that would have sent her away. The trouble with his wish was that his first patient was not Flossie but a little girl, and she was not much of a patient because she just made an appointment to see him on Wednesday. "That was doing well enough for my first day, right?"

Within a few months the patients were coming in at a good clip, Flossie was off in the mountains again and he wrote to say that he expected to be a "leading physician" in short order. There was joy in the words. He was busy, and happy with himself, and happy that she was to be his wife. By now he was speaking more plainly to her. He joked with her, argued with her. He trusted her and knew how far he could tease her. It was clear that she had toughened up and was not any longer easily offended — though her Rutherford was not Bloomsbury — so that he could say to her without fear that she would bristle:

> The three girls and I sat on the sand until half past ten last night but none of them believes in free love so I had to abandon them to their blind fates after a hard argument.

The two of them also looked at their common cultural future, and in one letter WCW composed a high-minded list of things they should see and do:

> Theater once every two weeks
> Opera.   Parsival
>   Russian Ballet, etc.
> Books to read.
>   Sartor Resartus
>   Ibsen's plays, etc.

After the high-mindedness came breathers:

> Dances at _____
> Parties
> Take a swim at Rockaway
> See a hockey game at Nicholas Rink
> Ball game
> Take a trip to West Point
> Take a walk about Fort Lee

Ending the list he said, "It may seem cold-blooded but it's the only way."

But the parents, on both sides, were sluggish. The parents were slow to say to themselves that the engagement was real, and slower to encourage the marriage proper. The doctor-poet was supposed to become a leading physician before, not after. WCW had no money even for rent, Pop refused to consider letting them live in the family house, Mother Elena lectured him about expenses and how he "would have to do this and the other and give up on this and the other." WCW looked ahead and could see some "hot times" before they settled down. Then Grandma Wellcome got sick; it was momentary but 1912 began slowly to slip away and the marriage began to have the look of something that would not happen.

Then it did happen, abruptly. In December 1912 they were married, not by one minister but two — a Presbyterian and a Unitarian. There was champagne at the Hermans. There was a quick honeymoon in Bermuda. And then there was a small apartment waiting for them in a house next door to the Williamses. In a year Flossie would be pregnant. Pa Herman would step in and help them with a mortgage. They would purchase 9 Ridge Road and move in.

WCW wrote at least four short plays during the long engagement years before the marriage — he was taking his dramatist future seriously — and two of the plays were about the relations of young lovers with parents. All four plays were historical, being set in American colonial times, but of the two plays about lovers one is set in the Salem of witchcraft days, the other in Nieu Amsterdam "after the Dutch have lost the town."

The Salem play is called *Betty Putnam*. In it Betty, a good strong-minded heroine, is thought by the puritans to be a witch because she writes poetry. The puritans of the play, especially the puritan daddy of the rather weak young man that Betty is engaged to, do not like poetry. Betty discovers that she can "not sing lest someone cry 'the Devil's in her,' " nor rhyme — "nay that's the devil too" — and so she has moments of despair in the middle of the play before the bad daddy's sinister designs are thwarted. The bad daddy is reminiscent of the bad daddy in WCW's earlier

Tragedy (see p. 48) ; he is not down on Betty for her poetry but he hankers for a piece of land belonging to her that is to be her dowry when she marries his son. He insists that the land be signed over to his son before they marry, his motive being to slicker son as well as Betty, since the son is in debt to daddy for an amount equivalent to the land. The play ends happily, the lovers keep the land and Betty is not hung for poetry — but it's nip and tuck to the last page.

The Nieu Amsterdam play, called *Sauerkraut for the Cultured,* has not a bad but a good daddy in it, a daddy who has no sinister designs upon anyone, a daddy who is a Dutchman, a plain man, a man with no aspirations to rise in the world and become a gentleman but one who wishes to be known for what he is. His name is Bach, he is distantly related to the musical Bach, and he himself plays bells, bells that he likes for their music and cares not how they look. His daughter is named Lina; she is lovely and is competed for by two young men in a manner suggesting the competition between WCW and Edgar for Charlotte Herman in 1909. But the two young men are not brothers.

One of them, by the name of Karl, is Dutch, honest, plain as an old shoe. He has the inside track to Lina at the outset but he willingly gives away his advantage in an effort to be fair in the competition. When he finds that the competition is going against him he displays resignation; he has no confidence in himself and is convinced that he can never win from the other in a contest.

The other is one Fred Pickel, an Englishman, a smarty with a long nose and red hair who, as one of the conquerors of Nieu Amsterdam, is anxious to bring culture to the Dutch. He is going to make Father Bach happier and bring him "in touch with the new world." He says grandly to Bach, "I will improve you because Lina is beautiful," but Bach doesn't want to be improved and doesn't like Fred. Fred plays not bells but a flute, and Bach finds flutes untrustworthy: "If you blow soft they play low if you blow hard they play high. What is solid in that?"

As for Lina, she may be beautiful but she does milk cows and admire the plainer virtues — she would seem to be a cross between Charlotte and Flossie. The contest for her hand turns into a lamp-design contest. The suitors are asked to suggest an appropriate design for a lamp to be hung in front of the Bach home, and Karl the unimaginative one is quick to disappoint Lina — he proposes a simple lamp on a simple nail right next to the front door.

A lamp on a nail? "To shine in a man's face on going up the steps? To leave the sill dark? To smoke the wall? To even start a fire?" No, the lamp on the nail won't do, and smart Fred proposes instead a fine lamp hung on a carved post — a post "of hickory turned . . . into elegant curves" — out by the curb. Lina likes that.

But Bach doesn't. He prefers the nail, and Karl. The nail is better because it is plain. It "is more modest and better in every way." An odd compromise is finally reached whereby Fred's plan for the lamp is accepted but Karl is accepted as future husband. Fred exits with minimal grace, saying, "what a waste of woman-hood — or perhaps not." He does have reason to be annoyed. End of play.

Is the character of Fred Pickel derived from WCW's smart brother, Edgar, who did such a fine "lamp" design that he won a *prix de Rome?* Probably, though in the original Charlotte-contest Edgar won. Edgar won only momentarily in that contest since Charlotte changed her mind while he was in Rome and went off with someone else. By the time of the writing of *Sauerkraut for the Cultured,* Edgar must have looked like the loser. In the end WCW was the successful suitor of the two in the Herman family.

If Edgar is Fred, WCW is Karl — and of course Bach is Pa Herman. Pa Herman fits the role well; he enjoyed his commonness and did not wish to be made over. But for WCW at this stage to have been thinking of himself as a plain unimaginative Dutch boy selling sauerkraut rather than culture is perhaps a put-on. He could have been exaggerating the differences between himself and Edgar, or he could even have been imagining that he contained within himself some of the qualities of both the suitors, with the plainness in him winning out over the smartness. Either way, Karl's victory is a victory for the homey and solid, a victory with ambiguities in it as Fred goes stumping off, ambiguities for Karl as well as Fred since Karl admires Fred and wishes he did have Fred's talents.

The bad daddy in *Betty Putnam* is also a troublesome character, for he must have been Pop Williams. Putting the plays together we come out with Pop Herman benevolently disposed toward the lovers, Pop Williams not. True? Fictions should not be converted to lives so readily but the autobiography does tend to confirm the conversion. It was Pa Herman who came to help the lovers with a mortgage after marriage (and so may be imagined to have been benevolent before) ; and it was Pop Williams who would not let WCW move in at 131 Passaic with his bride. Father and son had a fight as a result and WCW rushed out of the house and walked the night roads until dawn — this would have been early 1912. Pop may have felt that having already given off his front hall to the young doctor he did not need to provide a bridal suite too, but there it was, a sore between them — as was money. The play shows the father demanding that the son pay back a debt; the life does not show that clearly but suggests it, suggests that Pop planted in WCW's mind a strong sense of obligation to him for the expenses of WCW's education. In both the autobiography and the letters the indebtedness is consistently presented as natural and right, Pop having worked hard, made sacrifices for his children and generally conducted himself — except for suggestions of ineffectualness as a strong male figure in the household — as a father should. But even when WCW is being nice to Pop he does feel obliged to mention the indebtedness, and Pop must have had something to do with creating the obligation. In *Betty Putnam* that obligation is converted to an unwarranted burden imposed by father upon son to better his own lot. WCW hides behind his characters to bring the audience this underground message about Pop, and Pop may be imagined to have read the play and received the underground message too — there may even have been an amateur production of it at the Unitarian church or in the Williams backyard. Certainly it is hard for the outsider to leave the play without being reminded of WCW's darker thoughts about the parental marriage and the family box he had been brought up in.

So both *Betty Putnam* and *Sauerkraut for the Cultured* have biographical connections; they display character contours that look familiar because WCW always wrote, even in these early works, from a base of the familiar. But they are not personal in the way that his work was to become. They are set far off in colonial days — WCW must have boned up hard on his American history between patients — and they are neat and brittle in the manner of conventionally decorous theatrics of the period. If for the puritans poetry is the devil's work the audience is expected to say, so be it, but not work too hard to make contemporary application. And if a father is presented as a sinister figure and his young–lover son presented as insecure and unready to cope with the world, the father who is the possible model should not feel the circumstance pressing so closely that he need rise, like King Claudius, and rush from the theater. The threads that bind are there but they are only threads. In the main the plays are well-made contrivances that show us less of WCW's private life than of what he thought he had to do with a script to be a successful dramatist. As a dramatist he had, in these plays, the Mask and Wig world in mind. He was thinking of heroes and villains and story lines, and projecting for himself audiences with predictable bourgeois dramatic expectations. Especially since he is at this time in his life preparing himself quietly to jump on a quite different horse and ride off in a quite different direction and be radical, the plays are notable for their observances. Even the rebellious poet Betty Putnam is rebellious only in a conventional stage sense; the one example of her verse that WCW provides in the play is rhymed and jingly; he would not have wanted, even in 1912, to have claimed it as his own. And beyond the reaching for the typical in character and performance there is the deeper reaching, for the normal, social, familial. Before his marriage WCW was on his good behavior, with Hermans and Williamses and with Flossie.

His reaching in his poetry was not to be like that, though the difference would be hard to see until well after the marriage. In poetry WCW would not characteristically, when he became settled in the genre, establish two or three gregarious characters in a scene and have them debate politely about their past and future relations with each other. In poetry he would reach instead for the affairs of the private life, the solo sensibility taking in the world. The difference in the reaching went beyond the demands of the genres: drama became in effect his gesture toward Rutherford, poetry his gesture against it. It was in poetry that he was to let his Mr. Hyde out of the bag, his "strange me."

But Hyde wouldn't get out much until after the marriage — in the war years, and particularly in 1918–1919–1920 — when a great disaffection set in and doctoring was a burden and Rutherford was a burden and even his literary life, as he had lived it up to that point, was a burden, something to be got out from under, rejected, and replaced. Before the marriage there were traces of the disaffection but mostly he was a good boy. His 1912 book of poems, *The Tempers,* is a big step from the 1909 *Poems* but not a step toward disaffection. Except for the poem about the coroner's children it is creampuffs full of classical references borrowed from Pound, it is arty poems of distant cultural posturings, also borrowed from Pound, and it is safe poems that Rutherford would have thought highfalutin but not offensively so. He seems to have discussed some of the poems with Flossie, and once in a letter to her (1912) when she was off in the mountains with her family he mentioned getting a letter *from* her and a rejection slip for some of the poems in the same mail. He said, "I feel the glory of your love and the keenness of my disappointment together, side by side." At that point Rutherford and the verse were moving together.

Pound handled the publication of *The Tempers* in London (it cost WCW $50) and wrote an introduction to it and a review of it — he saw a fine talent lurking in it and regretted chiefly that the volume was so slim. But it was otherwise unattended, the rejection slips kept coming in. In 1913 he finally sold three poems to *Poetry,* for which Pound had become foreign editor — but the choice of the poems that had been sent to *Poetry* and accepted was Flossie's. Behind his efforts in both poetry and drama to serve other gods than his own, his "strange me" was sulking. The Rutherford muchness and the Pound muchness had driven it underground where it was sitting unhappily dreaming of a different muse.

In a long poem called *The Wanderer* it found it. *The Wanderer* seems to have been written over a period of years — it was not printed until 1914, and has a section in it referring to a strike in Paterson in 1913 — but in its final form it still retains some of the rhetorical flavor of his Keats period. WCW said it was an adaptation of one of his early epics but didn't elaborate. It is full of a kind of verbal extravagance that he would come to dislike, but it is also full of the later discontents. It is not about lovers in a medieval forest, it has no Greek goddesses. Its setting is his own local landscape — not Rutherford but the surrounding industrial wasteland — and though it has a genuine muse the muse is nobody remote and culturally pretentious, she is a strange combination of muse and antimuse, she is none other than Grandma Wellcome. Or so at least WCW said later:

> It is a story of growing up. The old woman in it is my grandmother, raised to heroic proportions. I endowed her with magic qualities. She had seized me from my mother as her special possession, adopted me, and her purpose in life was to make me her own. But my mother ended all that with a slap in the puss.

WCW was wrong. The mother had not "ended all that," with or without the slap, because here was Grandmother guiding him through life and literature as his muse when he was pushing thirty. But how strange that she should be doing so. Her ascendancy over the mother at this point is not strange but her ascendancy over Flossie, Rutherford and Pound is. Here was the young doctor-poet setting forth in his doctor-poet life with his young bride, and suddenly he was to be found climbing back out of all that into something deep in childhood. Was it a simple regression? Was it that he needed a momma again — and Grandma was Momma — because the world was too much with him?

There is something of that in the poem, something of a feeling of a lost child in a hostile place finding strength and comfort in the presence of the strong old gal. But that is a minor element in her role in the poem. She is much more than Momma there (as always it is dangerous to underestimate Grandma Wellcome), she is a genuine muse in the conventional muse sense — inspirer of verses, guide to the wisdom of the ages — and she is this in a world that seems to be otherwise empty of reliable guides. The poem is a poem of muse and poet battering at a hardness together alone.

It was perhaps the aloneness of Grandma that appealed most to the poet, the aloneness more than the motherliness — for he was writing the poem when he too, despite Rutherford and Flossie, felt alone. Grandma had always been a strange, set-apart figure for him; she had been in and out of his life, she had had her separate mysterious existence and persisted in her independent course. She was not Rutherford, she was none of what he was *in,* but was instead what he felt he himself was, or could be, an outsider, a wanderer. He needed a wanderer rather than Flossie for a hypothetical confidante and guide because it was to wandering that he was now addressing himself and there she was the original wanderer in his life. She had always been one, starting with her voyage from England with five-year-old Pop, and working through Brooklyn, the islands, Philadelphia, New York to an old age of isolation at the seashore in West Haven, having there as friends other wanderers, old sea captains. WCW needed her as that, but "raised to heroic proportions."

He also wanted her in the poem because she was temperamentally opposed to the equanimity of Rutherford. She was fierce, she was a wolf — he had outlandish words to describe her — and she had arrived at her fierceness by contending with, and being always contentious about, the forces of stable society. In the poem she and he together look at the "strivings" of persons in that stable society around them and he realizes that she is enormously wise about the strivings because she has always looked at them with the detachment of an outsider, a wanderer.

The strivings-theme that creeps into the poem has a possible start in the "delightful talk" he had with Grandma Wellcome in 1911, when she had insisted on "the worthlessness of all striving except for the expression of one's own individuality." Her new-found ability not even to want to keep up with the Joneses had impressed him; she had taken just the right tack with him about strivings as he was setting out on his own. He too wanted the strivings to do something for him inside, and as he puttered around his new office with stethoscope and stomach remedies he was not at all sure that that was what his Rutherford strivings were coming to.

So he wrote his wanderer poem with her as his life-guide in it. She comes to him first as a gull — there's a quantity of flying in the poem, a lingering function of muses — and he sees her while he is standing in the prow of his regular commuting ferry boat steaming across the Hudson for Manhattan. He then accompanies her, apparently himself flying, as she surveys Manhattan's busyness and then wings back to the Passaic River valley for a look there. Mostly she looks at people; she sees all kinds and mostly they are not happy. They are "dogged, quivering" characters to whom she points, asking him, "Are these the ones you envied?" Or they are worse than that. They are ugly, deformed:

> Faces all knotted up like burls on oaks,
> Grasping, fox-snouted, thick-lipped,
> Sagging breasts and protruding stomachs,
> Rasping voices, filthy habits with the hands.

An ugliness so ugly that it is grotesque is insisted upon throughout the poem. It is in the landscape as well as the people and it seems to be chiefly what she is showing him as they cruise about, showing him the hard facts of life, especially modern industrial life. But she is not showing it to him so that he will know what to reject, combat, avoid. She after all is ugly herself — she has majesty about her but is also a harridan with wild hair and torn clothes — and she is in her poetic, musey way a manifestation, an incarnation of the landscape. She shows him that she is a part of it all when finally she sits him down on the bank of the filthy Passaic River itself and communes with it as he listens:

> River, we are old, you and I,
> We are old and by bad luck, beggars.
> Lo, the filth in our hair, our bodies stink!

The river is a receptacle and she a product of the landscape's filth; they are there together in it rather as if they were in hell, but if it is hell it is also vital, real — a word he uses is "electric" — so that it is something to be reckoned with and at last lived with. Indeed living with it, becoming a part of it, is what she recommends to him in her final ministrations. She tells him to take the river into his own soul as she has done.

He does. He takes it in until the "utter depth of its rottenness" is in him, and he feels — and seems to love it — the "vile depth of its degradation." Then suddenly and confusingly she conjures up for him the image of a wholly different place. They are still sitting on the bank of the filthy Passaic place but she now holds up for his inspection an image of a fine pastoral scene, an opposed scene that is also hers and a part of her, a scene with "tallest oaks and yellow birches." She ends by suggesting that the one scene is contained within the other, or that from the one it is possible to reach out to the other — something muggily like that, the message being unclear.

This switch — from the ugly to the pastoral — comes off poorly in the poem. It has a false mysteriousness about it, as though having read someplace that beauty and the beast were one, he had decided to try to dramatize the possibility. But it is a possibility that he will not let go from here on. *The Wanderer* is the beginning of something.

The something seems to be, all in all, modernism. *The Wan-*

derer is the first of WCW's run-ins with that ubiquity. The big question that the hero-poet asks his muse in *The Wanderer* is, "How shall I be a mirror to all this modernity?" The word "modern" was in the wind. Pound was full of it, WCW's artist friends were full of it, everyone was rushing out into the streets to be modern, and so *The Wanderer* was WCW's first big reckoning with the word. But unlike his artist and poet friends WCW did not, in this first reckoning, interpret the word as an art word. To the question "How shall I be a mirror to all this modernity?" we do not find Pound's kind of answer. We do not find WCW's muse telling him that to be modern he should put down sharp images, or speak in the language of common speech, or dispose of iambic pentameter. Instead we find her whispering to him that if one aspired to modernity, and aspired particularly to bring Beauty to modernity, then one needed to look for the Beauty mystically within the material ugliness of the Passaic scene. There was the real, there was the modern, and there also, according to his new muse's gospel, was potentially the Beautiful.

From this poem forward WCW kept looking at, and mirroring, ugliness — ugliness as a regular font for the poetic. The ugliness that he found around him possessed him, drove him to his typewriter, and it was an ugliness that was not just ugly but freakish. It was in the Jersey landscape, it was underneath the Rutherford parlors, it was hiding in his own "strange me," his id sitting in the cellar not liking his clean-shaven, moon-faced ego. And his fascination with it seems to have come out of his own perceivings, not out of literature and art.

The grotesque has a long history but there is no evidence that at this time WCW was fussing with it. The grotesque was to become a feature of the modern, but at this time, except for the noises of the futurists (see next chapter), there was not much about except Beauty plain and capitalized. It would be some years later that Sherwood Anderson would write about a chicken farmer who collected chicken grotesques with "four legs, two pairs of wings, two heads or whatnot." And it would be some years later that other literary instances of the grotesque would proliferate, such as Pound's descriptions of earthly hell in his *Cantos* and T. S. Eliot's equivalent hell-imagery in *The Waste Land,* all contributing to a modernist gospel that rendered all the old norms of Beauty suspect, hence the abnormal necessary. In *The Wanderer* WCW was ahead of his literary peers.

Leader and guide Pound did not lead him that way. There is no ugliness, no grotesqueness except a medieval skull in *A Lume Spento,* and in the poems of his earliest collection of *Personae* the only possible grotesque is "Pierre Vidal Old," an archaic literary exercise about a medieval ex-wolf. Pound at the time was not looking at the landscapes around him much — his own later comment about *A Lume Spento* that it had only secondhand perceptions is just — and when he did look his inclination was not to be content to report on what he had seen but to convert whatever it was into something antique. He did a little piece, for example, about New York City in 1911 (he spent several months there then, with side trips to Rutherford) in which he too discovered a female presence lurking in the town — but no presence like Grandma Wellcome. No, his female was a capitalized Beauty, though she *was,* anatomically, a freak:

> My city, my beloved
> Thou art a maid with no breasts
> Thou art slender as a silver reed.
> Listen to me, attend me!
> And I will breathe into thee a soul,
> And thou shalt live forever.

Not the ugly idea at all! Pound didn't have it in him yet. Professor Gilbert Highet of Columbia, no friend of Pound's, once described this New York poem as kitsch, by which he meant a laboring after Beauty in the wrong places, hence an inadvertent ugliness. But that was not the same as a reaching after ugliness. Pound had labored hard at making the skyscrapers into females and the result was what Highet said it was. He had also labored

hard at importing to the New York scene the aged literary convention of the poet immortalizing that which was so fortunate as to
have been touched by him — another kitschean thought in the
context of all that glass, steel, and stone. But the result was nothing like *The Wanderer*. *The Wanderer* was not without kitsch; it
had Grandma as a sea gull and it had many laboriously rhetorical
passages but there was solidness underneath as there was not in
Pound's New York, the solidness of starting with the reality of a
scene and letting the art emerge from *that*.

Pound didn't like whatever it was that WCW said to him about
the New York poem, for he wrote back, "Would you have had me
say '12 years old and flat-chested'?" He knew that WCW was
working on something quite different though. WCW had written
him murkily about emanations from the real, and Pound, though
trying to be sympathetic, managed mostly to ridicule. He said,
"Your prose style is not remarkable for its lucidity. Still I am,
here and there, convinced that you are driving at something or
other. And that you usually mean something or other even when
you don't say it." WCW did get to say it, though it was still
murky, in *The Wanderer*.

Poor Pound. He couldn't join the revolution in Rutherford
but had to stay with it in London where he said — this was 1912 —
that he was now going to be *very* modern. He couldn't even come
to the Williams wedding, and because his publisher had gone bust
he regretted that he could send no present but only "felicitations
anent your approaching nuptials." WCW had sent him a card on
which was printed "Please present this card at the church."
Pound scribbled on it, "Dear Bill, I regret that I will be unable to
comply with the above request. Will you act for me in the matter?" WCW did.

CHAPTER THREE

The Revolution (in a Still Place)

Nineteen twelve is a convenient year to have the poetry revolution begin, whether in London or Rutherford. It did not begin in 1912 because Flossie and WCW were married then, and it did not begin then because Pound said then, in a letter to WCW, that he was about to go really modern, but it did begin then for reasons equally specious: *Poetry* magazine was begun in that year by Harriet Monroe in Chicago, and when she began it she asked Pound to be her foreign editor. Also in that year the imagists (or *imagistes*), who consisted of Pound and H.D. and one or two others, decided to create themselves and, having decided, issued announcements of their existence.

Earlier dates are needed for the revolutions in the other arts. Poetry was backward. Painting was in revolution in the nineties and before in Europe. America was slower but by 1903 it had a radical publication, *Camera Work,* that was more avant-garde in its paintings and art criticism than in photography. Prose had been receiving revolutionaries too for some time, with the Naturalists working on "the drab and the gross and the horrible," and with the Bloomsbury set trying to amalgamate prose and sex, and with Gertrude Stein in her drawing room amalgamating what might have been prose and cubism. ("Some ones knew this one to be expressing something being struggling. Some ones knew this one not to be expressing something being struggling. This one expressed something being struggling.") And there was modern dance and Isadora Duncan of whom WCW, while an intern, wrote that her "deft step" had "conferred no flaw."

Finally there was music. By 1900 Stravinsky was wandering around the University of St. Petersburg wishing to be emancipated from "unassailable dogma" and figuring out new things to do with counterpoint. In music there was also, among dozens of others, Charles Ives, who was ten years older than WCW and wandering around Connecticut and New Jersey busy at his own kind of counterpoint — which would be ignored for a long time.

But poetry was backward — at least poetry in English. There were the French poets with their vers libre and with the Rimbaud precedents for a kind of antipoetry as well as automatic writing (Rimbaud had said he was a spectator at the blossoming of his own thought and that he would make himself *"voyant"* by a "long, immense and calculated derailment of all the senses") but the French poets were across the Channel. Up to 1912 poetry in English was still hanging in as pretty much its ancient self. D. H. Lawrence thought he saw a revolution going in 1911 when he wrote a review of a book of Georgian verse, but he was wrong. His review was one of his first blood blasts. He was awfully pleased that poets like John Drinkwater and John Masefield were joining in the great work of demolition that artists everywhere were excited about. Looking at the Georgian verse he could believe that everything was "all smashed" and now everyone could "see the whole again." This pleased him. He felt that it was the return of blood, "quick, healthy, passionate blood . . . red blood running its way, sleuthing out Truth and pursuing it to eternity." Which was fine except that he was wrong. John Drinkwater and John Masefield were not the revolution. The revolution in poetry was still hanging fire, not because there was no red blood but because the old assumptions about what a poem should look like, sound like and say were still in the revolution's way.

He was not all wrong. Poetry did have to have the blood revolution; it had to join with the bigger thing, which by 1912 was deep into morals and politics and the labor movement — some said it was a revolution in consciousness — as well as the arts. Revolutionary pronouncements, in and out of the arts, were cheap. The futurists' pronouncements for example. The futurists proposed to "destroy the cult of the past" and "to extol every form of originality, however audacious, however violent." They said they despised imitation utterly and considered art critics "useless and harmful." They allowed that they enjoyed being called mad and they allied themselves with science, without asking science, because science was victorious in the "life of today" and it was the "life of today" that they wished to "render and glorify." During World War I the futurists would be succeeded by the Dadaists and others so that there would never be any shortage of persons saying it was necessary to smash everything and start over. The futurists were more sweeping than most but their assertions were not all bluster. Beyond the assertions there were true smashings going on that the war would be the climax of. Poetry did have to take in those.

But the poetry revolution also had to have its roots in poetry itself or poetry would remain like the poetry of John Drinkwater and John Masefield. And to get at the roots in poetry, though a technical undertaking, was hard. The old roots were hard, the old assumptions about what poetry was supposed to be and do were dug deep into Western culture and the education that preserved the culture.

It helped to be an American. The Americans were not as strong in the roots as the English, some of them having not even taken English Lit. at college. There had been Walt Whitman and his long loose lines in America. There had also been Emily Dickinson and her odd staggers. America was not without the roots wholly — the roots could be seen in the juvenilia of even the experimenters like WCW — but they were weak roots, weaker at least than those of a Britisher like Lawrence. Lawrence could spend his life being a blood revolutionary but in his poetry he remained prosodically a moderate; the voices of his education were with him whether he liked it or not, and they told him to stick with traditional verbal continuities.

The American schools did try to teach the English language and English prosody as the English taught it, and in the twentieth century the schools' teachings became targets of Americanists like H. L. Mencken and WCW who kept saying that what America needed was its own language and its own poetry. But even without the polemics the American poets would have found their way to the revolution more quickly than the English. Auden had it right when he brought forth the Wyoming image, that is, the image of American poetry being like flying over Wyoming at night.

Over Wyoming it seemed easy and natural to do what D. H. Lawrence said had to be done: start over. In fact it seemed the only thing there *was* to do, for the poets who had not taken English Lit.

The rootlessness was in the American sense of the language, and in the American sense of the nature of literary genres, but it was also in the American sense of what the man who sat down to write the poetry was undertaking to do and be. The American sense of the poet was strongly the sense of the poet as WCW described him in *The Wanderer*. Though the poet of *The Wanderer* had a revolution in prosody to worry about, that wasn't the main revolution for him at that time (later prosody would become obsessive with him) ; in the poem WCW said nothing about prosody. He was not then thinking of prosody when he thought of poetry but of the poet's life and the poet's mind; he was thinking — or his Grandma muse was thinking for him — that it was the poet's obligation to revolutionize what the sociologists now call life-style. That meant rearranging his own life so that he would come to know with great intimacy with his own senses the landscape of his life, not be distracted from what his eyes saw by prescriptions for what he should see. He was thinking of that kind of closeness as vital, and he was discovering that it was a kind of closeness not to be reached in settled, middle-class Rutherford, but he was still thinking of it mostly in terms of life not art.

He wanted closeness, then, intimacies with the real, but at the same time he was thinking that he should not be *too* close. He wanted it both ways; he thought the poet needed it both ways. There by the Passaic he wanted to be a fixture but he wanted to be a wanderer too, wanted to be set apart, wanted to see things from high in the air the way his Muse did (there was the Wyoming flying image again), wanted to be an observer, to think rather than act, and to think on his own in isolation. In other words, to the extent that he wanted to be a revolutionary at all, he wanted to be one on his own private terms. The private terms would give him the freedom he needed to break loose from the old assumptions, but they would also make him a poor revolutionary in any collective action. No solidarity forever. Just Grandma and poet on the river bank. That would turn the revolution into a very small one sometimes, more like a picnic.

But over in poetry itself — in the genre with its old forms, manners, and themes — the revolution was ready to be sweeping enough. What was needed was help from the other arts that were already mature at the labor of making themselves over. The poets needed to borrow. They did not need to borrow revolutionary feelings, revolutionary blood, but they had to be tipped off by the other arts that it was possible to violate a genre, and then had to be given a few clues on how to do it.

What did it mean in 1912 to listen to the other arts and then set about violating the genre of poetry? It meant many borrowings but two mostly, the two being both borrowings from the radicals in painting. It meant borrowing from the cubists the lovely thought that one should *assassinate* objects — the word seems to have been Picasso's — and it meant borrowing from a variety of other painting sources a new attentiveness to objects in their objectness, with or without assassination.

All the radicals thought that intergenre borrowings were fine. The poets were becoming painters, the painters poets. If a poet moved poetry in upon the spatial and a painter moved painting in upon the temporal, that was good because it made the genres richer. But the conservatives did not think so. There was Irving

Babbitt for example, a Harvard humanist, who felt the genre revolution in the air as early as 1910 and did not like it. He did not think that the old orders and assumptions of the different genres were tyrannical impositions of the establishment-culture. He did not think that the ancient rules of Aristotle — he was very strong on Aristotle — were arbitrary and senseless. No, he thought the prescriptions that had kept the genres in their places down the years were natural and reasonable, having arisen from the native characteristics of the genres. He thought that the spatial focus of painting and the temporal focus of poetry (or drama) were good instances of a natural and reasonable cubbyholing. The painter's art, he said, "has at its command but a single moment," and if the painter "attempts to paint two moments he is guilty of bad painting" (the cubist Marcel Duchamp, an acquaintance of WCW's, was about to paint not two but several "moments" in the career of a nude descending a staircase). On the other hand the poet, he said, necessarily works with words and the words "necessarily follow one another in time; anyone who would paint directly with words some visible object is forced to enumerate one after another the different parts of it." The moral was that painters should not be cubists and poets should not be imagists.

But they were going to be anyway despite Babbitt. And though cubism as described by Babbitt had the look of an art that ought to have started as a written art, the writers themselves didn't know that about it, and so picked it up from the painters, just as they did (though there is room to argue here) imagism. Imagism with many variants became the poets' way of escaping the tropes and coming to rely on their own perceptions. Cubism with many variants became the poets' way of escaping the logic of the old poetry.

Imagism and cubism. Those two — plus a boost from Kandinsky, perhaps, on the importance of improvisation. But it will be said that there was also impressionism, postimpressionism, fauvism, vorticism, futurism, constructivism, dadaism, surrealism, and a number of other -isms. There were, but imagism and cubism — together with improvisation theory — were the meat of it for the poets. They were the meat of it even though neither of them had the neat direct influence·upon the poetry that would be helpful for critics. The imagist movement as movement was a small parlor event that went away quickly, and anyway nobody in either painting or poetry who talked about images in the 1912 period seemed to mean exactly images. As for cubism, there came to be many verbal assassinations as well as pictorial ones but the verbal ones remained very different from what Picasso was doing with guitars (and noses). The connections all along the line between the genres were tenuous; the revolution that was modern poetry and began at the clanging of a Chicago bell in 1912 was not a clear product of any movement, and was not even clearly, until much later, a revolution. Still, whatever the revolution consisted of, improvisatory imagism and cubism were the meat of it and WCW's own poetry began, slowly and erratically after 1912, to show their presence.

2

Imagism. It was because Pound was so concentratedly literary in his Kensington flat with his London friends that he could imagine imagism was something that he and H.D. and Aldington concocted in Church Walk on a quiet afternoon to help H.D. sell five of her poems. Very late in his life he found out about and regretted his concentrations, particularly his habit of taking what he and his friends were doing to be what the world was doing. He said then, in a foreword to his *Selected Prose 1909–65,* that "the volume would be more presentable had it been possible to remove 80% of the sentences beginning with the pronoun 'I' and more especially those with 'we.' " If that had been done with his dozens of remarks about the local character of the imagist movement, the revolution would have been better served.

But then we would not have had his anecdote about H.D. and her five poems. Or his anecdotes about the *death* of the imagist movement. But even if he had been silenced about the death,

Margaret Anderson of *The Little Review* would have stepped in; it didn't matter. Margaret Anderson said of the death that it was Amy Lowell who did it. Amy wrote to Margaret to say "I've had a fight with Ezra Pound. When I was in London last fall I offered to join his group and put the imagists on the map. Ezra refused." Amy was incensed. She told Pound, said Margaret, that she would go back to America and advertise her own imagism so extensively that he'd wish he'd come in with her. And she did go back to America, and according to Margaret she then came to Margaret and *The Little Review* and said, "I love *The Little Review* . . . and I have money. You haven't. Take me in with you. I'll pay you $150 a month, you'll remain in full control, I'll merely direct the poetry department." But Margaret, said Margaret, said no the way Pound had, and so imagism was christened amygism and the real insiders went off into vorticism.

The anecdotes are deceiving. There were promotions, there were little plots, and there was Amy; but imagism in its essence was larger than that and Pound knew it. He just didn't like it. He wasn't an imagist himself much in his own work; he was a poet of the word and the music of the word. He could preach imagist gospel, that verse should be hard and sharp and that phrases like "dim lands of peace" should be avoided, but he was always looking for something beyond the advertised imagist don'ts, and beyond the (later) mystique of WCW's "no ideas but in things."

In a 1912 essay Pound made clear the larger, unimagistic dimensions of imagism, as he then thought of them. The essay is in the criticism volume with too many "I's" in it, and is one of his early learnednesses, very highbrow, called "I Gather the Limbs of Osiris." It is a brilliant bad-tempered piece in which imagism is not called imagism but "the method of Luminous Detail" and found to have been present in the world, though a rarity, since "the beginning of scholarship." Luminous detail is distinguished at length from detail. Detail is mud; there are too many details; but luminous detail is another matter. Luminous detail "governs knowledge as the switchboard the electric circuit." The sweep of the luminous detail's governance brings to mind Yeats and his remark in *A Vision* that he had been turning a symbol over and over in his mind for days, testing it, refining it, dreaming of its perfected completed state when it would catch Truth and Justice in a single instant. A luminous detail did not have to be a symbol like Yeats's great wheel — Pound avoided the word "symbol" — but its ramifications suggested symbolic functions and it did have to be big in the Yeatsian way. The weight in Pound's remarks was upon the luminosity, not the detail; as his essay went on he said less and less about detail. The luminousness of a whole poetic complex was what he was talking about. It was, as he put it elsewhere, "an intellectual and emotional complex" caught in an "instant of time"; but in the Osiris essay it was even bigger and better than that, it was the luminousness of the poet himself at his highest pitch, giving off his own particular virtu, that which he shared with no other:

> The soul of each man is compounded of all the elements of the cosmos of souls, but in each soul there is one element which predominates, which is in some peculiar and intense way the quality or *virtu* of the individual; in no two souls is this the same. It is by reason of this *virtu* that a given work of art persists.

The virtu of some poets, he acknowledged, was to think with objects more than with words (and some, he added, "progress by diagrams like those of the geometricians; some think, or construct, in rhythm, or by rhythms and sound") but even those with a natural feel for the object-world did not derive their luminousness from that alone. Pound praised his medieval poet-hero Arnaut Daniel for the precisions of his perceptions of the object-world — Daniel was not one to "babble of gardens where three birds sang on every bough" — but in the end the luminousness of Daniel was not to be localized in his perceptions of nature. He had more strings to his bow than detail. It was what he did with his perceptions in all ways that comprised his virtu.

Hugh Kenner has said that when Pound was in the American

prison camp outside Pisa at the end of World War II he came to believe of his own virtu what he had dreamed idly about it in better days, that he had actually become "possessed, beyond role, of the actual virtu of the great dead" upon whom he had "much pondered." Pound as Homer. Pound as Dante. The ultimate in luminousness, the climax of vorticist principle. Perhaps WCW could be said to have been possessed too in *The Wanderer* when he imagined that he and his Grandma-muse were at the business of catching the virtu of the Passaic. Then later in his *Paterson* epic he also seemed possessed, this time by the virtu of the city of Paterson. But both these WCW moments of possession were literary; they were deliberately entered-upon playings, not, as Kenner put it about Pound, beyond role. Though vorticist principle should not be confused with the thoughts of an unhappy Pound in the hot sun in Pisa, the identity confusion that Pound was led to there may be a lesson in the potential of vorticism to depart completely from the still center of luminousness where it began. Imagism is not like that; at least the ideas-in-things imagism that WCW labored toward is not. The WCW imagist is in love with emanations too but he has been told by his imagist god that he must not let the emanations escape their beginnings. His focus stays on the beginnings — in the things. The beginnings have a life of their own that cannot be taken from them; they have their own virtu that the artist's virtu does not displace; they cannot be merely used.

So Pound was not the one WCW learned his main trade from. Nor was H.D. H.D.'s trouble was like Pound's; she had to use images, not just put them down. From the beginning she could not leave alone a simple detail like a fruit tree but had to describe the bees going after its fruit as "honey-seeking" and "golden-banded" and had to bring herself into the thing by describing herself beside the tree, falling prostrate before it crying, "Thou hast flayed us with thy blossoms; / Spare us the beauty / Of fruit trees!" By the end of her life she was far beyond fruit trees and deep into myths, archetypes, Freudian connections. She mixed images out of literature with images from her own youth — great syntheses that the WCW imagist would walk in fear of. In a characteristic passage she spoke of "a wild moment that begot a child" in the Odyssean past, then moved as in psychoanalysis to a moment in a childhood closet,

> when long ago, the Virgo breasts swelled
> under the savage kiss of ravening Odysseus;
> yes, yes, grandam, but actually and in reality,
>
> small fists unclosed, small hands fondled me,
> and in the inmost dark
> small feet searched foot-hold . . .

Ideas-in-things imagism was not without its mysteries but they were homier.

Where then did the WCW thing come from? There is no telling finally because it came from many places. It even came from WCW's own work as he tried all manner of styles and slowly rejected those that were uncongenial, those like Pound's and H.D.'s with their heavy mythical imagery of busy gods and goddesses. He rejected those and gradually worked toward a simplicity of the local, the common, the immediate, the present — but it was by guess and by God, unprogrammed. He was not the first to arrive at the place that he came to, yet it is hard to know who and what to point to in the way of precedent. The painters seem the best ones to blame, not the poets, yet the painter influence was not simple and clear either.

Take Van Gogh for example. Van Gogh painted everything in sight and many of his portraits and landscapes have no bearing. But some of his works — maybe they are the lesser ones — do catch something that is imagist in the special way that WCW came to be imagist. Yet the ones that catch it are not centrally Van Gogh. There is a Van Gogh painting (1887) of a pair of old shoes for instance (the painting is called that: "Old Shoes"). The shoes are dirty, battered, unlaced; and they are just shoes, they are just there, there is nothing else. Then Van Gogh has another painting, done in the same year and called "Still Life with Apples," in which ten apples sit in a wicker tray. They are wizened apples. They are there in their appleness. They are apples merely.

Simplicities. Except that old shoes and apples are not simple. And even if they were simple, and even if it were imagist principle (as it is not) to render only the simple, there would still be nothing simple in carrying the shoes and apples through to art. The skill is of course a great skill that is needed to give the shoes their shoeness and the apples their appleness, but there is something beyond that and it *is* mystery though it is not pretentious mystery, it is not Eleusinian, not Orphic. It is the mystery of the emanations of old shoes and wrinkled apples. The shoes and the apples are charged with an energy beyond their thinginess. They are luminous in a common way but the luminousness is not less great for the commonness.

To put it differently, the luminousness is in the skill but it is in other things, particularly in the wonder that the painter, Van Gogh, should have *found* those shoes and apples. He may have in fact contrived and composed their finding. He may have taken the old shoes out of a closet and dumped them on the floor in front of his canvas — one shoe upright, one overturned (in another version of the same shoes they are both upright) — because it was his grand artistic purpose to make them look as if they had been dumped there. He may have faked the casualness of the apples too — who can tell what was going on in his mind up there in Montmartre? — but whether the scenes were in truth composed, or were in truth just happened-on as the paintings want to tell us, they remain art *made* of the happened-on. They are early examples of found art, what the dadaists came to call ready-mades.

They are fine examples but in the painting climate in which they were painted they are not common. The impulse behind them is not common, even for Van Gogh. Though it was true that the impressionists and postimpressionists were out to find luminous moments, moments in out-of-the-way corners even, they did not often reach into corners as remote as the shoes and apples.

Their landscapes and still lifes were tries at evoking the quiet speaking of things and places, but they were evocations by painters who were thinking, composing, directing the evocations. Painting was beginning to be impressions rather than stage sets but it was a slower beginning than the names of the movements suggest. The stage-set thoughts still came to the artists as they set up their equipment before the early-morning factory smokestacks; the artists would say to themselves, ah the smoke of the smokestacks will be a fine ironic pastoral diffuseness to balance against the sharp cruel rectangular solids of the industrial buildings underneath. When they said such things it did not go against emanations that they did so, but it did go against showing the wonder of what was there before they came.

To reach for that other ready-made kind of order, the inherent order, was hard. But it did not at first seem hard because it didn't seem different. Was not the order present whether the painter brought it with him or found it? Yes, and yet in the developing of the found-art mode a difference did slowly emerge and it was big. Found art is not just found. It is found unexpectedly; its recognition is abrupt, a surprise; there is no *time* for composition. Or at least the finished work must give the illusion of no time.

And because it is momentary, a brief and unplanned happening, it is also fragmentary. Whose are those old shoes and what is their place in the universe? The painting won't tell. (Van Gogh did paint an old chair though, and did tell — it was Gauguin's chair!) The fragmentariness is not only in the paintings of isolated, unframed images, it can also be seen in a number of Van Gogh's landscapes. He has for example a few bridge landscapes that show only part of the bridge. The bridge scene in the old mode would not have been *composed* until it had been extended to the right or left to its wholeness, but Van Gogh took part of the bridge only, as if to say that he had thought he was going to do a composition of the bridge but then had happened on an event near the bridge — a couple walking under the bridge, or a train starting to steam over it.

Van Gogh was not steadily interested in events in this sense, and these landscapes, like the shoes and apples, are not his most characteristic work. He was a painter of surprising deliberateness. Even in the wild canvases where a cypress tree has the look of a dervish and the moon is a curlicue and the stars are pinwheels spinning, there remains a sense of fixedness. The intensity is there but it is going to stay there. The spontaneous, the found, was not Van Gogh's game mostly. And it was even less the game of other impressionists.

Looking back now at collections of impressionist and post-impressionist paintings seems an excursion into the fixed. Occasionally the painters reached out for the happened-on, and they did have their own word "impression" to live with, a word that kept telling them that it was their job to deal with the happened-on; but their main attention was upon feelings deeply deliberated, not sudden impressions.

Pound insisted that the imagists were not impressionists, and perhaps that was partly because he thought that the impressionists did not reach out hard enough for the happened-on as he conceived it, a big instantaneous complex. But he did not dislike impressionist paintings and convictions — he complimented his friend F. M. Hueffer (later F. M. Ford) by calling him an impressionist — and his main reason for not wanting the *imagistes* confused with the impressionists was not that he disapproved of impressionism but that he didn't want the *imagistes* confused with any other -ism at all. He thought the *imagistes* were above -isms, and for the short time that he was pushing the *imagiste* cause he made the cause such a high one that a critic said it would better be called *snobisme*. For all his campaigning for the new he was, particularly in his brief imagist period, very much a campaigner for the old, "the sublime in the old sense." Imagism was for him hard to distinguish from a striving for poetic perfection.

As for Hueffer, he consented to be the impressionist Pound wanted him to be and wrote a long two-part essay for *Poetry* in 1913 on impressionism as a way for poetry to come alive and be read. But he did reach out for the less fashionable, less arty, less sublime impressionism, the kind of Van Gogh's apples and old shoes rather than the kind with mists. For the most part the poets printed in *Poetry* in its first two years were still with the mists. They were no more ready for apples and shoes than were the painters. Hueffer noticed that, which may have been why he wrote the essay. He was down on "love in country lanes, the song of birds, moonlight"; he said the "comfrey under the hedge . . . is just a plant, but the ashbucket at dawn is a symbol of poor humanity, of its aspirations, its romance, its ageing and its death . . . The orange peels with their bright colors represent all that is left of a little party the night before . . . the empty tin of infant's food stands for birth, the torn scrap of a doctor's prescription for death." He added that he would rather "read a picture in verse of the emotions and environment of a Goodge Street anarchist than recapture what songs the sirens sang." *Poetry* stayed strong on sirens though, despite his essay.

Or if the poets did search the happened-on and the common for their luminousness they were as sure as the painters that composing and elevating should still take place, that the sirens should be brought in somehow. H.D. was sure about the sirens because she was deep in Greek poetry. Amy Lowell was not sure about sirens but she felt the need for something *like* sirens. In a poem called "Cyclists" in 1914 she landed on the something with heavy feet. The something was Significance amid the commonplace.

Cyclists

Spread on the roadway
With open-blown jackets
Like black, soaring pinions
They sweep down the hillside,
  The Cyclists.

Seeming dark-plumaged
Birds, after carrion,
Careening and circling
Over the dying
  Of England.

She lies with her bosom
Beneath them, no longer
The Dominant Mother,
The Virile — but rotting
  Before time!

The smell of her, tainted,
Has bitten their nostrils.
Exultant they hover
And shadow the sun with
  Foreboding.

If that was to be imagism, then it was well to call it amygism. The poets in *Poetry* in its first years who were most nearly ready to let an image do its own work were Pound himself and Carl Sandburg. Pound wouldn't let the image alone completely — it had to be an equation with something else, it had to be directed — but he did respect it. Some of his best short poems appeared in *Poetry*'s early issues — "The Garret," "The Garden," "In a Station of the Metro," "Salutation" — but when his preoccupations with vorticism, Fenollosa, the ideograph and Confucius came to displace that simpler image-respect, he renewed his attention to images out of books, out of history, out of other cultures. As for Sandburg, he was for metaphor not image, but his figure for Chicago of a muscular "slugger" battling and building has the strength of sharpness and clarity that for the most part the poets and painters of the period missed.

WCW missed it too at first. He may have been ahead of Pound with his "Coroner's Children," and he did have *The Wanderer* up his sleeve, but the only poems he printed in *Poetry* in its first years were creampuffs laden with goddesses and Greek place names. The least pretentious of the group, "Sicilian Emigrant's Song," was the one he must have liked least since he left only it out of his next book. He was not ready for the happened-on yet; he still needed Significance and the sort of thing that Harriet Monroe kept speaking out for in her editorials, words that would "keep step with the ripple of waves and the beating of wings," cadences "delicate and elusive" that could attain "a haunting beauty."

What the painters weren't doing, or the poets, the photographers should have been doing. Photography was the perfect art for ready-mades. In time the enthusiasts with Leicas would come into their own and walk about all the countries trying to do for old shoes and apples with a focusing and a clicking what Van Gogh did at great labor with paint and brush. They would come around to the snapping of shadows of newel posts, the curves of urinals — perfections of the fragmentary. Especially they would come to the art of portraiture, hovering near their subjects with candid cameras, taking dozens of surreptitious quick shots in the hope of finding one perfect ready-made. Planned happenings, the best of both worlds. Dreaming of photography's potential at the turn of the century the prophets like G. B. Shaw could see it displacing painting wholly. Shaw said of the painters, "I snort defiance at them; their day of daubs is over." Then there was Maurice Maeterlinck who could find in photography a whole new artistic spirit; man was with photography's help coming to see that "everything around him begs to be allowed to come to his assistance and is ever ready to work with him and for him." In Maeterlinck's blurb, if the blurb was to be believed, was a beginning of "no ideas but in things."

But the blurb was a blurb. Photography at its beginning was practiced as an art of the composed like the other arts. It had first to be composed to be recognized *as* art. It was insecure. Its believers did not believe in it where it was most to be believed in but felt that if they were to compete with the daubers they would have to do what the daubers were doing, which was impressionism, the big murky kind.

Photographer Alfred Stieglitz started the magazine *Camera Work* in 1903 and that was a beginning. It was an expensively produced magazine and it had more in it than photography so that photography could mingle with the rest. It had painting, art criticism, news of the galleries, poetry. It went on for fifteen years in New York as a long-run highbrow announcement of the presence of photography as an art. And it was important in another way too; it was a sort of beginning of the little magazine thing that Pound and WCW and the rest were to carry forward. At least WCW thought so. When he made up a list of little magazines in the thirties he found that he had to put *Camera Work* at the top — the very first one in his chronology.

But the magazine was more conservative in its photography than it was in its art, just as Stieglitz himself was more conservative as a photographer than as art-entrepreneur in Manhattan. All the photographs that the magazine printed in the early years were in the murky impressionist mode. No snapshots of old shoes and apples. Stieglitz himself was one of the murkiest. He liked the smoke from the smokestacks balanced against the cruel factories. His friend Edward Steichen liked that too. Steichen turned New York's Flatiron Building into a pastoral emanation. He greeted modernity by catching a biplane and a dirigible in flight, but he caught them in studied relationship to hulking cloud formations. He also did impressionist portraits, with the faces looming out of the dark like apparitions.

It was not until 1911 that the murk began to clear — a couple of Stieglitz shots were printed of ordinary people at casual occupations in plain daylight. Then Stieglitz went on from these to crowd pictures, where he was also at last to be seen working for the casual, the unposed. By 1913 he won himself over all the way to naturalism with a flat shot of a sag-bellied dray horse standing behind a woodpile and in front of a wagon that didn't make it into the picture.

The other photographers in *Camera Work* began to do the murk-clearing at the same time, and by the last issue — in 1917 — the old impressionism was gone. The last issue had eleven photographs by Paul Strand, who was welcomed as the first new photographic spirit in ages and said to be "brutally direct, devoid of all flim-flam, devoid of any trickery and of any -ism, devoid of any attempt to mystify an ignorant public." The "flim-flam" referred to could have been directed at *Camera Work*'s own early work. Strand was feeling his way into a new mode as far as *Camera Work* was concerned but it was the old mode of Van Gogh's shoes and apples. Nine of his pictures were portraits — all casual, candid, sharp, and hard — of proletarian figures with distorted expressions. Then there were two close-ups of things, things so close to the camera that their thinginess cannot be identified, they are just lines and shapes. All hard and sharp. "Brutal."

In the year of these pictures, 1917, WCW's third book, *Al Que Quiere!* (translation: "To Him Who Wants It"), came out, and it too was announced as brutal. It was likely that WCW himself wrote the dust-jacket blurb (since he paid for publication), and it said, "You, gentle reader, will probably not like it. Because it is brutally powerful and scornfully crude." The year of the Brutal. The Brutal was displacing the Significant.

WCW didn't like Stieglitz much, any more than Flossie liked that "little tin god." Stieglitz was a big promoter of art on the New York art scene, several years WCW's senior, a man who brought the best-known European modernists like Picasso to New York for display in his Fifth Avenue gallery called "291" ("291" was the gallery's street number). "291" was a big thing and WCW was not. The magazine *Camera Work* was partly a front for "291" and for Stieglitz as art-benefactor. WCW sitting in Rutherford, commuting to the city regularly but as an outsider, could see the scope of the Stieglitz enterprise, could watch the big names entering and leaving, could feel neglected, not a part of the glitter when he wanted to be unhappy about his career — and he did want to. From 1910 to 1917 he had plenty of time to want to. He was trying to find his way in either poems or plays, but he was finding that he was not finding it. He was seeing that he was just a young doctor in Rutherford who happened to be on the arty side and who kept going in to shows and parties in Manhattan after a day at the office. It is an important fact in the history of WCW's morale that a poem by WCW never appeared in *Camera Work,* though dozens of very bad poems did appear there including some by his friends. And it is also an important fact in that history that when Alfred Stieglitz asked nearly a hundred persons to contribute to the next-to-last issue of *Camera Work* he did not ask WCW.

At least WCW was not in the issue. The issue was devoted to glorifying its editor's gallery, "291" — a characteristic New York venture. Everyone who contributed thought that "291" was wonderful, there was nothing else like it, its walls were "pregnant" (Man Ray), it was the center of the future. But no WCW. Twenty years later WCW wrote an obit for Stieglitz in which he damned him for several pages and praised him for one. Did WCW learn some of his imagist practices from this man? One critic thinks that WCW's "no ideas but in things" came heavily out of

Stieglitz but that WCW could never acknowledge the debt because he was envious of him and annoyed by him. There is a case here — WCW was an envious man and a man who had much to envy, commuting from Rutherford to Manhattan. But to look at *Camera Work*'s actual performance, until the late issues, is not to be sold on the case. All that is clear is that by 1916 and 1917 *Camera Work* was experimenting with the clear hard image and so was WCW.

In WCW's 1917 volume he had become allergic to arty posings. His revolution was taking a different route from H.D.'s and Pound's. He seemed to know now where the revolution, as far as he was concerned, was. In 1913 he had not known that; he had been full of revolution but aimless. In a 1913 verse letter to *Poetry* he complained of a publication called *Lyric Year* that it was a graveyard but he was then unable to give any solid information about what had brought on the death condition. He had the "unpleasant sense which one has when one smothers," but beyond that he couldn't go except to say that in poetry's graveyard everything was "socially well ordered" and the "socially well ordered" did not satisfy him. End of complaint. A year later, in a poem in *The Egoist* called "Aux Imagistes," he was no better off; he was well-ordered and arty in a pronounced *imagiste* manner, and while he seemed to be trying to be ironic about the manner the irony was muddled; his poor "frostbitten blossoms" were being conspired against by "envious black branches," it was all sad, but most composedly so. It was kitsch.

Yet by 1917 he had written "Dedication for a Plot of Ground" (see p. 10) and other poems approaching that poem in toughness and specificity. *Al Que Quiere!* was uneven. It was a book full of disaffection and the disaffection could be stagey, but he knew now at least what he was disaffected about: the neat and pretty and phony. He was looking, as he would soon say, for the "actual." His looking led him in *Al Que Quiere!* to too many ashcans, and made him patronizing to those — mostly his "townspeople" whom he knocked about in several poems — who had not yet learned about ashcans; but the book that came out of it was still a good book. The book was a big new moment for him because it was the moment of the real WCW coming out of the murk.

The newness was chiefly in the antiart, the art of the common and happened-on. The antiart motif showed up particularly in poems that seemed to be related in his mind to old-time pastorals. There is no indication in the book of what old-time pastorals he had been reading but three of the poems were actually called pastorals, and many of the others might well have been called that. They were at once assertions of life's simpler virtues as in the old-time pastorals, and denials that the old-time pastorals had actually located the virtues. He was laying out a pastoral philosophy while denying pastoral conventions. In one pastoral he described himself listening to the voices of nature but then settled on voices that were not the voices of wood nymphs or shepherds but "little frogs with puffed-out throats, singing in the slime." In another pastoral he set up natural voices against civilized voices but made the natural voices into (a) quarrelsome little sparrows and (b) an "old man who goes about gathering dog-lime." The old-time workers with pastoral would not have been happy at his disrespect for the idyllic — and WCW would have been happy that they were not. He was starting to make a profession of putting thorns on the roses, dung in the gutters, and starting also to develop a manner that would fit. Joseph Addison said of Virgil that "he delivers the meanest of his precepts with a kind of grandeur; he breaks the clods and tosses the dung about with an air of gracefulness." Not WCW. The graces had become targets too.

And yet the simple life, the life close to the earth, close to the bone, remained the object of wonder. What WCW was trying his hand at was, in William Empson's phrase, proletarian pastoral. Replace the shepherds with common industrial city folk, provide a city setting rather than a mountain retreat, put in the dung and the toughness; but keep the innocence of the old rural thing, keep the sense of the untainted life (in comparison with the monied, middle-class life) with all its honesties, its devotion to the good and the true.

The 1917 book was full of poems like these. It was strong on fact and hard image, it was against the fashionable and the misty, it wanted to be brutal — but it did still want to be composed too. It was not images merely, it was loaded with themes and shapings. And there was one particular shaping technique in the book that WCW was drawn to that he may have picked up either from Pound or the painters but was to become his staple: the quick juxtaposing of images. This was WCW reaching for "an intellectual and emotional complex in an instant of time"; it could be seen in other poems as well as in the pastorals (putting the sparrows in with the bird-lime man, setting them both against images of the civilized). One of the most successful of the book's poems was a sort of proletarian pastoral called "The Young Housewife," which was *imagiste* as Pound would have liked it to be but was also a good sample of a poem trying to put "planes" together, in other words trying quietly to be a cubist painting.

The Young Housewife

At ten a. m. the young housewife
moves about in negligee behind
the wooden walls of her husband's house.
I pass solitary in my car.

Then again she comes to the curb
to call the ice-man, fish-man, and stands
shy, uncorseted, tucking in
stray ends of hair, and I compare her
to a fallen leaf.

The noiseless wheels of my car
rush with a crackling sound over
dried leaves as I bow and pass smiling.

3

Cubism. Brutal ashcans have always been modern but they are as nothing in their modernity in comparison with the geometrical nose. When Picasso and the others invented the geometrical nose — as well as the profile portrait with both eyes on the one side, and the disassembled guitar — they became on the spot the best possible persons for the great unwashed to point to and say that there went the modern artists and they were mad. The musicians, dancers, and poets could earn for themselves similar compliments but they were always lesser compliments since the geometrical nose was so much easier to see than the other madnesses, so much easier to comprehend the incomprehensibility of. From 1908 on Picasso could not lose.

To be thought mad was fine. It was fine to be set apart. Most of the prominent painter radicals had a flair for being set apart. They were all on display in the big art show at the 69th Street Armory in 1913, and many of them worked as hard at their image as their images. The Armory Show was a good show but it was also a show to impress the unwashed with how great was the distance between them and the *artistes.* It did. Manhattan goggled as planned. Then the show moved to Chicago and Chicago goggled. When it was over modern art was in.

WCW goggled with the rest. Soon after the show he met Marcel Duchamp at a smaller show, Duchamp who had painted the nude descending the staircase in rectangles and was one of the best self-promoters. WCW went up to him and told him how much he liked one of his pictures at the smaller show. Duchamp stared him down, said "Do you?" and that was all he said. "I could have sunk through the floor, ground my teeth," WCW wrote later. "I realized then and there that there wasn't a possibility of my ever saying anything to anyone in that gang."

Aside from the posing there was seriousness. Cubism wanted to be thought modern for other reasons than that it was mad. There has been much written since about what it was, what it meant, and its sympathizers have been uniformly grand in explaining it. They have insisted that it more than any of the other movements and modes caught and encapsulated the revolution in consciousness that modernity stood for.

Picasso could talk about that revolution in terms of the immediacies of what he was himself doing — he was assassinating objects and reconstructing them; he was letting the mind reorganize what it saw as a demonstration of the mind's power — but the philosophers and aestheticians went further than that. They tied in the cubists' processes with industrialism and the theory of relativity and the end of God. To do so they had to go back in history first, and trace the great swings in human thought up through the ages, observing how the swings were mirrored in art and literature. Item: when Copernicus took over the world from Ptolemy the world was no longer the center of things, nor was it fixed; so painting became unfixed, full of perspective, and that was the Renaissance. Item: soon Newton came along with his laws and the world was fixed again. There were the hierarchies of the rigid societies and there was the Enlightenment, which was man's new capacity to know everything and put it in encyclopedias. Result? Watteau, Pope, rococo, neoclassicism. Item: the French Revolution, Marx, Darwin, and Boyle's air pump changed all *that,* so that in the nineteenth century the artists broke out again into open forms, into romanticism, leading at last to the wonder of all, cubism.

At least Wylie Sypher, one of the most learned of modern art critics, contends that in cubism all the experiments of the nineteenth century at last came home, in cubism the ideologies of the new world became artistically manifest, in cubism art and literature found a whole and complete style, not a stylization, not a mere technique.

Sypher has hung much on the geometrical nose. So have others, and the most far-fetched of the arguments for the modernity of cubism has been the one making the science connection. The argument runs that just as the scientists went below the surface of things, so the cubists broke up the surfaces of things to find *their* structures. Was there any connection between atomic structures and geometrical noses? There seems not to have been but that didn't matter; scientist and cubist were juxtaposed.

The science connection was always something of a put-on — there was analytical cubism for example, which was analytical because it broke up light into planes but sounded as if it had been invented by Pythagoras or Einstein — but there was a tradition for the connection in the long art revolution. The revolution had been especially long with regard to big consciousness changes, and in those the scientists had if anything led the artists; the artists had needed them. It had been the scientists who had insisted upon experimentation rather than the acceptance of hand-me-down knowledge. It had been the scientists who went to studying fossils though the religious establishment disapproved of fossils (to admit to fossils meant admitting to extinction, which was a criticism of divine wisdom) and the scientists (in the person of Robert Boyle with his air pump) who went to studying vacuum though nature was said piously to abhor one. It had been the scientists in other words who had led in questioning traditional assumptions, and since that was what the modern artists were at too it seemed good to make them allies.

And in the cubist revolution the scientific connection with atomic structure, though tenuous, did have the merit of pointing to something crucial about cubism, which was that it was more conceptual than perceptual. It was structures in the head sent to work outside the head. The scientist's atoms were like that too, since the scientist couldn't see the atoms, had to mock them up; but the scientist's job had always been heavy on conception. For the cubist to see in noses what was not to be seen in noses was a real novelty since the cubist was working in a seeing medium. He needed scientific support to do something crazy like that, but whether it was genuinely scientific or not wasn't the real point. The real point was that the strong conceptual thrust was a good way of fighting the old received notions of what painting had to, or ought to, be.

And so the cubists went at doing it, putting down on the canvases conceptions of noses that were not the same as the seeing of noses. In the process they affirmed the openness of the painting genre, and by doing that they affirmed the potential openness of all genres. It was a fine thrust. The only trouble with it was that

WCW (l.) and brother Edgar as children

WCW as a young man

Ezra Pound c. 1909. Frontispiece from *A Lume Spento*

WCW (l.) and brother Edgar, 1917

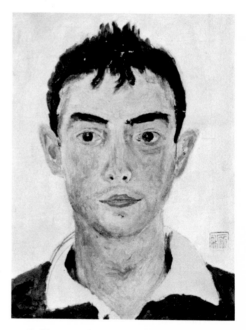

Self-portrait in oil by WCW, 1914

Charlotte Herman
in Hollywood, c. 1925

Florence Herman Williams
in the living room at
9 Ridge Road, 1925

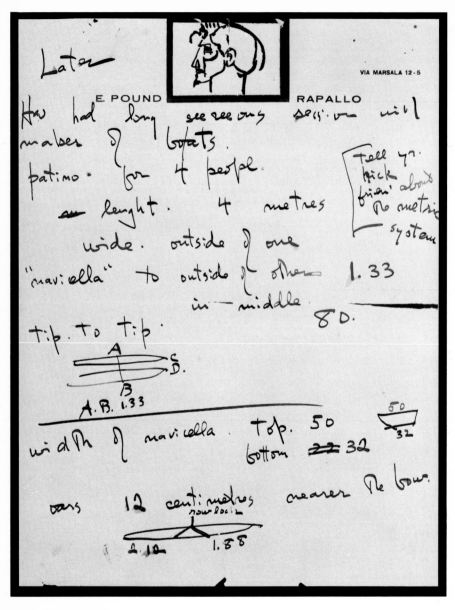

Second and last pages of a five-page letter from Ezra Pound,
apparently in response to a request from WCW for data on how
to build a small, two-hull boat that Pound designated a "navicella."
The "hick frien' " Pound wanted WCW to tell about the
metric system was Andrew Spence, a good Rutherford friend
of WCW's and a skilled craftsman with wood.

ya can
down near
stand em on end

water
level.

idiots on
a butt end
or sturn.

Sit
=

have been in very rough

surf here.

The frame house at 9 Ridge Road in Rutherford, which WCW
purchased in 1913

the unwashed would never come to believe that their doing it was anything but madness. After half a century of cubism they would still not cotton to the conceptual and the abstract but would stick to their received opinions that a genre was a genre and the visible ought to be painted as the visible. That left the consciousness revolution in the hands of the minority, the artists themselves, a condition that the critics of modernism were never slow to complain about wherever they found it and that they found specially criticizable in the geometrical nose.

So the geometrical nose, though revolutionary, was also a kind of *snobisme,* and when the radical poets took it unto themselves they were adding to their already large stake in *snobisme.* For poets like Eliot and Stevens — these are the poets in English Wylie Sypher singles out as most deeply influenced by cubism — the further commitment did not perhaps matter much since they did not at any time imagine that they were writing for the great unwashed anyway. But for WCW the cubist conceptual approach was something of an anomaly; he did have other dreams, Whitmanian dreams. In the very first poem in *Al Que Quiere!* called "Sub Terra," he bragged of his plain, earthy tastes; he pictured himself "poking into negro houses" and being at one with all the world's many "grotesque fellows." He could see that poetry did not have an audience of such fellows at the moment but he conjured one up anyway, just as Whitman would have, and the one that he conjured was the biggest ever; it was an audience of all the seven-year locusts ever; he saw them in his mind's eye suddenly "thrusting up through the grass." They were the common people, no doubt. Certainly in that poem and elsewhere he was making a large noise to the effect that he did not want *his* poetry to be an upper-class snob trade.

Yet he did move in upon the techniques of cubism. Or in upon the *idea* of the techniques of cubism — for it was as idea that cubism most lived. It was bigger as idea than as a specific movement. It was as idea that it was moved handily from one genre to another. As idea it was very malleable, so malleable that with a little twisting it could come to look like a dozen other ideas not called cubism. Wylie Sypher does well with it in *Rococo to Cubism* but to do so he has to keep tinkering with it to make it fit new places. It is the only way. And to fit it to the poets — WCW included — means putting aside the painter-cubist notion of the cubist making visible the conceptual — the poet has always done that — and shifting over to focus on the odd juxtaposings — not so much of images as of odd verbal patterns, thought patterns, experience patterns, patterns in time and mind. It has meant the assassinating and reconstituting of patterns, these at any rate more than of images.

Now *is* that cubism? Sometimes it looks like that, sometimes it looks more like automatic writing (a subject coming up) and a number of other associational techniques. If the juxtaposings are sharp, then the cubist "plane" effect is perhaps at work. WCW's "The Young Housewife" (see p. 113) does have that sharpness.

Call the poem cubist, and call in an analytical cubist to discuss its planes. There seem to be four. There is the plane of the housewife in her negligee inside the house, the plane of the housewife outside the house fussing with her hair and walking to the curb, the plane of the doctor-poet dreaming poetically of the housewife, and the plane of the car with the doctor-poet in it performing its odd ritual in front of the housewife. To imagine the poem on canvas helps; there the four planes would all have to be juxtaposed on the one surface, an instant mix.

But the poem is not on canvas, and even with the help of an analytical cubist would not be easy to put there. The time sequence in it would not be easy to put there. Perhaps the three stanzas with their separate times could be labeled as three more planes, but then these planes would have to be mixed with the image planes somehow — the picture would begin to get fussy. There is also the difficulty that the image planes are themselves not clean and static but contain movement in them, not to mention the difficulty that one of the image planes is not really an image at all, not paintable: how does one paint not a fallen leaf but a doctor-poet comparing a housewife to one?

All in all the poem becomes less and less explicable visually the more one looks at it. Its cubism is not to be thought of in mere visual terms. It is exactly what Pound would have called it, a complex.

No, not exactly, because it is not *exactly* anything. The scientifically inclined like Pound might like to measure the distances between the planes, or to construe the balancings of the poem's forces as an equation; but the poem resists such treatment. Though it is a complex, and though it is a complex worked out in (roughly) an instant of time, and though it is a complex that is imagistic in its hard clarity of both image and juxtaposition of image, it is not mathematical and has no affiliations with atoms or laboratories or men with slide rules. It does not even welcome the ministrations of English professors. It is that kind of complex, that kind of cubism.

Most of the cubists were like that. They were about as scientific as Groucho Marx playing doctor in a white coat and it was to them, the unscientific branch of the cubist mystery, that WCW looked. To men like Duchamp. Duchamp may have put WCW down in 1913 or 1914 but WCW did not then put him aside. He kept mentioning him thereafter as an instance of what the art and poetry revolution was all about; and what he remembered of Duchamp's art workings were the wild things Duchamp had said and done. Duchamp had said that "a stained-glass window that had fallen out and lay more or less together on the ground was of far greater interest than the thing conventionally composed *in situ*." Duchamp had touched up a photographic print of his own staircase nude, and by this "novelty" had made it into a new work of art. And Duchamp had one day decided that his composition for the day would be the first thing that he saw in a hardware store when he walked into it. He walked in, saw a pickax, bought it, took it home, hung it up. None of this was science but it was the sort of thing WCW was struck by.

In the years of the composing of *Al Que Quiere!* and WCW's next three or four books — a period of perhaps eight years — WCW never let go of the cubist thing. He did not use the word "cubist" much and when he did so he put it in quotes, but he was definitely making a connection in his own mind between the painters who in 1913 and right after were "roughly classed" as cubists, and himself — that is, between the kinds of things they were doing and what he was himself setting out to do — in prose and poetry — from about 1916 on. The connection that he saw was a mix of the spiritual and the technical. He saw the cubists, as he saw himself, rebelling against everything in sight that was bourgeois and establishmentarian and traditional; and he saw the results of the rebelling becoming visible as paintings or writings that gave themselves over to persons, places, thoughts, and happenings that didn't get into the old arts, and doing so with no bowing to the old arts' forms and sequences. He saw both the painters and the writers doing this, and doing it largely by hanging loose in their work, letting everything enter as it would enter. In his own work the result was what he called his "broken style." He saw himself as assassinating the old forms and sequences by ignoring them — that was the first big step — and by then wandering about the world "without master or method," being a good receiving-and-sending set. He compared his broken style to his mother in Rome, on a "rare journey always to be remembered," wandering around and getting lost. Getting lost was good, not bad. Getting lost was the whole idea. Whatever was before her was "sufficient to itself and so to be valued."

The broken style, he insisted, was a true manifestation of the imagination at work. What the imagination did, when it was not being bottled up by the establishment, was wander "from one thing to another." *It* hung loose, *it* was open. His mother was a "creature of great imagination" because in the first place she was capable of losing herself and wandering directionless, and because she was then able to deal with what she found "without forethought or afterthought but with great intensity of perception." There was imagination. Imagination was not Coleridgean.

Coleridge with his esemplastic power had thought, like WCW, of the putting together of things as the key imaginative act, but for

Coleridge there were ways and ways of putting them together and the differences were critical: if the things were put together without attention to the complicated justice of their *being* together (different and yet like, with great difference reaching out for great likeness), then the putting together was idle and fanciful. Had Coleridge been obliged to deal with such puttings together as WCW's he would have had to institute a new category of the idle and fanciful. WCW made himself busy putting together things that were in *no* way like but only together because WCW, like his mother, had happened upon them in sequence in his wanderings. WCW said he was not strong on the likeness principle at any level. He thought of that as a searching for one plane, whereas he was with the cubists in wanting to escape single-planeness. He said for example that "the coining of similes" was "a pastime of a very low order" and he found "much more keen . . . the power which discovers in things those inimitable particles of dissimilarity to all other things which are the peculiar perfections of the thing in question." Poor Coleridge.

But WCW was not able to practice what he preached here. He was constantly happening on likenesses, as in "The Young Housewife," which is a modest example of the broken style principle. "The Young Housewife" has only one simile in it (and that one is a mockery of similes, a characteristic WCW trick) but it does have a submerged metaphor (the wheels of the car over the dried leaves suggesting an aggression on the part of the doctor-poet upon the fallen-leaf housewife) that a Coleridgean might or might not be pleased with but would at least be ready to reckon with. It also has a very tight unity between the "planes" of a kind that WCW did not recommend in theory but continually practiced, with the housewife and the doctor-poet and the car converging simultaneously there at the curb. Many of WCW's other poems — some of his best — achieve like unity, and it would seem fair to say that in WCW's explanations of his broken-style he exaggerated his disrespect for the unities because he wanted to make his revolutionary point that the world's inherited unities had been a sell. Still, in the volume of his that followed *Al Que Quiere!*, **Kora in Hell** (written in 1917–1918, published in 1920) and the two books after that, he pushed the broken style as far as he could, to see what would happen; and after those books he was always pleased with the first one, *Kora,* because he felt he had in that volume broken loose.

The art critics and the literary critics have thought up many different phrases to describe the now ubiquitous broken-style principle, perhaps more phrases than there have been distinctive ways of practicing it. It is automatic writing, or stream of consciousness. It is a polyphony of simultaneous voices or it is simple collage. It is both analytical and synthetic cubism, and it is also dada, surrealism, and expressionism. In particular, however (aside from Duchamp) WCW singled out Stuart Davis at one point as an examplar of the principle. He said that what Davis had taught him was "an impressionistic view of the simultaneous," and that he had been so impressed by one Davis drawing that he and Flossie drove to Gloucester to get Davis' permission to use it as the frontispiece of *Kora in Hell.* Permission was granted, the drawing used.

Other influences were his close artist friends — Charles Demuth whom he had met over prunes across Mrs. Chain's boarding-house table on Locust Street in Philadelphia, and Marsden Hartley of Maine and 14th Street. Demuth was full of cubism in the war years, and a modest example of what he was doing then still hangs at 9 Ridge Road — factories, chimneys, smoke, with the various parts just slightly assassinated. Demuth and WCW once experimented together on a common subject — a fire engine with a big number five on it that they saw in Greenwich Village. Demuth's painting had a big "5" in the center and cubist shapes around it (including the words "Bill" and "Carlo") ; WCW's poem was more of the same, and not very good. A more successful example of WCW being deliberately cubist — and throwing in his lesson in the simultaneous from Stuart Davis too — was his "Overture to a Dance of Locomotives," which he read publicly at a painting show in New York, probably in 1917. It was a picture, in fragments, of a railroad station — the people, the clock, the sunlight streaming in high windows, engines, dining cars, all in a "dance."

Marsden Hartley tried all the painting styles, and he tried poetry too. His poetry was old-fashioned (just as WCW's painting, when he daubed the Passaic River, was unstylishly, plainly representational) but his painting could be wild, as could his words *about* painting. By 1921 he was solemnly into dada because he thought life was "essentially comic"; he was intellectually against the intellectual because the intellect was a manifestation of the cultivated man merely whereas the imagination was the natural man; and he spoke loftily and without clarity of achieving beauty in the old capitalized sense but doing it in the new sharp-image, actual-world way. His heroes in doing this were Whitman and Cezanne; it was they who had "clarified the sleeping eye." Hartley was a strange one. He was ugly, he was a homosexual ("he would climb all over you," said Flossie, speaking of the advances he made on WCW), he was alternately a warm friend and a cold acquaintance — but in the war years and for some time thereafter he was one of those WCW went to see regularly in the Village. What he seems to have supplied WCW — though WCW never mentioned it — was the Kandinsky connection.

By 1913 Kandinsky in Germany had done a good many paintings that he called improvisations. Only one of these made it to the Armory Show (Stieglitz bought it) but the improvisations notion got firmly planted in Hartley's head in 1913 or thereabouts when he was in Germany and studied under the man. As a result he took up improvisations himself — written ones — and came back to New York full of the theory of improvisations. In 1918 WCW decided to call his own *Kora in Hell* "improvisations." Kandinsky had tried his hand at the conventionally formal and the improvisatory, had decided that the latter had form too, though it was "a largely unconscious, spontaneous expression of inner character."

What was at the center of the improvisatory, no matter who may be said to have begun it, was the will to get out and do it. Just doing it was obsessive with WCW by 1918 — because he wasn't, then, doing it? was feeling dry, uncreative? In 1917 he set out to write *something*, as he put it, every day for 365 days. It was like his mother setting out in Rome to get lost. The improvisations for each day were a "reflection of the day's happenings more or less." Some were "pure nonsense" and were later rejected but the rest became *Kora*. *Kora* was as much anger and despair as cubism, imagination, and art, and was not scientific in any respect (any more than the little housewife poem had been), and was not a settled style but something that changed colors daily. After *Kora* came *Spring and All,* which was also the broken-style business, and soon after that came *The Great American Novel,* more of the same, more of the insistent juxtaposing of the happened-on. These were to be WCW's most experimental books. They were also to be the books where he was most explicit about what the experimenting was all about. When he had finished them he could settle down to plainnesses, but he had to do them first. He saw them as his own formula for the revolution.

4

He saw them as his own formula because he was very anxious in those years to have something in his art that was not Pound's or H.D.'s or anyone else's but truly his. He wanted the formula to be his own despite all the painter and poet connections because his own was what he was clutching for; and from the stridency of his complaints at the time about his friends — whom he thought of as competitors — it does seem that he was desperate in the clutching. But was the formula in the end truly his?

In its odd quirks and twists, yes. And in its working out in particular poems, yes. But in its general shape and direction it was not his private aesthetic but the aesthetic of the period, and the aesthetic of the period as it grew like Topsy on 14th Street, and the aesthetic of the period as it especially came out of painting.

The painting connection remained vital, and though the painting connection was not to be made to cubism merely it was a connection that the cubists had a big hand in. The connection was more than the planes and the juxtaposings; it was in the thinking behind the style. The connection was in the preoccupation with mind-and-thing, what the thing did to the mind, the mind to the thing. WCW was stuck with mind-and-thing for life after his rounds with the artists on 14th Street, stuck with it in its strengths and its weaknesses. It was what he needed, needed not only for his art but for food for his mind's workings. It was a mind that lived well with the mind-and-thing complex, sometimes better than with mind-and-person.

When Yeats turned his great symbol over and over in his mind looking for truth and justice he was doing his own version of mind-and-thing, and he was doing it not just because he wanted to find truth and justice but because he liked doing it. It was a good meditative occupation, symbol-turning. It was an occupation that suited his virtu. It was the sort of thing that went well with sitting in a tower, which Yeats would have done incessantly if his own tower in western Ireland had not been damp. It was a quietness, a withdrawing.

WCW's preoccupation was more with plain things than symbol things, at least until *Paterson,* and when he turned the things over in front of his mind he was much more abrupt and flighty about it than Yeats. He didn't like to stay in the tower long but to rush up and get the truth and justice and rush back down with them; but except for these differences he was with Yeats. He liked tower-sitting too, and he felt that the mind-and-thing relationship was what art was about.

Or what poetry was all about. Poetry was like painting here, and it was *un*like drama. Writing a poem and writing a play were never in the same league for him. For the poem-writing he went up to the mind-and-thing tower but for the play-writing he couldn't do that. For the play-writing he had to go into the parlor, and hear what people were saying, and stay with them to see what they did after the saying. The play-writing was a social art and an art that insisted on motion; the poem-writing was a solitary art, an art of Pound's complex instant. WCW tried both arts — they were two different roads to heaven for him — but in his writings about aesthetics he usually stuck close to poetry. That was the real center for him in the end. He was also a man with social concerns, and concerns for the actual, and he did not like to be thought of as an aesthete. Yes, it was so; he *was* busy, and concerned, and earthy. And because he was full of antiart impulses he had run-ins with the aesthetes on 14th Street when they exceeded his low tolerances for the highfalutin. But in his notion of what the act of the writing of a poem was he was not essentially different from them, and in fact 14th Street became in a sense his tower. Mind-and-thing were strong on 14th Street, while in Rutherford anybody caught staring a thing down was a nut. Mind-and-thing was a painter's stance and a poet's stance on 14th Street, and the poets and the painters were all there, and it was a nice trip from Rutherford, a short trip he was used to. He would take the Erie RR to Jersey City, take the ferry from there — and stand in the prow, the prow being like the tower, a proper place for a poet. Soon he would be at Marsden's, or Charlie's, or Walter Arensberg's, or Lola Ridge's, and there the tower would be that Rutherford could never understand.

Fourteenth Street and environs were not the only escape place. There was also a small artist's colony in the Palisades where some of the 14th Street set had summer shacks, notably Alfred Kreymborg. Kreymborg was a New Yorker, a city boy whose father owned a cigar store, and he had what he called a shack there — the place was called Grantwood — and he started a magazine there, *Others,* to which all of the 14th Street set contributed and to which Pound contributed too. It was Pound who told Kreymborg about WCW; soon Kreymborg and WCW were good friends and WCW was helping with the editing. Kreymborg's shack did not overlook the great Hudson River as a pastoral shack in the Palisades should have, but the Hackensack River; that is, it faced west rather than east — but it was pastoral enough for New Yorkers. It was on a slight rise and had a view to the west, and on a clear dry Sunday afternoon anyone who was out there for a Kreymborg literary picnic could look across the meadows to the Hackensack — and perhaps further to the Passaic — and if he were lucky he could also see a small cloud of dust traversing the meadows easterly. That was WCW in his Ford car, coming for mind-and-thing.

Pound sent not only WCW to *Others* but also T. S. Eliot in the form of his "Portrait of a Lady," which appeared in *Others* in 1915 within a month or two of the appearance of "Prufrock" in *Poetry*. Not content with sending poets Pound also shipped Kreymborg a printing press from England but the printing press had a tragedy. It arrived safely in New York, and it was safely carted to Grantwood, but in Grantwood in front of the shack the draymen dropped it off the truck. *Others* had to go on without *that* printing press.

It might have been good for WCW if *Others* itself had been dropped off the truck since the magazine and the people who worked on the magazine did give WCW a dose of mind-and-thing that he did not get over. But if *Others* had not existed there would have been some magazine like it — in fact there were many magazines like it, later in WCW's life — and for what it was it was a good one. Also it was his first little magazine — that is, the first magazine he was close to, could print his own work in at will and have some measure of control over the policies of — so it was important to him. He was to become, as his life extended, a little-magazine guru, and in that role he would live steadily with mind-and-thing as the staple view of art's nature. *Others* was an early and distinguished example of the little magazine breed.

In the first issue of *Others* Mina Loy described "pig cupid" and how his "rosy snout" was always busy "rooting erotic garbage." Orrick Johns imagined what fingers might say, and shoestrings might say, and a "beautiful mind" might say — the mind might say that it lost its mind "in a lot of frying pans and calendars and carpets." In the second issue of *Others* Amy Lowell pictured a man who was like "a mechanical toy which runs, and streaks, and veers over the carpet," Maxwell Bodenheim pictured four men playing dominoes on "sun-silenced afternoons" while their wives, who were "wide women," sat "in the backyard whispering tiny secrets and munching strings of grapes," and WCW made his first appearance with two of his pastorals — imagistic glimpses of proletarian innocence. The best poem in these issues was Wallace Stevens' "Peter Quince at the Clavier" and it was perhaps the only poem that was not a set piece. It had movement, development; it was a reflective poem radiating out from the preliminary image of a woman passing by to whom the poet was attracted; but that first image did remain the poem's occasion for being, and the radiations out from that, while bringing in music and dance as well as vision, were mental radiations, the poet seated in his tower turning the woman-image over and over.

In the third issue was Eliot's "Portrait of a Lady," which was a set piece if there ever was one but had the great merit of being also, like its companion piece "Prufrock," a complaint against settledness, against set pieces walking around in the flesh. The lady was too settled, Prufrock was too settled, they couldn't move and that was their trouble. Eliot was one of the few of the *Others* poets to escape the set-piece trap — another was Sandburg — but WCW would not like Eliot for it and anyway there were few poems like "Portrait of a Lady" in subsequent issues of *Others;* the Eliot mode was not its specialty. The characteristic *Others* poem was a static image, comparison, thought. "My mind," said Walter Arensberg, "is a naked child / Living in the little half-crimson garden of my soul." "The moon," said poet-sculptor William Zorach describing a night scene, is "like a great mouth opening to swallow the dead." Then there was the poet-painter Man Ray, who found beauty in "several small houses" that were "discreetly separated by foliage and the night." And there was the Australian poetess Lola Ridge, the proletarian one who gave poetry-reading parties. She put in a pitch for the beauty of the ugly in the image trade:

She is obesely beautiful
Her eyes are full of murky lights
Like little pools of tar spilled by a sailor in
    mad haste for shore . . .
And her mouth is scarlet and full — only a little
    crumpled,
Like a flower that has been pressed apart.

Others went on for five years. There were a few sallies into criticism in it and there was an occasional one-act play including one of WCW's — since Kreymborg like WCW lived a double life in art; but leaving the prose aside *Others* was a museum magazine. It was poems hanging on pages like paintings and asking to be looked at *as* art. It was poems asking to be awarded little medals for forcefulness, color, beauty, and then locked up for the night. An issue that WCW himself edited in 1916 was the most museumy of all the *Others* issues. It was an issue specifically billed as a "competitive" issue, and though no prizes were given out the competition-in-artfulness motif was clear enough. There were twenty-two contributors to the issue and each was allotted one page.

When *Others* folded in 1919 WCW was fed up with it and buried it with a big blast. He was angry at Kreymborg for having lost the manuscript of one of his plays, and still angrier at him for having passed WCW by when there was an opportunity with the Provincetown Players to produce a WCW play. He was angry at most of his other "competitors" too and his blast in the last issue of *Others* was not nice. *Others* was "vermine," *Others* was to be despised, *Others* was a lie that had existed in its "puling 4 × 6 dimension" and therefore its death should be an occasion for celebration. But when he got down to cases he did indicate, though vaguely, that he now knew what had been wrong with the magazine, he implicated himself as well as the others and singled out as the magazine's chief failing its museum quality. He did not use the word "museum," he did not make the painting connection, but he said what amounted to the same thing when he said that he

and the other contributors had been guilty of seeking "the seclusion of a style, of a technique" and had made "replicas of the
world" and lived "in them and not in the world," only seeing the
world "through a window."

He might have added that the "seclusion" of *Others* was such
that World War I was not thought worthy of mention in it,
though it was published during all of the war but three months.
Perhaps he didn't notice the omission because he omitted the war
too in the two books he himself wrote during the war. Some of the
other contributors to *Others* wrote war poems for other magazines — Amy Lowell had a stirring one for instance in *Poetry*
("Boom! the cathedral is a torch and the houses next to it begin to
scorch. Boom! the Bohemian glass on the étagère is no longer
there. Boom! . . .") and Kreymborg wrote one little piece that
appeared in a book of his, *Mushrooms,* in 1914, and seemed intended to dispose entirely of war as a serious issue:

> *Cheese 1914*
>
> Rats overrun his cellar.
> He salts their cheese with poison.
> The excellent cannibals eat each other,
> The eaters die with the eaten.
>
> Some such pleasant fodder
> (He claims it brings on asthma)
> Ought to be carelessly strewn about
> For those hungry inventors of war.

Looking at the war poems that came out elsewhere is evidence that
Others and WCW may have been well off without them. But the
omission remains striking; it was an omission like living on a rock
in the Atlantic and never mentioning the Atlantic. Yet it seems
not to have been the kind of omission WCW was talking about
when he described *Others* as unworldly.

The seclusion of *Others* — and WCW too at the time — was very
deep when it came to big human events, to history and politics
and the affairs of society, and it was a seclusion that other little
magazines — even magazines with greater professions of interest in

such things than *Others* — would share and that WCW would share despite his constant preaching of wishing to be close to the actual. At the spiritual level the sharing would be a sharing of a contempt perhaps for public events, a thinking of them as distractions from the intimacies and immediacies of the private life; but at the level of art it would probably simply be a sharing in some way of the mind-and-thing view of art. For that view did shut off the public. The seclusion of the artist in the tower turning the thing over and over was a closing of doors against other selves. It was also a closing of doors against time and the times. It was a closing off even though the thing that the mind chose to meditate upon might be something modern and up-to-date like an airplane or a dynamo. And it was a closing off even though the mind in the best modern way proceeded to assassinate the thing and reconstitute it so that it didn't look like a thing but a nonthing. The seclusion was in the stance itself, in the positing of a mind and a thing, alone together, making truth and justice. And though WCW would complain bitterly at odd intervals about aesthetic excesses resulting from the stance he would seldom penetrate to the center of its withdrawness. An exception was his book *The Great American Novel* (1923), but that was well after the *Others* period.

In 1914 Pound's friend T. E. Hulme gave a lecture on modern art (which he admitted stealing in part from a German named Worringer) in which he characterized the cubist kind of seclusion as a natural refuge for the modern mind. Art was either vital, he said, or geometrical. The vital showed itself in naturalism or some kind of realism, some kind of nature imitating, and it sprang out of an empathy with nature, a feeling at home there. The geometrical was not imitative; its forms were what could "always be described as stiff and lifeless"; and it was what it was because those who practiced the geometrical were not at home in nature, felt separate from it, were even fearful of it, had agoraphobia, were "space-shy." The primitives had been geometrically inclined, arbitrary and abstract in their cave drawings because they had plenty to fear in nature and were not at home in it but found it full of animals and gods that were out to get them. But the Greeks had felt at home and the artists of the Renaissance had felt at home, and had practiced the vital. It lay to the moderns to return to the other because the world had grown fearful and strange again.

A way of putting it. A way of describing the "revolution in consciousness." A way of describing the withdrawal symptoms and the *snobisme* of modern art. But what is curious here is that a revolution should be imagined to have been occurring at all — as so many persons including WCW imagined it to be occurring — when it occurred only in seclusion, only in the lonely place where the mind did its turnings and constructings. For if that was indeed what the revolution in consciousness was, then it was a revolution limited to the consciousnesses that did that sort of thing, to the artists, the tower folk, not to the great unwashed that sat around in their Rutherford parlors talking business and politics, and hating museums, hating art and poetry. The great unwashed may have hated the new arts *because* they demanded the new consciousness, but so long as the unwashed did nothing more than hate it — did nothing more than think of geometrical noses as crazy and of WCW's poems (as one of his Rutherford neighbors put it) as shitty little verses — then there wasn't much of a revolution, was there? Didn't one have to have a quorum for a consciousness revolution?

In the war years and after, in his experimental books, WCW was very hard on the Rutherford unwashed. He was with the aesthetic revolution though angry at its excesses, and that meant that he *had* to be against the unwashed. So he was. He called them his "townspeople" in a number of his poems and he lectured them like a Calvinist minister for their sins — chiefly the sin of insensibility. He was as intolerant of them and as annoyed by them as Pound could have been. He told them that they did not conduct their funerals properly because they refused to face up to death ("Tract" in *Al Que Quiere!*). He told them that it would be more profitable for him to live with a bunch of sea gulls than with them because the gulls were free in their thoughts as the citizenry was not ("Gulls" in *Al Que Quiere!*). He told them that their thoughts were so full of conventional claptrap that there was no chance that they would ever be able to learn to confront the actual; they would never be able to figure out at any "exact moment" where it was that they simply *were* (*Spring and All*). He told them that they were such a mess that he would just as soon destroy them all and start over (*Spring and All*).

He wasn't kind but in an odd way the poems were exercises in unkindness, to be taken at a discount. In the high-pitched tone of the attacks he was largely trying to convince the townspeople that he was in fact a revolutionary and not just a doctor delivering babies. And in directing the attacks at the townspeople he was telling them that his revolution had to be directed against *them* if it were to succeed. Meanwhile in placing the attacks in little poems that would appear in little magazines that they would never read he was showing them nothing; he wasn't even talking to them but to his fellow revolutionaries on 14th Street. Addressing the townspeople in the poems was a pose merely, part of the game of putting a poem together, part of the mind-and-thing game — but with the difference that the townspeople were themselves the thing, themselves the object that the poet had undertaken to contemplate in seclusion. That was not unkindness, that was art.

In other words WCW was having trouble locating the revolution and coming to grips with it as a public event. He didn't know where it was. Sometimes he put it on one side of the Hudson, sometimes on the other. But though he was confused — and some of his best friends, notably Pound and Robert McAlmon, kept saying he was — he had the solace that the confusion was built into the revolution as a whole. It was a revolution in seclusion, an anomaly. And WCW was if anything less committed to the anomaly than his 14th Street friends. He had more going for him on the Rutherford side than they. He was less in seclusion than they. He had his practice, he had his family, he had Rutherford itself, and all of this was too close and real to him for him to look at it as a collection of things merely. It was out of the Rutherford closeness in fact, rather than out of anything on 14th Street (or across the sea in Kensington) that another part of his revolution-aesthetic seems to have come. That part was more typically revolutionary in the social sense; it was the part that told him that for all their faults the townspeople were his artistic bread and butter; they were where the energy and life of art came from. It came from them haphazardly — they were undependable — but it did come from them finally, rather than from towers where minds contemplated things. Pound could never believe that part of the aesthetic, nor could Kreymborg.

It became a genuine mystique with him, the groping around for the human energy that was out there somewhere, out on his medical rounds, out on his car trips. He was sometimes a poor democrat, a poorer proletarian, but he was a working man, a family man, lived by the sweat of his brow, was a neighbor to poverty and sickness as well as to ball games and comic strips; so his groping went that way, went to the common folk. He would come to brag of his doctoring on "Guinea Hill," for instance, and the bragging would be ideological — he wanting it known that he was not a society doctor — but it would also slip over into aesthetic bragging because it was on Guinea Hill that beauty, *his* kind, could be found. No Greek goddesses, nothing even pretty, but the reverse, and yet it was beauty and it was, he would insist, over there. It was in the humanity there in the flab and the dirt — he would labor at the grotesqueness of it — and it was there perhaps more than in the middle-class places — though these too he could admire — because it was there that the human was nearest the raw human. That was it, the raw human. He was groping for *that* because he thought that in that was the art-spark.

In 1923 in *Spring and All* was a poem of his that caught the groping well, the groping that was his own — the wandering from thing to thing like his mother in Rome — but was also the groping of the world, the simply human. It was a poem that was critical of his homeland for lacking order, direction, good sense; it described the "pure products" of the country as idiots and blobs of flesh as if purification in America meant sifting down to the bottom in America; but then it proposed that somehow something from that was sometimes "given off." The giving off was in "isolate flecks" and there wasn't much of it, and except for the giving off the land was a chaos, and chaos was going to "destroy us" — there was nobody driving the car. But after all the reservations he still had to insist that the giving off was a fact, and crucial. It was like Yeats's truth and justice, the big thing that a poem or a life had to wander in search of.

So there in that poem was the mix of the raw human and the complex-in-an-instant-of-time that he was groping for. It was an "isolate fleck" in 1923. But seven years earlier in *Others,* when he was deeply committed to the competitions of 14th Street, he had had another "isolate fleck" — and that too had had the raw human in it. In that one the raw human had been himself, and his rawness was his genius and happiness, and though it was the rawness of the plain human it was a rawness best to be seen not in public, not en masse, but in seclusion. "Danse Russe" it was called, and aside from the happiness of the secluded rawness it was distinctive in that it managed to present the poet as both mind *and* thing. Doing so was a neat trick requiring only that a mirror be placed in the tower.

> If when my wife is sleeping
> and the baby and Kathleen
> are sleeping
> and the sun is a flame-white disc
> in silken mists
> above shining trees —
> if I in my north room
> dance naked, grotesquely
> before my mirror
> waving my shirt round my head
> and singing softly to myself
> "I am lonely, lonely.
> I was born to be lonely,

I am best so!"
If I admire my arms, my face,
my shoulders, flanks, buttocks
against the yellow drawn shade —

Who shall say I am not
the happy genius of the household?

CHAPTER FOUR

Stealing

H IS ROUTINE in the years after marriage did include the secluded moment, and that was the writing moment, the moment of the "happy genius," and it was apt to be late at night or early in the morning when Flossie, the servant Kathleen (whom he called a fine hunk of mud) and the baby — and then the second baby — were sleeping in the house and he was there too but there alone in his study, which was for a while on the second floor, then in the attic, then back on the second floor. But he also grabbed the moment in the ordinary hours; he grabbed it in the office between patients and would pull out the typewriter and pound away; he grabbed it in his Ford car, stopping by the side of the road and scribbling words on prescription blanks; and he even grabbed it in the parlor with Flossie talking to him. Once she was reading the magazine *Vanity Fair* to him, then paused in her reading and said, "You can't fool me." She meant that he was pretending to be there but wasn't there, was "stealing in order to write words."

He had to steal the moment to have the moment. His was that kind of life, or became so. But it was slow becoming so, giving him time to develop techniques for stealing. His medical practice grew erratically during the war years and he had troubles with it. He was not able to develop a solid local practice made up of Rutherford patients only — the "old line" in Rutherford, reports his son Bill, thought of him as a "whippersnapper" — and he rejected chances to move in with established doctors in New York offices. He also ran into tough competitive practices in the neighboring New Jersey hospitals making it hard for him to get a foothold. But he had, chiefly, trouble with himself. He came for a time to think that he was just not very good at certain kinds of medicine, especially surgery. In his intern years at French Hospital in New York he had been complimented as a "natural surgeon" with "a wonderfully steady and gentle hand," but a few bad experiences in the war years made him think, "My God how many bad surgeons there are — who knows better than I?" and he began slowly to pull in his sails and to figure out what he could and could not be, as doctor. When he was discouraged it was, he said, like drowning; he was out in the deep and did not have courage enough to keep swimming. It was not just the issue of competence, it was also the social texture of Rutherford: "I do not always get on well in this town. I am more than likely to turn out a bankrupt anyday . . . I especially cannot compete with other doctors. I refuse to join church, Elks, Royal Arcanium, club, Masons." His thoughts would go along like that, then would come to the solace that since there was no sense in his operating on people when they could "get a better man to do it cheaper in New York," and since he could not "safely lance every bulging eardrum," he had a special doctoring function, and it was a natural and good function in that small town. The doctor in that town, he decided, should think of himself as "primarily an outpost"; it was his role to be "keen on diagnosis, of the patient's ills as of his own limitations."

He did take that role, became a good diagnostician and referrer as well as baby deliverer and everyday pediatrician. He got his confidence back, and with the help of a few doctor friends — not the society doctors but the doctors who handled the poor, including one who was a tough warm dope addict — he at last found himself in business, especially in the "Guinea Hill" area of the neighboring town of Lyndhurst. Guinea Hill was where the raw humans were, and they were prolific raw humans who called him out in the small hours for usefully "brutal" deliveries. He also began to commute to New York three times a week to a pediatrics clinic, and when the twenties came he finally landed himself a nearby hospital position in the Passaic Hospital in the city of Passaic.

But to do that he had to set up residence in Passaic, which meant setting up an office in Passaic, so that then he had two offices to commute between, the one there and the one in the north wing of his home. By then the secluded moment really did have to be stolen. His oldest son, growing up then and headed for doctoring himself, remembers that sometimes the patient line stretched out of the door of the waiting room into the street and there were perambulators on the front lawn keeping the son from mowing it and doctoring was "a helluva way to make a living." The secluded moment had to be stolen, and it had to be stolen after the last perambulator had gone and the notes about each patient had been put down in the files — WCW was dutiful about the notes, so that when the moment was stolen it was apt to be stolen from family time.

The first baby came in early 1914, the second in 1916, which meant that Flossie was home holding the world together during the hard time when the practice grew. She could sometimes go into seclusion herself by falling asleep while WCW was talking, perhaps telling her that he had added "a new chapter to the art of writing" and was "truly a great man and a great poet," but she was on duty mostly, as mother, cook, housekeeper — and at the end of the day she was bookkeeper too. She would take the cash from WCW and listen to his forgetful account of the patients who had paid and the patients who had not, and record the figures so that at the end of the month she could send out bills. WCW had no receptionist, no secretary, no nurse in that north-wing office. He sat alone in his examining room that had his desk in it (with the typewriter always concealed inside) plus a glass instrument case and an examining table, and contended with the patients one by one out of the waiting room. Meanwhile Flossie was in the main part of the house doing her own contending and waiting to help him with his money and appointments. He had afternoon and evening office hours. In the mornings and in the late evenings he was out on house calls or at the clinics and hospitals. In between he would walk in from the office through the kitchen to the dining room and Flossie, contending, would have the right meal ready.

Flossie was regular and formal about meals. They were not secluded moments but full-scale family meals with napkins and napkin rings. The four of them — when there came to be four (and later there was also Mother Elena, who lived for a time with brother Ed, then WCW) — sat in their places and were family, and WCW liked that. He liked Flossie's food and Flossie's discipline about food, and liked the sitting there making a ceremony of eating. He never cooked himself and he never cleaned up a dish, but he ate what was put in front of him thoroughly and deliberately — and always with butter on it — favoring fish, lobster, clams, artichokes, mushrooms, celery, berries, in fact not really *not* favoring much; he ate it all, reports son Bill, "with relish and gusto" and knew as he ate it that he was lucky that it was Flossie presiding and not his mother who overcooked everything.

He felt lucky with that part of Flossie's governance but less lucky elsewhere. It was elsewhere that he would differ with her about how the family and the house were to be run; it was elsewhere that she would push him further than he was ready to be pushed, and he would react sometimes and take a secluded moment, and the great man and great poet would knock off a verse at her expense. One of the best poems, "Le Médecin Malgré Lui," suggests that she was too neat and wanted him to be too neat, and that the neatness was not just the neatness of the household but of the life that she was insisting he lead, including the doctoring life. In the poem he said that, with "Lady Happiness" guiding his thoughts, he had his work cut out, to wash the walls of the office, build shelves for the office, clean bottles for the office and put his journals in the office in order and catalogue important articles; he saw that if he were to follow her wishes he would even grow a beard and cultivate "a look of importance" because the image he was expected to project was part of the Lady Happiness scene too. In the Leipzig letters of 1909 he had said he wanted to marry Flossie because he thought she would push him into good habits and keep him from going "wild," but in this poem after the marriage he had shifted his ground. Though he truly wanted to be a "credit" to his Lady Happiness he also wanted sometimes to have something other than a "white thought."

So he had other-than-white thoughts constantly and wrote about them in the secluded moments. They were thoughts about sex, about chucking Rutherford and finding a new place to doctor, about chucking doctoring, about chucking family life, about chucking ways of writing and ways of the writing life, and occasionally (especially in his late years when he had been sick) about chucking life itself. They were thoughts that Flossie must have become accustomed to, and in the early marriage years they dominated the writing. They were the thoughts of the "strange me" that he had warned her about from Leipzig but that if anything he seemed to like to chide her with as soon as he was settled into the house with her. He wanted to chide her then because, despite her meals and discipline, he was unhappy with the range and magnitude of the white-thought life and unhappy with it for deeper reasons than that it was neat and clean. It was also, he once suggested to his mother, passionless.

Only a little more than three years after marriage he wrote a long letter to the mother in which he said that the original act of buying the 9 Ridge Road house had been a "high deed" (not too terribly high, he might have added, since Pa Herman had supplied the money) but that now the deed was "losing the force it had." He said that he felt he must dare higher, and then by implication suggested that though he was the one at fault the result was a failing of love on both sides. The earlier part of the letter had been a discussion of three kinds of love that the mother had herself proposed to WCW — a primitive furious love that burned out fast, then a longer-lasting love, then a democracy of love — and WCW had confessed that he felt that he and the rest of the Williamses were deficient in the first kind ("in our family the daring love of passion seems never quite to open its petals"). Then he went on to say that he had to struggle with this weakness in himself and that it was now time for him to refresh his life by "a deed of daring." It was not to be a deed of daring, though, in terms of renewed passion for Flossie and family. It was not to be the first or second kind of love but the third, "some deed of great love for humanity perhaps, some venture for the sake of poetry, the art I love." He ended melodramatically — the tone was that of letters written home from the University of Pennsylvania — that he felt "on the brink of a new change"; he said he had to "go or die." Go where? Not stated.

What is chiefly evident looking back on the strange letter is that he did not go and did not die either. The mother might have been disappointed that he did not go, since she did not like Flossie any more than Flossie liked her, but he did not go anyway and remained responsible in the not going. He remained good to Flossie, she to him, and if there was not the furious first kind of love between them there was the second kind, the fifty-year-marriage kind, and that was truly between them — despite the letter to the mother — and it was strong.

Perhaps it was strong on his side because he managed regularly to steal the secluded moment to work off, outside the house and in his own part of the house, what he thought to be the excesses of Lady Happiness, and perhaps it was strong on her side because she managed to do something of the same, make a life for herself (and the children) when he was off doctoring or doing 14th Street or writing; but there was strength in their life in common too. They delighted in working in the garden together; they were both intimate with flowers and plants and every trip in the car in growing seasons meant bringing home little plants and shoots in wet soil in newspaper on the car floor. Over the years they completed a 300-square-foot rock garden and they were always busy in it and they grew orchids even and entered flower competitions, and son Bill remembers their walking together daily in the garden, their arms linked, checking it out. They also did think of the house itself, despite their differences, as their house, not her house. Or if it was more her house than his, still he could be delighted in the her-ness of it when he wasn't angry with her. He could be anxious to help her remodel, repaint, refurbish it, add paintings to the walls of it. One of his happiest poems was an account of his *contributing* to the her-ness of the house — this was in the late twenties — and it was not only a poem that made a strong argument for the second kind of love, the homebody kind, but was a good poem as poem, one of his best.

The House

The house is yours
to wander in as you please —
Your breakfast will be kept
ready for you until

you choose to arise!
This is the front room
where we stood penniless
by the hogshead of crockery.

This is the kitchen —
we have a new
hotwater heater and a new
gas-stove to please you

and the front stairs
have been freshly painted —
white risers
and the treads mahogany.

Come upstairs
to the bedroom —
Your bed awaits you —
the chiffonier waits —

The whole house
is waiting — for you
to walk in it at your pleasure —
It is yours.

There is the suggestion in the poem that Flossie has been away and the house has been worked on in her absence, also the suggestion that she has been sick. This may have been after her 1927 year abroad with the children, but whenever it was it was solid tribute to the house as home. He wanted her in the house and he wanted to be in the house too. He had a stake in the house — it shows everywhere in the poem, even in the single exclamation point. The exclamation point is one of the details that lifts the poem off the page but it is not the kind of exclamation point he would have used in 1910. In 1910 he would have put several exclamation points in the poem and they would have been following oh's and ah's; they would have been exclamation points of the pull-out-the-stops kind. In "The House" the exclamation point points to a simple quiet moment and says *this* is where the passion is. His mother's second kind of love.

The house was a good place for that kind of love and WCW's commitments there must have been as great as Flossie's. It was not a commitment to Flossie only, or to the family only, though there was that; it was also a commitment that showed in his writing in the focusing on the at-home, the local, immediate, and everyday. The house's presence was to be felt even when he was sitting up in the attic being secluded and knocking off blasts at the settled middle-class life. It was a presence that took his rebellious modernity and molded it into something softer. It was what made his kind of modern Rutherford modern. Even now the mix can be seen in the paintings on the house's walls. The old radical 14th Street friends are hanging there but they are different there than in the art books and the galleries where they are still to be found. There is cubist Demuth represented in the living room by a factory scene with appropriate planes but the cubism subdued and the factory looking like factory; and there are two other Demuth paintings in the dining room with no planes at all but only simple still flowers. The wild romantic and expressionist Hartley is in the living room too but not wild and expressionist, with a mountain landscape in pastel over the couch. Then the precisionist Charles

Sheeler is there, with a bowl of fruit. Then there are numbers of other straight representational paintings — of a Roman fountain by WCW's brother, Edgar, of the white cliffs of Dover by Dorothy Pound, of a young girl's face by WCW's mother. The biggest picture is in the dining room over the sideboard, an Audubon print of a heron. If the revolution in consciousness is to be seen at all in these steady rooms it is to be seen dimly in an unlit corner in the hall where hangs a Ben Shahn, a late acquisition.

The house itself is not the likeliest place for revolution either. It is plain clapboard for two stories with tall unadorned windows; then it indulges itself with modest gingerbread across the third floor gables and has at that level also a semicircular window that Wylie Sypher might agree to call rococo. It is just a comfortable old Victorian frame house as it sits on the edge of the business district, a bastion against the stores, sheltered partly by trees and bushes but mostly by itself, its own plainness of presence. It is where it ought to be; it catches the spirit not of revolution but of old Rutherford, and it is still doing well at that sixty years after the Williamses moved in, though there are novelties creeping near — a clothing concern called "Schizophrenia," a restaurant called "Roadrunner."

It is doing well inside as well as out. There is no modernity in the furniture, the drapes, but the house reveals itself perfectly as itself wherever one looks. Why is there not an Eames chair or a free form table? Because Flossie did not like modern houses or modernity *in* houses, and all the evidence suggests that WCW did not either. His revolution remained confined and he didn't mind the confinement but assumed it without question, assumed that one could best and most comfortably conduct a revolution in consciousness from inside the solid, conventional and old. As a result, it was a matter of pride not just with Flossie but with him too that 9 Ridge Road was their roving friends' mail drop.

And now in her old age Flossie has had the satisfaction of finding the house declared a "state monument" so that now it can be a mail drop forever.

Fidelity, then, to the marriage was matched in WCW by fidelity to the house that the marriage survived in, with all its middle-class must. And it was also matched by children-fidelity. WCW was not the perfect Rutherford father and his older son remembers him as distant, withdrawn, "not there" (the younger son disagrees; the difference is striking) but he did do the things expected of Rutherford fathers. He told them bedtime stories. Aside from the one about the little Indian boy in East Rutherford who slew the dragon in the copper mine in the meadow the children remember best the one of a polar bear by the name of Spot who lived on an iceberg but it melted and so Spot swam ashore — in Maine. And WCW took them on trips in the car and they would sing as they went along through the corn — "Potatoes and corn, Blow your horn" (but he would also compete with the other drivers, and swear more than sing). And in the summers he would see to it that they all had weeks in the mountains or at the shore, where he frequently might be reclusive — he liked to go off and pick mushrooms by himself — but also took the kids on walks, or rowed them while they fished. And he did also dutifully tell them about life and sex, though the older one remembers that he did it by letter, was more intimate by letter than in the parlor. The older one, Bill Jr., has had a long love-hate affair with WCW, and has written his memories of him down in what may one day be a book, and thinks of their antagonisms as caused by likeness more than by difference, knowing himself to be disposed to withdraw, knowing himself how burdensome is the child scene; but even he can remember attentions.

The younger one, Paul, remembers more, that WCW was a friend, a confider, told him sex jokes, worried with him about school troubles. Even Paul admits though that WCW was "not there" in one manifestation of the father role, discipline. He spared the rod. Flossie took over the discipline and when Paul had girl-in-room trouble at the University of Pennsylvania it was Flossie who steamed down to Philadelphia, not WCW, and set him straight. Still, if the good doctor-poet missed a few family tricks he was, as poets go, a steady and dependable husband and father. He was much steadier for example than his wayward friend Pound, who set up one household in Rapallo, another in Venice (or San Ambrogia), and farmed out a child to a peasant family in the Italian hills.

2

But marriage remains prose, and infidelity poetry. This remark has been made in many ways but WCW made it in his own way after he had been married ten years. He said first that it was ridiculous for a poet to imagine that he had to have a poetic sweetheart rather than a wife ("My dear Miss Word let me hold your W. I love you. Of all the girls in school you alone are the one") but having ridiculed the notion, and having ridiculed Dante for his Beatrice, he went back to assert for himself what amounted to the same thing, that for the poet it was words that had to become his sweetheart. No matter how WCW sliced it the scene of the writer and his wife was for him the endless one of the writer stealing words while the wife was sleeping alone in the next room.

Stealing. It was a big metaphor for him and not all metaphor. His most famous poem on the subject is about stealing plums rather than words or moments, but he did steal the plums, stole them from his own icebox, stole them away from the breakfast that he might himself have had on them, and loved doing the stealing (and loved the confessing of stealing) :

This Is Just To Say

I have eaten
the plums
that were in
the icebox

and which
you were probably
saving
for breakfast

Forgive me
they were delicious
so sweet
and so cold

The stealing *motif* is so strong in WCW, especially in the early
marriage years when he was putting together his aesthetic, that it
is hard not to think of WCW as revolutionary without making the
revolutionary a thief in the night. But what kind of revolutionary
is that? If the revolutionary must steal time while the wife, the
servant and the baby are sleeping to look at his own nude body in
the mirror or eat the breakfast plums in the icebox, then either he
is a Caspar Milquetoast of a revolutionary or he has a restricted
notion of the nature of revolution.

Probably it was a little of both. WCW was not fierce and strong
but shy and mild in the presence of other people — though he
might later like to pretend to be fierce and make goggle eyes at a
little granddaughter sitting on his lap — and the power and extravagance of many of his written statements must have been compensation for the shyness. Also his revolutionary ideology was not
the big social kind. WCW was far from a spacious thinker. When
he thought of change he thought small about change — or at least
the G. B. Shaws and H. G. Wellses of the world would have
thought so if they had known him. It was of change in the consciousness alone in its study that he thought, but he thought constantly about that. And though he was physically alone in the
study — and thought he was spiritually alone too — there were
many who were thinking as he did. The direction his thoughts of
prized stolen moments took was a direction that the thoughts of an
age were taking, from the thoughts of rationalist Freud that truth
had to be stolen from under the nose of the ego to the sometimes
similar thoughts of the mystic Peter Ouspensky who had it that for
the most part man had no consciousness at all but was an automaton, a conditioned-reflex being who had to begin to work toward
consciousness by stealing moments from his automaton life. It was
a direction that the thoughts of the age were taking in both Europe

and America, a direction that would put revolution underground without guns in the hands of gurus, little magazine editors and psychoanalysts rather than Lenins or even Trotskys. It was a direction that would make the private life the whole bag while at the same time allowing the revolutionary to dream of changing the public life too. WCW's thoughts of revolution were most characteristic; they had dimensions beyond their obsessive literary center, and they were thoughts insisting upon their universal importance, but they were thoughts insisting that they were stolen thoughts, thoughts sneaked in moonlight.

The "Danse Russe" poem has the breadth and the narrowness of the stealing motif in good balance, and either explicitly or by suggestion touches most of the stolen life. It is a life of the moment since the wife, the child and the baby will soon wake up; it is a life in retirement that has to be conducted furtively behind closed doors and shades; and it is a life that even steals its *significance* from the other life, the daytime life that is being momentarily shut out. Significance in the poem adds up to genius and beauty. The happy genius in the poem is, by doing his dance, finding the beauty and expressing the beauty, and that is what geniuses do, and it is important for the world that geniuses do it — even the world agrees that far. But then the world and the happy genius part company; he is not doing it the way the world would have him do it, nor is he conceiving of beauty and genius as the world would conceive them. No, he is stealing the ideas of beauty and genius from the world and converting them, converting the genius figure from a fine figure of an upstanding public man to a "strange me," and converting the conventional image of beauty implicit in the poem — of the beautiful Narcissus gazing soulfully at himself in a woodland pool — to its satyric counterpart.

The satyr theme is strong. The body in the mirror is grotesque because it is naked; in nakedness is grotesqueness because the world does not approve of nakedness and beauty is clothed beauty. But more than mere nakedness is the issue. The satyr has been traditionally a sex figure, and has been thought grotesque because of his sex obsession, and has been represented in his grotesqueness in the old plays with a large tied-on phallus — a life force but hardly a beauty force or a moral force. And down the years, with or without the tied-on phallus (or the goat's feet), the satyr has been a mixed vision for the world of vice and ugliness. It is this vision of him that WCW has stolen from the world in "Danse Russe" and converted so that the vice becomes good and the ugliness beauty.

WCW is coy about nakedness in the poem. He does not mention the genitals but the omission merely calls attention to itself. This particular satyr standing before the mirror doing his dance shows the self-consciousness that an old-time Greek satyr would not have felt, a consciousness of his sex-being and of how that being is different from the daytime being who lives with the wife, Kathleen and the baby. It is in the contrast between dressed selves and the naked self that the specialness of the satyr self comes out. So the poem's self-consciousness turns out to be an asset for the poem, helping it to emphasize that in a world as messed up as this one the genius is always a loner and conscious of his loneness, conscious of his difference. Hamlet. Manfred. Ahab. "Strange me."

Next to WCW's preoccupation with stealing must be put an antistealing remark made by W. H. Auden in his conservative late years. It is a remark that this biographer thought at first to put on the title page because it is a caution against writing biographies at all when they are about happy writing geniuses and their private lives. Auden did not want to do his autobiography and he did not want anyone else to do it for him, and in defending his position about writing about writers he said (this was in a late book, a "commonplace book" or collection of poems and remarks culled from everywhere called *A Certain World*), "Biographies of writers, whether written by others or themselves, are always superfluous and usually in bad taste . . . A writer's private life is, or should be, of no concern to anybody except himself, his family and his friends." Chop chop to the WCW way of it.

Not chop chop to WCW specifically. Auden even came to like WCW's work. In the fifties he wrote him a kind letter, praising him for *Desert Music* and other late poems and in the very book in which he attacked writer-biographies he included a characteristically personal WCW poem. But the WCW poem happens to be "Asphodel, That Greeny Flower," and it is not only a late WCW poem, but a poem representing WCW the faithful, the nonstealer, a poem in praise of marriage and the long-term kind of love (love number two of WCW's mother). Auden would not have approved the early, stealing WCW, though he would have tolerated him; he was infinitely tolerant of poetic difference, as WCW was not. He would not have approved the extent of private revelation to which WCW was committed in *Kora in Hell, Spring and All* and *The Great American Novel,* the books in which his stealing motif is strongest, would not have approved either the preoccupation with details of the private lives of Flossie and WCW, or the constant ideological insistence that in the private life lay the key to it all. Auden's own art was the other kind; it was especially so in the late years but it was always partly so, even in 1939 when he was writing elegies for symbol-inspector Yeats and id-unveiler Freud; it was an art of the transmutation of private experience, fitting it to the public experience, which meant in practice adjudicating between the two, making a regular aboveboard connection. No stealing. Auden was thematically establishment; he was one of the faithful souls of the world even in verse, faithful to society, the culture, the traditions. He was faithful, though no prude, wherever touched. Of marriage he said that "happy or unhappy" it was "infinitely more interesting and significant than any romance, however passionate." Of the revising of the liturgy in the Episcopalian Church he said, "Why should we spit on our luck?" And of writing itself he said, "Even the purest poem, in the French sense, is made of words, which are not the poet's private property but the communal creation of the linguistic group to which he belongs, so that their meaning can be looked up in a dictionary." Similar upholdings of the communal and the traditional occur throughout *A Certain World* and WCW would have had trouble with all of them, just as he would have had trouble with Auden's beginning remark about biography. Writing for WCW began with the private life, and it never moved far away from it, and it thrived on its privacy because that was its independence, even from the dictionary: "Words. Words cannot progress . . . Words are indivisible crystals. One cannot break them — Awu tsst grang splith gra pragh og bm — Yes, one can break them." Auden would have said yes you can break them but after you have broken them you have nothing. WCW had it the other way. Along with the cubists and the others who favored breakings he believed that in the breaking was at least potentially the beginning of everything that the mind had any business being interested in.

The breaking. Or the breaking away. Or the stealing. They were all a part of his mixed-up though thematically consistent figure. But it was the stealing part that was most characteristically WCW because it brought in not only the illicitness — illicitness was at the root of any revolution — but also the privateness of the illicitness, changing the world by moonlight. For WCW stealing was, at least in his early days, the only way, and because it was the only way the biographer of WCW is stuck with denying Auden's premise that the private life of the writer should be off limits. WCW himself put it on limits, insisted on it, made an art of the private life. Also WCW delighted in trying to be in bad taste when he reported the private life, which was what Auden would have further disapproved. The biographer is stuck then with being in bad taste, too, as bad as WCW, and also stuck with the reporting of the personal because WCW seldom departed from it, seldom departed from what had actually "happened" to him in his own life or been reported directly to him as having "happened" to others. Many of the WCW critics have been insistently impersonal and the results have sometimes been comic — as when Vivienne Koch in her excellent early work on WCW mumbled of the persona of the doctor moving in on the character of Paterson in the poem of that name. Persona, no, that was WCW himself moving in.

Very well, but oddly the reporting of the personal does not make the biographer's job radical or racy in detail. WCW could not in practice bring himself to the pitch of stealing — or the reporting thereof — that he dreamed of and projected on paper.

He *was* always dreaming of stealing, just as Walter Mitty was always dreaming success, and it was big stealing that he dreamed, stealing far beyond plums; it was sexual stealing (stealing the time and the love from the marriage nest and putting them to work elsewhere) ; it was social stealing (stealing away with the mores, the tablets of laws and making them over, making them shine anew in the night) ; and it was literary stealing (the words stealing from the life). But though it was big stealing in its conception it was stealing that did have to be fitted to Rutherford and daily obligations in Rutherford; it was stealing that was moonlighting in the labor sense, something done after the rest of the day's business was done. Part-time work. And it was stealing that had other limits on it besides the time limit. There was an energy limit on it, for instance. WCW had sources of energy that made him productive and sleepless beyond the capacities of most, but he was still stuck with spending the energy where the revolution wasn't (he could be nasty with his telephone patients though, and conserve the energy: " 'Doctor, my child has swallowed a mouse!' 'Get him to swallow a cat then.' Bam!") And there was also a moral limit though he didn't like to admit it. The moral limit showed in the guilt that he felt about the stealing.

To put the guilt negatively, he would not have pinned the note that became the plum poem on the refrigerator door if he had not felt that in stealing the plums he had done something that he was not *supposed* to have done. And he would perhaps not have written his radical stealing books at all — the three he worked at between 1917 and 1923 — if he had not felt similarly that he was somehow stealing things that there were rules against stealing. His guilt was always plainly to be seen in his literary face as he confessed, and though he liked to confess, and felt that in the confessing lay part of the secret of illumination, he was not given to full and open confessing. After he was done confessing there was much that was still hidden. After he was done confessing he was still in part the faithful nonstealing husband and citizen; he still had a reserve of the proprieties — or so he hoped.

So he was not only a part-time and part-energy revolutionary but only a part-spirit revolutionary too. He had guilt feelings that a true flaming revolutionary would not have had, so that though he had strong urges to be extreme and shocking he felt constrained to be so ambiguously in obscure texts. Very square, very middle class it now seems, but in the context of Rutherford half a century ago it was not. And especially in the years 1917 to 1923 WCW must have felt very bold and bad, and very isolated accordingly.

3

There had of course been stealings for him before those years, before the radical books. The first recorded stealing was the one in the autobiography when he and brother Ed stole looks at the maid Georgia through a hole in the attic wall as she took a bath. Then there was the stealing away to spoon with someone named Kate on a porch overlooking Cranberry Lake the night after he had proposed to Flossie (the reporting of the spooning was his first marital confession). Then there were the intensities, also stolen, with Pound's discovery Viola Baxter. He had known Viola before he committed himself to Flossie but he continued to write her with passion after his engagement and after his marriage. It was probably Viola he was referring to in a 1918 story called "The Buffaloes" when he said,

> Once I had a beautiful friend whom I loved and who loved me. It was not easy for us to see each other, every moment that we would spend together having to be stolen.

But what is striking about his love for that beautiful friend is that after affirming the love in the first paragraph he backed off from love in the action of the story and made it into an intellectual engagement between a male chauvinist and a feminist (the male scored a point for men's lib). Similarly in his letters to Viola he would start by being intimate but would convert the intimacy to ideological musings. If Viola and WCW had been on a couch together the musings would have mostly put them at opposite ends of the couch. The most outspoken letter to Viola was in 1913 soon after his marriage, and in that he said to her that he regretted not having proposed to her four years before; but even that letter could be read more as yearning for lofty intellectual communings than as a love letter. When he wrote of Flossie to Viola he was loving but patronizing — he called Flossie his "beloved likeness" or "poor kid" but his manner with Viola was so brittle that despite his compliments to her she did not come off as a threat to "poor kid." Soon WCW and Viola lapsed into the state of old friends, with no further stealing.

And there were no other loudly recorded stealings from 1913 to 1917. Nineteen sixteen was even a happiness year for fidelity for WCW except for his letter to his mother meditating on his need for higher things. In 1916 he was busy in New York with *Others,* and busy with plays and acting; and Flossie would go in with him to New York frequently, once to see him in his big performance for the year, playing the lead opposite Mina Loy in a three-player skit called *Lima Beans* by Kreymborg (WCW was the husband and liked lima beans and only lima beans, and a vendor of fresh vegetables disturbed the marital calm by selling Mina a different vegetable — a characteristic Kreymborg plot). In return for the New York sociability the Williamses themselves threw one big party in Rutherford — Flossie was six months pregnant and "wonders today how she did it" — and the art crowd ventured out including Duchamp and Man Ray and Walter Arensberg, as well as the literary set. The party began Sunday morning and ended early Monday morning and nearly got the poet Skipwith Cannell killed leaping on a moving car racing off to get ice — but it was a "good party." So 1916 was a good year. In 1916 WCW went so far into amalgamating his lives that he made a playhouse out of his back lawn, complete with stage and a sort of orchestra pit. He put on one show in it with four song-and-dance numbers from Debussy to kids in bunny costumes.

Then something happened. In 1917 WCW ceased and desisted temporarily from *Others*, he immersed himself in a Rutherford fight in defense of his pro-German father-in-law, and he began the daily dark scribblings that became *Kora in Hell*.

Kora was not just an experiment in the broken style. *Kora* was his winter book, his unhappiness book. It had the literary slick of the Persephone story on it (and was followed, also literarily, by his rebirth book, *Spring and All*) but it was personal and it told of trouble. It was a book that pushed him into his stealing program. Partly he had to learn to steal then because it was time he was short on. In 1917–1918 he was a war doctor at home with a flu epidemic on his hands and with at one time his whole family down. But the stealing was brought on by more than busyness. It was a dark year. His father was dying of cancer (his death occurred Christmas 1918). The town was against WCW about the German business, and one of the local doctors wrote to the Rutherford paper recommending that patients not consult him. Meanwhile his own brother Ed had gone handsomely into uniform, brother Ed who was already a distinguished young architect and had, unlike WCW, "a European politeness and softness of speech that made him instinctively liked and listened to." What it came down to was that by 1917–1918 WCW was stealing away from his Rutherford self when he could because that self simply wasn't bearing up well.

And his literary self wasn't bearing up well either. *Al Que Quiere!* dropped in a big hole while T. S. Eliot the enemy received attention beyond what WCW thought his deservings, and the literary world in his neighborhood seemed to be progressing nicely without him. Isolation was his, like it or not, and on top of the isolation Flossie was after him. She was after him for stealing out with other women.

Kora was the scribbled result with the enemies always visible and the hero a vagrant, a wanderer looking at them. The book was an experiment in the broken style but the broken style kept producing ordered polarities, the neat whitenesses on one side, the warm darknesses on the other — and the hero regularly stealing into the darknesses, sometimes to be lonely and free, sometimes for trysts:

> How smoothly the car runs. This must be the road. Queer how a road juts in. How the dark catches among those trees! How the light clings to the canal! Yes, there's one table taken, we'll not be alone. This place has possibilities. Will you bring *her* here? Perhaps — and when we meet on the stair, shall we speak, say it is some acquaintance — or pass silent?

What the book was really saying that was personal and not literary was that WCW was out on the town now in his car. He was wandering through the Passaic world as his mother had wandered through Rome, searching out himself, truth, beauty, but in particular he was looking at girls' legs as they walked the sidewalks and hospital corridors; he was visiting with patients beyond patient time; he was using the pretext of patients to tryst with non-patients. Later he would be more open and direct in his descriptions of stealing love-time — in his play *Many Loves* for instance he created a doctor-figure who is woman-crazy and brags about it — but in *Kora* he was doing what he was doing with an excessive awareness that he wasn't supposed to be doing it, was alone doing it, was being frowned on for doing it. His guilt-sensibility was built deep into the murk of the book, a book of fog and darkness. And the murk was not merely impressionist murk. It was murk for camouflage and concealment. In 1917–1918 WCW felt he was a thief in the night.

And the concealment did not work. Flossie found out that year, and the town found out, though what they found out and how much are not stated. They found out and it was (figuratively) murder: "three bullets from wife's hand none kindlier: in the crown, in the nape and one lower." The marriage would survive the year but it was having a tense melodramatic moment ("the haggard husband pirouettes in tights. The wolf-lean wife is rolling butter pats") and Flossie and WCW could not have been communing much:

> The time never was when he could play more than mattress to the pretty feet of this woman who had been twice a mother without touching the meager pollen of their marriage intimacy. What more for him than to be a dandelion that could chirp with crickets . . .

So it was a bad year, 1917–1918. The stealings had become dark stealings, darker than Viola, stealings in the fog that he had to be quiet about with Flossie, and yet had to write about, and so stuffed in the pages of *Kora,* and murked up. Was that the year of the one-night hotel-room affair upon which his late play *Dream of Love* was based? Almost certainly not, but there were rooms in that year. They were dirty, hidden-away tenement rooms, and in them were not the likes of the intelligent typist of that play, nor of Viola. Viola was not only an intellectual. She was something of a prude, and complained of the "filthiness" in the little magazines, and talked about beauty as if she were Joyce Kilmer. The women in the rooms were women of less beauty and lower state such as the woman with "tawdry veined body" in his poem "Arrival," to whose "strange bedroom" he came and found himself "loosening the hooks of her dress." They were women in his grandmother's mold. They were precursors of the baroness.

The baroness seems to have come into his life a year or so after *Kora* but she could well have been in *Kora.* She was an aging nymphomaniac in Greenwich Village who lived in a filthy tenement with two filthy dogs and was herself filthy. WCW stole to her, then found he couldn't unsteal, couldn't dispose of her. She became his most conspicuous female stealing. He wrote a story about her in 1920, and later he covered his exploits with her thoroughly in the autobiography. By the time of the autobiography he could joke about her and how she wrote him obscene letters and sent him pictures of herself in the raw and came out to Rutherford to get him and Flossie threatened to call the cops (also how fearful Wallace Stevens was of her, so fearful that for a while

he wouldn't go below 14th Street) ; but at the time of his experience with her it wasn't funny. He was scared and worried. He
came to his friends for advice and help.

And *Kora* was two years before the baroness; it was not a book
of an experienced, worldly sinner. It *had* to be murked, had to be
a book of dark canals set up against white thoughts in clean
houses, with the women of the dark canals nameless, part of the
darkness. It was a book out of what he oddly called later his
presex period. Maybe the baroness was the caesura between before and after.

But the murk in *Kora* was essential for another reason than that
Flossie was a "lighthouse" whose beams kept finding him out and
showing him up as a liar. The murk was needed because some of
the stealings were not even real, that is, were not stealings with
real women but with dreams of women. He was out in his car in
the night with a dark second life that sometimes added up to
women and sometimes poems. And the connection between them
was itself murky. The connection was there in theory, having to
do with the stealer-wanderer's random way of achieving the illu-
minated moment. What he found when he found it was always in
some sense woman; WCW put it later that a man had to "create a
woman of some sort out of his imagination to prove himself," and
then added, to murk things up, "Oh it doesn't have to be a
woman, but she's the generic type. It's a woman — even if it's a
mathematical formula for relativity." But the theory is confusing
in practice in the murky *Kora;* the detail of the book does not
come clean to the outsider. It is referential detail with the references omitted. *Kora* is hermetic the wrong way, simply closed off
in many of its episodes to all but WCW himself. In 1917–1918
WCW needed it that way.

The next broken-style book, *Spring and All,* was sometimes
hermetic too but it had less darkness and there were poems in it
like "The Red Wheelbarrow" that could be readily excerpted. It
was a less personal book and for that reason less murky; it proposed that instead of stealing out of the house into the night the

poet steal away from the civilized to the primitive, a more conventionally romantic act and just as easy to do along the Passaic. The poet could steal away from the middle class in broad daylight like a good anthropologist and find the primitives out there, America's "pure products" — devil-care-men and young slatterns, deaf mutes, thieves, the lowly "hemmed round with disease or murder" — find them, and if lucky find *with* them the occasional illumination unpredictably "given off."

Then with *The Great American Novel* (also 1923) the stealing became domesticated. WCW could talk with Flossie about it (and she might go to sleep while he was talking about it). By the time of *The Great American Novel* he was over the hump of 1917–1918. *The Great American Novel* was a strong affirmative book for him, a new step, though it was much in the broken-style mode and did continue to make the case for stealing. It is a book to be discussed later, with his *In the American Grain,* because in it he fumbled his way through to the discovery that all America partook of the stealing life from its earliest beginnings. In *The Great American Novel* he at last found himself a community of stealers; he was not alone in his car at 3 A.M.

But he probably would not have found that community if the scene at 9 Ridge Road with its "alternate caresses and tongue lashings" had not become less tense by 1923. Between 1917 and 1923 a comfortable settling in to the marital complexities occurred, and WCW became no longer the haggard husband pirouetting in tights but a man on the earth in plain daylight who could go off to the New York Public Library and do his stealing — this time from history — there.

4

Flossie's mellowing in tolerance must have had something to do with it but his male friends must have helped too. There were some who became long-term cronies in art and literature like Charles Sheeler and Kenneth Burke, but there were two others

who were more than that, more in the sense that they stirred
WCW emotionally, reached in to his "strange me" and maybe
helped dispel the murk there.

The first was Emanuel Carnevali. He was a meteor in WCW's
life in 1918–1920. He came and went and they never knew each
other well, but what Carnevali knew of WCW he liked. He described WCW as a "big boy . . . naive to a great point, more
boyish than his lovely, earnest, almost-grave children" who "went
around in his Ford over the hills to pick wild flowers." As for
WCW he liked Carnevali too, liked him as soon as he met him at
Lola Ridge's, liked him because he was primal, a true apostle of
the artless, the lived. Carnevali had come to America from northern Italy very young, at the outbreak of World War I; had picked
up the language rapidly; had married "a girl who [had] happened
to live across the corridor some place where he was staying," who
partly supported him until he abandoned her; had worked at dish-
washer jobs around the Village but had also discovered the New
York poets in their dens and been printed in *Poetry* (after meeting WCW he went out to *Poetry* in Chicago and worked for a time
for Harriet Monroe). His prose and poetry had the gum of tenement life in it. He was frank, he made music out of ugliness and
misery, and he had the eloquence of a foreigner who has (nearly)
mastered the idiomatic in the new tongue. WCW was immediately taken by him. He dedicated the last issue of *Others* (1919)
to him. That was the issue WCW edited and took pot shots at all
his friends in for being too arty. Carnevali was announced in the
issue as the antidote to the arty, and he was represented in it by
several pieces the best of which showed Carnevali as an ashcan
realist living in a New York tenement with the world against him.
The world was represented by a neighbor who wanted to beat
him up for singing. It was an energy piece, all the stops out. It
and the other Carnevali selections in the issue proved to WCW
that everything *Others* had been doing had been preparing for
Carnevali's arrival. WCW said he had never seen a poem of
Carnevali's he wholly liked but that didn't matter. Who could

write a poem anyway that was "complete in every part" when "surrounded by this mess we're in"? WCW noted admiringly that Carnevali wouldn't let him edit his work though it was full of phrases in dubious taste like "eyes like spittle." Carnevali, thought WCW, was right all the way and he had been a fool, like the other editors of *Others,* for even mentioning technique to him:

> His poems will not be constructed. They cannot be. He is wide open, speckled with flashes, but he is wide, Wide, WIDE open. He is out of doors. He does not look through a window.

WCW said he also loved him because he screamed, screamed as if he thought "they" were going to gag him and throw him "in the outhouse." Could it have been that "they" were after WCW too, hence the sympathy? The communion must have had some such origin but the "openness" of Carnevali was good for WCW anyway. Carnevali was not one for camouflage like the murk in *Kora,* and he was always at the ready to complain about artifice, gentility, evasion, about not striking at the root. It didn't matter to WCW that Carnevali was himself a verbal exhibitionist and forever overwriting, and a great egotist, describing himself as "an enormous commonplace" rolling over the "delicate miniatures" that were his artist-friends. It didn't matter that he was always insulting his artist-friends — "My friends, Kreymborg, Bodenheim, Saphier, Williams and Ridge, I hate you. . . . I am disgusted with your little-review talk of technique and technicians. . . . Your black pens are ravens croaking over the stinking corpses of your wills." None of that mattered, at least for the moment, to WCW, because there Carnevali was and he was a strikingly dramatic figure and he was stirring the poetry pot as it needed to be stirred.

Then the poor man was taken with a dreadful disease, and he returned suddenly to his home in Italy where he lived in torment for years and wrote his friends including WCW for money, and came to think they all had betrayed him. He was wrong but some of them did stop sending him regular checks, including Harriet Monroe, who wrote to WCW in the thirties pleading with him to start a "group" to help Carnevali because she could no longer send him $10 monthly. The letters from Carnevali to WCW at the time were "dearest Bill" and "my dear sweet Bill" but in one of them he worried that WCW too had "abandoned" him; then he decided "yes, you are faithful, I love you, dear man" and went on to ask WCW if he had been successful in selling any of Carnevali's works. Carnevali did not die until 1942 but the years of his importance to WCW were just the two or three years after World War I when he was the meteor. Later WCW thought of him as a doomed one-book creature — "he was straight, slim, with a beautiful young man's head, keenly intelligent — an obviously lost soul" — but in the meteor years he brought brief solace to WCW in his isolation amid the loveliness crowd. WCW was a strong anti-Narcissus Narcissus in 1919–1920 and needed the likes of Carnevali whom he called, in praise, a "black" writer. The last issue of *Others* was full of WCW's own kind of blackness:

> Perhaps I am a sullen suburbanite, cowardly and alone. It is true that I have not seen the cocottes of Montmartre or the Lady Diana. Perhaps it is preposterous for the wealth of the world. I sit a blinded fool, with withered hands stretched out into the nothingness around me. Perhaps what I call my singing is a stench born of these sores. I deny that that makes any difference. AT LEAST I AM THAT.

At least he was that but that could not have been wholly consoling; nor could the self-centered exhibitionistic Carnevali have been. WCW needed a genuine companion in his literary misery, somebody to be desperate with him who would also reinforce him, someone who was also desperate and preferably younger because it was the older ones like Pound and brother Edgar (both of whom were really younger but from their authoritative ways didn't seem to be) who were reinforcing his sense of isolation. He needed a Childe Roland to blow a horn for both of them, and that was not to be Carnevali but another man, Robert McAlmon.

WCW was himself old enough when he met McAlmon to have had enough of preliminaries. He should have *arrived* by this time at some kind of public recognition, as well as at a clear sense of his own identity. But no, he was coming on forty and had not arrived, was still not settled, still not sure that he was at home at home. So he needed loyal young energy to guide him in new wanderings even if they would take him mostly to the old places. McAlmon was perfect for it.

McAlmon was a midwestern roamer whose literary credentials now seem contemporary. His formal education in literature had been spotty and he had been alienated by it. Bored by high school in Minneapolis, avoiding college for four years, he bummed around, took farm jobs, frequented pool halls. He even signed up for a night-school course in writing:

> The instructor told us to take a story of Hawthorne's, copy it three times, reproduce it nine, and then write a story of our own on the same plan. When I asked why not use an adding machine he looked blank. It infuriated me that my contempt didn't freeze his guts, so I walked out.

For a while he thought of bumming through Europe too, so that he would not have to be "part of the 100,000,000, just mud," but he couldn't make it to Europe. Instead he entered the University of Minnesota, soon switched to the University of Southern California, and from there switched to the armed services (1918) but not in time to go overseas. By then he had come to hate the academies and the books in them, but he had picked up a few friends in them, writer-friends. When he was demobilized in 1919 he tried USC again, and again education didn't take. He found himself on probation, dropped out, and roamed California for a few months taking odd jobs and working himself up to the discovery that what he was doing — roaming — was exactly what he should be doing to become what in fact he wanted to be: a writer. And so he kept at the roaming but headed east to Chicago, casually, keeping in mind that the establishments were poison for writers and that one did not go *into* writing when one went into writing:

One does not become an artist by going into the arts. One has some perception, some essential record that one must leave.

The statement could have been WCW's. It was the stealing way in, the pretending not to be there first, then by sleight of hand being there. For by the time McAlmon traveled casually to Chicago he had had a couple of poems printed in *Poetry* so that he was in a position to drop in on the offices of *Poetry* — casually, lest he appear to be going into the arts — and meet Harriet Monroe. He did, and there was Carnevali at work as well as Harriet, with the result it was not long before he was casually journeying eastward to the very parlor where WCW had met Carnevali. Lola Ridge's parlor. Everything happened at Lola's. At a party of Lola's McAlmon met WCW. He was a little over twenty, WCW was pushing thirty-seven.

"A coldly intense young man, with hard blue eyes," WCW called him but it was the intenseness and not the coldness that seemed to attract him. The two were instantly close and the closeness was not just spiritual since WCW was taken by McAlmon's physique: "He had an ideal youth's figure — such a build as might have served for the original of Donatello's youthful Medici in armor in the niche of the Palazzo Vecchio." The editor of WCW's *Selected Letters,* John Thirlwall, who knew WCW well and was, up to his death, still planning a WCW biography, said that WCW and McAlmon had a "sort of father-son relationship" but one of WCW's descriptions of how he felt toward McAlmon does not sound fatherly. WCW said that McAlmon had come into his life at a time when he needed him, had rescued him in America, rescued him "from much stupidity, from dullness," and then went on to talk about his love for him. The love as described was not just platonic, it was the real thing and because it was the real thing he had to write about it murkily as if he were still writing *Kora.* In the passage describing the love he worried about the "connota-

tions of his affections" for McAlmon; he was annoyed at the "slipping way" the world had of "getting out from under a difficulty,"
presumably the difficulty that homosexual love was real and
human like heterosexual love; but having suggested the difficulty
he didn't actually *say* what the difficulty was, he just kept worrying
it like a bone until the next page when he moved in close to it
again, and again backed off:

> Love. Everybody talks about love. It's the commonest thing in the
> world. There are no two kinds of love. Love is love. The moralist
> will tell you that. You love someone, that is all. If you love a girl,
> you want to have a baby. If you love a man, you want to have —
> what? If you love a girl, you don't want to have a baby at all. You
> just have one. You love her and after a while you have baby.

That is murky but does seem to say that loving the girl and loving
the man are the same. It suggests that the two loves' difference is
the creation of those who need the difference even though it is a
false one, need it to save family and morality, all the establishment
things. (The next paragraph complains about churches as a false
repository for love.)

But if the lines say this they do so with a mist over them, and
the mist is made mistier by the context, which is superficially a
novel context. The book is *A Voyage to Pagany,* WCW's account
of his own trip with Flossie to Europe in 1924 in which he called
himself Dr. Evans and gave his friends new names too (McAlmon
was Jack Murry). Occasionally he even truly fictionalized, giving
himself for instance a sister instead of a wife! — but the account of
"Jack" was wholly true to McAlmon in detail, as were the descriptions of WCW as Dr. Evans, so that the stuttering in the passages
about masculine love that the doctor felt for Jack does not seem
idle. McAlmon had reached him importantly and the important
part had to be slurred over.

The "baby" of their relationship had to be, in any event, a
magazine, *Contact,* which they began together. McAlmon had the

original idea for *Contact* and for the title. It was a shoestring project the money for which McAlmon supplied by "posing in the nude for mixed classes at Cooper Union" and the paper for which WCW's father-in-law supplied — such a big supply that WCW continued to use if for the rest of his life, mostly cheap yellow paper that is now cracking in the manuscript libraries. The first three issues were mimeographed and full of the ungrammatical and the misspelled. It was not an impressive publication; one of the more snobbish 14th Street writers, Djuna Barnes, said of it upon hearing its name that "the one thing about it you could be sure of was that there wouldn't be any contact," and about the first three issues of it she was right. It seems to have come into being out of a common desperateness in the two, a common feeling of isolation from the literary centers. That WCW should have felt as far out from the centers as young McAlmon was a comment on where WCW's first four books and his playwriting and acting and editing had taken him: nowhere. There were two other literary magazines of consequence in New York when *Contact* came out, *The Little Review* and *The Dial,* and WCW was a contributor to both and knew the editors of both — but he still felt himself an outsider to both. He needed a friend of a different order from the high-powered *littérateurs* and he needed a magazine powered by his own steam.

McAlmon at this time (1920) was an ignorant man, full of the wildest mouthings, but he was not without talent and he was especially good at putting down the "essential record," starting with descriptions of the parties at Lola's. In his novel *Post-Adolescence* he recalled that at two or three of them he and WCW were the outsiders, hating the artiness of the parlor poetry readings, wanting to escape to a coffee house. And he recalled also their being joined in the hating by Marsden Hartley and all three of them finally escaping to the coffee house, there to carp: "Yup, they give me the gut ache too, the arty art worshippers . . . There ought to be laws against talking about poetry, art or the social revolution." Those were words McAlmon gave to Hartley but he had WCW concur with them, having just escaped from the clutches of a woman at Lola's who had told him that his poetry would be better if more exalted. Lola's was full of the exalted. There was for example "that lady poetess Vere St. Vitus — the jumpy cooey little thing" who was in fact Edna St. Vincent Millay and whom McAlmon described as sitting off with a male and "gurgling." And there was also Lola herself who was very friendly but did like to spout poetry. Hers was proletarian tough-guy poetry that she rendered by "swaying and spouting with a super trance look in her eyes as she recited verses about the perspiring moon or the hot belly of that illegitimate child of industrialism, the city." There was reason to go to a coffee house to escape that, also reason to start a magazine. And so Hartley worked closely with McAlmon on the first issues. Hartley and WCW hadn't been getting on but McAlmon brought them back together, all of them in a dropout mood.

And of the three WCW, though a busy and seemingly settled doctor, was the one least settled in spirit, most confused about what he should do with himself. McAlmon described him as needing the strength and "stabilizing influence" of Flossie (called Nellie in the novel), but Hartley modified McAlmon's comment by saying that WCW (called Jim in the novel), would get unstable thinking about art and life, then would have to be stabilized, before going home, *for* Nellie. But both could agree that WCW was having identity trouble: he had "so much wild imagination, audacity and timidity mixed up in him indiscriminately that nobody could ever know where he is, least of all himself." Was WCW then the father-figure for *Contact?* Not clearly. And the magazine certainly needed one.

The three of them had sat in the coffee house complaining about the arty but the word "art" appeared in *Contact* in every other prose line and the poetry itself in the magazine was arty. The poetry was a mixture of overwrought description such as might have been heard at Lola's ("English chintz curtains scattered with prevaricating rosebuds" — Mina Loy) and trashy ashcan:

As an old priest mounted the steps to the pulpit
I looked under his robe.
He wore a union suit that sagged.

End of poem, Wallace Gould's. Wallace Gould was a marvelous eccentric from Maine who entered the Williamses' lives for a whole winter when he was broke, staying at 9 Ridge Road, trying to teach young Bill the piano, chain-smoking, and being genuine — but as a poet he was not much. And there was a good deal in *Contact* that was not much. And the poetry of the magazine was supplemented with vigorous but confused messages such as the one on the cover:

> . . . art may be the supreme hypocrisy
> of an information-cultured people . . . without
>
> C o n t a c t
>
> . . . justifiable perhaps if it becomes at last
> actually the way sensitive people live . . .

The dots were the magazine's and there were lots of them. There were also large-scale historical pronouncements such as McAlmon's on the state of civilization — "civilization, never more than a system for handling group needs, has now given up all pretense of an autocratic organization" — as well as doctrinaire aesthetic pronouncements, by WCW himself, against the doctrinaire:

> Joyce's method is a reaffirmation of the forever sought freedom of truth from usage. It is the modern world emerging among the living ancients by paying attention to the immediacy of its own contact: a classical method . . . We, Contact, aim to emphasize the local phase of the game of writing.

Reinforcing the two editors Hartley informed the *Contact* audience, which remained understandably tiny, that experience was "a horizontal of great severity, crossed in the center by a hypnotic vertical, with a tendency toward spiral. The rest is nerve." Kenneth Burke displayed an excess of learning about Laforgue. And Virgil Jordan — maybe a pseudonym for McAlmon or WCW — integrated sex and art by announcing that there were no big distinctions in life but only "a vast discharge of energy of innumerable patterns," a discharge that made Jordan think that "Sundays should be devoted to phallic worship." There was even in issue number three a bit of the great Pound himself. He had just discovered the economist Major Douglas (the one who promoted, in many pamphlets, a theory of Social Credit) and what was at the root of the world's troubles: usury. Everybody in issue number three was riding their hobbies hard.

By the fourth issue (1921) the magazine had turned into a promotional scheme for WCW's own work. WCW printed a long sample of his work, Marianne Moore contributed an endless eulogy of WCW's just printed *Kora* — she called it a superachievement — and a boxed announcement put up WCW's poems for sale through the magazine:

> Henceforth the writings of William Carlos Williams will be offered for sale at prices fixed by the author. Prospective purchasers will apply through CONTACT which at present is the sole agent. A minimum price of $50 will be charged for all poems, those of most excellence, as in all commercial transactions, being rated higher in price. Critical essays, imaginative prose and plays will be offered at prices varying according to the length and success of the work. The artist will however continue to contribute his work gratis to whatever publication, in his own opinion, furthers the interests of good writing in the United States.

The paragraph did not itself further the interests of good writing in the United States, the irony being too heavy and the grapes too sour. This *was* the period of sour grapes for WCW and his fourth book of poems was called *Sour Grapes* (1921), dedicated to Kreymborg for having, among other things, lost WCW's play. The sour grapes were generously spread around beyond Kreymborg — even Pound was not exempt — but they were saved especially for Eliot who came to personify for both McAlmon and WCW the kind of culture-and-civilization poet they didn't feel at ease with. WCW had managed to conclude from "Prufrock" that

Eliot was a "subtle conformist" but *The Waste Land* (1922) gave him darker thoughts about the man than that. *The Waste Land,* he said thirty years later when he was still steaming about it, "wiped out our world as if an atom bomb had been dropped upon it and our brave sallies into the unknown were turned to dust." He went on:

> To me especially it struck like a sardonic bullet. I felt at once that it had set me back twenty years, and I'm sure it did. Critically Eliot returned us to the classroom just at the moment when I felt that we were on the point of an escape to matters much closer to the essence of a new art form itself — rooted in the locality which should give it fruit . . . I had to watch him carry my world off with him, the fool, to the enemy.

It was the world that Eliot carried off that the magazine *Contact* at the time mostly represented, which was too bad because the magazine didn't represent it well. But *Sour Grapes* was a good book anyway — WCW knew what he was doing now in the short poem — and even *Contact* had WCW moments. In the fourth issue, for example, probably WCW's first successful story appeared, a story that showed not only that WCW could write a story but one that has biographical (sour-grapes biographical) interest.

.It told of a tired doctor who takes a small child — perhaps WCW's second son, Paul — on a daddy-son excursion and they meet a goat. The doctor oversees the meeting so that the goat will not hurt the child as the child paws it. The goat does not hurt the child but as they wander away from the goat the child trips in the street and falls on his head. The falling is described as if the child in falling were not a child but a plastic doll. The doll effect is what the reader is left with and the final implicit message seems severe: How did this baby get into the tired doctor's life anyway?

5

It was probably with other babies than real babies or with other women than real women that WCW was most steadily concerned, though the critics have been announcing for some time that he was a realist. He said himself frequently that his was a life of the imagination, said that he was not trafficking in flesh and blood primarily but with words, said he was a word machine; and though he sometimes said so to distract his readers from his flesh-and-blood affairs, still there is evidence in his works that he thought of the flesh-and-blood affairs as materials, grist for the writing mill. If he presented a real woman on page x he would convert her to a poem-of-a-woman on page y. He felt it his writing duty to make contact with the "actual" but having made contact his preoccupation was with the *use* of it; for he did want to use it, not just look at it and record it.

Also, in going out to meet the actual he stuck close to the local everyday scenes he inhabited, which placed a sharp limit on the simple dimensions of his realism. By aesthetic conviction and temperament he was a fan of the local — and in the pages of *Contact* both he and McAlmon made much of the fact that they were local, stay-at-home writers, then McAlmon rushed off to London and Paris — but while the local was actual enough and served him well it was a restricted actuality and did not encourage him to be "wide open" as he thought Carnevali was, wide open to the whole world of the actual. He was not taking in all of Rome or even the Passaic Valley as he went about his wanderings. He was taking in what he needed and felt he could use, no more.

Also, he was taking it in for works of more specific, controlled intent than he liked to admit. While he may truly have not at all times been conscious of *what* he needed as he improvised and did his broken-style dances, there remained a selective principle at work in him that kept him from the fullness of treatment of the actual that was characteristic of the commonest kind of realistic writing, that is, naturalism. WCW did have a naturalistic streak in him and he indulged it fitfully, especially in the proletarian thirties; but he always set limits for himself as a naturalist-realist. He did not move in on a slum family and write a trilogy about it covering every obscenity, every sad tearing of the flesh. Instead he made a life's profession of passing through such families, picking and choosing, holding up fragments, moments — a procedure that produced in the end an effect quite other than the naturalism of a Dreiser or James Farrell. It is not surprising that the literary critics who have admired and focused on naturalistic writers should have ignored WCW, critics like Vernon Parrington and Alfred Kazin. WCW preached contact and the actual steadily but he was never for long in the naturalistic camp. He was always pulled away from it by his own private third-floor and Ford-car aesthetic — the revolution in the tower — that told him that a little of the actual went a long way.

Late in his life he could be severe about his own withdrawal impulses; he could describe himself as "a prisoner, dim-witted, furious, raging at his prison," the prison being himself. But he did not seem to want to leave the prison. The prison was where he stole to do the writing, he put himself voluntarily in the prison, he found freedom in the prison that he did not find outside in the actual.

Anyway it was not what he was writing *about* that preoccupied him but the writing itself. He could chastise himself for the selfishness and coldness that the writing-need produced in him — he was abstracted, he was "not there" — but he remained confident of the result, confident that by the writing, the writing itself, he would come "through the obscurity of his surroundings to the flame." That flame in another context might be construed as naturalistic clarity but not where he used it in the play *Many Loves*. There the flame had an artier, more spiritual, certainly more subjective sense. There the flame was the gemlike flame of artifice, the illumination proceeding from little constructs written down on prescription blanks from behind the windshield. And it was that flame that WCW pursued throughout his career.

A naturalist writer does not conceive of himself constructing the actual behind the windshield. He does not imagine himself passing through the actual or stealing away from the actual to seek his flame, but inhabiting the actual and tirelessly recording the inhabiting.

So WCW was not a naturalist-realist. Nor was he a social realist, either in the Marxist sense or more loosely, though he did carry around an image of himself as a man of social concerns. He was against the money culture around him, against usury (like Pound, but not so strenuously), against the society doctors, against the crookedness in Washington; and he imagined that he was in his writings constantly a sort of spokesman of social protest; but in fact he almost never dealt with the society around him *as* society — at least until his thirties stories. He dealt with it individual by individual, and the individuals he chose were not chosen because they were representative of a class or some other social entity but because they were individuals and he had been with them and been impressed by them, impressed usually by their specialness, their detached, isolate, *un*social actuality. He liked his beings that way. He liked them unusual like his grandmother, grotesque if necessary, brutal and unbeautiful if he was feeling brutal and unbeautiful, but not representative. The odd were what attracted him, so that though he looked for them in common everyday local places it was not to their commonness that he addressed himself. He was that kind of writer, and in the end that may be the most American kind.

He had, for example, none of the impulses of communist John Reed. He met Reed in 1913 or thereabouts, knew him as a poet — Reed was a traditionalist in verse, busy with iambs — and as a social activist, and didn't think of him as the same breed as himself. In the autobiography he described him, at a party on 14th Street, as "a plump good-natured guy who had taken the bit in his teeth and was heading out." The heading out was courageous and not to be complained about but was odd nonetheless, WCW felt, *for a writer.* WCW could tell from Reed's heading out that he "was not primarily interested in writing," could see that at a party largely made up of writers Reed felt out of touch: "He looked at us as if he couldn't quite make out what we were up to."

In a thirties story called "Life Along the Passaic River" WCW was tougher on Reed. The story is as close to straight social-consciousness writing as WCW would come, and the sympathy for the proletariat of Passaic collectively is strong, yet he still had to take time out to complain about Reed's kind of activism. Reed was not a local boy but a professional outside agitator — that was a meaning for "outward bound" — and WCW didn't like him for that:

> When they had the big strike at the textile mills, and that bright boy from Boston came down and went shooting off his mouth around in the streets here telling us what to do: Who paid for having their kids and women beat up by the police? Did that guy take a room down on Monroe Street and offer his services for the next ten years at fifty cents a throw to help straighten out the messes he helped get us into? He did not. The Polacks paid for it all. Sure. And raised up sons to be cops too. I don't blame them.

WCW set himself up as an insider in that story, even to the extent of adopting a tough-guy dialect, which was unusual for him but he carried it off, and Reed was brought in as an example of an outsider who would never truly know or understand the local social scene and who should therefore not be regarded as a reliable type to entrust social affairs to. Yes, but it should be said that the outsider Reed did at least participate in the strike while WCW did not. It was the big Paterson strike that WCW wrote about in his poem *The Wanderer,* and Reed was an important figure in it, getting himself put in jail in Paterson briefly as a result and being largely responsible for a large mass meeting in Madison Square Garden to raise money for the strike (the meeting was a flop), while there is no record of WCW the insider having picketed anything, signed any petitions, gone to the meeting at the Garden, or contributed a penny. What WCW did about the strike was steal a poem out of it.

WCW never headed out the way Reed did because to head out as a writer meant for him to abandon the serious concerns of writing in favor of social concerns, to become in effect a journalist. That was death. Journalism was always a dirty word for WCW as well as Pound. Neither of them could stand writers like H. G. Wells. Wells was one whom WCW mentioned in 1923 as a good example of a writer who was not really a writer at all. "And what has anything Wells says to do with serious writing?" he asked in *The Great American Novel.* Wells had just been complaining about the modernist novelists around him, writers like Joyce who had, he felt, been paying too much attention to novelties of technique. What Wells was doing was carrying on — this was 1923 — with his old prewar anti*artiste* campaign, then fought chiefly against Henry James. Writing to James then he had said, "To you literature like painting is an end, to me literature like architecture is a means, has a use" — and the use for Wells was always essentially a social use, the betterment of society, he being one of the greater betterers. Therefore, Wells concluded, he would rather be called a journalist than an artist; that was the "essence of it." WCW thought that was nonsense just as James did, and was not nearly so polite as James. To look at writing the Wells way, he said, was to insure that the writing would be enslaved to saving the empire or the proletariat. That was wrong. Words, he said, "cannot, must not, will not be mustered of the people, by the people, for the people. They are words. They will have their way." Pound had put it another way, had characterized journalism as writing that brought people what people expected and wanted, and had said he wanted none of that. Neither Pound nor WCW wanted any of that. All their lives both of them were persistent in celebrating, in their own eccentric fashion, the familiar American Horatio Alger dream of do-it-yourself success. That is not a dream that makes social realists.

Frederick Lewis Allen once wrote an essay debunking the Horatio Alger dream as it had been presented in the Horatio Alger stories themselves. Allen showed that although each of the stories *seemed* to be a story of how by hard work and grit and persistence the hero won his way to riches, actually each story had a sort of trap door through which the hero slipped to pick up the riches after the hard work and grit and persistence had not, not quite, done it for him. The hero would work honestly and diligently for two dollars a week for a few years and, discovering that he had amassed by his labors something less than the million he wished for, would then happen on a gold mine or rich uncle. What Allen neglected to say was that deep in his heart *every* Horatio Alger American knows about that trap door, knows that it is not the honest persistence that does it, not the labor and the saving of pennies, but some freakish unplanned event or, more darkly, some financial coup or killing, usually illicit. If there is social realism in the Horatio Alger dream it is there, in the recognition of the economic reality, in the recognition that one does not make a million dollars by hard labor but by finding it in a hole or taking it from somebody else. That is a realistic understanding but it is not a social understanding; it is antisocial; it is a vision of human affairs that puts individual rights before group rights, Adam Smith and company notwithstanding. In this sense the Horatio Alger dream has been antisocial from the beginning and is still being so. "I am lonely, I am lonely, I was born to be lonely," sang WCW as he danced happily before the mirror in his study, and when he did it he was being, but for the money side, Horatio, asserting the great American principle that forever flummoxes communists and other earnest social reformers. They look at the American scene and try to renovate it or abscond with it, not believing that Americans, the honest ones, *really* believe that you should take what you can get and get there fustest with the mostest. They can't believe that anybody would be committed to such a life code and still profess to be moral and upright and neighborly, but they should believe because Americans do so profess. They profess to it and create a hundred or so new millionaires weekly who rob the multitude blind and are admired for it.

It is odd that the poets and little magazine editors of America — the editors in the ideological camp of Pound and WCW — have shared the Horatio dream with the aspiring hungry millionaires, because they have not been money people; they have had to transfer the dream from economics to aesthetics. But this they have done. In their art they have come to be as insistent as the millionaires that the way to success is the trap-door way. WCW was like that and modernist literature in general has been like that. Modernism has been a movement that has made loud revolutionary noises but kept to its stealing. Unlike the millionaires' stealing it has been principled stealing mostly; it has been stealing that cannot be readily construed as exploitation; but stealing it has been, stealing that has taken some of the best and worst, certainly some of the most radical, literary minds out of the world of radical social movements. Pound writing his antiusury blasts from the fastnesses of Rapallo for decades is an extreme instance of the breed but WCW seems to have been hardly more capable of conceiving of concerted collective social activity, or of an activist literature connected with it. In the thirties he put his feet in the water timidly — and was told by the editors of the *Partisan Review* that he was an ignoramus for doing so — but everybody was doing it then and WCW didn't do it very far and when he did it he kept saying that he didn't like it much; and in the early years he was even less socially oriented. He had no interest for example in the literary-political crowd in the Village that gathered around Mabel Dodge and printed *The Masses*. His friends Hartley and Demuth seemed to pass readily from Lola Ridge's house to the other but not WCW. He cut himself off in other words not just from John Reed but from the likes of Walter Lippmann, Emma Goldman, Margaret Sanger, Frances Perkins, and many others whose vision of the connection between literature and society was not the individual-sensibility modernist vision that WCW educated himself to. It is no coincidence that the journalists and the radical activists have not in general been sympathetic to modernism but have favored traditional literary forms even as they set about to destroy other traditions. The focus of the modernist has always annoyed them as it annoyed H. G. Wells, and in turn the focus of the activists has annoyed the modernists.

Those who have followed Horatio Alger into literary modernism have put themselves out of social play — the revolution in the tower — though sometimes unwittingly, by concentrating on their own peculiar effort to the exclusion of the social connections that the activists have insisted on, and they have done so without anything like the chances for success that the ordinary aspiring Horatio Alger millionaire has in the U.S. America may be able to sustain a hundred new millionaires weekly but not a hundred new poets. The trap door does not let a hundred a week through but only a score or so a decade.

There are some poets who do know that. WCW did not know it at first but he came to know it. By 1923 at least he knew it and his trap-door aesthetic took on a kind of fatalism that said in effect the trap-door way is a poor way but the only way. In *Spring and All* he said that; he set himself a rebirth theme and determined that he would accentuate the positive, but in one of the very strongest poems of the book — the one already mentioned in chapter three about the "pure products of America" — he came out asserting that in the general mess of imbecility and thievery that America's "purity" consisted of, it was impossible to conceive of any order that would be a good order, any directedness that would be a good directedness. The old orders of Europe — called in the poem the "peasant traditions" — were not with us (and oddly he seemed rather to regret their loss in the poem though elsewhere he was constantly disposing of Europe) and we had nothing to replace them. We were not therefore lost, we would go on with our purities, but it would be only in the "isolate flecks" that something would be "given off," and what was given off could not be anticipated or planned. It was random, haphazard since there was "no one to drive the car." It was random at the root, and no John Reeds or reformers of any kind could take effective control.

Maybe in the end it has been resignation rather than hope that has given strength to the trap-door theory in America. Certainly living in the social miasma of the industrial Passaic Valley does not encourage hope in order and directedness. Paterson itself is the original home of American robber barons and should have a sign at the city limits to that effect. It began as an "industrial park," a bright idea of Alexander Hamilton's to compete with European industry. Hamilton was unable to get government money for the project, raised private capital, turned it over to an entrepreneur who bled it and left it bankrupt in the first four years, starting America's first depression and the great traditon of bleeding. New money was raised, and with the war of 1812 prosperity settled into Paterson. It became a boom town for the industrialists there who made everything from submarines to textiles but did not think of it as a town, disclaimed social responsibility for it. When at last it picked up a city government the government was always beholden to the industrialists whose feelings about the town were well caught by the man who ran the locomotive works there. Refusing to release a small piece of land to the town needed to complete a hospital project he said, "I owe nothing to Paterson." The industrialists fought the unions, fought social reform, fought civic betterment, even fought cleaning up the Passaic River that they polluted. They kept the town down and when the nineteenth-century boom days were over the town was a sick slum town quickly, prototype of America's urban mess, and there was still nobody in charge, nobody driving the car. If you lived there, Allen Ginsberg observed, you didn't see any connection between yourself as private citizen and the city's affairs, didn't see any connection at any rate unless you were one of the very few on top:

> In a city the size of Paterson there are maybe 150 people who really know what's going on. They're the ones who are involved in it or who have access to the gossip. As for everyone else, their basic civic relations are cut off . . . In the end, people are walking around in the midst of a clearly defined hell. But they can't put their fingers on its causes or structure. Finally, they just decide that life itself is hell.

Ginsberg was brought up in Paterson, was more nearly one of the 150 than WCW would ever be, knew the mayor, even got the mayor to read parts of WCW's *Paterson* in 1949 plus his Sacco-and-Vanzetti poem, with the result that the mayor said he thought WCW was a "right guy" and "for the people, like Sandburg" and proposed to give him a key to the city, so Ginsberg had a feel for the place. His sense of the cut-offness of the people from anybody imaginably driving the car has been trustworthy, and it has been a feel for more than Paterson, a feel for the whole of the American cut-offness finally, as manifest in the Paterson condition, a cut-offness that Ginsberg has been socially more angry about than WCW ever was. Yet it is that cut-offness that WCW also knew deep, felt in his aesthetic bones and based his own social fatalism on. The real, the actual for WCW — as for Ginsberg — seldom rose to the social city-hall level but only kept walking the streets, inhabiting the tenements. If the argument for the modernists against the activists has a valid starting point it is probably in the truth of such feelings.

But where do such feelings put WCW as a realist? J. Hillis Miller, a critic who has written extensively about WCW, has said that the realism of WCW is the realism of one who has identified himself completely with the world around him in the sense of the world as things rather than systems, has merged word with object, fused the subjective and objective. Certainly WCW said such things many times about his aesthetic intentions, and tried to effect such mergers, and this theory of the nature of his realism needs attention. Yet a poem about a waterfall and a waterfall remain distinct despite the remarks of poet or critic and it is to be doubted that efforts at fusion or identification can ever result in other than some variant on the *illusion* of fusion that art has always practiced. WCW was no more a realist of fusions than he was a naturalist or a social realist — though he liked to theorize that he was — and in fact if he is to be called a realist at all it would seem best to think of him in connection with illusion, that is, the art side, first. He kept insisting that the art side was first — that poetry was words first and painting was paint first — and though he also wanted the other, wanted the words or the paint to be kissing cousins to the immediacies of perception they were meant to evoke, he could never get around the difficulty that the words or the paint were not the same as the immediacies but approximations; nor can anyone get around it. WCW's art was in the approximating; his realism was in the approximating. It was a significant art, and it remains a significant art much practiced by WCW's successors but it is an art of approximation only, an art that will not make waterfalls but only poems dreaming on water-falls — which is what poems did before WCW too.

What they did not do before — or did not do before to the extent that WCW and his successors have done it — was assume that the approximating was strictly a one-man Horatio Alger show. They did not think that to achieve their approximations, their illusions of the real, they were prohibited from using the traditional resources of their art that existed outside themselves. They did not see the necessity of keeping the poetic transaction wholly at home in the singular poet's singular mind. But WCW did see the necessity; those outside resources of language and form were mere blockage for him, *keeping* him from his work, and so he struggled at the unblocking for decades, struggled at getting closer to what he conceived to be the actual by insisting on his isolation, the primacy of it. Very American and very modernist. And, though it liberated poets from iambs and the like it was in some respects limiting.

It was limiting because it led to wholesale rejection of civiliza-tion's leavings, not just the iambs. McAlmon's remark that civili-zation had never been anything more than a system for handling "group needs" and was in any event now dead was characteristic. Whatever may be the merit of the throw-civilization-away view it is one that when seriously adopted puts aside a lot that may be detestable but is also real and actual. Stealing away into the immediacies of the self inevitably does that, and WCW's stealings did that.

6

His isolation during the year or so of the publishing of *Contact* showed in the civilization-busting hysteria of *Contact*, a little mimeographed thing standing against the world; and when Mc-

Almon left him he must have felt lonely indeed. McAlmon left him for a woman, a rich woman as it turned out, by the name of Bryher who proposed to him and soon carted him off to London and Paris. When WCW heard of the romance he "literally felt the tears come to [his] eyes," but WCW and Flossie were instrumental anyway in giving the young-marrieds a big sendoff in New York — there were orchids and orchids and Marsden Hartley proposed that the newspaper heading about the party read "Poets Pawing Orchids" — and soon McAlmon was abroad with the expatriate set. Bryher quickly abandoned him for a woman, namely H.D., but he had money now and so he went on with *Contact* but made it a book-publishing venture. He visited all the great ones including Pound, T. S. Eliot, and James Joyce. He liked Pound and called him a man of good will but said he felt "more than generations apart" from him. He was surprised to find that he liked Eliot too but he managed not to let his liking him interfere with the WCW-McAlmon party line about him that he was a literary disaster. As for Joyce, he wrote WCW that Joyce and he could "touch" — he added, "as you and I can" — but that even Joyce talked "a lot of erudite theological and learned talk" that had "nothing to do with real states." From his literary joustings he emerged with *Contact Editions,* a series of books by Pound, Gertrude Stein, Hemingway, H.D., Ford Madox Ford, and Robert Coates as well as WCW (his *Spring and All* as well as *The Great American Novel*). But his presence abroad was, for WCW, just one more reason to devise a way to carry through with the biggest stealing of all, the stealing he had dreamed of intermittently since he became an intern, the stealing away completely from medicine and Rutherford.

Pound had been dreaming of it for him for a long time. Pound had tried first to get Eliot stolen away from the bank in London and had set up a curious enterprise named *Le Bel Esprit* designed to get money from his friends for Eliot — and therefore save civilization. After Eliot he thought he would save WCW — and civilization — but WCW seems not to have received any money from

Bel Esprit. WCW had to steal away on his own financially, and he chose to take Flossie with him, a new kind of stealing for him. Oddly it was McAlmon who strongly advised him to take Flossie. He wrote a fatherly letter to WCW from Paris telling WCW how much WCW needed "Florence and the youngsters." He said, "Like Joyce like myself and like many a sensible person you aren't a strong will and you need a ballast. Joyce is the victim of anybody that has him out to dinner — ready to be dragged from one drink to another. He'd go to hell but for his family." And so Flossie and WCW together stole out but first they had to find a doctor to take over the practice, then they had to find the right person to take care of the children, and then they had to move out experimentally for a few months to New York, visiting the children on weekends to see if the plan was working. While they were in New York WCW began going to the New York Library and reading up on the historical figures that he would write about in *In the American Grain.* Flossie helped him here. She was in on the stealing now and she did *"all* the reading on the Aaron Burr, Alexander Hamilton theme." Stealing was good sport, especially from books, but if you were doing it at the New York Public Library you had to be sure that you really did have the books. One day WCW was sitting there without a book, having the De-Soto chapter "burning" in his head and writing "furiously." An attendant came up to him, tapped him on the shoulder, and said he couldn't write in that room:

> "I'm writing a thesis," I said.
> "You have no book," he said.
> "I'll get one in a minute," I said.
> "You can't write here without one," he said.
> So I had to get up, go to the desk, get out a book, put it on the table before I could go on. My day was ruined.

That was 1924, or perhaps late 1923, a dividing point. WCW was forty, he was off and away with Flossie, he was getting started on another book that was a different kind of book than anything he had ever done, and he was also headed out to see a part of the literary world that he had been isolated from. But it was also, and more importantly, a dividing point in his writing. By 1923 with *The Great American Novel* he had by hook and crook and many a devious route really learned to write, that is, learned all the essential competence that he would display. He had caught on to the short poem's mysteries earlier as well as the disciplines of plays, but the broken-style books had led him into prose and eventually into narrative prose so that there he was, suddenly a grownup in prose too. Could he have learned such things from writing instructors like the one who wanted McAlmon to copy down reams of Hawthorne? No, the learning of these arts was not like that in his aesthetic; it was something that you grew into, the way a beaver grows into building dams, a natural process, writer and the world contending. He was a slow bloomer this way — and to some kinds of writing he never bloomed; never mastered methods of argument, for instance, and would have been unable to tell a syllogism from a claw hammer — but he got there, and the getting there by his route was part of the necessary game. He knew that he had to steal there, and knew that sometimes the civilized conditions for stealing there were so bad that he even had to pretend to read a book in the library, but he always felt, except in low moments, that he could make it there anyway if he just kept at it long enough. On some of the stationery he used for his 1910 letters from Leipzig there was a drawing of a turtle in the upper left-hand corner, and under the turtle, *"j'arriverai."* He was right at last, though where he had arrived was to prove a forbidding place. Also, since for another twenty-five years only a select few in the literary world would find out that he had arrived, it was hard for him to know that he had done so himself.

CHAPTER FIVE

Moment of the Twenties

IN 1958 Robert Lowell wrote to WCW congratulating him on his autobiography. "Rushed perhaps in places," he said, "but blazing fire in others. You and Fitzgerald catch the moment of the 20s better than anybody except Lawrence." WCW had no interest in Fitzgerald but Lowell could have seen a Fitzgerald connection in the way WCW began the twenties part of his autobiography: "I suppose the vile bathtub gin we put away was an incentive to art." And he could have seen a Lawrence connection — Lawrence *was* important to WCW — in the way WCW promoted revolutionary literary behavior, issuing pronouncements like those in Lawrence's *Studies in Classic American Literature.* But other connections are harder. The "moment of the 20s" that WCW caught was in so many ways so different from either the Fitzgerald or the Lawrence moment that WCW could well have been writing about a different decade.

WCW was not used to wading in the fountain at the Plaza at 3 A.M., or to going to expensive parties on Long Island, or to selling stories to the *Saturday Evening Post,* or to begging his publisher for large advances on his books. Once when he was younger he had proposed to himself to write his autobiography but his notes on the subject must have discouraged him since they went dully along like this: "1. All my lief [sic] briefly. 2. What else did I do (all over with different material) . 3. What did I think? 4. Details more in particular: France, Switzerland, Leipzig, London, Spain.

The sea. Puerto Rico. 5. After all, what did I *do?"* And aside from the lack of doing there were other deficiencies in his existence, compared to Fitzgerald. He was not a writer of the lives of the rich, he seldom troubled himself with middle- or upper-class mores or manners, and the nearest thing he had in his writings to a virile gamekeeper was his tough pregnant mothers on Guinea Hill. He had his own milieu, his own twenties set apart from theirs, and while what he wrote sometimes reached to theirs he mostly kept his distance.

But he did not always want the distance — and here is perhaps where the Lowell remark applies. Even in the mellow autobiography WCW can sometimes be seen looking in on the literary great from outside, the way one of Fitzgerald's characters once looked in on a glittery Princeton party with his nose pressed against the window. It does not matter that Fitzgerald went to more of the glittery parties than WCW did but only that there was the want in both of them — and in Lawrence too — to go to them. For all three writers the world was a sick, oppressive society needing an overhaul, especially when one didn't go to the parties.

There were parties and parties. There were not only the Princeton parties and Plaza parties and Long Island parties and parties in southern France, but there were ideological parties too — and those were the ones that Lawrence and Williams went to more than the others. There were, for instance, the parties, mostly talk, of sexual liberation that Lawrence kept attending even as his own sex life went to pieces, and the parties of the new literature that WCW kept attending even though sometimes he felt that he was outside looking in the window, felt that he was the doctor-hick from the country among highbrows. In the end it was not so much what the composition of the parties was as whether you were invited and felt at home at them or were not invited, and if so what you suffered. The insiders who went to the parties might discover their emptiness — Fitzgerald did, and came to write of how little there was at the heart of them — but those who didn't go were left to suffer their martyrdoms. Both Lawrence and

WCW led martyrs' lives largely, and though Lawrence was if anything less buoyant a martyr than WCW, WCW was as strong as
Lawrence in the service of reporting on the suffering, and reporting on who it was at the parties causing the suffering.

For those inside as well as out the party life was a nervous one,
on an edge, but as a whole the outsiders with their martyrdoms
were *more* nervous and driven than the insiders. No insider was
worthy of respect because the insides were always corrupt, but that
didn't help the outsiders much because the outside though pure
was never wholly livable — no outside can be. Those on the outside though querulous wanted as much as the insiders to be inside,
and when they did on occasion arrive there as gate crashers or
wallflowers or hicks they were full of the tensions between accept-
ing and rejecting what they found. If the parties were, for instance, to be drunk at — and WCW did sometimes drink his full
poet-quota despite protestations in the autobiography — the
martyr could do his drinking at them but he had to be more
serious about it than the insiders to remain a martyr. And if he
did the drinking in Paris, where all the insiders went to be insiders in the twenties, then the seriousness problem was greater.
Flossie and WCW made it to the Parisian inside in 1924, and they
frequented for a few brief days the Dome and the Trianon and the
other insider places, but while WCW was there he was conscious
that he had a big obligation to his art not to like what he was
doing.

No, he had to wish that James Joyce would stop singing Irish
songs at the Dome and settle down to a "profound discussion." He
had to believe that there was too little time left for saving what
had to be saved, and too much to be done in the time there was,
not to call a halt at some point to Irish songs.

There was this kind of martyrdom in WCW. He was better off
than Lawrence perhaps. His intensities were tidal and when they
were down he could be humorous and easy, devoid of the stern
missionary spirit and the ironic aggressiveness in Lawrence. But
when they were up he not only had to save the world but he had a

fierce quick temper for doing it. Once he was theatened with a suit for hitting a neighbor child wildly in a fury, and on artistic occasions he could be equally instant, either writing off thoughtless midnight letters to editors who had annoyed him, or filling up his private notebooks with bitterness at whatever happened to be out on the publishing front to be bitter about. In 1924 for example his intensities were up for a week or more while he was in Rome with Flossie, and he stole time to scribble a journal that was all the angriest darkness and pornography, apparently provoked by his outsider feelings about the art and art culture he found surrounding him in Europe.

It was fifty pages labeled just "Rome," and while it began as an exercise in letting himself go, after the manner of *Kora*, it picked up most of its steam from anger. The anger was anger at all the old things he had been angry at, suddenly surfacing again, but the anger had also moved out from literature and the academies to settle on New York money and middle-class American life plus the Roman equivalents. A characteristic blast in it, characteristic in its spaciousness, was, "There can be but one object in life for us: to kill the damned thing as it exists now, to get out," with the "damned thing" not further specified, being just the kulch. He was in other words full of a heavy disillusionment that went far beyond his private predicament. He called America "one monstrous grotesque" that would go on being that, and looking around Rome he swiftly traced the trouble back before America to Christianity, which he said was "a bastardization of paganism . . . sucking the cock of art clandestinely." In the old days in contrast Venus "gloried as a fucker."

He cleaned up these thoughts when he wrote *A Voyage to Pagany* but kept them in their Roman context. Rome was a darkness for him that year, and he had many such darknesses, and they were the darknesses of a martyr who had tried very hard to bring the light to his time and nothing had happened.

His martyrdom was hard on him when it was with him. It left him not only with little time for parties at the *Dome* but with disappointment with his friends when they didn't aid him with his martyr duties. He was annoyed for example with McAlmon in that year because McAlmon in Paris didn't arrange for him to meet some of the French surrealists who were "moved by a significant impetus"; and in the absence of friends' help WCW set up a tight, uplifting tourist schedule for himself and Flossie that took in not just Paris but southern France, and not just Rome but northern and southern Italy, plus Austria (where he even took medical courses) and Germany. And during the travels he constantly drove himself to writing, not only the writing of the angry Rome journal but the finishing up of the book he was working on, *In the American Grain,* so that he could then move on without dilettantish pause or delay to the book that would be about the traveling, *A Voyage to Pagany.*

The schedule left few nights for Irish singing. If he had not been a constant preacher against puritanism an observer might well have pinned the puritan label on WCW's own chest that year.

2

And perhaps the label should have been pinned on anyway. He did protest too much about the puritanism not to have been aware of it in himself, though erratically. The puritans were his prime villains throughout the twenties and they could not have earned such enmity easily. He had nothing good to say about them. They were the font of all American vice and he would have been happy if he could have discovered that they had not only destroyed America but Europe too. Obviously he needed somebody like the puritans to beat over the head though it sometimes meant beating himself.

It helped him that in the twenties the puritans were a common target for the literary insiders as well as for outsiders like himself. Someone could always be found to complain about Irving Babbitt at Harvard, for instance, as he beat the drums for literary law, order and decorum; and the whole American literary community was up in arms for years against the establishment New England figures in the Sacco-Vanzetti case, a case that provoked hundreds of protest poems including one by WCW. Very well, but the anti-puritanism began in WCW long before the outrage at Babbitt and Sacco-Vanzetti. It began before he had mounted his hate campaign against his long-time favorite literary puritan, T. S. Eliot, or before he had read Lawrence on the evils to American literature of puritanism, or had been subjected to any of the twenties flood of generalized superior slander of the puritans such as this little blast in a magazine, *Broom,* that WCW became involved with soon after *Contact:*

> America, made of the Puritan, by the Puritan, for the Puritan, re-made of the Machine, by the Machine, for the Machine.

The hatred of the puritans in WCW was to be found way back in his play *Betty Putnam* that he wrote before his marriage, where the puritans were made out to be opponents of all good things, and particularly poetry. In that play the worst puritan person of all, the bad daddy of the play, wanted to cheat his own son out of property and may be imagined to have had a psychic connection with WCW's own Pop. Was it perhaps with Pop that the anti-puritanism began?

There is evidence that WCW thought of Pop as a puritan though Pop professed to be a poetry lover and does not seem to have tried to cheat WCW out of property. WCW reported a dream he had in 1919 in which Pop *was* a hater of poetry, WCW's own poetry. It was a dream he had soon after Pop's death, and in it Pop came down the steps to him from his New York office and said to him, "You know all that poetry you're writing it's *no good.*" The dream must have come from someplace, but Pop did like Shakespeare and did bring serious poesy to the Williams parlor — his aesthetic knowledge even impressed Pound — so he had to have other qualifications for puritanism than a generalized hatred of the art. The poetry focus between Pop and WCW was probably not so much on the poetry itself, even WCW's, as upon poetry as a profession. Pop was a puritan about work. At least there is plenty of evidence that WCW saw that kind of puritanism in him outside of dreams, evidence that WCW thought Pop had a work ethic lodged in his bone marrow, an ethic that he probably imposed upon WCW by regularly disapproving of artists' hours.

WCW had a poem about Pop, "Adam," in which he was very much the Englishman who, though living among Latins in the islands, and marrying one, could never unbend and was always driven from tasting paradise to tasting instead "the death that duty brings so mincingly," duty "that enslaved him all his life." The duty kept him from himself, demanded of him that he obey his ideological inheritance, and obviously WCW himself felt threatened by that inheritance. Once Pop asked WCW what every American father at some point asks his son, namely what did WCW want to *do?* WCW replied that he wanted to do *nothing* — which was a lie if there ever was one, though a dramatic one — and was thereupon pleased to discover that his father was shocked, pleased that he had said the offensive thing, had asserted a different ethic. But when later WCW was to keep finding the offensive thing in himself, and to see that even if he took six months off in Europe he couldn't take all of it off but had to make use of it, improve the shining hours, then it was impossible for him to bury the puritanism with Pop. WCW had to learn to live with it instead, and ever after it would come out of him in odd shapes. There was a poem of his, for instance, fairly late in life that would have shocked any puritan of Pop's vintage and yet was, beyond the shock word in it, a call to duty as clear as the call attributed to Pop in "Adam." The refrain stanza went,

> Any way you walk
> Any way you turn
> Any way you stand
> Any way you lie
> You have pissed your life

Then there had been not only Pop to reckon with on the puritan front but also brother Edgar — brother Edgar who from the day he won the prestigious Rome prize had been a model of the artist as a successful social adjuster. Along with Edgar's adjusting had come a slight British accent and a measure of prudery — or so at least WCW seems to have felt. The prudery must have been incipient in his early life when he and WCW were close but it blossomed with age just as WCW's rebelliousness blossomed. Also it came sometimes to be directed straight at WCW for his rebelliousness as if Edgar, discovering that WCW was the family bad boy, had felt moved to take over Pop's function in the family after Pop's death. Edgar, who had supplanted WCW as elder brother, served on important committees. He had been president of the Architectural League, vice-president of the Fine Arts Federation, president of the National Academy of Design and president of the Municipal Art Society. He was strong on the preserving and remodeling of old buildings, particularly libraries, and had remodeled part of the interior of the New York Public Library as well as designing a new wing for the Rutherford Library one block from 9 Ridge Road. He was a trustee of the American Scenic and Historic Preservation Society and in all ways a pillar of respectability in the community. WCW respected him for being what he was, and in the novel *The Build-Up,* in which he described their strange competition for the hand of Charlotte Herman, he went out of his way to indicate that he shared with the rest of the Williamses a delight in Edgar's triumphs. In turn Edgar tried hard to like what WCW wrote, with the result that the two brothers saw each other frequently, and aside from coping together with family problems, such as what to do with Mother Elena, they did occasionally talk literature. But while Edgar tried to be sympathetic with the literary revolution that WCW kept conducting it was not a revolution that was finally to his taste at all. How far apart the two were, even though they partook of the same puritan root, shows in two of Edgar's letters written to WCW when both of them were coming on seventy and their long-term differences were fixed, letters that unfortunately are not available for reproduction here even in part but which may be summarized.

The occasion for the letters was WCW's autobiography. WCW had just finished it and had stuffed a copy of his foreword to it in Edgar's mailbox. Edgar came home, read it, and wrote a quick note to WCW saying he had liked it but felt paragraph three should be omitted. Here was paragraph three:

> I don't intend to tell the particulars of the women I have been to bed with or anything about them or the men either, if I have been to bed with any. That has nothing to do with me. What relations I have had with men and women, such encounters as have interested me most profoundly have not occurred in bed. I am extremely sexual in my desires. I carry it everywhere and at all times. I think that from that arises the drive which empowers us all. Given that drive a man does with it what his mind directs him to do. In the manner in which he directs that power lies his secret. We always try to hide the secret of our lives from the general stare. The hidden core of what I believe to be my life will not easily be deciphered, even when I tell, as here, the outer circumstance.

After recommending the elimination of the paragraph Edgar was careful to compliment WCW again, but then he went firmly to his point, which was that WCW had, in the paragraph, violated standards of decorum that were important in art as well as life. WCW seems to have replied expressing annoyance, since Edgar then wrote a second letter reiterating his position and observing as well that he felt it was a writer's duty to provide his readers with uplifting thoughts. It seems unlikely that WCW was impressed but Edgar was friendly enough, and also persuasive enough, to effect at least one slight change in the paragraph, the omission of the words, ". . . or the men either, if I have been to bed with any." That much of a concession WCW was willing to make to puritanism.

Aside from Edgar and Pop there was Mother Elena with her own Latin versions of puritanism, fortunately mixed with a good earthiness. In his book about her WCW emphasized the earthiness and was careful to put down in full the stories she told him that made his kind of good copy, stories such as this one:

> I'll tell you a story, it is true — not very clean, but — one time there were a lot of men at a supper I suppose and they were pulling

corks from bottles of beer — or wine, I don't know. Poor Toledo was pulling hard at a cork when a little wind escaped him. Blup! Don Sebastian Sedo quickly turned to him and offered him a cork on the end of a cork screw. That is a true story.

But there was another side to her too. She had been bred up in a culture respectful of propriety in dress and conduct that Pop and then Edgar could only have approved, and before she had married Pop and been caged in the middle classness of Rutherford she had imagined herself living in fine houses surrounded by servants, elegance and good manners. She remembered going to "a very fine affair" in Paris where "they were all nobility" and she was introduced as *"la soeur du plus grand médécin de Puerto Rico"* and she had worn a dress made specially for the occasion "of pongee silk with little ruffles of lace all over." With such memories and faded aspirations she was bound to have feelings that literature should be genteel too, and she did, and she was not at all sure that the new modernism in WCW with its emphasis on the ugly and rude was what a son of hers should be trafficking in. In the late twenties when she was old as the hills and severely crippled, though she would live yet for many years, she undertook to read his *Voyage to Pagany*. Her comment on it was that the first quarter of it was "all sex, sensual, no love the sublime" and had "too much damns and hells, I am sure you were not brought up on that coarse language." She added, much as Edgar would some years later, that she looked forward to a WCW book with uplift. As she put it, "Before I die I would like you to write a book following your noble character and intellect."

So WCW was surrounded by his own familial puritanism as well as that which he conceived to be part of Rutherford society. Rutherford was hardly populated by old Bostonians or even by Englishmen like Pop, but by the twenties WCW had made the connection. Puritanism he saw as no longer a local New England phenomenon but the pervasive American ill that the New Englanders particularly but many other groups in their social and religious diligence had brought upon the country, starting way back. It was an ill that showed in prudery about sex, in Prohibition, in fear of plain talk, in all the usual manifestations of fastidiousness and decorum that WCW came to hate, but most conspicuously showed itself in incessant pressure for conformity. As WCW struggled to find and assert his own private artistic identity he more and more came to imagine that the unfriendliness he felt around him, whether in the form of familial chidings or in the publishing silences that met his works as they came out, was in the end all puritan in origin. He was hipped on the puritan connection, and *In the American Grain* showed his obsession, though it was in other respects a fine historical effort, an important experiment for him in deselfing. Perhaps it was in his antipuritan obsession that WCW most caught "the moment of the 20s"?

3

The Great American Novel (1923) had been witty and good-tempered and he had kept his good temper even as he blasted away in it at H. G. Wells and the Mormons and the general American shoddy (he used "shoddy" as a noun and described it as a cheap cloth made from woolen rags and blown into the warp and woof of the system, insuring that everybody would get less for their money). He had begun the book as another exercise in his broken style, with unannounced jumps from meditations about the form of the novel to descriptions of an amorous car (WCW himself, on four wheels) falling in love with a beautiful green and red truck. Then suddenly in the middle of the meandering he had happened upon a historical mission for himself, a mission that he later carried over into *In the American Grain*. Out of the blue he began describing Columbus and his arrival in the New World, and the prose jumped with energy on the page. *"Nuevo Mundo!"* he had Columbus's sailors shout happily, and before WCW knew it his tale had spread out to all sorts of historical manifestations of *Nuevo Mundo,* skipping haphazardly from place to place in the American past but keeping hold of the key idea: that it was always the new that had had to be sought out in America, that the seeking had itself been the great American mission whether in poetry or geography. That was to be the key idea of *In the American Grain* too, but in the latter the bright horizons of the new were to be clouded up by puritans.

In the American Grain also had some good humor in it, though no amorous car, but such humor as it had was more aggressive, Lawrencian; behind it the Williams anger smoked. Kay Boyle once said of him that there was "no venom, no imbalance" in him but she could not have said that if she had read his Rome journal, and it would have been hard for her to say it if she had read *In the American Grain* not just as history, which it was, but also as a personal document. She knew, as most of his friends did, the part of him that was shy and gentle of manner. Also she knew him to be full of fine enthusiasms and able to bring forth great generosity of feeling for other kindred-spirited writers. But apparently she didn't know the part of him that held the venom. It was there and it was a driving force in *In the American Grain*.

Beyond the venom the book had many subjects, being a series of short biographies or character sketches of some twenty American figures from Eric the Red to Abraham Lincoln. Occasionally the prose was fragmented as in the earlier books but its verbal modernity was not conspicuous. It was a solid historical venture that encouraged him to remove himself from his attic and hurry to the New York Public Library, which he did, and encouraged him to reach for a kind of objective truth about the historical figures covered that he felt the old academic historians had failed to achieve, which he did also. But even in the library, and even in the finished words of a book that tried to keep history honest and without false orderings by going back to prime sources like journals, or back to early and simple secondary sources, still the self kept creeping in. It was the 1924 self, the martyrdom self, feeling isolated, ignored, beleaguered. In *Kora* the self had been oppressed by Rutherford merely but the 1924 self was oppressed by all America plus points east, America and Europe being finally by then both puritan continents for him. Furthermore the 1924 self looked into American history and found many earlier selves like itself which had been similarly oppressed. The 1924 self discovered that it was not alone in its oppression but had troubles built deep in the American grain.

To the obsessive oppression theme WCW added one other that served as palliative, a grand sexual-ideological explanation of the weakness in himself that helped the oppressors to their advantage. He had of course long worried about his tendency to remove himself from the fray, especially when depressed; he had come to lean on Flossie to keep him from disturbing chores and details and to carry on with normal family life with the steadiness he lacked. By the twenties Flossie was good at normalcy. She would take the children off and away to the country when he was nervous, and pay the bills, and tell him when he needed a new suit. But by the twenties he was full of his theory of the male psyche that he had dabbled with earlier and that made his weakness not just a private thing inherited from his melancholy mother but the general masculine inheritance. The theory was fuzzily out of Otto Weininger (he described it as Weininger in reverse) and told him that the male in isolation from the female was abstract and impractical, was a rootless tumbling weed, and hence needed constantly the female presence to keep him from that kind of tumbling. He had been convinced of the male need for years and had written about it in a letter to *The Egoist* in 1917 where he said that males were by their nature troubled by "insufficient attachment to the objective world" since their only "positive connection with the earth" was in "the fleeting sex function." In between the performance of the function the male, he was persuaded, had nothing to do except stargaze and be idle, and the idleness was what led primitive males, when they were not "busied with women," to be "either hunting, fighting, loafing or drunk." He was persuaded of this ideologically in 1917 but in 1924 he set about applying his belief to history. He had always imagined that he himself needed other women than Flossie, needed all women, needed the female principle, but in

1924 in his history he looked for the need in others too, in the old heroes.

Where did he find it? The point does need to be made that he did not find it in Columbus's journal or in the old Icelandic sagas or in town records in Massachusetts or in any other sources that he and Flossie went to — for Flossie helped him — in putting together *In the American Grain*. It was his own finding, his own conceiving of the heroes. He found that the heroes too needed the female principle to keep them from being "either hunting, fighting, loafing or drunk" and found that they spent their lives as he did wandering about the world in search of the principle.

It was definitely a principle as he conceived it, not just a female, and he was persuaded that the principle could manifest itself in land as well as a female body. His conviction helped him resurrect his old wanderer theme, and just as his poet in *The Wanderer* had come to earth at last in a particular spot next to the Passaic, so the wanderers in his history came at last home to the female earthiness of some part of *Nuevo Mundo*. Each particular hero had his particular earth to quest for but the nature of the quest was always the same. Always the earth discovered and explored was female, with the consequence that the history of the exploration of the *Nuevo Mundo* became, throughout *In the American Grain*, a history of man chasing woman. When Columbus and his sailors shouted, "*Nuevo Mundo*," they were shouting, after all, for a girl.

Sometimes the territory that the explorers of *In the American Grain* quested for was only suggestively identified as woman but it was always in some way beauty (though not of course to be capitalized in the radical anti-Beauty twenties) and it was also always physical, material, real, a thing. ("No ideas but in things" has this male-female background.) Eric the Red driven from his former home by the bastardizing Christians was described as wandering lonely and sad through the north looking "toward summer," which would be warm female country where he would be "whole" again. Columbus "floated with luck and in sunshine on that tropic sea toward adventure and discovery" as if he were about to be sexually bedded down. And after Columbus came many other males in search of female wanderers, Cortez, Ponce de Léon, Sir Walter Raleigh, Samuel de Champlain, but particularly De Soto to whom the land spoke loud and clear as a woman saying, "I am beautiful . . . You will not dare to cease following me." All of these explorers were good and heroic though they were weak with the male weakness and needed the strength of the female land. Even Cortez was good; he was not to be blamed for the destruction of Tenochtitlán; the old world was to be blamed, the old world rushing "inevitably to revenge itself" upon the "orchidean beauty" of the new. WCW did not explain clearly why Cortez should have been admired for taking his signals from the old world but otherwise the admiration for Cortez, even for his slaughters, was not out of line with WCW's male theme. He was not averse to praising violence when it came naturally as he thought it did to Cortez, whom he described as "a conqueror like other conquerors, a genius superbly suited to his task." That was to say that the violence was an authentic part of his being, part of the mystery that drove him on, as was the violence of a later hero of the book, Père Sébastien Rasles, a French Catholic who sided with the Indians against the British and in his own authenticity encouraged the Indians to authentic violence. "Did one expect the Indians not to be fighters? Not Rasles at any rate." So naturally Daniel Boone's violence also seemed to please WCW when Boone took "the lives of the beasts into his quiet, murderous hands" and lived "with the sense of the Indian." At least the Indians and murderers were not puritans.

By the WCW thesis, so long as a man was essentially his own man struggling to come to terms in his own way with his own basic primitive male self by finding the female somehow somewhere, he was good, he was authentic, he was probably heroic. Sometimes WCW's approval came out so strong that it was a bit thick, designed to shock:

> So they strangled and hanged de Val and stuck his head upon a pike. To me the whole thing's marvelous — all through.

But if it was sometimes thick it was consistent. The male drive uninhibited and left to itself for fulfillment was by his credo a life force, an energy to be respected as much as the female force it sought; and what was bad was not the authentic violence that sometimes attended the male drive but the impediments put in the way of the drive by the puritans.

Most of the evil men in *In the American Grain* were literally puritans except Benjamin Franklin and Alexander Hamilton, and those two might as well have been puritans since they had all the qualities WCW hated in puritans. The puritans were bad when they were violent as well as bad when they were calm. They were just bad. They were bad because they were not lonely wanderer souls like WCW in his attic or Eric the Red "a marked man, beyond the law," fending off the old Scandinavian culture in the Greenland wilderness. They were bad guys because they were not individual questers at all but craven collectivites looking for leaders to follow, meanwhile impeding or oppressing those who did not need such leaders and who had the courage and strength to go solo. They were bad because they were not in "the pursuit of beauty," were not like Raleigh busy at "plunging their lust into the body of the new world" but were emasculated beings possessed of none of the lovely lonely male drive. "Each shrank from an imagination that would sever him from the rest." They were even — WCW was speaking then of the Mayflower pilgrims — bad spellers.

How could a speller like WCW have sought out evil spelling among the puritans? It was a sign of his obsession. If he had been thinking clearly he might first have noticed that the puritan "misspellings" were scattered beyond the Pilgrims throughout the seventeenth century, and he might secondly have conceived that misspellings were a form of independence and individualism; but he had villainy keeping him from thinking clearly, villainy that insatiably took the form of repressive spirits, spirits who drove the good independent world wanderers out on the oceans searching for freedom, out on quests for *Nuevo Mundo*. Drove them in effect to stealing. Stealing was not good in itself perhaps but it remained in his eyes a necessary evil in a world run by insistent conformists who had the free spirits bottled up if they didn't steal. Franklin, though no puritan, was a conformist example. He had some of the good maleness in him, some of the explorer's or stealer's raw energy, but he hoarded it, being always one to play safe and to scatter precepts about for playing safe, so that the "force of the new world" was never open in him but "sly, covert, almost cringing." Similarly Hamilton, also no puritan, was the same as a puritan and an oppressive spirit because he wanted to "harness the whole young aspiring genius to a treadmill," the genius being the young country itself and the treadmill being Hamilton's national industry project at the Paterson Great Falls. Both Hamilton and Franklin were oppressors, and so were Cotton Mather and all the real puritans; and faced with their powers the free spirit would not have done badly to have indulged in a bit of misspelling.

In the American Grain was impressive, thematically, though elephantine. In it WCW pulled his polemic together for the first time. Its twenty separate essays were not really separate but were all working the common ground of what WCW thought to be the basic American tragedy, the tragedy of a great and endlessly rich *Nuevo Mundo* being captured by conformists. WCW would never be more eloquent — but he would also perhaps never be ideologically more driven. If the obsessions in it be thought of in terms of his own life, then the book does look, for all its virtues, a wee bit paranoid. Perhaps the paranoia was also a part of "the moment of the 20s."

4

Paranoia: in psychiatry, a mental disorder characterized by systematized delusions of grandeur or, especially, persecution. Laymen should not use words like "paranoia" lightly but there it is, a word that is used lightly. Let us say that there became evident a slight literary paranoia in WCW at this point, and let us say this while not worrying about the childhood origins when Pop and Edgar and Mother Elena, all looking suspiciously like the Pilgrim Fathers, menaced him. Let us look at it as a delusion that was not just WCW's, not terribly private, but the delusion of dozens of other like-minded literary people who for one literary reason or another had not made it to the glittery parties, the delusion that the world was out to get them because they were free spirits.

Pause for a *New Yorker* joke. A sensible-looking female is being lectured to by her analyst who says, "Mrs. Smith, you have nothing to worry about. Yours is not a delusion. The grocery stores and banks *are* passing on their higher costs to you."

The free spirits have been oppressed; there have been cases and cases. WCW was himself close to some of the most celebrated cases, particularly the censoring of *Ulysses* as it appeared serially in *The Little Review,* and then the hunting down of Pound as traitor at the end of World War II; and toward the close of his life WCW was to find himself at the center of a genuine case, a small one but big to him, a case having to do with his connection with the Library of Congress, a case that hurt deeply and was true oppression, no delusion. For all that the book *In the American Grain* remains so loaded with persecution polemic that "delusion" is an appropriate word.

The delusion was there not only in WCW's presentation of the puritans and their equivalents but also in his choice and handling of the heroes of the book, especially the two he most clearly personally identified with, Aaron Burr and (the only poet represented) Edgar Allan Poe. WCW lovingly lavished all his own problems on both of these gentlemen, and lovingly provided them with his virtues too.

WCW would have given, his essay suggests, his right arm to be Burr. Burr was such a wonder that when the beautiful and commanding Indian princess Jacataqua, she who could well have stood all by herself for the whole female principle in the whole of the beautiful *Nuevo Mundo,* when she saw Burr for the first time she was instantly struck and said, "That, that Anglese! Who?" and when she was told who Burr was she sent all the other Angleses except Burr off to eat, and then turned to Burr and asked him if he would hunt with her! Burr was, said WCW, "admired by women," which was above all else what WCW needed; and Burr was also "a subversive force where liberty was waning" so that "they nearly hanged him for it," which WCW felt was nearly happening to himself. And since they were also trying "to torture him to death with their small slanders on his private life" Burr could well have been living in Rutherford. Burr was grand and Burr had been misrepresented by stupid academic historians who thought of him as a "frightful danger to the young state" because he was at odds with the Feds. Obviously what the country needed was not less but more Burrs, more opposition to the Feds. George Washington had started as a good man but he had been sucked in to the big system "with shrewd dog Hamilton at his side" and had gone to "locking the doors, closing the windows, building fences and providing walls." But Burr, loved by women, Burr supreme in "clarity and disrespect for the applause of the world," the wonderful Burr was "not tractable." Burr was a freedom man, Burr was "immoral as a satyr" — could he have been one to dance before his mirror? — Burr was open, immediate in his responses; Burr had a "delicious sincerity," Burr gave off, as WCW always aspired to give off, "careless truth." Burr also did a good job in killing Hamilton, which was a job WCW would apparently have liked for himself.

Then there was Poe. WCW's Poe essay seems to have picked up some of its energy from Lawrence's remarks about Poe but it was a personal piece too and it showed a reading of Poe on WCW's part that went beyond the Poe that Lawrence had been talking about, the deathy Poe. WCW went to the lesser-known Poe and to his own fancy to find *his* Poe, and that Poe predictably shared many of WCW's own preoccupations and problems. That Poe lived in a world where love did not thrive, surrounded by a "formless population drifting and feeding." That Poe could have lived in Rutherford too.

One of the oddest of WCW's attributions to Poe was that Poe was an apostle of the local. WCW was obviously thinking of himself, at least his ideal self, when he said that Poe was "a genius intimately shaped by his locality and time" but the localness WCW meant was not a localness of a particular region but a localness of the mind, a localness that was local in the simple negative sense that it didn't take its cues from somewhere *else* like Greece or London or Tibet.

Whatever the merits of WCW's Poe theme — and he was picked on for it in a review by Laura Riding who found nothing local about Poe's House of Usher or his misty midregion of Weir — it was a theme that fitted Poe neatly to WCW's attic, made Poe an abstract male like WCW who had figured out a way to be a local boy anyway. According to WCW Poe was a local boy because like WCW he made everything originate in his own place and his own head, not on some foreign Parnassus. He was a local boy even in the ghoulish unearthly works, was a local boy though he had a mathematical mind and constructed his stories and poems as if they were theorems. He was a local boy because he took the creative act unto himself — like the explorers in the book — and therefore was one who made *Nuevo Mundo* his own. That was the real gist of the Poe localness: "Either the New World must be mine as I will have it, or it is a worthless bog," WCW had Poe say, and those words contained WCW's 1924 persecution sentiments too.

And what made the Poe-WCW connection even more earnest was that Poe, as WCW presented him, was scarily surrounded with enemies who would not let him *have* the world as his. Poe tried to avoid them, keep clear of them. He tried to live in the air and to imagine that the world was not there, was "a morose, dead world, peopled by shadows and silence"; but that wouldn't work, the world kept after him. His wife defended him against the world but when she died he was defenseless and "the place itself attacked him . . . a huge terror possessed him" and *Nuevo Mundo* became for him a sort of hell, a "pure essence" of lovelessness against which he struggled with his own purities of method and technique.

Was Rutherford that for WCW in the midtwenties? Apparently he thought it was and that was what mattered. He finished off the *American Grain* with that kind of thinking and when the book, for which he had high hopes, didn't sell he had further reason to think he was being persecuted — it was the publisher's fault that it didn't sell; he didn't promote it — and so he scuttled his tentative plans for a sequel. He went on to other kinds of writing and they turned sour too. The most sour was the case of a story he wrote called "The Five Dollar Guy," a sad case that had only the merit that it gave him a good solid reason — a lawsuit — to think he was in fact being attacked by "the place itself."

The suit was no delusion, yet it *was* his fault. The case was quite simple. As he put it in the autobiography he had been told a story "by a young person" of his "acquaintance" that he found so good that he rushed home and wrote it down, using the actual names he had heard. It was the story of a woman who was propositioned by her boss to come to his office, the boss being known as a "five-dollar guy." WCW finished the story, slipped it into his drawer with no revising, and forgot about it until a magazine — he doesn't mention the name in the autobiography but it was *The New Masses* — wrote him asking for contributions. He then thought of the story again, slipped it into an envelope without reading it, and the magazine proceeded to publish it fast in its first issue without notifying him or sending proof.

He was then sued for $15,000 libel. The "young person" who told him the story denied having done so, and WCW's knees began to shake. From the evidence in his notebooks he imagined the worst. He thought he would go bankrupt and he plotted nightmarishly to save himself by using up all his funds by some quick extravagance before *they* got hold of them. He also meditated on ways of paying the sum, and following through with those thoughts came up with his most anticipatable conclusion: that he would write. "Writing will save the day. Pay for the damage if it's good enough to read and to sell. *Must* make it readable." He projected a novel that was to be about his trouble, his "brush with the law," and that dangerous scheme led him to memories of

Pound and how Pound had always told him true about America and what America would do to him. He imagined what Pound would say to him when he heard of the suit — "America! ho ho. Serves you right. Serve it? Ho, ho. Get it up the pooper for the good you seek. Serves you right for staying there, lost all you had? Now have nothing." He even imagined that the novel, which apparently never got further than this sketchy dream, would be a history of his relationship with Pound, the novel's theme apparently shaping in his mind as the rightness of getting up and getting out of America.

But the case was settled out of court for $5000. At the time he observed in the notebooks that he was exhilarated by his wife's courage. Later in the autobiography he said, "Floss, of course, was marvelous, but she let me have it, all right.

" 'I've told you, time and time again, not to use real names.'

" 'But I've got to,' I said, 'if I'm going to write convincingly.'

" 'That's ridiculous!' "

5

There were normalcies too. They need to be remembered and reinvoked. There were the normalcies of Flossie and of the medical practice, and there were also the two children moving on normally in school, having the normal diseases and delights, learning to write and to draw and to have their accomplishments appreciated normally by their parents. By the midtwenties there was even the middle-class parental normalcy of having the two kids regularly in camp in the summer and writing the predictably extraordinary letters home. Bill and Paul both were sent to the same camp near Bennington, Camp Enejerog for Boys, and each year the camp put the boys through the same big four-day hike. Bill did his hike in 1924 and wrote home about it and how he *went* to "a" and *went* to "b" and *went* to "c," a cascade of *wents;* and when Paul came along in 1926 he outdid his older brother:

Monday morning we went on the four day hike . . . we went
through Wilmington and from there we went to Arlington High
School and had dinner and went to Bennington monument we went
to the top from there we went to Lake Bomoseen and stayed on
Crystal Beach. In the morning we went to Lake Dumnmoore from
there we went to Middelbury Gap from there we went to [inde-
cipherable]. In the morning we went we went [sic] to one of the
deepest marbel quarrys in the world then we went . . .

Paul was bright but slower with the English tongue than Bill, and
there was a brief time when, though enamored by "went," he
didn't know how to spell it. What he did know was how to have a
good time on Halloween. Writing to his "best friend," who was
named Harvey, he said,

we busted all the milk bottles we could find. We hong'ed all the
horns of cars on the road and let the air out of tires. Then we ran
down to Rutherford Ave and we raided a party. Everybody got a
glass of cider and a dime. Then four kids from the gang went away.
So we whent by ourselves. We whent down to Oriont way and got a
chair and put it up a telephone pole. Then we raided another
party . . .

It must have been hard not to have felt centrally American,
whether puritan or antipuritan, when in the receipt of such documents, and WCW had plenty of other forces and events around
him pushing him steadily toward center. But as always he was
divided in himself about where he was and what he stood for, and
the bad events of the twenties like the case of "The Five Dollar
Guy" and the publishing failures enhanced the divisions in him,
accentuated his ups and downs. If he had kept a chart of his
emotional moods, as he did of the New York stock market in the
late twenties, it would have been clear that his private economy
was unstable.

He kept the real stock market chart on his attic wall and the
children wondered at it. The boom had reached Flossie and him
too, he admitted in the autobiography: "We invested moderately,
buying what we could." He did not say what happened to the

investments when the crash came except that there were losses, but the investing at least makes clear that by the late twenties he was able to invest. Also by then, despite the 1924 sabbatical, his practice was bringing in enough for the extravagance of a year abroad for Flossie and the children, though not enough so that he needed to moderate his antagonism to the rich. But the chart on the wall that showed the market and his own bank account going up would not have been applicable to his emotional state. Charted in the period of the boom, that would have looked like the great depression.

His depression began in 1917 and continued through to 1929, a big trough with a modest upswing in the center for 1921–1925 but even the upswing marred by a sell-off in Rome in 1924 — his Rome journal. It was the puritans who were after him pushing his stock down, and once he had firmly in mind what they were doing to him he was unable to let them stop persecuting him. The puritans in their various shapes were his furies even after *In the American Grain,* and drove him to his typewriter. There he sometimes wrote well and sometimes badly, but consistently had an enemy-image in his mind as he wrote. The enemy of course was everywhere, even sometimes at home in the form of Flossie. The year's separation from her in 1927–1928 was necessary and a good thing, though his writings were filled with sadness the whole year. The year was a vacation from marriage.

A vacation, not a separation, not a marital blow-off. Flossie was the one who proposed it, arguing that the parents needed it for their health and the children for their education (the children went to the same school in Switzerland that Ed and WCW had). WCW sailed abroad with them for the '27 summer, and they all had a good time touring and a good fling in Paris before WCW returned. On the boat returning WCW was so affectionate that he wrote Flossie twelve letters in nine days on shipboard. He told her that he never stopped thinking of her. He said he was heartbroken in her absence. He confessed that she was the one who had converted his unhappy childhood life to the contented life he now had. He doubted that he could last the year out without her but he praised her, calling her a "corker" for having thought up the year's separation. He said that he knew that he was difficult, that he had done many things to "lessen" himself in her eyes, but he felt that what he had done, because she was so generous and understanding, had in the end only brought him back to her "the stronger." In this state of marital exaltation he debarked, and went back to Rutherford to live with his mother and be unhappy.

He should have been happy about *The Dial* award, which came to him in late 1926. It was not only that the $2000 helped pay the $5000 settlement for "The Five Dollar Guy," it was also by far the biggest honor he had received. Wallace Stevens wrote to him that as girls passed the great Williams on the street they were surely nudging each other and saying "the golden boy." But WCW didn't have to analyze the award very deeply to see that it was an award from old friends, and an award in time of trouble, therefore slightly though pleasantly tainted. It was hardly, that is, like winning the Pulitzer, which he would do only much later, only when dead. The loyalty of Marianne Moore at *The Dial* office and of Pound across the sea was impressive but not enough, not enough for someone being determinedly despondent.

Nor was a forty-page spread in one of Pound's magazines enough. The magazine was *The Exile* and Pound arranged (in 1928) to have printed in it a despondent broken-style piece by WCW called *Descent of Winter,* modeled after *Spring and All* in its mixture of prose and verse. WCW was grateful but being printed in *The Exile* still left him with an awareness that the literary bells were not ringing for him outside the charmed little magazine circle where he had begun. Even up to 1930 almost all his published work first appeared in magazines (numbering by then about thirty) that were Pound-edited or Pound-nudged. The two exceptions were his own *Contact,* which only made his Pound dependency seem greater since *Contact* was a flop, and *Broom.* *Broom* (which Kreymborg helped start, but soon left) was a big if short-lived venture (1921–1924) but it proved a disappointment too. It was in *Broom* that he had a chance to air his historical practices, practices which seemed promising before the book flopped and were even reinforced in *Broom* by the great Joe Gould. Joe Gould received play in *Broom* too with his "prodigiously long cigaret holder which heave[d] into view like the bow sprit of a large schooner" followed by the "bent wire spectacles . . . the sparse and goatish beard" and finally the whole head. Gould was the Greenwich Village sidewalk genius with a Harvard degree who was writing an "omnivorous history" of the world and his history sounded not only radical and twentyish but quite like what WCW was doing, at first. Gould was taking notes of the actual in "a number of grimy notebooks," his only requirement being "that no fact [should] enter his history which he [had] not seen with his own eyes or heard with his own ears." WCW could not have obeyed that principle with Columbus and Eric the Red but he admired it in spirit and then poof, *Broom* was down the drain and *In the American Grain* was gone and WCW had abandoned his planned historical sequel. The bells were not ringing.

While publishing the early *Contact* he had thought that self-promotion was the solution to literary obscurity, but he soon found out that promoting himself in *Contact* was like selling Fuller Brushes in a museum at midnight. By the late twenties he was temporarily too world-weary about literary politics and the road to fame to have many bright new promotion plans. All he knew was little magazines, having discovered that the literary people in the big publishing places kept insisting on not knowing *him*. What to do? He went back to his attic.

Especially in the year 1927–1928, of Flossie's absence. He went back to the attic with the persecution thoughts so common to American writerdom, and he wrote notes to himself in notebooks to the effect that good writing wouldn't sell, ever — wouldn't sell because *they* didn't want it to. And he wrote the notes in his inward attic broken style, being convinced as always that a preliminary and absolutely basic condition for good writing was that it be as far away from what *they* wanted as a typewriter or pencil

would allow. *Descent of Winter* was one result, the best; another
was a new private journal resembling the 1924 Rome journal that
was wild and sometimes darkly incoherent.

The journal did have its light moments, with flashes of wit:

> Every time she puts her fingers
> in her mouth we say
>   no no   no no
>   so now she sucks her
>
> toes

There were also good comments in the journal about naturalism,
with which at the time he had decided to do battle ("the philosophy of stupid people is stupid and realistic novels of stupid
people are still more stupid than the people themselves").
Further, there was a perceptive remark about Eugene O'Neill,
whose *Strange Interlude* WCW had just attended: O'Neill's distortions, he said, were great though they were inadvertent;
O'Neill thought he was being realistic but he wasn't; his badness
saved him from realism. And there was even, late in the journal, a
poem to Flossie that was not as soft in the underbelly as the letters
from shipboard and caught well the unpredictable mixture of
penitence and belligerence that he brought to marriage, brought
to it even when he was being happy at it:

> Christ I have
> lied to you about
> small things
>   whoring and
> whatnot
>   but never
> did I unknow that your love
> is in me and I
> in it
>   Love me
> while I am not disgusting
> like that —
> while I am still warm
> and a liar
> and a poet and a sometimes

devoted lover
>   who
> loves you and will lie
> to you
>   always

But the tone of the journal as a whole was far from loving. He was sometimes (though perhaps only experimentally) drinking heavily — remember that the male when not with women was destined to be "either hunting, fighting, loafing or drunk" — and when he drank he would waver between being confident that the drinking was the release that would bring on the art (it might also, he observed like somebody in a comic strip, bring on the wife, and that would be hell because she was "all tongue") and being defensive about his bad reputation as a drunkard. He may have made up some of the badness of the reputation since he was in effect bragging to himself of his badness, but he could not have made it all up. Perhaps he made up a patient saying, "How, sir, by the way do you expect to observe really what people are when you are nothing but a drunkard and a loafer?" But there were other incidents that seemed real that he lingered on, particularly one that he wrote into an early version of *Paterson* that he labored and labored over, couldn't put down but finally left out of *Paterson* entirely, a dialogue that rang obsessively true on the drinking, being full of such lines as "You're a brilliant physician, sir, and a drunkard." Sometimes he would justify drink as helping to loosen him up, but he was more apt to wallow in his condition than praise it, wallow in his good-for-nothingness. And always of course he had to write the weak moments down:

> It tastes good and it has a good effect too. There were two apples almost together on the tree in front of the house. After I had my drink I could plainly see three of them. I was half seas over. If I had been whole seas over I would have seen four.

In the drinking parts of the journal he went after the academics and the Eliots and the "sons of bitches that run theaters and publishing houses," and he was also full of sex talk. Late in the journal he went so far as to retreat to the memory of his dear old baroness, observing, "Never save when sex has been fed in the bedroom is the rest of the house liveable. This I observed with the baroness. Out with it, in with it. Have done with it and then the world is open." There was also the account of a certain child who shall be nameless.

He noted down her name, the date of her birth and its auspiciousness, then egged himself on to "use her" in his future writings, use "all ties with her . . . the locality and the time," because she was "real." Insisting that everything about her had to be included (in a work that would not in the end be written) he went through her prenatal past and infant present as if he were projecting a story or play about her. He went so far as to tell himself that her "pukes and shits" were important, and ended up,

> The thought of her illegitimate conception fills me with joy. I conceived her. I begat her — under the powdery light in the falling leaves — the day I coughed and spat at the telephone and nearly choked when the liquor went down my windpipe.

Real? The "moment of the 20s"? It does seem so, but that is all there was in the journal about the child, and in the other chief works of Flossie's absent year, *The Descent of Winter* and *A Voyage to Pagany,* he was more restrained. Perhaps the chief literary mark of his depression at the time was not the drunken confidentiality of the journal (the journal may well have misrepresented the magnitude of his drinking) but the way he kept reaching out in his poems and other writings for unlikely connections, reaching out not to obviously kindred spirits like Lawrence or other writers but to almost any person or thing that might somehow give him reinforcement. Lawrence he of course did admire, and wrote an elegy for him at his death saying that "it grows clearer what bitterness drove him" and that he had passed "unwanted from England" — WCW perhaps thinking as he wrote that he would himself one day pass unwanted from the U.S.; but Lawrence and other such heroes were remote figures for him. He needed nearer ones, he needed connections of any kind, he needed even connections with nature, and so went about indulging in what every college English major used to know as the pathetic fallacy — that is, the attributing of thoughts and feelings to trees and the like — in ways that did not become an objective imagist. He would project his feelings on the big Other out beyond him without a qualm, finding there all sorts of self-likenesses to comfort him. It didn't matter that in print he had always been opposed to the usual literary ways of working with such projections, the metaphor and simile; he kept sneaking in likenesses anyway, likenesses that made the chosen objects into little versions of himself — a black flag in the wind writhing, like himself, to be free, a "red cold world" of a Russian dawn that turned out to be his own bleak heart.

And when he came to people he was even more possessive. People he could convert with the greatest dispatch to his own camp, his own kind of art, his own oppressions. He was especially strong on converting Shakespeare to his side. Shakespeare he suddenly discovered to be "an ignorant, instinctive man" who "turned to verse, and did it well, because he couldn't write sentences, couldn't do prose." He also learned of Shakespeare, though where is not recorded, that Shakespeare was "drunk in the gutter that he might create." As for Shakespeare's artistic processes he found not surprisingly that they were not those of a dramatist schooled in theatrical conventions but of an actualist dealing directly with life like WCW himself. Shakespeare "took the print and reversed the film, as it went in so it came out. Certainly he never repeated himself since he did nothing but repeat what he heard and nobody ever hears the same words twice the same." Was it not presumptuous to have Shakespeare the genius of the conventional and the master-user of other people's plays and histories, to have Shakespeare suddenly standing on a street corner with WCW and listening, drunk and illiterate, to the actual as it walked by? — WCW was in trouble, was reaching out everywhere for help, for allies.

6

The literary exception to all this inwardness was his *Voyage to Pagany*, which he had begun before Flossie's year abroad but seems to have finished off then (it was published as a book in 1928). It really wasn't an exception though it was meant to be. It was meant to be a travel book and a novel. It was meant to be a moneymaker. It was meant to be another venture out of the attic like *In the American Grain*. But it didn't quite make it out of the attic, and it didn't make money, and as a travel book it was too breathless, and as a novel it lacked pace and conflict — so it was a minor exception. Still it was healthier than the 1927 journal, and more readable than *The Descent of Winter*, and as another exercise in extended straightforward prose it paved the way for the successes to come like *White Mule* and the short stories.

It was dedicated to Pound and a few of its chapters appeared in *The Dial* and in an important little magazine published in Paris in the late twenties, *transition*. As a travel book it was about the 1924 European trip of WCW and Flossie, but it took its travel manners from other less sophisticated sources than the expatriate crowd they met in that year. If it was a manifestation of the moment of the twenties in travel it was less like Hemingway in Spain or the café lizards in Paris than Richard Halliburton in India, Halliburton whose *Royal Road to Romance* (1925) was full of the ecstasies of seeing the Taj Mahal by moonlight. WCW plodded through his whole 1924 trip day by day and place by place but he tried to make up for the plod rhetorically. Later he was slightly embarrassed by the lushness of the prose — he thought it "more romantic" than he had intended — but he continued to like it, like it perhaps more than he should have. Many of the descriptive passages were themselves ego trips:

> He . . . lay upon the powdery white sand, picking up the paper-thin yellow and orange shells there and looking out over the pale-green hardly stirring sea whose thin wavelets broke in long overlapping crescents beside him — widely, icily along the shore.

Pound, if he had been given a chance, would surely have knocked out half or more of the dozen adjectives and adverbs in that sentence, but WCW was experimenting as usual; there were yards and yards of such excess in the book and he would have been better off taking as a model not Halliburton but Mark Twain. Years before Halliburton, Mark Twain made fun of such tourist prose in *Innocents Abroad;* he was amused by what he called the "industrious night schools" of keepers of journals in ship cabins and hotel rooms, those who later imagined the whole world later reading their heated accounts of sunsets and the Mona Lisa. Like everyone else Twain had to fight the organ impulse and occasionally he would let go and talk of the dying sunlight gilding the clustering spires and ramparts — but he always had the good sense to recover quickly and put in parenthesis some rhetorical antidote like "Copyright secured according to law." WCW in *A Voyage to Pagany* uniformly failed to recover. He was too bound up in himself in the year of its writing to be aware of excess.

Excess was evident in the book as novel too. It was sometimes painfully investigative of characters' feelings, and nowhere did it achieve understatement. WCW said of it that he didn't know anything about the novel form when he wrote it, and had always in the past hated the novel form because it was too romantic, but that he thought he ought to "write one of the damned things" anyway to see what he could get out of it. What he got was a characteristic first novel, deficient in story, heavy on feeling and, beneath a thin fictional veneer, largely autobiographical. Yet there was a plot or plan of sorts imbedded in it that did put it in the novel league, a plan by which the doctor-writer protagonist (whose name was Evans — nickname Dev) was methodically made subject to various different kinds of love! A true WCW plan.

The first kind of love represented was man-to-man love, with the figure of McAlmon as faithfully represented as the doctor's love object as the figure of WCW was faithfully represented as the doctor — but this love was swiftly put aside as a thing of the past and the novel moved on to women. There were a number of them in sequence, each distinctive physically and thematically, and none clearly identifiable like McAlmon (WCW said of them later that they were "frequently" his conception of his wife but also imaginary, "women the American might have desired to go to bed with"). The women were interspersed with four even headier romances for busy Dev, romances with medical knowledge, with pagan art, with music, and with writing. All in all the book contained a lot of Others to be passionate about, even an old baroness who had "few teeth" and "could not control her spittle well." But the baroness, who was not the original 14th Street baroness, was not clearly a figure in the romance sequence.

Dev had affairs of different degrees of intimacy with the four main women. The first woman was Dev's sister Bess who, when not being sensible and family-loving like Flossie, was wildly drinking and carrying on like Nancy Cunard whom Flossie and WCW had met and become good friends with in Paris (and whom WCW called in the autobiography a "perfect bitch") and who, after behaving very unsisterly, refused to return to America with him. The second was named Lou Adams, an American Dev thought he was engaged to and with whom he lived briefly in southern France until she discovered that she didn't understand him and needed a simple rich man instead. (Could she have been the early Flossie, the Flossie who drove WCW wild by going out with a boy with a car and a boat when penniless WCW was in Leipzig?) The third woman was a Fräulein with slightly thicker ankles than the "dance hall type" and a slight peasant look but "shining mistlike palegold hair" whom Dev compared to Botticelli's Venus on the half shell. She was also compared to the Venus Anadyomene of Cyrene but seems to have been modeled after persons closer, possibly another Parisian acquaintance of WCW's named Iris Tree and possibly also "a character in a Roman pension" who, said WCW, actually flirted with him on his Rome trip though he was with Flossie. In other words the Fräulein, whoever the model for her was, was more "actual" than the others and seems to have had no Flossie in her. She found Dev to be an exotic foreigner, "a savage not quite civilized," and Dev confirmed her impression by showing her a flint arrowhead he always carried in his pocket. The arrowhead ended the affair.

The fourth and last of the women, Grace Black, was another American but with Indian blood and imperious ways. She was not in physical appearance clearly identifiable as a WCW acquaintance but she could have been ideologically any number of Americans who had told WCW to dispose of his bourgeois life and go into writing in earnest. She described Dev to himself calling him an aristocrat under the touristy surface, and said of him that it was too bad that he liked the America of the Wops and Polacks and feared the "fine people." She told him that he should not let the fine people cause him any strain but she knew that they did, knew that they made him want to run "to America where there are no really fine people — or they are buried, voiceless, lost." He offered her marriage but she rejected him because of his American commitment, she wanting to keep her freedom by staying in Europe. Four women, then, the whole of the female principle on the hoof, and poor Dev ended up with none of them, ended up sailing home alone to resume his not quite believable bachelorhood in the not quite livable United States.

Of the four women it was sister Bess who finally made the least sense. As a sister first she was a chastely loving wife, and as a sister second she was suddenly incestuous — WCW doubtless feeling that he had to get *that* into the female principle — and drunkenly propositioned Dev and talked about having children (then she toned it down to child adoption). WCW later said that the brother-sister idea had been suggested to him by watching a couple in Paris, Clotilda and Lawrence Vail, and possibly those two were in real life really so intimate as brother and sister that he was able to say to himself, Yes, there is another kind of love to put in the book's pantheon. But that love didn't make it to the page, possibly because Lawrence Vail was not Dev. Dev was always inexorably WCW who didn't have a sister and knew it.

There would not be much sense in playing the identity game with this book if WCW had been a steady long-time writer of genuine fictions, but he was not. *A Voyage to Pagany* was an oddity for him and his experiments in creating rather than recording characters, though tentative, made a great impression on him. He later kept emphasizing the characters' fictional side, thinking of them as a slightly foolish but amusing literary adventure that put him for a moment in an entirely different writing game; but if he had gone farther with the fictionalizing the novel might have been better. Oddly it was not the fictions that damaged the book but the actualities intruding behind them. The actualities that were most damaging were the interminably truthful travel pages, including many of the specific dates of WCW's own 1924 trip and the character of Dev.

Dev was a disaster. Dev was WCW and was therefore the disaster that was WCW in 1927 and 1928 when he was alone and dwelling within himself and writing his tortured journal. Dev was sorry for himself and preoccupied with America's neglect of him, Dev felt out of things with the "fine people," Dev found that the Christians — he had moved up from puritans merely — had swaddled the world in hypocrisy, Dev wished to get out of doctoring and write, Dev wanted to make a life of writing, Dev paused to announce that T. S. Eliot (concealed by no fictional name) was a menace to poetry, Dev felt a yearning for the vulgar, and of course Dev saw in each woman the archetypal female without whom the male was doomed. All of WCW's preoccupations were present in Dev's words and thoughts, and the fictional veneer quite failed to reduce the confessional pity-me effect.

Yet one of the most "actual" sections of the book, though only fuzzily fictional in the novel's romance sequence, had the merit of illuminating a part of WCW's own life, his intellectual medical life, that is hard to find details about elsewhere. It was a description of the month that Dev spent in Vienna freshening up on doctor lore with the great specialists of that city — and particularly a certain Walter Mitty–sounding von Knobloch who must have been real — so that he might return to his practice in the U.S. full again of the "wonder of abandon to the pursuit of knowledge."

The editor of the paperback edition of *Voyage to Pagany,* Harry Levin, suggests that the experience was derived from memories of Leipzig back in 1909, but though that may have been so there was also a closer source. WCW did in fact go to Vienna in 1924 and take courses there — he reported on the episode specifically in the autobiography — and Dev's words about the month, that he had planned it as "a month of concentrated scientific effort" and had hoped it would be "the apex of his tour" would seem to have been straight WCW gospel. Then too the descriptions of the other American doctors in Vienna showed WCW's low opinions of his colleagues and, quite inadvertently, showed also WCW as an incurable romantic despite himself, even in his own professional backyard — romantic in his vision of the ways and means of doctoring, puritan in his doctor work ethic. The section presented the revolution in medicine that WCW would have liked to have imagined occurring, a revolution that was the equivalent for him in medicine of disposing of the sonnet in poesy.

For it was the great von Knobloc and his colleagues who had the revolution in hand. The Viennese view of medicine was that it should be pitiless in its search for truth, and Dev though a soft Westerner could only agree. The Viennese were so dedicated to truth that they sometimes were cruel to their patients, and Dev loved that too:

> There was no feeling but the presence of the truth. It hurt an American. Old, deformed, or young and unfortunate, they came there and were stripped to be inspected . . . One especially Evans was fascinated to see — a girl, barely fifteen — with the pock. Poor child, she was brought in cowering, the tears streaming down her face from anguish and shame, her body marked all over with recent syphilis. Kern patted her, but there she stood and was turned and inspected — studied while she cried and bit her lips. It seemed pitiless but there it was. She was taken out to be cured.

Dev was too western to be able to take very much of the pitilessness, couldn't really dare the adventure of "the great science of unhappy flesh" since he had nerves that "had never permitted him to get fully past the smells, the unsightly acts of pathology," but he could see the wonder of it in Vienna, could see what Vienna meant, Vienna where the great von Knobloch was fighting the general paresis brought on by syphilis by giving the patient malaria! Dev knew enough to see how backward America was in contrast, and how disinclined were its inhabitants to face up to essentials at any level. The other American doctors in Vienna were instances of the American failing. In the first place they were idle, unlike Dev who was always busy taking notes, taking it all in; they were "a smoking, story swapping crew" who had no conception of the dimensions of medicine but were "blatant ignoramuses" seeking merely to acquire a skill they could turn into cash. And in the second place they were professional snobs, more concerned with status than truth. Dev recalled the annoyance of a colleague from the States upon hearing Dev acknowledge that he did not belong to the County Medical Society: "What, not a member?" (And yet WCW ended up as the head of the doctors' association at Passaic General.) Essentials? It was a persistent theme of *A Voyage to Pagany* that if there was to be any improvement in the soft west it had to come through a new perceiving of essentials — and that went for doctors as well as poets. The doctors could learn from von Knobloch, the poets could learn from the pagan remnants of the old cultures in Europe; and for all of them the learning meant, as Levin put it in his introduction, setting up shop as a *paganus,* that is, "a person who did not share prevailing beliefs." There was Dev, and there was WCW, in a nutshell, but being there was not easy. Being there left both of them with enormous America-saving obligations and no time for small talk.

It left them also, finally, alone, an aloneness that was peculiarly WCW's "moment of the 20s." Dev sailed home alone, having committed himself irrevocably to the return to his benighted country and his own martyrdom. Similarly WCW alone in Rutherford had his martyrdom, thinking, as he must many times have been thinking, that he had been deserted by both literary and medical America, had been left to carry on solo with the cause of truth. It was thinking like this that made *A Voyage to Pagany* a painful book, and made the late twenties a painful time for him.

7

What did he want that was not being granted? He wanted the sun and moon and stars of course as everyone does, wanted a share in the future of man; and when the want was upon him he was, as a young friend said of him in 1926, his own wild poem. But he was a reasonable, hardworking man in everyday life, and paid his bills, and served on hospital committees, and kept his dreams mostly in harness — so that much of the 1927 journal's wildness and *A Voyage to Pagan*'s pretentiousness should be taken at a discount. Yet his literary dreams always remained grandiose for him, hard to bring down to earth. His talk about them was wild, and true in its wildness, and here the journal — the journal particularly — was reliable. WCW remained convinced through the twenties that writing was at its best a primal instinctive thing like love, and he kept trying to get at the primalcy with a whirl of words as if writing were a physical thing like swimming or running and one simply poured on the muscle power. He felt that if he could himself somehow be primal at the process he could in his own writing bring off instances in which the poetry would live like the thing or the person or the event that occasioned it, would live not as a mock-up but as a manifestation of the actual, would live naturally, organically with the words and the form of the words proceeding out of the actual like a living, growing thing. He believed this, he struggled with the realizing of it — it was behind all the automatic writing that had started with *Kora* and proceeded through *Spring and All* and *The Great American Novel* and then, in the late twenties, *Novelette* and *The Descent of Winter,* not to mention the scribbled journals — he struggled with this most romantic of literary dreams over and over again at his typewriter in his attic, even though Pound himself, his most faithful backer, was skeptical and cautioned him at one point that his improvisations were old hat.

Yeats put it once that the shape of a poem should be "from the seed" but Yeats was a traditionalist and didn't believe the seed theory literally, believed instead in the agreed-upon seemings of poetic form, in conventional equivalences. In the extreme days of the twenties WCW did go for the seed theory literally, actually, really; he was truly convinced — or so at least he kept saying — that poetic creation could be spontaneous on the page like a flower growing. It was this conviction that made him go to great lengths to dispose of the literary baggage that stood in the way of naturalness and spontaneity, made him sit down again and again to the writing act as if he were undressing and going Neanderthal, and then drove him to write as fast and as heedlessly as he could, letting rip. As he put it, "To write is to write because it is to write." That he could be as well a writer in the other sense, a craftsman, a careful shaper — all that would be forgotten when his romance was upon him.

But the romance would not have been as intense in him as it was in the twenties if the puritans had not been steadily sitting on his real or imaginary doorstep tormenting him. The romance was an aesthetic adventure but as an unfriendly psychologist might say, it was also a way of getting back at *them*. When the puritans were learned academicians he sought to beat them by making a virtue of not knowing, when they were doctors he sought to beat them by knowing *more*, when they were traditional artists he sought to beat them by throwing away the traditional, and when they were simply the social puritans of the Rutherford neighborhood — perhaps in the form of successful, upright members of the community like his own brother — he sought to beat them by being a natural man, a man with the usual frailties but unusual in having the honesty to admit to them. By this kind of analysis his romance with primal writing emerges as a defensiveness that helped save him from competition he felt unable to face.

He was basically as competitive at the typewriter, however, as at the wheel of a car, and when his competitions were going badly it hurt him. He needed success, needed the trophies in the bookcase, having been indoctrinated early that rewards like his brother's Prix de Rome were the true source of self-esteem. The indoctrination applied even if one set out to be a rebel and unconcerned with the world's opinions. WCW was not unusual here. Much of the rebellious modernism in art has always, especially to the young, had such a base, which is why so many students who ought to be taking Bonehead English are to be found instead doing Cummingsy-Williamsy things (and Ginsbergy-Snydery-Olseny things) in Creative Writing. WCW must have himself had some of that fierce need to convert weakness to strength by a trick, by changing the game rules.

Wylie Sypher said of the romantic painters of the nineteenth century that unlike their predecessors they were "obliged to carry the burden of self into their shops," that their chief need was to have their own perceptions, that they had to bring "their consciousness directly to bear upon the world" to achieve authenticity, their vision of the actual. The words could well be applied to the large body of WCW's work as well because he was at all times preoccupied with the integrity of private perceptions as opposed to hand-me-downs; but it was in the twenties that the "burden of the self" that tags along with such an aesthetic was most heavy for him. It was in the twenties that his work and he suffered from self-excess, with the result that the authentic or the actual or the real or the true — those words slipped and slid but kept getting down on paper — was constantly being worried and chomped on by his doubts and anxieties — and sometimes seriously distorted too. The distortions were inevitable, part of the chaotic process of his growth.

Describing WCW's unpredictable genius Robert Lowell said, very late in WCW's life (some years after his praise of the autobiography as catching the moment of the twenties), that "it was as though some homemade ship, part Spanish galleon, part paddle wheels, kitchen pots and elastic bands and worked by hand, had anchored to a filling station." Lowell was not being insulting but kind; his theme was that the world needed more of WCW's home-madeness since the not-homemade had gone to warp and mold — and he was probably right: the world needed the homemade at the moment of the twenties, and needed it also in the sixties moment when Lowell wrote, and needs it at the moment now. But if there remains a lesson in the moment as WCW homemade it in the twenties it is that the moment is *always* a hard moment for its creator to live with and perhaps hardest when it is most success-fully homemade, least obviously affected by all the pressures the artist of the homemade fears. WCW's notebooks and journals of the twenties are testimony. The twenties were a hard moment for him because the homemade then was made at great home cost.

CHAPTER SIX

Causes

BUT IN 1928 Flossie came back with her normalcy, and the children came back, and the house was no longer totally in the mother's domain, and the food was again edible. The worst of the isolation was over and when in the winter of 1929 the East Coast had a good flu epidemic WCW and Flossie were, as he said to a friend, "thrown violently into each other's arms" again by the heavy survival pressure on their harassed doctor-house. The year's separation had apparently been good for them, and anyway Flossie was talented at adjusting and coping. She was not only a good cook and a good housewife and a good bookkeeper but she could make fine martinis, and because it was prohibition time she made the gin too, what came to be called simply "Mom's Gin." She made it well. She took medical alcohol that trickled in from WCW's office, and she added lemon and juniper, and then she filtered it carefully through a paper filter filled with calcium oxide (lime) and boneblack (fine charcoal) and it was excellent.

Also the children had grown and were doing well. Bill's voice was deepening; he had learned to speak "rather good French" and reported of his own maturity that sometimes he felt "years and years older" than the adults. As for Paul, "when asked by Floss if he would lie to her his reply was: 'I've already done it.'" They were both going dutifully through the schools and retaining respect for the family scene. They were also in the summers learning a good deal more about basic things like cows and pigs than suburban children are expected to. Flossie's family's 300-acre farm in New York was where they went, to be worked hard but otherwise treated with deference and love by the grandparents. There was family closeness at root and it extended through the generations though WCW himself later felt guilty about his father role and wrote Bill, when Bill was in the navy in the Pacific, that he had been angry with him too much and for too little. He also recalled an occasion when he had cruelly laughed at Bill because Bill, then a small child, had lost a canoe race and cried about it. Fathers always have much to feel guilty for.

As for WCW's own life and with medicine, it was babies, babies. At the office they were trundled in by the parents and he would look at their ills and end up looking at the parents' ills. At the hospitals the rigors were sterner; many of the kids were derelict kids, "poor brats" who had been dumped there and were "almost dead sometimes, just living skeletons . . . wrapped in rags, their heads caked with dirt, their eyes stuck together with pus" but the nurses would clean them up and WCW would come around and look at each one and perhaps indulge in a little of his own brand of toughness: " 'Give it an enema, maybe it will get well and grow up into a cheap prostitute or something.' " And in the houses of the poor at 3:00 A.M. the life was sterner yet with the sleepy doctor trudging up the stairs with his leather bag containing Argyrol and sterile umbilical ties and artery clamps and sutures, and finding the woman with cervix fully dilated but not quite ready. He would wait, doze in a chair, at dawn perhaps trying to hasten the birth with pituitrin until the birth at last took place and he "tied the cord, cut it and lifted the baby . . . to hand it to the woman." WCW knew what he was about now, and treated his patients with ease and rough love, admiring them not for their beauty and virtue but for their ills, for "every distortion to which the flesh is susceptible, every disease, every amputation."

The trouble was he was also tired of the doctoring business, as well as jealous, as always, of the time that doctoring took away from writing time. By 1928 he had a regular assistant in his offices but that was not enough. In the early thirties he gave up the Passaic office. He was tapering off a little, very little, and he wrote Pound to say that he was loafing "under the guise of becoming a specialist," also that he was giving up his evening office hours, "that hellish drag." If he did give them up for a time in the thirties he certainly had them back by World War II; but aside from the hours he and Flossie began to try to be more civilized by taking regular extended summer auto trips, mostly to New England, especially Maine. In 1931 they even took a summer excursion on a boat, starting in Montreal and steaming down the St. Lawrence past Quebec, then north to Newfoundland. Williams William he was called on his immigration identification card for that trip and he enjoyed the trip greatly — and of course wrote it up. When they were at the trip's outer reaches there was "nothing, nothing clear to the Pole" and that was fine, and when there were people around them feeding them cod livers and showing them their diseases that was fine too. They had a good captain, they danced on shipboard, WCW sat in attendance on a birth with a local doctor on a tiny island, and when Flossie and he took walks on shore they could both think warmly of their rich garden plantings at home as they walked among "small ferns, mosses and dwarfed shrubs and vines" that "put to shame every rock garden in the world."

But when at home there was also — though not in charge — the mother, who did not improve civilization. The mother lingered on into the late 1940s and by the thirties she had moved in with them for good. First she was nearly blinded by cataracts, then had them removed and it helped only a little. Then she broke her hip slipping on the ice because she had refused to stay in on a wintry day as WCW had told her to — and was never able to walk again but was just there, there in the house, growing deaf also, being impossible and being particularly Flossie's burden and best enemy. She was there in her room with her possessions "to the last spool of thread" neatly placed so that she could find them by herself in her blindness; she was there, impossible, and there was nothing to do about her, and since it was "bestial in a man to want to slaughter his old mother" WCW cast about for diversions. Soon he and she were busy translating together a battered sixteenth-century Spanish book that Pound had long ago left at 9 Ridge Road, something "with the title in crooked gilt letters all but completely obliterated" that became in English *The Dog and the Fever* by Quevedo. She would lean over the book with a large reading glass and struggle with the hard old Spanish words, and WCW would listen to her and take down her translations — and then he began to discover her again.

It was the way she mixed Spanish and French with her English that fascinated him. It was her own language, wholly distinctive; he wanted to catch it and put it on paper, just as he always wanted to catch the phrases and cadences of ordinary American speech on street corners; he wanted to catch her phrases and make a collection of them — but she didn't want him to, didn't want him to write her biography because she thought her life was "too mixed up" so he had to resort to his old trade, stealing. He would be seated beside her and they would both be using a sewing board, she to spread the Spanish book on and he to write on, and he would sometimes put down the translations she gave him but more often just put *her* down. Out of it came *Yes, Mrs. Williams.*

It was found art really, the sort of thing he liked and found basic because actual, uncontrived. It had the double virtue of being real and yet not ordinary. She talked of her childhood in the islands mostly — the sights and sounds, the big events, the odd anecdotes — and when she did she displayed the kind of specificity WCW was always reaching for in his own writing — how to eat a particular kind of fruit that was difficult because "the inside near the skin sticks all around the mouth all white and you cannot get it off," or what you did for asthma if you were an island native — you would take little turtles and "cut their heads and drink the blood." She talked and talked, he wrote and wrote, and eventually both books were done, the translation (which was not published until 1954) and the book about, or of, her. Doing the books made it possible to abide poor old Elena.

So that was the home life, with the doctoring and the children and the mother, and the occasional vacation with Flossie. WCW was aging gracefully now, losing the hair that had bothered him in his youth because it insisted on his youth, leaving him with a bespectacled freckled baldness that was not severe and contained few wrinkles, a roundness and openness that still could break readily into smiles. In most of the pictures taken of him he is looking head-on at the lens, conscious of its presence and trying to be photogenic — like one who is resigned, but not unhappily, to not being. Still slim and wiry, still agile, he is also still failing to look poetic. In a way he always had to steal away from his own physical being to be poetic; but by the 1930s the writing was not otherwise a stealing but an accepted part of the dailiness. And as he turned fifty he was even by his own standards most prolific.

In the decade following *A Voyage to Pagany* WCW published a volume of his collected poems that showed for the first time — though the book was not at the time well received — the dimensions of his poetic talent. He also produced two of the best collections of short stories that would come out of the thirties (*The Knife of the Times* and *Life Along the Passaic River*). Further, he wrote and had published *White Mule*, his first real novel and a novel that did show, unlike *A Voyage to Pagany*, his underlying commitment to a flat, controlled naturalism. It was life on the page without rhetoric; it was also life without the faults — or mostly without them — of the "realistic novels of stupid people" he despised, the novels that were "more stupid than the people themselves." It was a good novel and led to two others; and not content with all that he also in the thirties undertook the libretto of an opera. He was not idle literarily.

And to the production of poems and stories and the rest he kept adding to his typewriter's load an always growing quantity of correspondence. His correspondence life had always been busy — he could say things in letters to people that he could not say well in their presence — but in the late twenties it began to expand greatly. Dev of *A Voyage to Pagany* did not return lonely and martyrly to his native land just to join the puritans, ignoramus doctors, and dollar chasers. He came back from Europe to be a dissident, to try to do with his life in America what the expatriates were trying to do with their lives in Paris, and for his dissidence the correspondence life was crucial. He had to find a society at home *within* the dollar-chasing society to live with, a society of writing spirits like himself; and they turned out to be people in out-of-the-way places like Rutherford to whom he wrote letters and received warm, cooperatively dissenting replies. As Pound put it, the idea, if you were surrounded by puritan America, was to see a human being once in a while. WCW shared Pound's *snobisme* mostly about what constituted a human being, only differing from him in believing that there were a few human beings on the west side of the Atlantic too.

The human beings he settled on were of the little magazine world, which was growing, becoming a social phenomenon, moving out beyond the New York and London entrepreneurs to the boondocks. His new pen pals were not as distinguished and established as Pound or Marianne Moore or Alfred Kreymborg but they were serious literary folk who could be found working at saving the literary world out of their own respective attics, serious in the sense that they had no visible commercial or political aspirations. (That has been what "serious" has mostly meant for little magazine people.) They were a separate and elevated species, and though some of them were in Europe as Pound thought all humans had to be, there were others who were really in America and could really be located — located, that is, if one looked up with binoculars to the craggy cliffs. WCW felt isolated in the twenties and thirties, but by the thirties he had constantly increasing compensation for his isolation as he exchanged his miseries with isolated editor-writer friends. He always dealt with his correspondents faithfully, compulsively. They replied in kind, the missives flew back and forth, and the contents were so full of a friendly small-townness that the whole state of literature became pleasantly diminished. Or perhaps the pen-pal community was not so much a small town as an island, an island where a select and pure few could together curse the dollar-chasing many, meanwhile talking aesthetic shop.

To a cynical mainlander the proceedings always seemed to be those of a mutual-admiration and positive-reinforcement society. A big part of the game was to encourage the other writer, the writer at the opposite end of the island who was also sitting at his typewriter staring at a wall covered with rejection slips. WCW was good at encouragement. He had quick genuine enthusiasms for other writers, at least for those who thought as he did. He could say to Kenneth Burke, "Do you think me a fool if I say that at present I find you to be the only interesting character writing in America today?" To Bob McAlmon, "It's a damned good book. I like the book immensely and have made up my mind to go to some trouble about getting it printed." To a poet named Alva Turner who had written to him out of the blue of Wisconsin: "You are a genius. BUT you don't yet know how to write. If you are not too old to learn you can take my word for it (which you don't give a damn for, of course) you have the goods." To Charlie Demuth, praising a particular painting: "the most distinguished American painting that I have seen in years. I enjoy it for five or six distinct reasons, color, composition, clarity, thought, emotional force, ingenuity — and its completeness." To Marianne Moore, of her work: "Why should I not use superlatives? It couldn't be to a more discerning listener: there is no work in verse being done in any language which I can read which I find more to my liking and which I find to be so thoroughly excellent. You have everything that satisfies me." To a little magazine, *Furioso:* "We had a gang of lights and less lights here last night, and many of them saw my copy of your baby and liked it . . . Someone said it was the best little mag he'd seen in years. It is. Go to it."

For the great Pound himself there was always warmth and respect in the mail, but these two knew each other so well that the complimenting was less extravagant and the criticism sometimes hard. WCW's best praise of Pound in the twenties was not by letter but in the dedicating of *A Voyage to Pagany* to him. When he dedicated it he was embarrassed and wrote the news to Pound in Pound's own manner, mixed with Huck Finn, saying that he had asked himself who among his acquaintances he should "hang it onto" and had received from himself the answer, "Why, who else but my old friend and college chum Ezrie . . . So this is to let you know that I writ it all out fine and high sountin and it'll be print in the front of that there novel, as nice as you please . . . I hope you likes it. But if you don't why you can tear out the dedication page in the copy I'm a goin to have them send you."

Of course Pound did like it, and he immediately responded by writing for *The Dial* his most considerate account of WCW's writings, "Dr. Williams' Position," which in turn pleased WCW who wrote back, "Nothing will ever be said of better understanding regarding my work than your article." It was (sometimes) a very nice island society to belong to.

But if some of the praise on the island was excessive the general drift was honest. The islanders might have been wrong but they mostly believed what they were saying to each other if only because everyone on the island had a common view of the state of literature — it was deplorable — and common difficulties, so that they could hardly help finding each other important and valuable — valuable so long as each played his part in praising the work, or the promise of the work, of the others. Late in life WCW said that he thought of all the little magazines as one continuous magazine. The remark was a good one, and because each of the little magazines was run by just one or two people it was a remark that could also have been applied to his dozens of correspondents. In the end they added up to the same person, the same with respect to what they did with their energies and paranoias.

It has been because of this kind of closeness that the hundreds of separate little magazine enterprises of the last half century have many times been lumped together and characterized as a literary *movement*. It has not been a movement really but something has kept holding it together, some kind of psychic literary glue. Perhaps just living on the island has been enough, that and the chief island premise, uniformly agreed upon, that access to a printing machine is all that is needed to start the revolution. As Kenneth Burke put it, "The print shop in the cellar is the only way." And as Pound put it, a circulation of eighty is all right if the eighty are the right eighty. Whatever the reason the solidarity has been there, and has been passed on from one little magazine generation to another. Through several of these generations WCW was a dominant figure.

Yet it was Pound — it was pretty much always Pound — who established for WCW the ground rules for island life. He was not only one of the great letter writers the literary world has seen but he wrote *more* letters than anyone except Richardson's Pamela. He flooded the island with letters. Also he established the tone and direction of the letters, making it clear that though small talk was permitted — and particularly sex talk was permitted, and asides at the enemy — the letters were supposed to be in the main about literature, and serious about it without rhetoric. Pound created his own letter-language over the years, and when he began to lose his senses in the late thirties the language became so much his own that it was undecipherable except by close friends but it was always an antirhetorical language, the language of insiders. WCW took his cues from Pound as his own pen-pal society widened; he too became good at mixing the informal with the important. And both WCW and Pound displayed in their letters the quality basic to the success of island life, a capacity for affection and concern. Sometimes it was only literary concern, sometimes it went deeper, but always it was present. Pound was perhaps more affectionate with WCW than any other pen pal — he addressed him as everything from "My Dear Old Sawbuck von Grump" to "Deer Willyum the Wumpus" — but all his few true island friends received similar warmnesses. WCW, though more reserved, learned the mode from him and nightly at his typewriter served the cause of keeping the island community close.

Close it was. Just reading the letters between Pound and WCW is a half-century lesson in how human beings with an ocean between them can treat each other as if they were next door. Yet the warmth did have something synthetic about it even in the best years because they were *not* next door. The reference points between them were not the daily events of putting the garbage on the curb and taking the children to the dentist but the entrepreneurial details of calling particular manuscripts to the attention of particular editors, or of demolishing enemies for what they said in the last issue of whatever magazine Pound and WCW were at the moment reading. Pound was very concrete and businesslike on the literary scene, and he had a mind that could be most attentive to housekeeping details as well, but as he was separated from WCW and many of his other "intimates" by three thousand miles of water he was driven to concentrate on the only local homey details available to him, which usually turned out to be some stupidity of Harriet's in Chicago or perhaps of a usurer in ancient Tuscany.

And WCW in his attic, though nearer to the daily, was not that much nearer. Perhaps it was the distance, the real distance that produced the main distortions in island life. The distance eliminated everything except literature and literary people, making the island society special and partial like Swift's philosophers on the floating island of Gulliver's third book. It became not so much an island as a fort surrounded by enemies. WCW had his own enemies, and he picked up some of his enemy manners from Pound, but beside Pound he was a Quaker. For Pound the fort was surrounded by philistines, puritans, usurers, academics, iambicists, and other inferior *littérateurs* in such density of villainy that one couldn't even see to the woods beyond, *littérateurs* like G. K. Chesterton ("a vile scum on the pond"), and G. B. Shaw ("fundamentally trivial"), and scores of others. This large body of evil had to be beaten off by the slings and arrows of sometimes just Pound himself, with the result that he would write piteously to WCW, "I really can't do the whole show. Besides I am not supposed to run the American end." The whole show was civilization really, which was a big thing for one man — and by letter — to save. If WCW's enemy-paranoia came from anybody but himself it came from Pound.

Pound of course spread his enemy gospel far beyond WCW, all through the island (or fort) community. Even so, for Pound the community remained tiny so the gospel didn't spread far. Early in the community's life Pound wrote to Marianne Moore in New York, "entre nooz: is there anyone except you, Bill and Mina Loy who can write anything of interest in verse?" At about the same time he wrote his friend and patron John Quinn, also in New York, that he had been turned down "by about every editor in England and America," but the point of the letter was that he had been turned down by one magazine, *The Outlook,* and he was looking to Quinn for help in wreaking appropriate "vengeance" upon that sheet. Two decades later he was still thinking big while dealing small and he would refer to some tiny just starting little magazine as America's only hope, or would single out, as he had in the days of *Le Bel Esprit,* isolated literary figures as leading the world's future. WCW had a firmer grip on the big outside than this.

But WCW did not have a firmer grip on the nature of literary talent on the island at the basic level of whether a poem was good or not. Here Pound was discriminating, a tough clear-headed analyst, while WCW tended to the sentimental, approving of island folk because they were island folk. WCW corresponded endlessly with writers and editors who had little or no talent — or whose talent he could only guess at — while Pound was always busy alienating the weak ones with his absolutist evaluations, measuring their lines with arrogance but precision. He would tell the losers to their face that they *were* losers. He could even call WCW a loser, especially during his "improvisations" period, and his targets included the very best poets he knew, from his dear genius friend T. S. Eliot — whose *Waste Land* he said was the greatest thing of the century while at the same time advising Eliot that he was no Alexander Pope and shouldn't be so foolish as to try to imitate him — to E. E. Cummings whom he liked but thought a minor figure and tried to straighten out by saying, "you needn't feel obliged to keep up to your godawful reputation for cleverness. . . .There were bits of *The E. Room* that were good and not in the least bit clever."

2

But of course Pound was not the only letter-writing addict on WCW's string. In the Yale files there are letters to WCW from the editors of well over a hundred little magazines and in few cases was WCW's connection with them perfunctory. He would generally send on a poem if the editor wrote for one; he would suggest other contributors; he would read the issues as they came to him and comment on them, usually favorably. They were magazines with names like *Seven, Cronos, Factotum, Galaxy, Insert, Voyager, The Rebel Poet, Nimrod, Yugen, Neurotica, Magick, Wake, Lirica, Naked Ear, Contour, Phoenix, Spectrum, Between Worlds, Matrix, Hika, The James Joyce Review, Botteghe Oscure, Spearhead, Origin.* They were magazines that gave WCW a steady attic outlet not only for poems and stories but for wisdom and polemic *about* poems and stories. It was in the thirties and forties that he became deeply involved, reached out beyond Pound's magazines, became a fatherly impresario of the magazines on his own. And it was then also that he became mellower. Perhaps the awareness helped that after all the isolation-feelings he had nursed through the twenties he now had a following. The correspondents would come to him in the form of close friends like Burke, addressing him as "ole dopo" and asking him, "what kind of pests are anapests?" or strangers such as a student editor asking him to contribute to an undergraduate magazine or sending on odd new insights into WCW's own work — like this one about "The Red Wheelbarrow":

> So much depends upon
> The ovum and the sperm (chicken)
> Man's ingenuity (wheel)
> His labor (barrow)
> And the elements (rain)

But whether they were strangers or intimates they were out there, enthusiasts of the island, and WCW joined them in their causes.

The causes went many ways, especially in the thirties. Objectivism, Marxism, and Social Credit were the big three in WCW's thirties life, but he also mingled tentatively with other oddities — notably something called Aesthetic Realism that nobody has even yet understood though it is still alive and kicking — and managed in the end not to be taken in by any (except perhaps his own cause, the "variable foot") since he was not a joiner. What the causes did for him chiefly was get him out of himself, turning his writing away from the subjectivity of the improvisations and back upon thinginess. Objectivism was particularly useful here, though only its enthusiasts can now see it as much more than a reaffirmation of the tenets of imagism. Objectivism was Louis Zukofsky.

Like most of WCW's literary friends Zukofsky came into his life via Pound. Zukofsky had been corresponding with Pound in the late twenties, had impressed Pound with his poetry, and had joined with Pound in the publishing of a magazine called *Exile,* provoking Pound to write WCW to say that Zukofsky was talented and lived right in New York and couldn't they get together? Meanwhile Pound wrote Zukofsky about WCW, mentioning the wealth of "human values" to be found lurking in WCW's bosom. Zukofsky wrote to WCW about his reported "human values" and WCW replied, "By 'human values' I suppose Ezrie means that in his opinion I can't write." The friendship began, with WCW inviting Zukofsky to Rutherford for a meal and adding as a come-on that he had a good cook. Within a week WCW had read some of Zukofsky and was complimenting him extravagantly ("Yes yes. You have the rare gift").

The friendship persisted over a long period, and though WCW became severe about Zukofsky's own work — which was eccentric and difficult in ways that WCW could sympathize with less in others than in himself — he continued to respect Zukofsky's critical powers. For years Zukofsky had an important hand with a red pencil on WCW's work. His Objectivism may not have been in the long run a significant -ism but Zukofsky was a significant force in WCW's career.

The trouble with Objectivism was that it sounded like a new and glorious imagism but didn't work out that way on the page, didn't in fact emerge with any distinctness at all. Zukofsky tended to describe it metaphorically. He said that one should think of it in optical terms as "the lens bringing the rays from an object to a focus," but the poetic samplings he provided did not show anything new in the focus line; and he said similarly that Objectivism was like a military campaign in which the general-poet picked out an objective and aimed at it, but the Objectivists' generalship didn't seem distinctive either. Zukofsky's first big chance to bring Objectivism to the world came in February 1931 when Harriet Monroe allowed him to be guest editor of *Poetry* for an issue. It was here that he "explained" Objectivism, and printed a dozen poets whom he thought Objectivist including WCW. He also dismissed all the poets not included in the issue, thereby outraging Harriet.

WCW's poem in the issue was "The Botticellian Trees," which was not primarily imagistic — but what was Objectivist about it either? It was a metaphorical description of trees containing within themselves words and sentences, the bare branches being "the thin letters that spelled winter" and the leaved branches being sensual and full of love "as a woman's limbs under cloth." Then there were contributions of diverse sorts by Carl Rakosi, Robert McAlmon, Charles Reznikoff, Kenneth Rexroth, George Oppen and a number of others, especially Whittaker Chambers, who contributed a modest poem that did *not* have as an objective a pumpkin. All of the chosen poets were there together happily in what was called the Objectivist Issue, and their Objectivist ranks were reinforced soon after in a small book edited by Zukofsky called *The Objectivist Anthology;* but why these poets and not others were there under the Objectivist label remained a hard question. Harriet Monroe accordingly got after Zukofsky in her next issue objecting that he had consigned too many poets to "outer darkness" and declaring, with more than usual good sense for Harriet, that they had been sent out there simply because they did "not fit into a theoretic scheme spun out of brain fabric by a group of empirical young rule makers." She then wrote her own polemic, against each of the poets whom Zukofsky had included. Even WCW didn't fare well, he being WCW "of the eccentric orbit," but McAlmon fared worst: "well anyone who wants him should have him." The critical noise then went on in *Poetry* for several more issues from many other islanders but was unmarked by illumination. Most made speeches and thought they knew what they were saying, but Zukofsky made it clear that he at least no longer knew by retreating from his discriminatory original position: he announced that all good poets from Homer on had always been Objectivists.

Years later in the fifties WCW, who had had trouble finding in Zukofsky's own work "the objective clarities of image" that he supposed Objectivism reached for, asked Zukofsky to remind him again what Objectivism was, and Zukofsky told him learnedly that "Objectivist poetry equals poetry and that's that." The defining seemed in other words not to have progressed very much in twenty years though Zukofsky then did add something not evident in his earlier commentary, something that sounded fuzzily like the gestalt theories of poetry that WCW by then had become involved in with Charles Olson and others; he said, "A poem has an expressed shape, form, love, music (or what other word have you?) and that goes for a poem in anytime, for any time." Objectivism was opposed, clearly, to received traditional forms and shapes as WCW had always been, but how it arrived at what it was *not* opposed to was not clear.

Luckily Zukofsky was not just an Objectivist but also a friend, and as a friend didn't have to talk aesthetics all the time but could share with WCW the pleasures of battering the establishments. WCW went through the Metropolitan Museum of Art one afternoon in 1931 and wrote off busily to Z, "Isn't it a shitting crime that a big stone heap like that should sit on life and keep it under?" And between the two of them for a time a plan was toyed with for a collectivist publishing venture, Cooperative Publishers, which would stand against the world by having "membership" limited to those with a good book manuscript on hand, presumably themselves and one or two other poets. Cooperative Publishers may or may not have been the same project as the one that came to be called the Objectivist Press. The Objectivist Press was largely Zukofsky's baby (with George Oppen as angel) and had a limited but significant run, producing among others WCW's *Collected Poems 1921–31.*

Another good literary entrepreneuring friend of the late twenties and early thirties was Richard Johns, née Johnson, who wrote WCW out of the blue from Boston to say that he was starting up a new magazine, *Pagany,* that had picked up its title from WCW's book. Johns thought WCW was great, asked WCW to be an editor; WCW was flattered, accepted, and the result was a magazine that, though short-lived, pushed WCW into the writing of *White Mule,* which appeared serially there, as well as a number of short stories. Johns was a great enthusiast about WCW's prose, and later WCW said he thought he would not have written *White Mule* without him. When the first chapter of *White Mule* appeared Erskine Caldwell, who was also a contributor to *Pagany,* wrote Johns to say, "Williams gives me an inelegant puke with his *White Mule* but he's got something (God knows I don't know what it is) that nobody else has ever had." Feeling that he had overdone the compliment Caldwell added, "He's as creative as a bull jumping a fence but I don't like the windward smell." The chapter was a description of childbirth, probably WCW's best. Johns and *Pagany* pushed WCW back on his medical experience and on good reportage, a useful antidote to the artiness of Zukofsky and Pound, and with Johns's encouragement WCW found himself for a brief period writing freely, quickly and without inhibition as he always hoped to write. He said to Johns that he had a "crazy bug" on "short stories, quite short ones . . . I've written six of them as fast as I can write . . . Lord I could write a hun-

dred if anyone would read them . . . I know Ezra would pass out
if he could see them." He had, he said, been reworking and refining a longer story, "that damned Doc Rivers thing," and it had
been driving him crazy because he couldn't, he was convinced,
"work that way," and suddenly he found himself doing a story
about a red-headed woman. It "tickled me pink. And then I got a
perfect diarrhea. I wrote so fast I couldn't see straight . . . I love
to write when it drips off my fingers." The result in the end was
his two volumes of short stories of the thirties, stories that were not
all, as he recollected later, about the poor, but were all clearly
incidents from life. John Crowe Ransom was to say of one of
WCW's later stories in the same mode, as he rejected it for *The
Kenyon Review,* that it was "clean, stripped and adequate" but
that he didn't think of it as a story but as an episode or anecdote.
That was the sort of thing that went well with Johns and *Pagany,*
however, and because it was clean and stripped it had the merit,
whether it was formally complete enough to be put in the traditional story bin, of not being politically loaded as so many prole
stories of the thirties came to be.

Pagany was not at root one of the proletarian magazines and it
probably suffered for not being. It went on handsomely but without great success for a couple of years with WCW contributing a
story or two beyond the serialization of *White Mule* and sneaking
in three of Pound's *Cantos;* then Johns ran out of money and
folded his literary tent contritely, provoking WCW to ask him
"what in heck" he felt so guilty about. It was true that Johns
had paid Pound with a bad check but Pound had not been angry.
He was used to impoverished publishers and replied mildly that
he would simply prefer not to have any more of those bad
checks as it might "unduly complicate foreign relations." The
folding of little magazines was something one got used to, and in
fact WCW's own venture of the period lasted less long and made
less of a dent than *Pagany.*

It was a revival of *Contact,* and this time it was chiefly WCW's
baby with McAlmon acting as his literary scout abroad and with

Nathanael West, a new acquaintance, helping at home. West put some of *Miss Lonelyhearts* into the magazine, and he also helped with the dirty work of composing a bibliography of literary magazines that ran through the first two issues, and McAlmon tried to get together an art issue (it never gelled), and a New York publisher named Kamin not only picked up the tab but took over the dirty work of composition and proofreading so that WCW in his attic could concentrate on editing and entrepreneuring (he briefly became enthusiastic and went so far as to send out a few night letters to likely contributors). The announced "program" in the first issue was "to cut a trail through the American jungle without the use of a European compass" and inside to cut the trail were three fine poems by Cummings and lesser verses by Zukofsky, Charles Reznikoff, and Parker Tyler, plus fiction by WCW, West, and McAlmon. Also featured was Diego Rivera on Mickey Mouse, three slim pages announcing that Mickey Mouse was "one of the genuine heroes of American Art in the first half of the 20th century." (What would Rivera think now if he visited Disney World?) Issues two and three were similar, and in each WCW had a short editorial, one complaining that because he was trying to focus on American literature he was being taken for a regionalist, the other complaining about Eliot and academic poetry. But nothing worked well and after three issues the publisher soured on WCW. WCW resigned and for a moment had the impression that the fourth issue would be issued "under the editorship of a group, proletarian in feeling," but then the magazine folded completely and WCW himself went sour. *Pagany* had restored his faith in little magazining briefly, as had another magazine of the time, *Blues,* edited by Charles Henri Ford, into which both he and Pound had jumped with both feet in 1929 playing daddy roles and talking about what "the young writers today" should, if they were wise, do ("they should not play around with trite forms, trite rhythms, trite images"); but the collapse of *Contact* made him write to yet another literary friend one of his less generous observations about the state of magazines and literature:

A gathering on the side lawn at 9 Ridge Road, c. 1916.

Male group. Front row, from l.: Alanson Hartpence, Alfred Kreymborg, WCW (with Mother Kitty), Skip Cannell; back row: Jean Crotti, Marcel Duchamp, Walter Arensberg, Man Ray, R. A. Sanborn, Maxwell Bodenheim

Female group. From l.: Helen Slade, Mary Caroline Davis, Yvonne Crotti(?), Flossie, Kittie Cannell, Mrs. Davis (mother of Kittie Cannell), Gertrude Kreymborg, Mrs. Walter Arensberg

WCW with his English grandmother and sons
Paul (in lap) and Bill, 1917

Mother Elena, c. 1940

WCW with Bill (l.) and Paul in a quickie photo gallery on the "strip" at the Savin Rock, Connecticut, amusement area, 1928

Robert McAlmon in England in the early 1920s

WCW in the late 1920s

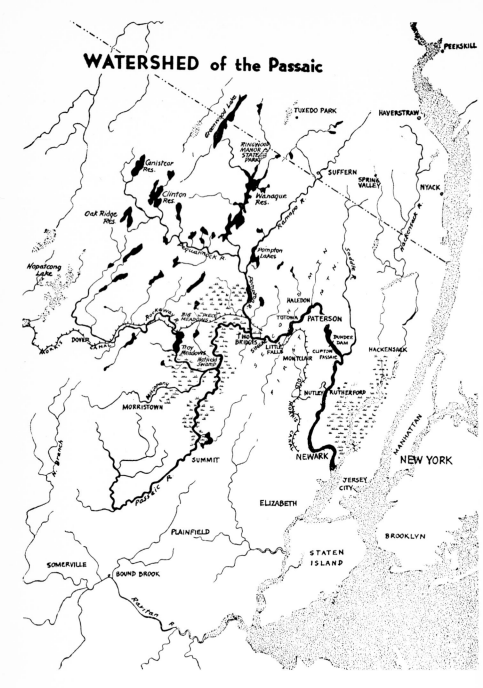

Watershed of the Passaic

Flossie at Irvington, New York, about 1942

WCW in the late 1940s

There isn't enough good writing in the entire U. S. to keep one good magazine going for a year. It's true. We're positively nauseated by the crap that came into the *Contact* office . . . Why should I at my age waste any more time seeking for others that which I have never been able to find for myself. I can't find a publisher. All the mags turn me down . . . There is no real desire for united effort. Never has been. We shit away every chance we have by putting out little piddling magazines here and there.

3

Perhaps the trouble with *Contact,* as well as *Pagany* and *Blues,* was that such publishing wasn't proletarian enough for the times. WCW was managing to be unfashionable again. He was listening to the socialists and looking at their magazines, he was trying to be in favor of the poor and against the rich, and he was trying not to be an intellectual snob (he had another anti-Eliot tantrum when Eliot was invited to Harvard in 1931, writing to Pound suggesting that he come over as Eliot's valet) ; but he was also trying to be, as always, his own man — and that was something he kept discovering the Marxists didn't want him to be.

Anyway listening to the Objectivists and other aesthetes on the one hand, and to the Marxists on the other must have been like having two radios on. WCW did try to listen to them both, and it was lucky for him that he did not have to listen to them literally but could sit up in his attic and hear them by mail. Zukofsky wrote him several folders' worth of Objectivist illumination in the late twenties and early thirties, and WCW had no single wholly dedicated Marxist friend who was nearly so prolific; but after the crash there were so *many* Marxists, especially among artists and writers, that even Zukofsky was outnumbered. And what the Marxists had to say was that aesthetes like Zukofsky were too, well, aesthetic.

The Marxists in their brief rule tried to politicize the little magazine island. Marxism meant what came to be called socialist realism, meant a turning away from matters of literary technique, meant frowning at self and the individualist excesses of island or attic life. Of the magazines that WCW had lived with in the twenties, only the determinedly nonpolitical *Poetry* survived the thirties as itself. Plenty of magazines like *Poetry* sprang up again after the Moscow purges, but during the big Marxist period before 1937 there seemed to be something indecent about little mags indulging in Zukofskian quibbles about whether a line like "the ceaseless weaving of uneven water" was "sincere." What was decent was bringing the masses to literature or literature to the masses, and doing it so that the masses would be enlightened and led toward the heavenly city of classlessness. The hopes for a literary base among the proles were never to be realized but in the brief period when they were entertained the John Reed clubs of the land went in hard for small publications, each club imagining that it was printing in its cellar a future media giant.

The New Masses, which had begun in 1926 by printing WCW's unlucky "Five Dollar Guy," became the nearest-to-giant of the lot and was the most persistent. It lasted through the purges and through World War II, only dying with (or of) McCarthyism — but its big days were the first years of the thirties. At that time it drew from all corners of American literature, as well as from big-time journalism. It was readable and predictable. William Saroyan could be found there writing about "the well-dressed punkos" and proposing the writing of a symphony with a strike movement in it and "screaming N.R.A. eagles." Erskine Caldwell could be found there reporting on the killers of blacks by the hands of "parties unknown" in Bartow, Georgia. Dorothy Parker could be found there, late, during the Spanish War, reporting on the "magnificent achievement" of the Spanish Republican government and finding "incredible . . . fantastic . . . absolutely beyond all belief" that these people could not live decently "without the murder of their children" — incredible "except that it [was] true." Dozens of determined cartoonists could be found there portraying the bloated capitalists with their bloated stomachs. Sample: a bloated capitalist was pictured riding by as one bystander whispered to another, "they say he owns 25 sweatshops but never perspires." And Theodore Dreiser could be found there writing that World War I had made America safe for Standard Oil, Ernest Hemingway could be found there reporting on Vets in Key West dying in government camps in a hurricane, Richard Wright could be found there reporting on Joe Louis's discovery of white racism in the form of Max Baer, and S. J. Perelman could be found there with a thoroughly Perelman piece: the Red Menace under siege by the Rover Boys.

There was poetry too, and fiction. WCW's friends Bodenheim and Matthew Josephson appeared, surrounded by Kenneth Fearing, Lorca, Genevieve Taggard, James Agee, and others. No issue of the *New Masses* failed to remind the reader that this *was* the Depression, with the unemployed selling apples on street corners, the Vets marching on Washington and being fought by their own kind, the Wall Streeters jumping out of windows. Sometimes the writers' best way of emphasizing the magnitude of the country's troubles was just to make great listings of woes, which was Fearing's best trick:

> . . . who shot down the man in the blue overalls? Who stopped the mill? Who took the mattress, the table, the birdcage, and piled them in the street? Who drove teargas in the picket's face? Who burned the crops? Who killed the herd? Who levelled the walls of the packing box city? Who held the torch to the Negro pyre? Who stuffed the windows and turned on the gas for the family of three?

And sometimes the best way was to pick a case, as WCW himself did with a man wrongfully jailed (in his poem "An Early Martyr") and as so many including WCW did with the Sacco-Vanzetti trial — pick the case, tell the story of it in verse or prose, and then perhaps do a bit of special pleading to wind the thing up. The special pleading was always important in *New Masses*. Art was either activist art or it was bad art.

But WCW was not good at activist art though he tried his hand at it in a few poems. He may have been lucky not to be good at it because in its place he had something else, but he was not good at it and *New Masses* was therefore never really for him. His capacity for straightforward rendering of experience, a capacity that was handsomely suited for the Depression times, kept him at arm's length from the true activists, especially in fiction where *New Masses* writers seemed phoniest. The *New Masses* story writers managed to convert every incident into melodrama or allegory whereas WCW's movement in his stories and in *White Mule* was consistently away from that. It was in fiction that WCW shone in the thirties: the proles were in his fiction but they were in there as people not pawns.

The difference between WCW and the others was not so much in matter or texture as intent. WCW was doing as they were in trying to catch the talk of the poor, to put glimpses of their lives on the page, bring their actuality into print; but he was avoiding the easy social-political tags and conclusions that the others invariably rushed to. He was avoiding, when he wrote of the poor, saying that the bloated capitalists had done the poor in, avoiding sentimentality about their troubles, avoiding the building of a utopia in which the pimply young heroine or bowlegged varicose-veined mother would be suddenly healthy, happy, and political.

An Albert Maltz story in *New Masses* in 1934 was just the kind that WCW could not have written. It had the necessary hitchhiker in it with the necessary woe — this one had picked up silicosis by working for evil exploiters in an ill-ventilated tunnel — and it ended with a tear-jerking letter that the hitchhiker had written to his wife explaining why he had left her: he had been told by the doctors that he was going to die in four months so he thought he should be kind to her and get out of the way, let her try to "git another man" since she was "a young woman yit." Now WCW was capable of writing hitchhiker stories too — because everyone in the thirties wrote hitchhiker stories or riding-the-rails stories — but he was incapable of bringing a story to such a conclusion. It was more to his taste that the hitchhiker be down on his luck and penniless but carelessly, unpolitically so. Thus in one of his stories the penniless hitchhiker was a carefree young blade who

proposed not that the doctor and he save the world together but
that the doctor come swimming with him in the raw in a nearby
pond.

Similarly WCW could not have written a melodramatic thing
that Thomas Wolfe contributed to *New Masses* in 1938. Wolfe
pulled out all the stops on the evils of big-company labor practices,
with such speeches as this one:

> "You deliver or you go right out upon your can! See? The Com-
> pany doesn't give a damn about you. It's after the business. You've
> been around a long time, but you don't mean a damn bit more to
> the Company than anybody else . . . I've given you fair warning
> now. You get the business or out you go!"

WCW's characters had to be more human with each other than
that. And WCW's message had to be less pat than that. In his
novel *White Mule* the company he portrayed was indeed a bad
company but the union he portrayed was a bad union, with the
result that the hero of the novel, who happened to have been
WCW's father-in-law and who happened actually to have dealt
with the bad company and the bad union, went off to be antiso-
cialist in a big way by starting his own company. Such a dénoue-
ment was death at *New Masses*.

All in all WCW would sooner have been a vegetarian or a
Martian than a Marxist, though the furthest left he would reach
was considerably farther than to vote for Al Smith, as he did in
1928. His aesthetic and social impulses were uniformly anticollec-
tivist, and when under the pressure of the times he dabbled in
thirties social doctrine he mostly managed to indicate that he
should have stayed home. Even in *White Mule,* which was well
controlled otherwise, the union talk was naive and melodramatic.
White Mule was the story of the birth and early years of Flossie,
and when it was on Flossie it was a fine story because WCW knew
about babies and mothers; but when it switched over to the
father's troubles at the print shop it took on doctrinal social matter at a primitive level with the capitalist saying, "Money can be

made, big money, quickly and with complete honesty in this country," the father saying, "We're up against a lot of dirty crooks just the same," the capitalist liking him for that and asking him about his union practices, and the father replying:

> Open shop . . . Good pay as much as the business can stand, decent appointments, protect the machinery — give them everything they need to do good work. And stick to them as long as they stick to me.

At that point the capitalist asked the father what he would do if his employees turned out "no good." The father said instantly that he would fire them, that he "wouldn't have a shop under any other conditions." Luckily the novel did have Flossie and the parents' family life as antidote to such talk, and WCW had the good sense to begin and end the novel with Flossie, making her though an infant the controlling character. At the beginning she was being born; at the end she was toddling about on a farm surrounded by her elders with her "face smeared with berry juice, her hands sooty," feeling "quite part of it all." At the *New Masses* at the time a flat ending like that, an ending proposing in effect that a baby getting smeared with blueberries was as central an event as one charged with political dynamite, would have probably been classified as decadent individualism.

White Mule was lucky that it had its decadent privacies but their prevalence wasn't *all* luck. Though WCW was frequently swayed by the radical talk of the time, and though he felt that he had to insert a large hunk of it in *White Mule,* he must have realized that it was not native to him. His faith was like his father-in-law's except that unlike his father-in-law, who was once deep in union affairs, WCW only knew about company-union conflicts at second hand. He was a writer of letters to newspapers, an outsider with an angry pen. Once he grew angry at the trucks on the roads blocking his private way as he drove about in his car, and so proposed to the *New York Times* that all buses and trucks be taken over by the railroads and "confined to special roads paralleling the r.r.'s on their existing rights of way." Hurrah for the private car. And if that proposal had actually been legislated he would have been against it as a form of collectivization. His faith, even when he was writing to his Marxist friends, was always totally with the individual and with local government against the Feds. In the late twenties the most political subject he could seriously discuss was Prohibition (which he was wildly against), and in the thirties his most political subject was probably Social Credit, which was Pound's anti–Marxist-oriented money idea. Yet he was surrounded by Marxist writers as well as the industrial poor. In the thirties' climate he naturally *started* where the other writers did, but he seldom ended there.

None of the stories of his that appeared in his two story collections of the thirties, *Knife of the Times* (1932) and *Life Along the Passaic River* (1938), appeared in *New Masses*. The stories dealt with dailiness rather than climactic social moments. Perhaps half the stories were from a doctor's point of view (the brief visitation was his strength, and fitted well the kind of story he mostly undertook, the story with a single incident or point but not an O. Henry point — a quiet point rather). The doctor's view was usually close in, and though occasionally (as in "Jean Beicke" and "Life Along the Passaic River") he would generalize about conditions, mostly his focus was upon the private event. (Typical was his most anthologized story, "The Use of Force," in which a little girl tries to keep the doctor from looking at her infected throat.) If the individuals of the stories did happen to talk politics and social injustice they would throw that kind of talk away before the story's end and move to the more urgent problems of their lives, problems like whether or not to pay the doctor, and how. (Why in beer, of course.) Life along the Passaic River was rough in the thirties and WCW left no doubt of that; but he also left no doubt that life was being lived there. Children were being born in dirty back rooms but they were being born. The unemployed were sitting idly on their stoops in the city of Passaic, but as they sat there a lot of them could unpolitically smile and joke, and once in a while they could scrape up the necessary dollar to take the little excursion boat from Passaic to Coney Island down the newly cleaned-up Passaic River and out through Newark Bay. In a way the Depression became for WCW a vindication of his aesthetic of the ugly; it gave him a chance to affirm, with the evidence all around him, that life as well as art thrived under conditions that the old literary conventions as well as the new Marxist social conventions said it wasn't supposed to thrive under. WCW never betrayed his aesthetic by being teary for the lame halt and blind. He thought they too could be vital, beautiful.

But he did have several good Marxist pen pals, such as John Beecher, a fine journalist-poet whose *Collected Poems* has recently appeared, and more intimately a midwestern socialist named H. H. Lewis. Lewis was a farmer from Missouri and WCW's relations with him showed how confused WCW's political position could be. WCW described Lewis as first cousin to a mule and reviewed a book of his most favorably, saying of him that he was a man who spoke directly as a man should speak, and a writer who had the good sense to do away with "the putrescence of symbolism." Lewis happened also to be a poet full of rhymes but he didn't always rhyme and anyway rhyming by Lewis seemed, to WCW, all right, as did Lewis's love of Russia. WCW said, "It doesn't matter that Lewis comes out openly, passionately for Russia," and went on at length to assert the primacy of Lewis's Americanness. Lewis was simple. He did story poems of local injustice and did thesis poems about new wonders in the U.S.S.R. such as the reported Soviet success in developing — "by crossbreeding horticulture to socialism" — oranges that could be grown in cold country. He had a good if heavy wit, he kept abreast of the daily Depression crises in the papers, and he was always busy writing to the magazines to tell them what they had done wrong. WCW's friendship and backing was natural and healthy but, as always, ideologically confused.

4

Not that there was nothing to be confused about in thirties' leftist politics. There were the indoor and outdoor radicals, the city slickers like Philip Rahv and William Phillips and the grass-root bellowers like H. H. Lewis. WCW seemed to favor the latter, and aside from Lewis he became a good pen pal of an undogmatic grass-roots type named Fred Miller who was actually a poor boy from Greenwich Village who edited a pleasant thirties' sheet called *Blast* (no connection with Wyndham Lewis's magazine *Blast*) in which WCW, who became an associate editor, could sound off at the other leftists, the wrong-headed ones. Eventually the Spanish War and the Moscow purges put most of the American left into the confused category of Trotskyite, with *New Masses* and the *Daily Worker* holding out as Stalinist. But the Stalinist-Trotskyite simplification did not take hold until late in the decade and was not even then a satisfactory explanation of leftist divisions, especially the temperamental split between the high theorists and the muddlers-through.

WCW was always a muddler-through. He had muddling built into his aesthetic theory and into daily life too. But there were times when he wanted to combat Pound's opinion of him as the most incoherent gargling animal and wanted to be thought the Thinker. In leftist politics his thinking-urge meant that he couldn't always be satisfied muddling along with comfortable down-to-earth Marxists like Lewis and Miller but had to aim at the highbrows who congregated around the *Partisan Review* and then *The New Leader,* and who organized in the late thirties an intellectual political instrument called The Committee for Cultural Freedom. Not being an orderly thinker and not knowing the machinations of the dialectical part of Dialectical Materialism, he was not on safe ground in the theorists' presence, and before the end of the decade he had earned their annoyance.

He should have stuck with *Blast. Blast* featured "Proletarian Short Stories" and its first issue began with WCW's story "Jean Beicke," a beautiful example of a proletarian story not for *New Masses.* It was about an unwanted baby, one of those who come into the hospital "with pneumonia, a temperature of a hundred and six, maybe, and before you can do a thing, they're dead." The trouble with the story politically was that the capitalist system wasn't the cause of the child's death but the doctors, including WCW, who had failed to diagnose the child's ailment. Nor was the medical failure brought on by the doctors' overwork or inattention or callousness. The doctors tried hard but just plain missed, and were disgusted with themselves afterward when they conducted an autopsy and discovered that "the left lateral sinus was completely thrombosed and on going into the left temporal bone from the inside the mastoid process was all broken down." How could such a story end? The "ear man" came down, was told what had killed the child and said he thought that if they had "gone in there earlier" they would have saved her, at which point WCW said, "For what?" adding that if they had saved her they would have saved her to "vote the straight communist ticket." To WCW's piece of cynicism the ear man added his own, asking, "Would it make us any dumber?" and that was the story's end.

WCW had several other stories with the same lack of respect for formulas in issues of *Blast,* and editor Miller, who was a short-story writer too, occasionally contributed one of his own. He was more orthodox than WCW — he had a tale for example about the purchase of a superfluous upperclass Abercrombie & Fitch item at Abercrombie & Fitch's itself while that store was being picketed by the angry unemployed shouting "No Work No Rent" — but neither Miller nor WCW were ideologically intense enough to subscribe to the kind of rhetoric displayed in an advertisement for the first issue of *Partisan Review.* In that it was proclaimed that within *PR's* pages "the leftward moving professional writers and the young revolutionary writers from factory and farm [would] meet in a common effort to forge new literary values." Not many of the revolutionary factory and farm writers were to come within ten miles of a copy of *PR,* and WCW and Miller were scornful of such pretensions. When WCW had a story rejected by another heavily ideological magazine, *Dynamo,* he and Miller printed in *Blast* with contempt the reasons the *Dynamo* editors gave for rejecting the story. The story, *Dynamo* had said, was not leftward-moving enough, not sufficiently warm to the common effort; the doctor of the story "seemed unaware of the implications of giving the girl a prescription that would cost not less than fifty cents when her father was receiving ten dollars a week." Implications? A prescription was a prescription for WCW except when he was using the blanks for poems.

But *Blast* couldn't last, and anyway WCW had to have his rounds with the theorists. He contributed to a symposium in 1936 in *PR* in a way that brought epithets down on his head and affected — though how much is not finally clear — *PR*'s handling of WCW's subsequent Lewis review. In 1936 *PR* had merged temporarily with another leftist sheet, *Anvil,* and the superideologue's question to which the ten symposium contributors were asked to reply was, How could Marxism be ideologically related, if it could be related, to the American tradition?

Seven of the contributors said it could be related and explained how, including Theodore Dreiser, who thought the shift from capitalism to socialism was inevitable and therefore a good thing to get going on, and Newton Arvin, who also thought things were switching nicely but worried about a lingering cosmopolitanism left over from "the age of Eliot" (there were other Eliot-haters too), and Josephine Herbst, who bragged that in 1932, at a point near where Washington crossed the Delaware, she had voted the straight communist ticket, and even Kenneth Burke, who made his position characteristically difficult but ended with hope for "the good philosophy, the philosophy of communism." Three contributors however said no, Marxism and Americanism were not reconcilable. WCW was one and his negative was the sternest.

Marxism, he said, was a "static philosophy" out of the past, the opposite of the American democracy of the admittedly frequently deluded "self seeker," and because Marxism could not catch the American spirit the revolutionary literature that was written with a Marxist base was merely "tolerated by most Americans." WCW found Marxism definitely in conflict with the country's "deep-seated ideals," though by so doing he in effect took the opposite position that he took in his Lewis review, which he must have written at almost the same time.

WCW's symposium comments brought forth a number of angry letters to the *PR* editors, of which one was printed with the heading "Sanctions against Williams" (the word "sanctions" being supplied by the *PR* editors) and asked where Williams had been living all these years. It announced that "the whole school of modernist writing of which Mr. Williams [was] such a shining light [had made] no dent on the American consciousness." The editors of *PR* contributed their opinion in a note after the letter, saying that *PR* was "utterly opposed to the direction of thought" shown by WCW. Before this complaint was printed they rejected WCW's Lewis review.

WCW and Lewis later comforted themselves that the review's rejection was indeed an actual form of sanctions against WCW since the review had been rejected by *PR* after the editors had seen and digested WCW's contribution to the symposium; but in fact the *PR* editors had a rather good *other* reason for rejecting the review, a reason that WCW and Lewis chose to underplay: a shorter version of the review had appeared in *Poetry* at about the time that the review was received by *PR*. Oddly, Lewis himself seems to have submitted WCW's review to *PR*, a fact that exonerated WCW from the sin of double submission but not from the sin of letting Lewis figure out ways to promote himself with WCW's words. Anyway *PR*, having received the review and perhaps having accepted it, then found a shorter version of it in the February 1936 *Poetry*. They sent a blast either to Lewis or to WCW, Lewis blasted back, and then four *PR* editors replied in unison to Lewis in a letter (dated February 4, 1936) now in the WCW files at Yale, a reply that Lewis scribbled over angrily and forwarded to WCW.

The four editors were Ben Field, Edwin Rolfe, William Phillips, and Philip Rahv. If they had been content to complain about the double submission they would have been on firmer ground than they finally achieved, but they had read by then WCW's symposium piece (printed in the April 1936 issue) and were mad in several directions. First they did complain about the double submission and beside their complaint Lewis scribbled angrily that this was "a face saving excuse" since he had himself told the *PR* editors about the "partial prepublication" in *Poetry* and suggested that maybe WCW could rework that part (it would have been hard; the duplication was extensive). Then they denied an earlier accusation Lewis had thrown their way, that *PR* had said of Lewis that his "polysyllabic verse cannot be understood by either workers or peasants" — and beside this Lewis wrote, "Philip Rahv, one of the editors of *PR*, said it in *Dynamo*, so what's the difference?" After a number of other complaints the editors wrote, "Here is something else for you [Lewis] to chew over" and proceeded to quote from WCW's symposium contribution, adding,

> This will show you that Williams has no right to pass judgment on revolutionary poetry because he is opposed to it and doesn't understand it. You know perfectly well that people like yourself have always considered Williams a bourgeois decadent and lo, suddenly he emerges in your eyes as another Plekhanov.

Apparently Lewis did not think that WCW was a bourgeois decadent but that the *PR* editors were the villains. He wrote beside their signatures, "complete horses' rectums, the four of them!" Such were WCW's happy early days with the highbrows.

Three years later he put his foot into the city slickers' camp again, first by signing up with the Committee for Cultural Freedom, then by resigning from the Committee, and then by objecting, to Sidney Hook, to what *The New Leader* had said about his resignation. His letter to Hook brought Hook out of a hole to counterattack, saying that he had nothing to do with *The New Leader* but that the aspersions WCW had cast on the C.C.F. were "demonstrably false." The interchange was another, though smaller, squabble tending mostly to show that politically WCW was at the time giving off more heat than light.

Not that many were being illuminating in 1939 and *The New Leader* itself made the most muddled reading. It was full of hot headlines purporting to show that the eventual triumph of social-ism and justice was assured if left to *The New Leader*'s investi-gative reporters, headlines like "Tories Keep Food, Guns from Loyalists," "800 U.S. Organizations Work to Build a Fascist America," "Utility Subsidy Revealed Behind Press War in TVA," "The Truth About the Exlax Co," and "Louisiana Fascist Re-ported Paid by Hearst to Smear FD"; but the purport went off in a number of directions since the *New Leader* editors were not only against the Fascists but the Russians and yet nothing enraged them more than to be called Trotskyites. "Trotsky as Ruthless as Stalin," one editorial was headed, and when in late spring they discovered "May Day's Early Traditions Perverted by U.S.S.R., Nazis, Fascists" there was probably nobody aboard who could have said with clarity what May Day's early traditions had *not* been perverted by. Their confusion did not reduce their stridency and when the Russo-German Pact led to the divvying up of Poland they pushed hard for isolation and for the Committee for Cultural Freedom (there was a big headline when Sinclair Lewis joined) meanwhile doing their best to knock off another writers group that looked "Stalinoid," namely the League of American Writers. They bitterly identified the League with the *New Republic* and with a long list of distinguished leftists including Lillian Hellman, Lewis Mumford, I. F. Stone, Upton Sinclair, Van Wyck Brooks, and WCW.

It was name-calling time, listing time, but if there was any WCW lesson in it at all it was probably that WCW's own mean-derings were not politically listable. His responses might be naive but they were always genuinely his. They were also apt to be temporary, and afterward he would usually make up with those he opposed. By the 1940s, for example, he was contributing to *PR* again and waxing indignant with them again but on a different matter. It was no longer their Marxism that was bugging him but the Eliotism that was creeping into *PR* (*PR* must have been the only magazine after the early *Poetry* to which both Eliot and WCW were contributing simultaneously) in the form of the *Four*

Quartets and other offenses against poetic spontaneity. WCW sat down busily in his anti-Eliot chair and wrote off to Dwight Macdonald that T.S.E. had "no creative intelligence whatever."

There were, of course, many cantankerous individualists like himself stirring about in leftist ranks and finding them uncongenial. Some of them had no activist impulses, and some were fanatics briefly, then lapsed. One of his female leftist acquaintances was a momentary fanatic whom he had to caution — was he frightened *then?* — against calling him "comrade," while other acquaintances like Kenneth Burke dipped in and out of the revolution without getting more than damp. But whatever the degree of commitment the persons whom WCW found himself most commonly leagued with were not the organizers but the lonely ones of the little magazine world who remained islanders throughout the upheaval period. They were earnest in their social feelings and aware of the dimensions of the social struggle around them but in the long run they were psychologically and ideologically anarchist. The heart of the American thirties may well have resided in them.

Their faith was not to be confined to platforms and manifestos, but to be found in their continuous backing and filling, in their finding socialism a fine thing except impossible, in their fighting Henry Ford on Tuesday and their own comrades on Wednesday. The thirties may have been confused ideologically but the confusion had a kind of health and vigor to it and the health was here rather than in the movements. The big issues did keep coming up to be wrestled with by earnest and singular and sometimes wildly eccentric minds, each mind working out the whole revolution on its own. If a typical American thirties radical could have been produced out of a computer he might have been found to look like WCW.

And WCW carried his confusion pretty far. At the height of it he could be found panicking not only the Marxist ranks but also those who later came to be called fascists, Pound's Social Credit bunch. Pound brought WCW Social Credit and WCW gargled about it even as he was being pals with Lewis and Miller. Pound never had any time for the proletarians or their writing, yet Pound with his *snobisme* was as attractive to WCW as Miller or Lewis. In fact Pound and WCW exchanged witticisms about the faults of proletarian writing. As far as Pound was concerned the "rugged ole lady's doc from Ruggerforg" was the only American writing decent prole stories, the rest being "bloody bores" because all they ever discovered was that there was "NOT enuff money." (Pound added, "it is so monot that it bores me to mention it.")

Pound, of course, happened to be one who knew what should be done about there not being enough money, but until the thirties he was too busy being literary to be political. Then suddenly in the middle of the Depression and from Rapallo he jumped into political action, writing WCW that "in yewth we cd set in the daisy fields but at fifty we got to take the white man's / I mean we have got to work ON the bastuds who are actually making the laws and deciding what is to be done NOW, this week." Pound wrote and WCW harkened.

What he wrote was the Major Douglas line about credit that the state should take control of its issuance, that is, take away the control of capital from the banks and therefore the banks' capacity to loan money at interest rates the banks could establish. It was an antiusury theory and WCW liked it, and before long he was working on the "bastuds" too by talking up Social Credit and by writing at least one article in its praise and against the "money cancer." What he had to go on when he wrote, aside from Pound's comments in letters, was apparently only a one-column summary of Social Credit that Pound had written for *The New English Weekly* and sent on a copy of. The column observed that it was ridiculous for any state to run into debt to individuals, that many states were beginning to realize their powers and their obligations to improve the distribution of money, that a state could have a double standard for currency, one for home and one for foreign use, that a state could issue money in the form of certificates for work done thereby making taxes unnecessary, that a state could also issue money for commodities as it pleased, and finally that a state could with its unlimited money powers dispose of its evil middlemen and see to it that commodities could be exchanged at par without "being impeded or taxed by a third party." It was a fine document, a fine theory. Also, when Pound first put his talents to the service of the theory he was in a mellow mood that made his words the more persuasive. There was no fascist connection yet; Major Douglas and Pound seemed to have just another labor theory of value to compete with Marx's.

Pound was so mellow in fact that for a time he could write comic verse about Social Credit, mostly in cockney. He submitted the verses week by week to the editor of *The New English Weekly* for publication on the letters page. He attached to the poems coy remarks like, "it would tickle my missus to see this new bit in print," and the remarks were printed too. The poems would easily have passed muster in *New Masses,* though Pound would never have sent them there. Sample:

> We yare 'ere met together
> in this momentous hower,
> Ter lick the bankers' dirty boots
> and keep the Bank in power.

> We are 'ere met together
> ter grind the same old axes
> And keep the people in its place
> a 'payin' us the taxes.

Soon the poems were published together in a little pamphlet, still under the pseudonym. The pseudonym was Alfred Venison. Not only that but Alfred Venison was "Alfred Venison, the Poet of Titchfield Street," and on the cover of the pamphlet was printed a statement about the poet Venison by Pound himself: "Only Social Credit could have produced this poet." That was 1935. Within a year or so it became harder for Pound to be comic and he was not any longer able to deny, as he had to an old professor friend in

1934, that he was losing his composure: "No, doc, it won't do. You ask anyone who has met me or any one of a hundred correspondents about my being embittered. Disgust is one thing but letting it get into one's own private Anschauung is another."

WCW was at first mellow with Pound's own mellowness about the "money cancer" and as a preliminary to writing his own essay he wrote approvingly to Pound (1936) of Pound's words on Social Credit and said that now was the time to bring the scheme to the American public since "the American political upheaval" had "practically eliminated the Communist Party" (as much as anything he was still angry at *PR*) so that it seemed to him to be "THE moment for directing sane minds toward the need for an actual radicalism." Writing his essay he then made most of Pound's Social Credit points. He made no fascist connection, any more than Pound had done in his *New English Weekly* summary. That was not in the cards yet but he did distinguish between the Social Credit route to the millennium and the nasty alternative of the Dictatorship of Labor. In other words the *PR* episode was over and he was letting all the Marxists go hang except H. H. Lewis while he tried, not very successfully, to figure out how he himself could sit on a political fence.

He delivered his Social Credit essay as a lecture in Charlottesville to members of an institute of public affairs. In it he was particularly insistent — perhaps because he felt he was speaking to conservatives? — that Social Credit would not destroy but would reinforce and preserve individual freedoms even as it went about knocking down the usurers and big monopolists. He labored hard and managed literally to praise rugged individualism, though qualifying its virtue by admitting that it sometimes was antisocial. He cited three modern examples of rugged individuals — Lenin, Mussolini, and his own grandmother — then went back to punching the bankers. It was not only that the bankers controlled the government and controlled (and bled) the poor, but also that they controlled literature by encouraging commercial potboilers — the lowest thing they could do.

The speech was strong, and he was as right as rain about the bankers, and he could expect as little result from speaking out against them as American reformers can ever expect; but whatever the members of the public affairs institute may have thought of the speech they probably wondered what movement the good doctor represented. Major Douglas and Pound had had a hand in the speech but in the end it was a speech describing WCW's own private movement.

Which was probably lucky. Pound, following Major Douglas and Social Credit, was soon deep in a bog from which he would never emerge safe. Had WCW accompanied him he might not have been safe either, but he did not and soon the letters between them tapered off. By the late thirties Pound had been living in Italy for more than a decade, was enamored of Mussolini and the strength of his government, was behind on — though convinced that he was ahead of — the literary and cultural affairs of both England and America, and had little on his mind *except* Social Credit. He had written three economic documents — his *ABC of Economics,* something called *Impact,* and his *Jefferson and/or Mussolini* — but getting them published was another matter. Even Eliot, by then an editor at Faber and Faber in London, was not interested in Pound's money schemes and tried to divert him from them by asking him to write an essay on Robert Bridges. Pound could still be comic about *that* and Robert Bridges immediately became his old enemy Rabbit Britches, someone who had written perhaps ten lines of Worse Libre. In a letter written on Monday Pound thought he might actually do the Britches article, but on Tuesday he wrote Eliot again to say no, he could not write about Britches because "the number of putrid pigs in England" was so large that to dig one up for reburial was inexcusable "unless one were absolutely in need of feed." At about the same time he wrote dozens of other persons urgently, and with less humor, about money and how to deal with it, including Ernest Hemingway. "Waal, me deah Hembo," it began and then advised Hembo to reflect on how money started wars:

Banks make 90% of all buggaring money, of all exploding gun-
runnun gunselling jawbreaking and eviscerating and . . . amputat-
ing money that goes into buggarin shells for the bloody, was it a
WAR

Pound's wit was deteriorating by then, as his letter style began to
show, and when he came to the U.S. in the summer of 1939 with
nothing in his head but money and the determination single-
handedly to swing American opinion — in the right place, mostly
in Congress — over against usury and America's anti-Axis stand, he
could only be violently anti-Semitic in his polemics against keeping America out of an evil war. He visited WCW briefly in that
time — they must not have seen each other since 1927 — and that
visit may well have been the real end of their mellowness together
though WCW was still trying to listen:

> I found, unfortunately, that he has acquired a habit of avoiding the
> question at issue when he is pressed for a direct answer. Not so
> good. But he does go, he does see the important faces and he does
> have some worthwhile thoughts and projects in hand. I like him
> immensely as always, he is inspiring and has much information to
> impart but he gets nowhere with it, "a static explosion in a granite
> quarry" is the way Munson spoke of him. The man is sunk, in my
> opinion, unless he can shake the fog of fascism out of his brain dur-
> ing the next few years, which I seriously doubt that he can do. The
> logicality of fascist rationalization is soon going to kill him. You
> can't argue away wanton slaughter of innocent women and children
> by the neoscholasticism of a controlled economy program. To hell
> with a Hitler who lauds the work of his airmen in Spain and so to
> hell with Pound too if he can't stand up and face his questioners
> on the point.

WCW was not speaking like an inarticulate animal in that letter,
and he had Pound well diagnosed. Pound, after failing in his
congressional mission, went back angrily to Italy. Both before and
after the United States entered the war he made his celebrated
speeches on Rome radio protesting American involvement in the
war, speeches which became the chief immediate occasion for his

being declared a traitor. When the American soldiers moved into northern Italy at the end of the war in 1945, Pound turned himself in to them and was for his pains put in an outdoor pen at Pisa with other prisoners. Then he was returned to the United States, first under indictment as a traitor and then as a mental patient in St. Elizabeth's Hospital in Washington. During the course of that terrible decade — a decade that extended to nearly two decades before he was finally released to go back "home" to Italy in the care and custody of his daughter — WCW sat on the sidelines wondering what had happened to his old college chum.

Pound's fate was not pleasant and must have had much bearing upon the fate of WCW's own politics. Eliot had been an obsession with him, now Pound became one. In 1938 Pound gave him merely a "more than usually severe pain in the ass over his pro-fascist sympathies" but by 1944 Pound and Eliot were paired in his mind as elitists, "having turned their backs on . . . coarse language" and by 1946 Pound was a "bastard and a son of a bitch in the fullest vulgar meaning of the terms." Yet the progression even then was not all down and away; in 1946 he also wrote to Pound himself in St. Elizabeth's and apologized for having been so nasty: "I feel ashamed when I lose my temper over you . . . it's a shabby business, you in an asylum and I much too occupied with my own affairs, to carry on this way — like two children."

CHAPTER SEVEN

Imperative Without Closure

By THE LATE THIRTIES the children, the real children, were both heading out into the world. Young Bill had been a roamer since 1931 when he spent a summer as a bellhop on a ship that sailed through the Panama Canal. As an undergraduate at Williams he wrote home letters not unlike WCW's University of Pennsylvania enthusiasms, saying that he was in with a swell gang and the food was swell and the courses a snap. He went on to Cornell Medical School as brother Paul made the most of the University of Pennsylvania, catching an enormous catfish at dawn, after an all-night party, in the tiny pond behind the dormitories that Pound had been thrown into by seniors in perhaps 1903. After Pennsylvania Paul went on to Harvard Business School and beat Bill into marriage. Both were ripe for the war in 1941.

To liven things up came, in 1938, the greatest hurricane of the century for the Northeast, and WCW was caught in it with his mother, Elena. Elena had been staying at the shore in West Haven, WCW had driven up to return her to 9 Ridge Road for the winter, it was a fine clear early fall day; but as they drove west and south on the old Boston Post Road suddenly it was not fine and clear but raining and blowing, trees were falling in the streets, electricity was failing, gas pumps were not running, a policeman waved madly at them to beware (how, he didn't say) the dam of a reservoir that might burst — but WCW and Elena drove through it and Elena, who had been bred up in hurricane country in the islands, was heard to observe that it was really a very big storm, wasn't it, almost like a hurricane.

The Depression tapered off. WCW and Flossie discovered that they had money again when a bank they had lost savings in decided to pay sixty cents on the dollar. And although literature was not yet ready to contribute more than pennies to the family kitty WCW was able to have published, in the late thirties, two books that by his previous sales standards were wild best sellers, *White Mule* and *Life Along the Passaic River.* The success story was beginning that would move in less than a decade to *Paterson.* But WCW was coming on sixty.

He had a new publisher for his books starting with *White Mule,* James Laughlin, a Harvard boy with money who skied and played tennis and wrote poems and looked up to the avant garde. WCW had failed for some years to sell *White Mule* in book form when Laughlin came into his life — introduced as always by Pound — and made an offer for it that sent WCW to his typewriter to exclaim, "My God! It must be that you are so tall that separate clouds circle around that head." Laughlin was tall but the offer was merely that he would pay for the book's publication and then share the profits if there were any — and it seemed unlikely that there would be. WCW was so accustomed to the deficit financing of literature that the offer sounded fine to him, and when the book appeared the next year (1937) it was well received by a few reviewers and that was fine too. The small first printing of 800 was soon marvelously gone, making WCW delighted with sales and New Directions until he discovered that that meant there were no more copies to sell (like any greedy author he had traveled to Macy's and found that Macy's had none) and that his tall young publisher-hero was in New Zealand skiing where he could not be reached to order a new printing. A delay occurred that in WCW's opinion lost the big sales moment. The New Directions glow dimmed.

But a second printing finally took place — though Laughlin hedged on it and had only 300 copies actually bound — and then the short stories were published (1000 copies, 1938) followed by a new volume of collected poems (1500 copies, 1938) that was twice as big as the 1931 Objectivist Press book. WCW kept glancing hopefully in the direction of Madison Avenue for a publisher with really serious distributional intentions but he didn't find one — not at least until the fifties — with the result that he stayed with Laughlin for many years. Sometimes Laughlin was "the one publisher, creator of the earth and of the spirit of literature amen," and sometimes he was an annoyance because he didn't spend enough time at his publishing business; but all in all he was (and both Pound and WCW from their long miseries with other publishers knew it) a big new force in American publishing.

Laughlin had gone into publishing casually, taking the name "New Directions" from the title of a poetry section he had edited in a magazine while at college. His first book effort was the publishing of an anthology of modernist poems and stories that he announced would be annual. Annual it was to be (and it is still going), testimony that though he might be casual he was also persistent. WCW was to appear in the annual many times and to sponsor other poets' appearances there, and Laughlin as editor was to meet half of literary America in the process of bringing it out. It was simply at root another literary magazine but since it was bound as a book and distributed as a book it added another dimension to little magazine enterprising. Chiefly it gave Laughlin an "in" to experimental writing that big commercial publishers tended to neglect.

And aside from the anthology Laughlin had from the beginning Pound and WCW. They were the heart of New Directions. Like WCW Pound was pleased with Laughlin from the beginning, nor did he defect (perhaps he didn't have the chance) as WCW did. In Laughlin Pound finally saw his dream realized: a publishing house that would not only print reams of Pound but also serve the cause of literature in other ways that Pound wanted it served. Laughlin did avoid the potboilers, did stick with the new, did publish works that had no dollar signs sticking out (though he could pennypinch as he did so) , did respect the authors' wishes and not aspire like Harriet Monroe to improve all of God's literary creation with a red pencil, did in other words listen to Pound and WCW. The results are now evident in any good bookstore and they are impressive: a five- or six-shelf spread of ND paperbacks of which about two shelves are Pound (fourteen books) and WCW (fourteen books) .

Of WCW's books *Paterson* is the big work, the epic. He began laboring at it soon after he signed on with Laughlin, and he was gratified to watch Laughlin bring out each of its five books separately in handsome editions on good paper with big print as WCW completed them, and to follow up with publication of the first two books together, then the first three, then the first four, in cheaper editions. The final paperback, containing all five books and the fragments of a sixth book that WCW was working on at his death, was published in the year of his death, 1963. By then *Paterson* was a much celebrated phenomenon in literary circles and though it was perhaps more celebrated than read it was celebrated for other than the usual reason for epic celebration, that it simply was an epic (all writers need to write an epic, even if unreadable, to prove to the world that they are serious and important) ; it was celebrated because it contained the WCW aesthetic in a loose 246-page nutshell, an aesthetic that by the time of the fifties and sixties had suddenly been discovered to be of the essence of true modernism.

For readers who are not wholly persuaded that *Paterson* is absolute mint-and-vintage WCW there is the temptation to regret WCW's creative expenditures on it, to ask if he would not have been better off if he had kept pounding away at the modes of the early poems, the thirties short stories and the late plays. But WCW had to do *Paterson* the way Pound had to do his *Cantos,* and though Pound worked longer on his *Cantos* and perhaps suffered more in their writing than WCW did with *Paterson* — suffered because of the energy pouring out to the insatiable and finally unfinishable work — still the two men's relations to their respective efforts were similar, as were the works themselves though an ocean flowed between them. For both poets their epics were their *necessary* works, necessary not only because every poet is owed an epic by his muse but also because both epics were efforts to put everything between two covers. Pound's biography could be written out of the *Cantos*. *Paterson* is smaller and its actual creation did not begin early with WCW as the *Cantos* did with Pound; yet the background of *Paterson*, like that of the *Cantos,* is all of the poet's life and thought. It is a dissertation on aesthetics and on knowledge as well as a poem. Or perhaps it should be described as an antiaesthetic or an antidote to conventional knowledge since it has the muddle-throughness of WCW at its ideological heart as well as his lifetime anger at the orderly unmuddled ones.

2

The *Paterson* beginnings precede WCW's thirties angers at the *PR* highbrows, and even his Eliot obsession that began with *The Waste Land,* going way back to *The Wanderer* before World War I. It was in *The Wanderer* that he announced he was going to root his poetic life in the Passaic Valley in all its stench and ugliness, and in *Paterson* thirty years later he did that; but the first poem that he actually wrote about the city of Paterson and called "Paterson" appeared in *The Dial* in 1926 — it was what won him *The Dial* award. In that poem he presented the central image of the later poem, the image of the city as a man, a man lying on his side by the river peopling the place with his thoughts:

> Inside the bus one sees
> his thoughts sitting and standing. His thoughts
> alight and scatter . . .
> that they may live
> his thought is listed in the telephone directory.

But the place was not just a manifestation of the thoughts. The thoughts were also a manifestation of the place, hence the poem's key line, repeated several times: "no ideas but in things."

There was the conception then, twenty years before the first book of *Paterson* was completed; but at the time the conception had little meat on it. Perhaps his most cogent aesthetic remark in the twenties was to a young friend, John Riordan, after Riordan and he had had an uncomfortable evening together and Riordan had stimulated him to think about his own thought processes:

> I can't take a situation for what it is, that's why I was "dead" in the studio. I must look and digest, swallow and break up a situation inside myself before it can get to me. It is due to my wanting to encircle too much. It is due to my lack of pattern . . . As I exist, omniverous, everything I touch seems incomplete until I can swallow, digest and make it a part of myself. I thank you for making this clear to me, you have been an invaluable friend.
>
> But my failure to work inside a pattern — a positive sin — is the cause of my virtues. I cannot work inside a pattern because I can't find a pattern that will have me.

In other words it was not only ideas and things that had to be interlocked but form and experience. If *Paterson* were to have a shape to it the shape would have to be something that he would come upon by living with the town, making it a part of himself. He could not be arbitrary and impose a shape but had to wait for the shape to announce itself. *Paterson* had to just grow.

And it did just grow, in his mind, for another fifteen years before he began really to work on it, but there were many steps in the mental growing. One small incident in the late twenties was especially productive, demonstrating to him that the arbitrary ones around him who could and did work within prescribed patterns could be more foolish than he. In 1929 his son Bill, who had learned a good deal of French in his year in Switzerland, found himself flunking French in Rutherford because he didn't know French the American way, the way the teacher did. The occasion was one to make of Bill's parents instant advocates of organic learning.

Both WCW and Flossie seethed. Eventually the teacher was appropriately chastised but that was not the end of it for WCW. Soon he was busy composing 130 densely typed pages of educational philosophy that he entitled "The Embodiment of Knowledge" — and he actually put an account of young Bill's trouble in as chapter two.

The essay, or collection of essays, was heavily a polemic against the knowledge establishments. It went through the deficiencies of science, philosophy, and education as if those three were soldiers who had been bad and had luckily been detected, and then it proposed an alternative to them all, namely poetry, poetry the true way to knowledge, poetry as WCW conceived poetry. Poetry was the good soldier, poetry had the truth. Or at least it had the truth if it began with things, with the actual, and never lost touch with those immediacies. Poetry that was properly beholden to the immediacies did not allow the cultural interferers to take over, interferers like young Bill's French teacher.

WCW had high hopes for "The Embodiment of Knowledge" and wrote Kenneth Burke, among others, that he thought it one of his most important efforts, but it rested quietly and unpublished among his papers for forty years until Laughlin decided to bring it out. In 1974 it was finally put into print with an introduction by an academic convert to WCW's theory of how knowledge should be embodied, Ron Loewinsohn, who drew a three-page analogy between WCW and a black basketball player, Bill Russell. Loewinsohn said that both demonstrated their knowledge in action and both had learned what they knew by their struggles against the conventional; Russell against the stereotype of blacks, WCW against conventions of "poetic decorum." Loewinsohn praised "The Embodiment of Knowledge" as a landmark in the history of organic theories of language and learning, finding in it William James, Dewey, Whitehead, and Jean Piaget as well as poets; but he failed to stress what any reader coming to the book would benefit by being told (especially since the price tag was $18.75), that it was deadly reading. It was WCW at his most abstract and least coherent. As far as WCW's career was concerned it was not a success but it did point toward *Paterson*.

Among the intellectuals WCW was taking issue with at the time of composing "The Embodiment of Knowledge" there was at the top of the list, as always, Eliot — he would never lay off Eliot — but beyond Eliot there were the academic literary folk whom WCW thought Eliot represented, those busy becoming New Critics who were good at analyzing poems and stacking them up against the tradition but had, he felt, no sense of the thing itself, the basic raw poem. These intellectuals plus the *PR* people and other highbrow politicos in the little magazine business comprised a body of good minds that he would be in and out with for years, being grateful for their praise of him (the praise did at last come) and angry with them for their blindness or smallness or prudery. They were the orderly minds who drove him to his disorders, but behind his running ideological war with them there was an underlying psychological discomfort; he did not feel at home with them even when they were on *his* side. Thus in 1948 when his reputation was suddenly shooting skyward and he had been invited to be a distinguished presence in a summer writing program in Utah with the formidable Eliot-lover Allen Tate, he sat down, became orderly and read a book on prosody. To catch up with Tate.

He seemed always mildly astonished that academic people could like him, being convinced that they thought him a member of "the lunatic fringe." His surprise at academic acceptance was part of his general astonishment, touching in him, that he was what he was at all and that there were human receiving sets in the world who would listen to him. After giving a poetry reading in 1940 he wrote off to a friend, one of his plebeian kind:

> I watched them closely and what do you suppose I saw? The MEN leaning forward eagerly in their folding sunday school chairs LISTENING with their mouths open, fascinated. I could hardly believe it. You could have heard a pin drop as I told them about my wife's new pink slippers etc.

His modesty, mixed in with his determination and his strong defensive assurance that there were things that he could do that the great ones and the much educated ones could not, stood him in good stead in the end; but along the way the ambiguities of his intellectual life kept showing.

A pleasant manifestation of the confusion came about just before *Paterson*, in 1939, when Ford Madox Ford suddenly singled WCW out as a model of American imagination and intelligence. The Ford episode was eccentric in the best Ford way and it could have become either a great joke or a significant moment for American culture if Ford himself had not been desperately ill — he died less than a year later — when he proposed that WCW be the titular head of a new cultural society based in New York City. Ford had been in the U.S. for some time trying to make an honest dollar at writing and at an occasional academic job. He found himself in 1938 at a small college, Olivet, in the middle of the flats of Michigan saving, as he conceived it, the curriculum there while he scribbled eccentricities in his vast and arbitrary history of literature soon to be published as *The March of Literature*. All his life he had loved to tell whoppers and at Olivet he kept on telling them, reporting to a friend, "I am in demand for reorganizing the literary departments of several universities." He then performed the first specific act that he could think of that might give the reorganizing a boost, namely the hiring of Pound at Olivet. The WCW episode, also something of a whopper, was to come a few months later.

In early 1938 Ford wrote Pound that he should seriously consider coming to the U.S. He said that Pound had been too hard on American educators and should give them a chance to be educated. He offered Pound his own job, despite the curricular challenges he said he was facing, and sat down to wait for Pound's answer so that he, Ford, might be sprung from Olivet and enabled to go to New York. But Pound's reply was discouraging. Pound wanted to know if Olivet was using any of Pound's texts in its reformable curriculum (it presumably was not and would not be) and he also said that he wouldn't under any conditions take his friend's job. Ford pled with him, announced his own deathly sickness, but Pound was unmoved, would not come (though he did sail for America a year later in the spring of 1939 to save not

Olivet but the country — only to be told by Senator Bankhead in Washington that there was nothing a man like Pound could find to *do* in Washington) . Ford then set about departing from Olivet anyway, was given an honorary degree there in June of 1938, and traveled to New York to try to finish off two books. He also went there to set up, perhaps as an antidote to the Olivet failure, the small but amazing organization called "The Friends of William Carlos Williams."

It was amazing to WCW anyway. He reported in his autobiography that he never understood the reason for the group and that it "horribly embarrassed" him, but Ford's biographer Arthur Mizener located a grand educational reason for the group in the letters Ford sent out to people he wanted to become members. "Between ourselves, but see that it is strictly between ourselves," he wrote the president of Olivet, "I am trying to get a kind of academic Goncourt in this country for the benefit of more thoughtful and widely read writers . . . and if the funds should run to it we would probably give an annual prize like the Prix Goncourt." Obviously Ford had in mind something like Pound's *Bel Esprit* of the twenties when Pound undertook to save civilization by saving Eliot and others *from* the civilization, and so it was to be expected that Pound would like the scheme. He did, though with skepticism about its workability:

> A "sort" of Academie Goncourt *could* be used as prod to the useless Institute of Letters . . . THAT body if seriously criticized/ Murry Butler strangled and Canby educated or drowned *could* be useful . . .

WCW seems not to have realized that the organization was more than it professed to be, a group of friends, though he should have smelled a rat since the friends were about half not friends at all but simply big names like Archibald MacLeish, Mary Colum, Waldo Frank, Sherwood Anderson. But at least if he had known he could have taken consolation in having been chosen as a fourteen-carat symbol of an antiacademic intellectual ("thoughtful and widely read"), the kind of person Olivet and the other moribund brain centers needed. "The Friends of William Carlos Williams" did not do much more than eat and drink, and WCW remembered the eating occasions as embarrassing because dollars were laboriously collected, but one of the parties was at Carl Van Doren's apartment and Ford himself cooked the meal. "That night," said WCW, "the fried plantain was fine and we had a good time of it."

3

And then Ford died. WCW wrote a fine poem in his honor and "The Friends of WCW" lapsed and the war came along with the war's reinforcement of WCW's antiacademicism, all of which would appear in *Paterson*. It was first the quiet war when the Germans and the Russians were being friends and dividing up Poland, and when England was threatened and FDR was trying to give it fifty destroyers. On the question of U.S. involvement WCW sat hard on the fence with scores of others. He became a member of the Committee for Cultural Freedom, which was isolationist and, the Stalinists said, Trotskyite, and then resigned from it because it was *too* anti-Russian (for his pains he was immediately labeled a Stalinoid warmonger by *The New Leader*). Then when the Russians began invading Finland he had second or third thoughts about his stance and rejoined the isolationists by signing a document printed in *PR* and attributed to "The League for Cultural Freedom and Socialism" (not distinguishable ideologically from "The Committee for Cultural Freedom" he had just resigned from) in which the signators swore "implacable opposition to this dance of war in which Wall Street joins with the Roosevelt Administration." But though he did not know it he was readying himself to be a hawk and to deliver, as hawk, a blast against not only the academic establishments but intellectuals themselves, a blast that would not improve his image as a model of the "thoughtful and widely read."

His switch was slow. In mid-1941 when the Germans attacked the Russians WCW decided that "implacable opposition" to U.S. involvement was too strong but he did not, as so many at that point did, swing completely over. He did not at any rate swing completely over to the position known as (and scorned among intellectuals as) the MacLeish–Van Wyck Brooks American Front. For more than two years MacLeish and Brooks had been preaching a patriotic gospel that found the country's academic and literary intellectuals "irresponsible" in the face of the fascist threat, insisting in passing that most American writers were hopelessly isolated from serious social concerns and anyway much too highbrow. WCW shared some of these sentiments and would soon display them, but at the time of the German invasion of Russia in 1941 he was not quite ready. Instead he sided with Dwight Macdonald, who was attacking MacLeish and Brooks hard.

One of WCW's troubles in 1940 and 1941 was that he was looking so intensely at what was happening in England that he couldn't think straight about what was happening in America, whether among hawks or doves. The English were being bombed nightly by the Luftwaffe and he knew that he didn't like *that,* but he also knew that Eliot had sold out to the English and he didn't like *that.* So there he was, stuck with disapproving of the Nazis yet unsecretly pleased that England was getting her deservings. The unsecret part was in a poem he wrote for *PR* just before Macdonald attacked MacLeish and Brooks.

The poem was called "Exultation." WCW wisely did not reprint it in his books since few readers would have been confident later that there had been something to exult about. He announced in it that the bombing of Britain was an effective purge of British imperialism, "destroying the rottenness" of the London slums and giving Britain an opportunity to emerge purified. He had a long footnote to the poem about his own English heritage and how his old Grandma Emily had hated British imperialism; and in the footnote he could not refrain from mentioning "his contempt for and distrust of T. S. Eliot." The trouble with Eliot was that "he and others like him" had allied themselves "with that part of the English character" that deserved the bombing.

That was summer 1941, with Pearl Harbor approaching. In being isolationist WCW was on the side of many intellectuals he knew, but in being against a certain American-English intellectual he was also being, in the opinion of the same intellectuals, a troublesome antintellectual. His obstreperousness about Eliot hardly helped his intellectual credibility with fellow isolationists and when after Pearl Harbor he became a hawk like nearly everyone else he became such a very complete hawk that he alienated them further, that is, he wrote a short piece for *PR* in which he criticized less complete hawks than himself.

It was the time for that sort of thing, midwar. Both his sons went into the war, Bill first, a young doctor fresh out of Cornell into the Pacific where the land crabs would cart off his socks and to which WCW wrote him long letters full of medical pedagogy but little poetry ("You say you'd like to see my book of poems. What the hell? Let 'em go") and then Paul into destroyer service in the Atlantic. Paul had married before sailing into the unknown and had left his pregnant wife at home with WCW and Flossie. The absence of the sons and the presence of the wife brought the war close, as did the wartime medical pressures and all the local furor about what to do when bombed. WCW was in the war, everybody was in it, it was an undeniable presence and he was quite right to say (in an introduction to a small book of poems that he was lucky to get published in 1944) that the war was "the first and only thing in the world." Whether he was right to say what he said in *PR* was another matter.

The piece was called "A Fault of Learning." It was not a piece designed to endear him to brains and Delmore Schwartz of *PR* took strong exception to it. Though it was a wartime piece the essential message of it would not go away after the war but be incorporated in *Paterson*. He was working on *Paterson* during the war; he kept writing his friends about it and how difficult he was finding the writing of it, and clearly as he was writing it he was thinking of it as his one-man attack on the intellectual establishments. He said as much in a letter in 1943 to Laughlin, described it as an "assault" on the intellectual cults, an "infiltration into the dry mass of those principles of knowledge and culture which the universities and their cripples have cloistered." But *Paterson* was his long-term assault and could wait, whereas "A Fault of Learning" could not. It was a temporal blast and began by trying to demolish the writer Max Eastman for qualifying his support of the Russians at a time when their backs were against the wall and all the Allies were in the conflict to the death.

Eastman had been one of the American radicals most violently disillusioned by Russian conduct in the late thirties. He was no acquaintance of WCW's; WCW singled him out as simply a representative intellectual (though he had been writing not for *PR* but *The Reader's Digest*) and said of him that his hedging on the Russians was the sort of thing intellectuals always did. Then he went on to his big general point, which was that America had not been made strong by the intellectuals but by the nonintellectuals. The nonintellectuals, he said, had been "our greatest leaders"; they had "never been the brightest men of their times" but they had known what to do in a crisis. He celebrated Washington and Lincoln chiefly, noting their small intellectual accomplishments yet their enormous practical strength, and observed that intellectuals were not like Washington and Lincoln; they had brains but their views were "circumscribed" by "their passion for 'order' at all costs, how it stinks!" The wrong-headedness about order of the academics was something he was full of in that year; he had said to Laughlin in a letter for example (in connection with the writing of *Paterson*) that order should be thought of as what was "discovered after the fact, not a little piss pot for us all to urinate into." In brief, in "A Fault of Learning" he took the intellectual hedging about Russia to be a manifestation of all the mental vices he had been complaining about for some time.

Replying to WCW, Schwartz, who was no Eastman fan, wrote first a private letter to Rutherford as warning that a public statement against "A Fault of Learning" would appear in *PR* in the same issue as WCW's piece:

As one with intense admiration for your work for a long time I'd like to say that I have been unable for ten years to understand your hatred of intellectuals.

Obviously Schwartz knew that he was getting into hot water (it is too bad that WCW's replies to Schwartz are not in the Williams files; WCW must have been furious) but his words showed him deeply distressed and feeling an absolute obligation to speak out. In the magazine itself he elaborated on the letter and he characterized WCW's "hatred of intellectuals" by identifying it, though cautiously, with the common sentiments of a variety of tyrants. Then in an extended conclusion he sought out the reason why a "writer like Williams" — a phrase clearly intended as a compliment — should have undertaken "to reject outright the cultural functions peculiar to the intellectuals" and sadly discovered that the reason was the "debased cultural situation" that America found itself in in 1943.

Schwartz was not wrong. "A Fault of Learning" had gone about as far in dispraising qualities of mind as WCW could go and still not join the backslapping Chamber of Commerce Americans he had been so bitter about in *A Voyage to Pagany*. Even as a war document its urgencies were darkly misplaced. They made Eastman's complicated anti-Russian position a foible native to the intellectual mind, any intellectual mind, rather than a commonplace political stance in one of history's most complicated ideological moments. Schwartz felt the venom in the piece and justified his complaints with firmness and no malice, and the merit of his remarks was to be sustained when the war ended and the urgencies ended and WCW was to be found still beating the intellectuals over the head in *Paterson*.

4

And so Paterson the man, who was also a city, lay on his side by the Passaic River. In the first book he lived in the past; in the second he confronted the present; in the third and subsequent books he meandered; but in none of the books except the first was his character as the city dwelt upon. WCW settled on the man-city early, but having introduced him he was content thereafter to let him rest in the reader's imagination while the hero of the poem became the one he had always been for WCW, namely, the doctor-poet walking about and experiencing what he was experiencing. WCW was not good at personae; he had to be on stage in person in any extended effort. And since it was he in his own experiential shell who was the one quite openly receiving through his own senses all the thinginess that would lead to the poem's ideas and shapes, the character of Paterson was something of a dodge, though an important one. It was an aesthetic dodge to make the big ideological and psychological point of the epic, that each of us is our environment, a part of it, not separable from it. Each of us creates the world even as the world creates us and we must not seek to separate our private sensibilities from the big outside other.

We must not and yet do. A fault of learning. In his verse preface to Book One WCW insisted instantly that *he* did not wish separation; he pictured himself as "just another dog among a lot of dogs," learning "by defective means" but learning the natural way, "sniffing the trees." And throughout Book One he evoked nostalgically the early primitive man-city Paterson (before the craft of poetry was "subverted by thought" and "minds like beds" had become "always made up") when mind itself was a green and dove gray country and the Great Falls of Paterson spoke Paterson's language and the country above the Falls was the female in Paterson's life. But also in Book One he suggested the dark questions: why could the interlock between man and nature not continue? why did the natural language come to fail Paterson and his (its) inhabitants? why did "marriage come to have a shuddering implication," namely, divorce, and the ear of Paterson become a stone ear not hearing the Falls and their meanings? Oddly, these complaints about "divorce" were not personally connected in the text to WCW's own private solitude except in the letters included in the poem from a woman, "C," who raged murkily at WCW's failure to commune with her; but the general impersonality of the divorce remarks were of a piece with *Paterson* as a whole, which simply did not draw steady sustenance, like the rest of his work, from daily life. In any event the reason given in *Paterson* for the failure of "interlock" was that knowledge in the modern sense of knowledge had moved in on the primitive idyll and made divorce rather than unity the sign of knowledge. Though the true ingredients of knowledge remained at hand and so strong that their "stinking breath would fell us" if we had not removed ourselves intellectually from their presence, still we ignored them, insisted upon separation, and it was the custodians of the universities who had seen chiefly to the separation. The universities were run by "clerks" who had forgotten to whom they were beholden, "knowledgeable idiots" whose least sin was the negative one of failing to devise "means to leap the gap." A fault of learning.

In WCW's view the fault of learning was the imposition not only of a false and separate language upon men's minds but also of false orderings of art and experience. In constructing *Paterson,* therefore, he kept searching for a natural order, an order implicit in the mind of Paterson and the environment of Paterson. The search led him eventually to a collage form, a collecting and juxtaposing of incidents, memories, letters, newspaper reports, and conversations that were sometimes sifted and commented on by the doctor-poet and sometimes just deposited on the page as found things. It had the randomness of the old *Kora in Hell* form and it was the inherent form that he had long been campaigning for — yet, curiously in the constructing of *Paterson* he did not start with it.

When he first worked on the poem's parts he experimented instead with an arbitrary frame for them as if he were not sure whether he was playing the role of WCW the organic poet or WCW the conventional playwright. The frame he tried — and he went through several versions of it — was dramatic, a dialogue between a plain-spoken democratic character called Willie and an alcoholic medico called Doc. Willie and Doc were always busy talking and drinking, and arguing about drinking ("You're a brilliant physician, sir, and a contemptible drunkard") and Willie took on the big burden of the talk by reading to the drinking doctor passages from various histories of Paterson. In a few places in the manuscript the name of Willie became not Willie but Paterson but the frame was not otherwise violated. The passages that Willie read to Doc from the histories were to become the central ingredients of *Paterson*'s first book but they were presented in this early version as subordinate to Willie and Doc.

It was a commonplace scheme for order. If WCW had retained it the whole poem would have been hung on a conversational string in the mode, say, of Wilder's *Our Town* (ironically his enemy Eliot conceived of a similar string to hang the first draft of *The Waste Land* on, then at Pound's suggestion abandoned it). The poem then with its temporal progression would have been easier to follow and the temporal order might have urged order elsewhere. The poem would have been a discursive event, a long evening's chat with dozens of illustrations — in other words a rational chat. But after struggling with Doc and Willie through several drafts — and after comparing in his own mind the Doc-Willie stratagem to the plan for *The Canterbury Tales* — WCW must have realized that a rational chat was just what he didn't want. A rational chat would have been a fault of learning, an imposing of a false order from above.

And so he scrapped Doc and Willie and switched over to building the *Paterson* collage from moment to moment. The collage of Book One became largely a clustering around the word "divorce," with ancient instances. What he was reaching for was an order that existed within the experience, the life of the city of Paterson itself, an order that he would discover rather than impose. In reaching for that order — which the philosophers would perhaps call an experiential or phenomenological order — he was trying to do with his epic what had been part of his modernist gospel for small poems for decades; but the epic's dimensions made the project a new kind of labor for him, new in the magnitude of the intuiting needed. It was all very well to fiddle with the parts of a short poem until the poem was "right" somehow and the poet could feel its rightness by just reading it and going away from it and coming back to read it again; but to intuit the whole of the man-city in all of its manifestations from its earliest historical beginnings? That was a big intuiting.

He had to proceed in that manner anyway. That was part of the imperative of the poem for him, to open himself to the possibilities of the city and the falls and the hills above, to open and receive whatever there was to receive. He had begun with a plan but the plan was gossamer. He had casually studied the history but the history was anecdotal and partial, at best only a small contributory stream to the flow that the poem had to be. What he had chiefly done, and had chiefly to continue to do to finish the poem, was live close and long with the "stinking breath" of the city of Paterson, and then live close and long with his own private and mysterious attic energies as they worked on *Paterson*. It was a passiveness in the end that he had to cultivate, not a passiveness of sense but mind. Antiintellectual?

The conservative critic Yvor Winters was for many years fascinated by WCW's work, being alternately repelled by what he thought the failures of mind and attracted by the "sensuous and emotional awareness" and the "beauty of execution." He felt even more strongly than did Schwartz that WCW was distrustful of the intellect, and he went further than Schwartz in dispraising him for it, calling him "a foolish and ignorant man" who "did not know what the intellect was." And because Winters prided himself so much on his own rationality he had only at last the option of seeing WCW as a sort of poetic cripple, one who could do very well what he could do but was kept from the larger enterprises of art by his handicap. Was Winters right? No disciples of WCW would now agree and yet the passivity to order in *Paterson*, and the insistence in it upon living with the stinking breath, could probably not have pleased old friend Pound much more than Winters. In the end Pound was one of the damned intellectuals too. *Paterson* did not, despite many connections, go the way of the *Cantos*.

5

It is not clear whether WCW and Pound thought of each other, as they grew apart, as unable to commune because they were of different species or because they were separated by force of circumstance. Pound had always been patronizing about WCW's incoherence and WCW had always been mildly contemptuous of Pound's intellectual pretensions, but they remained sympathetic despite these opinions until the late thirties, and praised each other's work in public and private as if they were basically working for the same ends. They both had long agreed for example that the educational establishments were corrupt and the managers of high literary destinies misbegotten. They both had said yes there must be no iambic, no gumming together of stock responses, no polite verses about God and trees. And for decades they had written each other comforting letters in which the assumption was always that they were both indeed in on the same poetry revolution and possessed of the same aesthetic gods even though Pound was the expatriate with the grand foreign ways and WCW the simple American homebody. They had in other words lived with each other as brothers in their art and had both moved to the big works in their lives with a sense that they were sharers. How could it be that those big works should turn out in the end to have little in common?

It is a curious lesson in human nature to watch two persons who think they are in agreement — because they were born in the same block or belonged to the same fraternity in college — commune with each other up to the moment of truth when they discover that they are miles apart. WCW and Pound discovered each other to be miles apart because of Pound's obsessive fascism — it could not have been pleasant for WCW to find himself quizzed by the FBI during the war because Pound had mentioned his name over Rome radio — but from a distance, now, the difference between them seems to have have gone deeper than the politics and the obsession. The difference in the end was a difference built deep into the two poets' conceptions, as seen in Pound's *Cantos* and WCW's *Paterson,* of what a poet was and did.

When Pound was just beginning with his *Cantos* his exotic friend Yeats reported of the poems that Pound had a wholly arbitrary rational plan for their ordering, a mathematical plan by which their main themes would be run up and down against each other through all the possible mathematical permutations and the essential architectural unity would be visible at Canto 100. That was Yeats talk of course, big, and Yeats was reporting on Pound talk, also big; and since the *Cantos'* big hypothetical order never did emerge it might be sensible to imagine that the two poets were at the time simply reinforcing each other in their schemes as Yeats dabbled with his own mystical numbering system and Pound wondered how the dickens to hold an epic together. But beyond the big talk there was probably a truth. Pound was a schemer, synthesizer, maker of mental bundles, and when he began the *Cantos* he was taking on everything. Later he lowered his sights and the *Cantos* became a history of money but even that was a big intellectual order, a history of money in Greece, China, medieval Italy, and contemporary America and Europe.

In contrast, though he was trying to think big too, and though as will be seen in his mental gyrations about the "variable foot" he too could be mystical about numbers, still WCW scaled his epic to what he could take in with his own senses — plus a few study trips to the eccentric Paterson castle-museum in the hills above town where hung nineteenth-century firearms and pictures of President McKinley staring down benignly on Paterson's primal capitalists. When WCW read at all as a scholar-poet doing research for his work he read local history, history accumulating in a single county in Jersey, and anyway he did not need to read widely because the main action of the poem was not historical but contemporary and the prime sources were on the streets of Paterson. Where was the world? The world was for WCW a hereness, a thereness for Pound, and though Pound was as dutiful as WCW in the enterprise of putting sensuous immediacies on the page he was like a painter copying the old masters in the Louvre rather than one setting up his easel on a river bank. There were traditions that Pound was contemptuous of, but of tradition itself and of the past he was continuously and bookishly aware. WCW the complete American was not.

And Pound was ideologically bookish too, *not* believing that ideas began in things. Ideas began in heads and then the heads went around looking for things to reinforce the ideas. What was it that the *Cantos* were aimed at and dedicated to? — at putting over an idea, a single luminous idea that one could document and back up from all the histories of all the cultures but remained something that first and last needed to be known as idea, an idea that Pound thought was the *key* to everything, an idea that he kept shouting to the hills and discovering that the hills refused to understand. At the beginning of the late group of *Cantos* called *Pisan Cantos* he summed it up: "and with one day's reading a man may have the key in his hands."

What was the reading to be? It could have been selections from Major Douglas or John Adams, or Pound's own *ABC of Economics* or the *Cantos* themselves (those parts dedicated to pointing out what John Adams had pointed out, that "every bank of discount is downright corruption/taxing the public for private individuals' gain") but these particular readings could have been other readings and the key another key and still have displayed Pound's distinctive quality of mind, a quality WCW did not share.

The quality was not particularly evident in Pound's first 30 *Cantos,* and accordingly WCW had admired those, had admired Pound's technique of "cracking up . . . words and natural word sequences" to get away from the made-up-like-beds mental world of conventional poetry. But the middle *Cantos* (those numbered

30 to 70 and written mostly in the thirties) found Pound steadily
driving home a message, and accordingly ordering the *Cantos*
largely as loaded chronology. There were pages and pages of perfectly sequential, sometimes boringly sequential historical narrative without breaks or shifts, narrative whose forward movement
was reinforced by endless three-and-four-stress lines with end stops
that made the music as steady as a church recitative. Some of these
regularities rose to grace and elegance, as in Canto 55 ("with
usura/wool comes not to market," etc.) , and some of them sank to
unedited tedious listings of trivial facts and figures, but they were
all steadily indicative of the rationalist bent in Pound that had at
last been let out of the bag.

Paterson was destined to go the other way, like WCW. Pound
was a reformer and had a key. WCW was a reformer too but had
no key; he had only a process or a theory of process. There was
nothing that could be read in a day that would sum up everything
that he had to say, and there was no order that he could find in
the library in somebody else's book that he could apply to his own
book. There was only the living and the writing and that was endless and undirected — and for him crucial in its endlessness and
undirectedness. So when he got into *Paterson* he felt that the
writing and the living were going on concurrently in him as they
had done in *Kora*. As he wrote he went to the river for relief from
"meaning"; he went to the falls to make a verbal replica of them
that his word "disease" might be cured; and he went to his desk
and wrote just to write, hoping but not planning for something
productive, something beyond the mere writing. As he wrote he
raged against those who had grand plans beyond the writing. It
was his "assault" on the old learning, and on Pound, Eliot, the lot.

It was also an assault on the Englishness of American literature,
and here too he split off from Pound. In the early days it had been
Pound who had led him in the fight with the language traditionalists, Pound with his "ear for the sea surge" (as he said of Homer in
Canto II) , that is, the mysterious natural properties of language
not mentioned in textbooks. But from the American sea surge

Pound had become detached; he had no recourse to language on
the streets of Paterson or any other American town. Also he had
long immersed himself extravagantly in the languages of the old
cultures that jammed his shelves, a further distraction from the
immediacies of everyday speech. In his *Cantos* the sea surge became not only uncontemporary but it took on cadences from all
over — a bit of the Bible, a bit of Longfellow (the insistent femi-
nine endings), a bit of eighteenth-century prose. The poems still
had the *spirit* of the rebellious American aesthete in them but the
sounds were from afar. Not so *Paterson.*

WCW conceived of *Paterson* as American to the last syllable.
The language in it was to be the American language whether it
was the beautiful natural language of the Falls or the unbeautiful
language of American bureaucrats. It was to be the American
language with none of the cadences of the wicked Mr. Eliot in it.
WCW was with H. L. Mencken on this, Mencken whom he had
come to admire in the thirties. In reviewing Mencken's *American
Language* he paraphrased Mencken's position approvingly: "we're
still a colony as far as our badly tutored minds are concerned. We
don't quite dare, do we? to say that we have a language that is our
own." In return, Mencken shared WCW's anti-English view and
also his contempt for English teachers: "the great majority of
English teachers avoid [common speech] as if it were poisonous."
But built into WCW's insistence on the integrity of American
speech was something beyond what Mencken was campaigning
for; WCW would have been delighted for example with the recent
efforts of linguists in both England and America to demonstrate
that language is learned almost everywhere *except* in the class-
room, that it arises out of the primal and social and familial scenes.
He would have loved such experimentation as that in London in
the sixties by a linguist who strapped little tape recorders on little
children from different parts of the big city and took the results
home and listened. Listening was the thing. WCW felt deeply
that the trouble with languages in the schools, beginning with
young Bill's French teacher, was that the language teachers didn't

listen. They issued orders instead. They prescribed the languages. They took it upon themselves to fit the languages to predetermined molds when all the time the languages were unmoldable, were organic essences growing according to their own rules and destinies. WCW had believed in language as a growing thing for years and it was in *Paterson* that he both promoted the belief and tried to let the poem be a sort of exempluum of the growing principle. Pound could never have carried his sea-surge faith that far; he preferred to have the language emerge not out of the people but the *right* people.

6

Aside from the ideological strands weaving their way into *Paterson* there was the practical side of just getting the thing together. It was, after all, partly a research project and WCW was no researcher. He had had Flossie's help with his other historical venture, *In the American Grain;* now for *Paterson* he had the help of a young Irish woman who had come to him for a good diet for her baby, Priscilla, and revealed herself as a playwright and aspiring novelist. Her name was Kathleen (Kitty) Hoaglund. She and WCW met socially for the first time, she reports, in 1935 over creamed chicken and after the chicken he read poems. Soon WCW had her performing editorial functions with *White Mule* and the short stories. She was married to a literary journalist, Clayton Hoaglund, who worked on the editorial page of the *New York Sun* but also wrote book reviews and brought to Rutherford such literary giants as the 6'9" Minnesota novelist Feike Feikema (of him WCW said, "Where did you get that big fellow?"). The Hoaglunds lived within a few blocks of the Williamses, and Kitty's presence as a literary assistant as well as speller and typist gave the WCW production line what it needed, especially with *Paterson* and the plays. To WCW's playwrighting Kitty contributed practical (and conservative) stage concerns — she being active in the Rutherford Little Theater, which before World War II was intense and lively (among her projects for it was a play version of WCW's story "Life Along the Passaic River") — and for *Paterson* she did some of the legwork and helped paste the pieces together. She reports that much of the historical matter for the early books was taken verbatim from a WPA historical project in New Jersey called *The Prospector,* that she herself wrote up one of the prose passages, that she took it upon herself to cut down on the interminable letters from "C" that WCW wished included (after her cutting they were still interminable) and perform other severities for which he was grateful. Her comments on the constructing of the poem suggest that the collage impulse was fully in charge as WCW brought Book One into its last stages, that he was little concerned with the details of the "found" passages but thought of them as items to be pasted randomly on his big poetic canvas to perform vague services for the poem's texture. He busied himself with the poetry itself, he walked occasionally on Garret Mountain above Paterson trying to make it a part of himself, and Kitty helped with the pastings. At last Book One was done (1945). Would it work?

He was not himself optimistic. As he read proof on Book One he wrote his proletarian friend Fred Miller that he felt he had worked on it too hard and too long; he thought that "it had no flow" and that "diarrhoea would have been a little better." When Miller read it and praised it WCW was most grateful for the reinforcement, saying that it would help with the three parts to come: "I'll do them with greater confidence if I feel as I am coming to feel that a couple of friends are behind me." He was in other words not thinking he was off the island yet, nor could he see in his crystal ball that he would be soon. He had just been conspicuously omitted from the highest-powered poetry anthology in the country, Conrad Aiken's collection for Modern Library, and he had no reason to suppose that *Paterson* would change things. How isolated he felt shows in a project that he and Fred Miller concocted together at the same time that Miller was reading *Paterson* One, a concoction that had all the marks of literature as therapy.

The two had a jazz evening together listening to Bunk Johnson in Greenwich Village and met there a strange editor-novelist-jazzman named Moon whom Miller thought would be a good model for the central figure of a novel. WCW thought so too and soon they were writing the novel together and WCW had located a third scribbler needing therapy to add to the mash, a female with a flair for Victorian sentences. The idea as WCW put it was to "run wild . . . no holds barred" and they did. Soon they had three different stories going about "Moon" in three different styles and WCW was pleased with the game, thinking it would be "a lot of fun" though perhaps not "grreat litrachoor," and announcing that the chapters should be allowed "to fall where they will." As for WCW's version of "Moon" it was definitely not great literature but it was predictably a WCW character, one whose primary interest was writing, who started writing at midnight and did not stop until breakfast, who thought that the place for Eliot's *Waste Land* was in the WASTE basket, and who generally conducted himself as a knower of the dog-sniffing-the-trees kind, meanwhile scorning the "well groomed campuses." The whole document came to be called *Man Orchid* (with a subtitle, "Lives on Air") and as a sample of WCW's sourness on intellect, on intellectual establishments, and on the impossibility of an audience coming to be interested in his work it was convincing. Yet in the letters WCW wrote to Miller about it at the time there did linger a defiant hope that something might happen sometime to beat "the Alan [sic] Tates, the T. S. Eliots and their little *PR* pupils." As the events of the fall of 1946 began to prove, *Paterson* One was the something.

Paterson One came out in all its doggy antiintellectualness in June 1946, and in the fall with great prescience the University of Buffalo gave WCW an honorary degree. That degree was the first of a series of capitulations to dogginess on the part of the intellectuals, and it was the work of Charles Abbott of the university's Lockwood Library. WCW was delighted. He had already been persuaded to give an atticful of papers to Buffalo, and he and Flossie had been feted by Abbott at a fine country house east of Buffalo belonging to Abbott's wife's family, the Gratwicks, where one day WCW was made Poet Laureate of the Tree Peonies (he was driven on a tractor to a lily pond and crowned). Becoming a genuine L.L.D. was an even mightier distinction, especially for an antiintellectual. Then came the reviews.

The first big one appeared right in the enemy camp, in *PR,* and was unstinting in praise and set the tone for the general critical reception of Book One. One of the delights of the review was that it had been written by a poet WCW had regarded as a frivolous academic. WCW had been furious with him in 1940, calling him a "professional literary sophomore," and now the sophomore was grown up and had been won over completely. He was Randall Jarrell.

Jarrell did not have a mind like a made-up bed but he had been snippy in 1940 about the uncerebral works of the poet Kenneth Patchen and also about the kind words that WCW had spoken about Patchen. WCW read the Jarrell complaints (which were also in *PR*) and sat down right away to have a letter-to-the-editor day for himself. His letter was printed in the magazine's next issue, describing Jarrell as "one of those who turn up from the universities now and then to instruct us out of the book in our errors." He added, "I for one detest them as I detest plant lice." So now this particular louse was saying that *Paterson* was the best thing WCW had written and that if WCW could keep it up he thought the complete work would be "far and away the best long poem any American has written."

Another poet reviewer was Howard Moss, who announced in *The Kenyon Review* that *Paterson,* as judicable by Book One, was the "ultimate justification" of everything WCW had written and a poem founded on "very major premises" that everyone needed to attend to. And hard after Moss came Robert Lowell in *The Sewanee Review,* outdoing everyone in praise. *Paterson* was better and more important than anything written by "any living English or American poet" and if WCW kept up the pace in the next books the work promised to be "better than anything since The Prelude."

It was not a landslide; someone in the Newark paper panned it

for its incoherence and WCW wrote Kitty Hoaglund that the review "tickled" him, adding, "Let 'em flounder, that's part of my
intention"; but the big (and scholarly) were now suddenly aston-
ishingly on his side so that he in old age would perhaps after all be
able to sit comfortably in his attic and glow with the thought of all
the seven-year locusts finally discovering his work He could also
proceed with Book Two.

He did. Book Two was published within two years. It was less
well received by reviewers than Book One but brought down on
his head a new intellectual honor, The Loines Award of the
National Institute of Arts and Letters. Wallace Stevens wrote
immediately to explain what a distinction the award was and what
a fine person Loines had been and WCW replied thankfully and
humbly, asking Stevens what he should wear to the ceremony.
Stevens replied, "You should wear what you wear every day," but
WCW had been so smitten with the highbrowness of the award
that he had written not only Stevens but Tate about what he
should wear. Tate's reply:

> Faded vine leaves as a billet around the brow; a breech clout tied at
> the navel with sea weed; the staff of Hermes, a caduceus, in the left
> hand, and in the right a bunch of sour grapes.

All this attention was fine and it led to the writing and publishing
of both Book Three and Book Four within the next three years,
books that were attended by still more attention, with Book Three
winning him the National Book Award and putting his picture in
the papers standing beside Nelson Algren, another winner, and
Eleanor Roosevelt. The only trouble with Books Three and Four
was that they did not live up to the hopes that Jarrell and Lowell
had had for them. In fact despite the honors they were disasters.

Books One and Two had been loosely ordered but they had not
been merely miscellaneous. Book One had had a mishmash of the
Paterson past in it — the natural setting, the early settlers, Alexander Hamilton and his national-industry plan — but it was not
without clearly controlling themes, notably the dog-sniffing-the-

trees and the divorce theme. It went on for forty scattery collage pages but it ended with a series of demonstrations of a single premise, that "earth the chatterer" was the "father of all speech." Howard Moss in his review of Book One might have been overstating the case when he called it "beautifully ordered" but it had the feel of order about it, being much more carefully put together than, say, *Kora* or *Spring and All,* and it also had the promise of future order since WCW announced with Book One's appearance that there were to be four books in all and that the general composition of the four parts was to be as follows:

> Part One introduces the elemental character of the place. The Second Part comprises the modern replicas. Three will seek a language to make them vocal, and Four, the river below the falls, will be reminiscent of episodes — all that any one man may achieve in a lifetime.

That was hardly a detailed plan but it was something, and Book Two in presenting the "modern replicas" was perhaps more straightforward in its shape and direction than Book One. It brought the female principle in thoroughly, giving Paterson a woman to live with in the form of the public park above the falls, and it reinforced the abstract female with the letters from "C," a real female writing annoying letters about the blockage between people, this being Book Two's version of the divorce theme. Most of all Book Two had a clarity of time and place that Book One had not had and that subsequent books would not come close to; its action occurred mostly on a single Sunday afternoon in the park above the falls, with the Paterson working people out in the park in force and an evangelist preacher orating to them of the evils of money as they stretched out in the grass and drank and made love. Beside such formal simplicity Books Three and Four were collages in earnest.

Book Three tried to be, as advertised, the seeking of the language and it did say a great deal about language — but did not find what it sought. Of all the books it was the most firmly antiaca-

demic — was this because the academies were by then (1949) giving WCW degrees and medals? — and it could not leave off
battering at the "stagnation and death" of libraries, at symbols, at
the "stain of sense." What it tried to do was balance the canned
qualities of art and culture as found in the learneries (Pound's old
word) with the real beauties of flesh and earth but the trouble was
that it was itself full of a straining after the kinds of meaning that
the learneries were being criticized for encouraging. It was full of
symbols like a burning library that burned for pages as prepara-
tion for something better than libraries, and an enormous tapestry
with a dog and a unicorn on it that seemed like a detail out of
the wrong poet.

There were two or three interesting personal notes about writing in Book Three, such as an ironic mimicking of what WCW's
neighbors must have been saying about his writing ("We're so
proud of you!/A wonderful gift! How do you find the time for
it/in your busy life?"), and there were also one or two good gen-
eralizations about the organic writing process, notably,

> What is more clear than that of all things nothing is so unclear, be-
> tween man and his writing, as to which is the man and which is
> the thing and of them both which is the more to be valued.

But the chief fault of the book, and it was a grievous one, was that
the book was given over largely to pleading the organic language
cause; it was argument concealed as collage, and since WCW had
never been a master of argument anyway, and since argument was
pretty much all that held the book together, it was not held together.

And Book Four (1951) was the same except longer, denser and
more miscellaneous. It was academically pretentious in its antiacademicism, having a pastoral dialogue in it between two Renaissance lovers named Corydon and Phyllis who were up to date and
talked American, and drawing misty highbrow analogies between
the uranium atom and a city (or money) (or love). It had complaints about usury, it had quotations from WCW's mother, from

Norman Douglas, from Billy Sunday, it had a page of miscellaneous quotations printed droopingly slantwise and a page of statistics about soil layers to the depth of 2000 feet. It had in fact everything because it had been programmed to have everything, having been designed in the original plan to be "reminiscent of episodes, all that any one man may achieve in his lifetime." And because it had everything it showed that its order was finally not order at all. It showed, that is, what had not been evident to Jarrell and Lowell when they reviewed Book One, that the movement of the whole construct was necessarily *away* from the wonderfully mysterious organic order that WCW reached for in the early states to mere episodes, perpetual collage. WCW had not foreseen the total formal collapse in the early stages, imagining four books and an end; but after he had passed the planned end he himself discovered the truth about what he was doing and put it well when he said, some years later:

> I have come to understand not only that many changes have occurred in me and the world, but I have been forced to recognize that there can be no end to such a story [as] I have envisioned with the terms which I had laid down for myself.

That was his explanation for deciding that Book Four was not an end after all and that he would write a Book Five. Which he did. And he was at work on a Book Six at the time of his death. *Paterson* was scheduled to return and return, to maintain the essentially formless form of the work in its final five-book printing; and the endlessness of it was in the end the real imperative for him. The imperative was deep in the "form" and he knew at heart that it was — and sometimes he even bragged that it was — the imperative being his basic existentialist writing stance — but he was not willing to accept the cruel fact of the imperative that though it was an imperative to action it was not an imperative to ordered action. It was the old imperative that drove him to write every day when he was doing *Kora,* write to get something down, write to bolster his inexhaustible hope that if he kept putting it down something would come of it; but unlike his old aesthetic his *Paterson* aesthetic had large formal pretensions too, pretensions that he was encouraged to cultivate by new disciples who congregated about him in the fifties.

He was not encouraged long by his earlier encourager Jarrell. Jarrell backed off on *Paterson* after his praise of Book One. He was sorry to do so; he still felt that WCW was "one of the best poets alive" but he found that the three books following Book One were "worse organized, more eccentric and idiosyncratic, more self indulgent, than the first" and he quoted Flossie herself against the later sections, Flossie as WCW had quoted her in Book Four saying that she missed "the poetry, the pure poem of the first parts." Jarrell concluded in 1952 that WCW was "a very good but very limited poet," being a "notably unreasoning, intuitive writer" and "not, of course, an intellectual in any sense of the word." The louse from the academy had become a louse again. He was reinforced by a British reviewer in *The Times Literary Supplement* who admired WCW's short poems that had attended to "the sharpness of things, to smallness and accuracy of detail" but was skeptical of the new larger effort, "the kaleidoscopic quality, the lack of verbal density — even the absence of memorable and quotable passages." Fortunately the louse from the American Academy and the British reviewer could be written off as manifestations of WCW's old Eliotesque enemy. *Paterson* went on.

CHAPTER EIGHT

The Romance of Writing

Iɴ 1940, when Flossie was off on a vacation, WCW wrote to her of growing old and said he thought the best thing was to discount the ills and be thankful for having lived at all. Off and on he had been worrying about his chief ill, a heart weakness, ever since a doctor at Horace Mann School had told him he had strained his heart while out for track and should never again indulge in violent exercise. The doctor had been wrong, WCW had been able to play tennis and baseball as well as to swim and hike into middle age, and had had no further attacks following the school episode, and little other sickness, until he was past sixty. As late as 1939 he professed to be happy about his physical condition, and while he was vacationing with Flossie at her parents' farm in New York he bragged of digging, using a scythe, and even like Frost of cleaning a spring (though he didn't mention Frost, didn't like Frost), and said he felt it was right in his bones to work with his hands: "I suppose I'm a masochist. I love to take a beating that way." But he was not fated to be able to take a beating that way much longer; soon he began to think sickness and age.

In a play that he finished in 1940, called first *Trial Horse # 1* and then *Many Loves,* he presented three of the main male characters as moving in rapidly on decrepitude while the major female characters remained comparatively young and without physical blemish. One of his males was a senile comic-strip-reading uncle who died unobtrusively on stage of a heart seizure, the second as a doctor who lapsed gracefully into drinking and reflecting upon his lifelong female attachments, and the third was an aging homosexual patron of the arts who watched his young man, a poet, go off with a woman. This last character, the young man, also had a good measure of WCW in him though he was young, for he was destined to leave his woman to cool her heels while he wrote, and wrote. The psychological burden of the play — as distinguished from its on-stage concern with presenting "many loves" and showing that each love had a flaw — would seem to have been that WCW was thinking of himself as an aging parent with deteriorating physical equipment and loaded with life's obligations, yet also a poet in spirit, hence young in spirit, and radical, and obligated to no one. The romance of writing did not desert WCW, and unlike many of those who followed his lead in the fifties and sixties he was able to realize many of his writing ambitions. Of course he wished for more than he achieved, and many of those who succeeded him in poesy wished for more yet — there being no end for the wishings as he and his most loyal backers conceived poesy — but as he not only wished for writing but really did write, his was a romance with a happy (mostly) ending.

But for that ending to be a properly mellow twilight of writing and talking of writing it seemed first necessary to have free time, which meant disposing of the doctoring. But the doctoring was cruel again in the war years with all the young doctors being shipped off like son Bill to remote posts. There were doctoring rewards such as the young soldier who came to WCW about his sex life, then wrote him a painfully intimate letter describing what he had done with the girl to make him sure, yet not sure, that it must have been somebody else who had made her pregnant; but if WCW was good at playing father confessor to naive and straightforward lovers he was also reaching an end of his patience with the role. He was once more faced with long evening office hours, house calls, and interminable hospital visitations that pushed him too hard physically. In 1942 he canceled a poetry reading at the Young Men's Hebrew Association in New York — a big opportunity and of a kind that he was increasingly enjoying — because his "very shoulders" ached. He was able to take a short vacation that year at the Gratwicks' estate but the vacation only served to remind him that he wanted a vacation that didn't stop. He was surrounded there, he reported, by 18,000 volumes, a number he found "terrifying," and in various visits to these volumes over the next few years he took on a good many opuses that a dedicated antiintellectual would have been wise to omit, such as Butcher's translation of Aristotle's *Poetics* ("thrilled me beyond words") and Henry James's *Wings of the Dove* ("I won't go far in *that*") ; but chiefly when he was able to retire from his intensities he was reminded (when he was not dreaming of new ways to restore the intensities) that he was old, that he had worked hard, that the time was upon him to slow down. After the 1942 visit he wrote Abbott,

> If the mind permitted it I'd hire myself out at food and lodging to be your gardener for the next ten years with the special privilege only — to write . . . I'm good at caring for children though. I'll bet I could fit in.

That was not the letter of a young revolutionary though it is true that at the same time he was also busying himself with angry letters to *PR*. He was as always pulled several ways but certainly the consciousness of his physical need to respect his heart was strong upon him, as was the old middle-class pull, now renewed, to be a docile husband and father. He found himself in his new oldness looking reflectively back at the longevity of his marital state and liking it mostly, saying to Flossie, "we've gotten used to each other. It's been a hard time breaking down our diverse resistances," then essaying the extravagance that they were probably nearer together than they had ever been (and then withdrawing it: "That's a typical declaration of love on my part. I'm a hell of a declarer of love"). He had plenty of angry energy left in him to fill the bins of *Paterson* One and Two but the caution signals were up. The first health storm hit him in 1946 when he had to have a hernia operation.

It was just at the time of the publishing of *Paterson* One. The first operation didn't take and had to be repeated. For the second he moved from his own hospital, Passaic General, to New York Hospital, where he reported like a hick from the country on the hospital's wide doors and on the amazingness of knowing "nothing about the whole matter" but of waking up just where he had been when he "passed out." His recovery then was good; he and Flossie had a healthy 1947 during which they drove across the country at about 400 miles a day to the Utah Writers' Conference where he competed with Tate about prosody (and made, it should be added, friends with him. Would he not have done the same with Eliot?) ; but in 1948 he was truly stricken, stricken with the first of the steady series of heart attacks that darkened his last fifteen years. That was February 1948. He first described what had happened as a minor anginal attack but the attack proved to be serious enough to lay him up for three months and make him pleased that after the three months he was able to drive and move about at all. He then wrote to Abbott, "They tell me that IF I BEHAVE I'll be all right pretty soon." He soon was sufficiently well to take on a semester's teaching job at the University of Washington but the end of well-being was upon him. It was an end that came in the middle of *Paterson,* in the middle of praise, citations, and awards, in the middle of what in a better world would have been a beautiful place to begin.

How heavily the heart trouble lay upon him in the late forties was especially evident in probably the best play he ever wrote, *A Dream of Love* (first called *Trial Horse* #2), which appeared in print eight months after the attack and was staged a year later. In the final version of the play the doctor hero who had an eye for the women and a wife who had put up with the eye for years, was taken with a heart seizure while making love to a certain Dottie in a New York hotel room — and died on the spot. His death left the play heroless in the middle of Act II (though the hero was resurrected in a dream for part of Act III) and gave the heroine the job of converting the play to her own, making it the story of her coming to terms with the husband's infidelity *and* death. In an early version, however, the hotel scene was present without the death and the wife's problem was infidelity only. If an actual event of this kind occurred in the lives of Flossie and WCW it must have been smoothed over swiftly in 1948 — that, or it must have occurred well before 1948 and simply been combined in the play with the heart seizure — since there is no indication in the 1948 correspondence that there was any marital crisis of the dimensions approached in the play. Yet the play remains otherwise so close, so characteristically close, to the WCW-Flossie scene that its biographical relevance is hard to dismiss. The Doc in the play is a poet and a doctor who wants to get out of medicine; he is absent-minded and loses his car keys; he is short-tempered and furious about losing them; he is calmed by the efficient wife who finds them for him. He is also ready at the drop of a hat to confuse women and poems, and to say that he needs both women and poems to prove his worth. Meanwhile the wife is annoyed that the Doc throws himself away on worthless women who take advantage of him, and on literary deadbeats who do the same. She can't control herself sometimes and gives it to him:

> Oh, come out of it, you dirty, lying cheap guy! If you don't want me why don't you say so and let me get out? Go with this woman or that woman — or man or boy or little girl or anyone your mind will lead you to. I don't care what you do but I demand that you tell me, in so many words, what you promised this woman before you dropped dead in bed with her.

Yet the two of them together, having been kicked around by all kinds of people (kicked around, as the wife puts it, by "your literary friends and the shits of this town") are tough in the marital service and would clearly have been able to make up and go on if it had not been for the heart attack. The play ends with the wife taking hold of herself, beginning again to cope.

Particularly close to home was the following scene, omitted in the final version:

She: We've been so particularly happy . . . I've forgiven you what
you have done in the past. I've never felt so close to you or so
happy.
   We've shed the two old women. The boys are independent.
We're not old. Why now? and can't you contain your self. It
isn't what you do it's the betrayal of our love not mine.
He: Is it that
She: Is it not that
He: I can't tell
She: Can't you really tell? To me it is so clear. Something I have
[not clear] wanted for all my life. Since the first shocks of our
married life.
He: Is it that? Is it really that? To me it's more a kind of game
when I am closest to you. Then I wanted to be [away?] I say to
myself, the better to return. When you are away I am indifferent
to all others. Why when you are closest do I want to break and
run. To tempt disaster, and I am not even particularly able . . .

In a letter to Flossie at the end of 1948, when he had recovered
and had gone out to Seattle [so that he could be away from her
and therefore be close?] he wrote that he might have been over-
doing it but that his head was clear and his "guts comfortable" and
that he had given a poetry reading in which he had really had a
sense of being a performer — and as for their love? "I kiss you
sweetheart and have only one hope, to live with you a little while
longer in peace and see the boys get a little rooted in this world."

2

   The boys did get a little rooted. By 1949 they were both married, with Paul in business and Bill, having completed his New
York internship, preparing to move in on his father's practice, and
one of the daughters-in-law praising WCW's writing for being the
difference between steak and beef stew — "straight and clear — all
meat — thank you I love it." WCW was especially confident that
having Bill in the office would help bring the peace that he wished
for, and he and Flossie were therefore unhappy in 1948 when Bill
flunked by two points his Jersey state medical exam (he had
passed the New York exams seven years earlier but neglected to

make a conventional credit transfer before the deadline, and had then been too busy to cram for the Jersey exams). What flunked him was pharmacology, with parental indignation extreme and Flossie penning a draft of a furious letter to the bureaucrats starting with "your honor" but quickly descending to the spectacle of Bill being made "to sit here like a bad boy until October" for a rotten two points. WCW scribbled at the top of the letter, which was presumably never sent, "any time during those seven years he could have got his transfer to Jersey for one hundred dollars." Bill did at last make it into Jersey.

And once Bill was installed the pressure in the office receded. He and WCW worked together for a year or two until the transfer was complete, and in that final doctoring period WCW seemed ebullient, sassy, his old self. Or so at least Brendan Gill has reported. Gill interviewed him for a *New Yorker* Profile around 1950, and even went with him on his rounds, discovering that "despite his age and damaged heart he was lacerated by sexual excitement; every young mother . . . encountered seemed to strike him as a Venus." Gill went on:

> Williams and I would pull up in his car in front of some not very savory looking bungalow, and Williams would slap my knee and say, "Wait till you get a look at this one!" We would ring the bell, and the door would be opened by some slatternly woman in her late 20s or early 30s, wearing a soiled rayon dressing gown and with her dyed hair done up in a dozen or so pink plastic curlers. She would have an infant in her arms, purple faced from screaming and with diapers unpleasantly tapestried, and the odds were that however sick the infant was, the mother was suffering from something equally unpleasant at the very least, so I seem to remember, a severe case of postnasal drip. Williams wouldn't be daunted. He would examine the baby, write out a prescription, and then spend five or ten minutes in happy banter with the dull, distracted, and wholly undesirable mother. Back in the car, he would be breathing hard and radiant. "What a girl!"

Shades of the nighttime doctoring described in *Kora in Hell,* and of such stories as "The Girl with the Pimply Face" and "A Night in June." Shades also of the scene in *Many Loves* where the amorous doctor sits around with Clara, drinks wine, admires her, and confesses to her,

> Women! With their small heads and big lustrous eyes. All my life
> I have never been able to escape them.

Gill reported that he decided against doing the *New Yorker* Profile at the time because he felt there was "no way to tell the truth," at least in public print, of WCW's "joyful, indiscriminate amorousness." Yet WCW had been bragging of that "truth" — and probably exaggerating it — for decades. In any event he still felt himself healthy enough in 1950 to keep confirming his yearning for *nuevo mundo* females.

And the presence of young Bill on the scene made it possible for WCW to try out his health in another way, by taking trips. Aside from the 1948 term of teaching at the University of Washington (he was alone on that excursion and wrote Flossie his worries about staying up late drinking with Ted Roethke) he made two other trips to the West Coast, both with Flossie. One found him on the poetry circuit starting in Seattle and moving south; the other put him in Los Angeles for a single engagement after which he and Flossie returned via El Paso where they visited the ailing and sad Bob McAlmon who was working for his brother — and they partied with McAlmon in Mexico and, returning across the Rio Grande bridge, saw a small heap of humanity beside the bridge railing ("an inhuman shapelessness, knees hugged tight up into the belly") that became the dominant image of a long poem that he wrote for a Harvard appearance, *The Desert Music* (Flossie reported loyally that the poem in its straightforward frankness offended Harvard). And one summer they even embarked in Cincinnati on a refurbished paddle-wheel boat that steamed them to New Orleans.

But of all the possible projects that came WCW's way as he moved into retirement the most attractive — or so it first seemed — was an invitation to be Poetry Consultant at the Library of Congress. A sinecure it was described as — and it was meant to be;

there was nothing to do, it was an honor; one didn't "consult" but pontificated on a few formal occasions and otherwise just wrote — and so he looked forward to it as a year away from Rutherford which would also be the occasion for formally hanging up his stethoscope. But the Library offering did not in the end bring peace. Nor did a new three-book contract that he signed with Random House in 1949. At a time when his health required that he be quiet he managed not only to pin himself down to writing obligations without precedent in his life but to become involved suddenly in a brouhaha with the Library of Congress about his alleged communist past.

The Random House contract was the result of a falling out with Laughlin together with the move of one of Laughlin's editors, David McDowell, to Random House. In the end the contract was fulfilled by a book of short stores called *Make Light of It* containing stories from two earlier books plus new ones, the *Autobiography,* and the last and least novel in the Stecher trilogy about Flossie's family, *The Build-Up* (Laughlin had printed *White Mule* and *In the Money* before the war). Putting together the short-story collection was easy but the other two books were tough assignments and were written against short deadlines. "I had the respect of any businessman for a contract," said WCW. He wrote "rapidly and carelessly," said Flossie. He completed the autobiography (1000 pages in manuscript) in considerably less than a year, had another stroke as a result of it, recovered, and went on to do the novel at the same speed.

The affair with the Library of Congress was even more debilitating but in a different way. He was invited first to the Consultantship by Librarian Luther Evans in 1948 (for 1949–1950) but was obliged to postpone taking the job because of his health. In 1949 he was made one of the Fellows of the Library, too late to be in on the awarding by the Fellows (including Eliot) of the Bollingen Prize to Pound for his *Pisan Cantos* but not too late to come to admire Librarian Evans for his conduct during the Bollingen affair. At the time the affair seemed likely to destroy the Library and it did cause the removal of the Award from the Library's jurisdiction (the money for the Award was private money and the Fellows were private poets, but Congressmen and others were outraged anyway that an award should be given through a Federal agency to a man who had been indicted as a traitor) but Evans stood by the Fellows and the Award was at least not revoked. A year later WCW said of Evans, "Had he not stood like a rock for the Fellows they would have been wiped out." And yet two years after that statement WCW regarded Evans as the chief villain in his life.

WCW liked being a Fellow, and from the one or two meetings he attended concluded that the Fellows were a "good gang" (he did not have to include Fellow Eliot in the goodness since Eliot, in London, did not attend the meetings). He could see, he said to a friend, that the Fellows wanted to do something for literature though they had little power to do what needed to be done, especially at "our schools of learning." Meanwhile Elizabeth Bishop became the Poetry Consultant in place of WCW in 1949–1950, followed by Conrad Aiken, and when in early 1952 WCW indicated to Evans that he was now well enough to take on the job he was invited to come in September. He arranged with Aiken to rent Aiken's apartment near the Library on Capitol Hill, and he began to wind up his medical affairs; but then once more his health betrayed him. First he became inordinately depressed, writing Charles Abbott,

> Something's come over me that has knocked me off my feet, something personal, you might properly call it an illness — of a nervous sort. It's been going on for the past two weeks . . . My illness, my nervous instability has me seriously disturbed . . . I know I'm a coward, many have greater burdens to bear than I, in fact I have none, but I am nevertheless in trouble.

What had come over him bothered him so much that he travelled to Boston to see his poet-doctor acquaintance Merrill Moore, a psychoanalyst, about it. The episode passed, he and Flossie went off on vacation to the Gratwick estate near Buffalo, and it was there that he had what Flossie later described as a severe stroke and suffered temporary loss of speech. Flossie, writing immediately to Merrill Moore, was told that the speech loss definitely indicated another "vascular accident," that WCW was going to have a series of them and that they would be followed by "one great big one" after which he wouldn't get out of bed. Moore recommended, however, that he take on the Library job anyway — "he could take it easy there" — and so it was arranged with the Library that WCW arrive in Washington for his sinecure three months late, in December (a press announcement of the appointment had already been issued by the Library in August).

But in October a busy poetess who read of WCW's appointment made the news by announcing that WCW was a Red. This was at the heart of the time of the naming of Reds, the Hiss time, the McCarthy-Cohn-Nixon time (Hiss was in jail but the papers were still full of it) and the busy poetess suddenly felt that it was her duty to write an open letter to the subscribers and contributors to the little poetry magazine *Lyric,* of which she was editor and publisher (one of the few little magazines in the country WCW had had no connections with) to tell them of the wickedness of WCW. She said that the appointment of WCW to the Library was "an insult to American poetry and American citizenship." WCW had lent his name, she said, to various communist causes and he had written lines of verse that were "the very voice of Communism." She cited as a communist line, "Oh Russia, Russia, come with me into my dream," which had appeared in a WCW poem entitled "Russia" that had been printed in *The New Republic* in 1946. Apparently she did not approve of WCW bringing Russia into his dream, and she managed to miss the main point of the poem, which was that Russia had long been a dream to Americans and WCW wished that Russia would now live up to the dream. Certainly the poem did not proclaim, as she suggested, that Russia had lived up to the dream *yet.*

Her letter was summarized in a brief piece in Washington's Hearst paper of the time, the *Times Herald,* and that account was followed up by a nasty reference to WCW's appointment by the

Red-hunting journalist and radio commentator Fulton Lewis. Nothing about these accusations appeared, however, in either the Washington *Post* or the *New York Times,* and since at the time the *Post* and the *Times* were preoccupied, as was the rest of American journalism, with the Red issue, and since Adlai Stevenson, running for President against Eisenhower, was being Reddened daily by the right (typical headlines: "Nixon Declares Adlai 'Color Blind' on Reds"; "McCarthy Makes Scathing Attack on Adlai") it seems clear that the non–Red-baiting press was not impressed with the *Lyric* editor's charges, and that there was nothing at first particularly unusual or newsworthy about them, such charges being standard daily fare at the time in the lives of many Americans with little or nothing of the Communist Party in them. Why the Library of Congress should have been impressed is therefore not clear, especially since Librarian Evans was famed for having "stood like a rock" during the Pound trauma. But the Library was impressed. The evidence that it was impressed was brought to WCW and Flossie in the form of a letter from Assistant Librarian Verner Clapp that was addressed to Flossie and arrived in Rutherford in mid-December, about a week before WCW planned to assume the Consultantship.

The details of what happened from this point on would not be worth recounting if they did not have bearing upon more than the ways of bureaucracy, but they do. They show WCW at bay in the land of those he had always called puritans and they show these puritans reacting, just as brother Edgar reacted, to WCW's inveterate gift for impropriety. Furthermore, what the Washington bureaucratic puritans did to WCW in December 1952 and thereafter would have driven persons far less gifted in impropriety than WCW to be ill-bred, and so the affair has implications beyond WCW. A spokesman for the Library, Roy Basler, has described the affair as "much misunderstood," meaning that the Library did not conduct itself as heartlessly as friends of WCW have imagined; but even when reading Basler's version of what happened one is hard put to find anything to misunderstand.

Assistant Librarian Clapp's letter was written to Flossie rather than WCW out of concern, reports Basler, for WCW's health, but if that was so it was the only concern the Library showed. The letter informed Flossie that the Library had suddenly been obliged to await a "full investigation" of WCW through the channels of the Civil Service Commission before allowing WCW to take office. The full investigation was necessary because the preliminary and normally perfunctory loyalty investigation of WCW that was required (then and now) by law for anyone receiving a federal appointment had, for reasons not given in Clapp's letter, not cleared him. Clapp did not of course mention the editor of *Lyric* — he may have been unaware of the existence of an editor of a *Lyric* — but what he also did not mention was whether the Library had any stake at all in backing up its own appointment in the face of the investigatory people's action. Apparently Clapp, and subsequently Evans, thought the Library had no stake in it. Otherwise they surely would have reassured WCW at this point that they were going to do what they could to see to it that the job remained his. WCW and Flossie traveled to Washington after receiving the letter, met with Clapp and others and received no such assurance, even according to Basler's account. What they were told was that "a hearing before the Library's Loyalty Board would be afforded if necessary after the full report had been received and evaluated." Basler reported that "the visit terminated on a friendly note" but then acknowledged that WCW "seemed to be understandably annoyed and nonplussed." Who would not have been? WCW went home and hired a lawyer.

The lawyer and WCW composed a statement to Librarian Evans to the effect that "WCW had been ready to take up his duties on December 15 and that he did not waive the right to either the job or the salary." It was this action that converted Librarian Evans to a fierce rock of another color than during the Pound episode. In a letter of January 13, written perhaps not coincidentally two days after WCW had won, with Archibald MacLeish, the Bollingen Prize — now emanating from Yale — Evans called the whole thing off including the loyalty investigation: "After full consideration I have determined that the condition no longer exists which at an earlier date made your appointment appear desirable and profitable . . . I accordingly hereby revoke the offer of appointment heretofore made to you." He added, twisting the knife in the wound, that his action had "nothing to do with the allegations about your loyalty" but was brought about by the "Library's view" of WCW's health and by WCW's hiring of the lawyer. In other words nobody was going to hire a lawyer to preserve his rights and get away with it with Evans.

WCW's adrenalin did not need this sort of encouragement, and even in retrospect Evans' action seems as uncivil and dictatorial as it could well have been — but it was only the beginning. WCW's lawyer wrote Evans back that WCW was not happy about Evans' "self-appointment as an expert" on WCW's health and said that WCW would now "not permit the FBI investigation to lapse." David McDowell of Random House followed the letter up at the FBI itself, pleading with them to investigate WCW "relentlessly" — but the FBI took instant refuge in bureaucratic procedures, saying that since WCW was "no longer on Civil Service rolls [had he ever made it *to* them?] they could not investigate him further." There then came flurries of meetings of Library Fellows in New York, commiserating letters from Fellows to WCW and at last a "heated talk" with Evans for several hours by two of the Fellows, Leonie Adams and Cleanth Brooks, with the result that Evans agreed to be less of an expert on WCW's health if a statement by a "qualified physician" vouching for his health was put into play, and to revive the loyalty investigation if WCW undertook to "disavow" his claim of a right to the disputed appointment. It was like Gilbert and Sullivan, but not funny, with Evans in effect making no concessions at all. WCW gave in, obtained a physician's certificate and wrote the Library to say that he had no intention of suing anyone. And on April 24, 1953 — two months before the period of the Consultantship would be for practical purposes over anyway (the office was vacant in the summer) and four months before it would be officially over — Evans wrote to say that WCW had been appointed to the job again, the appointment to become effective May 15 "or as soon thereafter as loyalty and security procedures are successfully completed." The investigation was in fact completed on June 26 but was never "evaluated" by the Library.

And WCW was not told. Months and months later he went to his lawyer again, complained (the complaint reached the pages of the *Times*), and was advised by the Library that the case was closed.

Did it matter? Any of it? In March 1953, during the course of these unpleasantnesses, WCW had another heart attack, and he also suffered another siege of mental depression, this time so severe that he was put in a mental hospital on Long Island and Merrill Moore wrote a letter advising Flossie of the merits and demerits of shock treatment. WCW did leave the hospital before June and he would have been able to sit in his Library office for a June day or two before the summer holidays and the end of the appointment — but what good would a day or two have been?

In the first place it need not have been just a day or two. Considering the nature of the case Evans' most reasonable and benevolent gesture would have been to make the appointment effective through the *following* year; he could readily have done this in his April letter if he had wanted to, since there was no other poetry consultant lurking in the wings and there would *be* none for four years so traumatized was the Library by its poet troubles. And in the second place, even if the appointment had been for just a day it would have been an important day, a day of WCW's exoneration from whatever it was the appointment had been kept from him for, a day of being removed from limbo. In other words it could have been a day for Evans to mend fences with WCW if he had been so disposed. But he was not so disposed, a point that Basler's paragraph describing the June events managed to avoid:

A full report was received from the Civil Service Commission on June 26, 1953.

In the interim, however, on June 15, 1953, the Executive Board of Unesco, meeting in Paris, had nominated Luther H. Evans to be Director General of Unesco, and on July 1, 1953, the General Conference confirmed the selection. On that date, Dr. Evans resigned as Librarian of Congress, effective July 5, 1953. The President of the United States did not nominate a successor to the post of Librarian of Congress until April 1954. Meanwhile, the term of Dr. Evans' offer of an appointment to Dr. Williams expired in September 1953. Thus, the investigative report received on June 26, 1953, was never evaluated.

Since the clearing of WCW's name was of the order of unfinished business the departure of Evans (which did not anyway occur until after the receipt of the loyalty report) should have made no difference in the handling of the "evaluation," and if Evans had been in Paris or Timbuktu at the time he should still have arranged that action be taken.

WCW made up with the next Librarian, Quincy Mumford, and received from Mumford a letter, which he was able to make public, that he had not failed to receive security clearance. And nearly twenty years later the *Quarterly Journal* of the Library published an anthology of poems by the Library's poetry consultants in which poems by WCW were included (with no acknowledgment of permission having been received, the only exception in the anthology). Unfortunately WCW was described there merely as a consultant who did not serve. If WCW had been alive he might well have gone to his lawyer about *that.*

3

Beyond the Library's angers and mincings there was of course the Communist Party charge itself. It was wrong, like most of the Communist Party charges of the time, but the wrongness was based on more than a misunderstanding of what it meant to sign an antiwar statement in 1939 or to write a poem called "Russia" in 1946. The wrongness was in the view that the *Lyric* editor, not being of any modernist persuasion, seems to have had of modernist poetry. Modernist poetry was radical stuff, therefore communist. In fact the communists had for decades disliked modernism more than they disliked the likes of *Lyric,* and for them WCW was a characteristic modernist (except perhaps for his thirties stories). Back in the thirties the most typical Party response to what WCW stood for appeared in a letter to *PR* when WCW had disgraced himself by finding incompatible the American tradition and Marxism. (The angry letter writer said, "the whole school of modernist writing of which Mr. Williams is such a shining light has made no dent on the American consciousness." See page 256 of this text.) WCW had put himself out of play then ideologically by his individualistic disrespect for party lines, and aesthetically by his insistent experimentalism, which inevitably made his verses difficult and unpopular whether the populace was the proletariat or his middle-class neighbors who didn't like his "shitty little verses." And there was no change in his basic art in the forties and fifties when he was writing *Paterson;* he was then still making no dent on the American consciousness when the American consciousness was represented by a patient of his reported on in *Time,* who thought *Paterson* swell but what the hell did it mean. There were plenty of readers like that patient and there always would be, and the Party line about him, like the Chamber of Commerce line, was and would remain like the patient's. But the editor of *Lyric* identified radicalism of any kind with communism. She did not understand that what WCW stood for first of all was himself and his own perceptual integrity, and that in standing for himself he was, among other things, as American as apple pie.

As for his experimenting, that too was thoroughly American though not American the *Lyric* way, and in his old age as he read poems and talked poetry at various colleges (Rutgers, Dartmouth, Bennington, Oregon, Reed, Washington, Harvard, to name a few) he insisted over and over again that what he had himself at last arrived at prosodically, his "variable foot," would probably prove to be his most important contribution to the art. Sometimes when he was feeling grand and messianic he sounded as if the world revolution was beginning with the variable foot, and in this expectation also he was displaying not a Marxist line but the line of an old-fashioned American entrepreneur, one setting forth into the future with his own better mousetrap.

He didn't like to acknowledge that there had been variable feet before but there had been, even in his own poetry. His conservative not-quite-friend Yvor Winters had described them in the forties in an essay on free verse, observing that free verse did in fact have feet and that they were rather bigger feet than iambic feet or the feet of the other -ics. A foot in free verse consisted, said Winters, "of one heavily accented syllable, an unlimited number of unaccented syllables, and an unlimited number of syllables of secondary accent." Winters was not sure that he approved of the unlimits but he had tried his hand at free verse feet in a few of his own poems and he proceeded, in his essay, to mark up two of them and number them before demonstrating that the same numbering system could be applied to free-verse poems by true free-verse advocates. The poem of WCW's that he chose to scan was "The Widow's Lament in Springtime," vintage 1922, beginning,

> Sorrow is my ówn yárd
> Where the néw gráss
> Flámes as it has flámed
> Often befóre but nót
> with the cóld fíre
> that clóses round me thís year.

If WCW had written those lines in 1955 he probably would have made them more variable in ways that will be seen, but the big change would not have been in the syllable count but the spacing, thus:

> Sorrow is my own yard
> Where the new grass
> Flames as it has flamed

        Often before but not
            with the cold fire
                that closes round me this year.

The difference? In the first place Winters thought of each of the
lines in "The Widow's Lament" as consisting of two feet (marked
in the text are the stressed syllables only) whereas WCW's variable foot of the fifties was the whole line. And in the second place
the new placement emphasis in the variable foot triad that became
the stanza base for "Asphodel" and other fifties poems made
Winters' kind of counting old-fashioned. WCW in the fifties was
not thinking syllable by syllable but unit by unit so that each triad
was really a threesome of ones. He could by such measurings
justify even greater variations within the foot than those Winters
tried to describe — for example, a foot could have one or two or
more dominant stresses and still be a foot — and he could at the
same time assert, and frequently did, that he had achieved a
greater rigor of measure than had been possible in the free-verse
days. Here is a characteristic group of lines in the new mode —
note the metrical irregularity of the line or foot units and at the
same time the spatial insistence on their regular triadic placement:

        I was on my way uptown
            to a meeting.
                He kept looking at me
        and I at him:
            He had a worn knobbed stick
                between his knees
        suitable
            to keep off dogs,
                a man of perhaps forty.

If the change from what Winters was talking about to the new
mode does not from these examples now look like revolution, still
it seemed like one to WCW at the time; he was as much taken
with the potential of the mode as with the lines he was actually
producing. He had always had "invent" as one of his big words,
and when he came upon his variable foot he thought of it as an

invention so specific that he could practically make application for a patent. It was important in itself, it would have repercussions beyond itself, it would change lives; and even more delightfully, at least from his private point of view, it was an invention that showed that he, an old man, was still *capable* of invention — which was the same thing as saying that he was still a poet.

Because he was so pleased with his aged precocity he was occasionally vain in suggesting invidious comparisons between himself and other poets with less of the explorer in them, notably Sandburg and Walt Whitman. Sandburg's collected poems appeared in 1951 and WCW, reviewing the volume for *Poetry,* said plainly that poor Sandburg no longer had any prosodic inventiveness in him. The "drive for new form seemed to be lacking" and so Sandburg had "petered out as a poet" ten years earlier. By implication WCW had not petered out, was still searching out the new prosodic forms that fitted the new world around him, was not committed like Sandburg to endless repetition of youthful triumphs — and at this point WCW cited Sandburg's "Chicago" as a poem the poet had never moved beyond.

There was truth in what he said about Sandburg — and Sandburg was scheduled not to like him for saying it, muttering some years later that WCW wasn't as good as he thought he was — but if it was true that Sandburg had stood still while the world moved on it was also true that WCW exaggerated the magnitude of his own moves. Not only had he once observed to himself that breaking up a foot was like cracking the atom but he based one of his first published briefs for his variable foot upon the foot's connection to Relativity Theory. He thought of his foot as a thoroughly measurable foot, and having decided that it was measurable he became most enthusiastic about measurement, saying eventually in *Paterson* Five that "to measure is all we know" and professing to be no longer satisfied with intuitive countings: "it is all over the page at the mere whim of the man who has composed it" — yet after all these protestations of the need for measuring precision he did not set about actually measuring his feet. Instead he preached that the old ways of counting were dead and the new countings vital, but as for what the new countings were, well, they were, he alleged in 1953, matters that he was experimenting with and the experiment's results would soon appear in a new book (*The Desert Music*). He did not think the experiments were final and definitive, and he tried to be cautious and judicious about them; but his enthusiasm wouldn't stay down even as his measurements wouldn't come out:

> There will be other experiments but all will be directed toward the discovery of a new measure, I repeat, a new measure by which may be ordered our poems as well as our lives.

It was this sort of heady optimism that led to his 1955 comments about Whitman, the occasion being the one-hundredth anniversary of the publication of *Leaves of Grass* and a book of essays in Whitman's praise. WCW was full of praise like the other contributors, but he was patronizing too because he was feeling that he had now himself gone far beyond Whitman. Whitman had been good in his time but like Sandburg he had gone downhill in old age. Whitman was a "worthy and courageous man of his age and, to boot, a farseeing one," but after seeing the "great light" that the "matter was largely technical" and that free verse rather than the old forms was the order of the American day he had made the mistake of forgetting his own great discovery and concentrating instead on "message." He therefore "took his eyes off the words themselves which should have held him," forgetting that "poems are made of words not ideas."

Yet WCW allowed that Whitman despite his limitations made a strong beginning at equating the language of poetry with "the new order that had hit the world, a relative order, a new measure with which no one was familiar." And though Whitman's verses seemed disorderly (WCW missed Whitman's insistent and dominant rhetorical patterns and said he had "abandoned all sequence" so that "it was as if a tornado had struck") still WCW maintained that there was a subtle and hard-to-analyze order in them:

. . . it has to be insisted on that it was not disorder. Whitman's verses seemed disorderly, but ran according to an unfamiliar and difficult measure. It was an order which was essential to the new world, not only of the poem, but to the world of chemistry and of physics. In this way the man was more of a prophet than he knew.

But what was the new measure? It was a relative measure. It took the place, said WCW, of Shakespeare's measure, which had been great in its time but was now outmoded; it was now abroad in the world waiting to be improved on, with the hoped-for improvements sadly delayed by the maneuverings of the wicked Eliot who went British and took poetry backward for a time so that it lost Whitman's forward thrust. By implication WCW was now ready to resume the Whitman thrust, resume it and do it, as Whitman hadn't quite, right.

These were pretentious remarks but timely. A revolution *was* in fact brewing and though the variable foot may have been incidental to its triumph WCW himself was not. WCW with his organic theories and his Eliot obsession proved to be one of its strongest prophets: a prophet of what might be called the fifties Revolution of the Word.

The fifties revolution was a big thing though not Marxist. It was the revolution that WCW had sourly prophesied to Fred Miller in 1945, the one to rid the world of the Tates and the Eliots and their *"PR* pupils." In the fifties these intellectuals were still riding high; and as the revolutionaries beat drums in San Francisco the old villain Eliot could be heard addressing 16,000 in a basketball emporium in Minneapolis (the Eliot influence was so strong that Delmore Schwartz, himself an Eliot pupil, could be read lamenting in the pages of *PR* Eliot's literary "dictatorship") ; but the rough beast had been activated, was slouching through the desert toward the English departments. In another decade he would have so completely slouched as to leave few in those departments who could believe their memories of a time when the Tates, Eliots and *PR* pupils had themselves been thought revolutionaries.

For WCW the new antiacademic rough beast showed up in the

form of Allen Ginsberg and a few other comparatively young poets who appeared on his doorstep to praise him, talk with him, and learn from him, they having found in him suddenly an image of themselves or what they would like to be. They were not poets like Jarrell; they placed no limits on the intuitive; they had mostly seen something of the college liberal-arts routine (as WCW had not) but they had found it wanting and believed as he did that knowledge had to be "embodied." There is nothing more remarkable in WCW's life than this postwar clustering around him of a new group of poetic allies — notably Ginsberg, Charles Olson, Denise Levertov, Robert Creeley and Cid Corman, though the list could be extended indefinitely. WCW had a way of corresponding with everybody in poetry but these particular poets were more than casual pen pals; they were WCW enthusiasts and in varying degrees followers. Their attraction for him was partly ideological — all of them must also have been anathema to the *Lyric* editor — but it was also simply an attraction to the man WCW, the good gray individualist who stood outside the system and spoke his mind.

And their attraction was a tribute too to his success as a writer in keeping up with the young and the new. In 1942 he had said of Van Wyck Brooks, as he thought of reasons for not liking him, that Brooks had "lost the power to recognize" the new age, adding, "let him go to school again to the young." In the fifties WCW himself did just that. Particularly with Olson and Ginsberg he leaned over backward to persuade them that he had done just that. And of course they went to school to him too, he having practiced their intuitive art for decades before them.

Ginsberg was perhaps the least of his followers prosodically. Though an apostle of unimpeded writing flow and a dedicated antipuritan, his verse had been corrupted by Columbia College where he practiced traditional literary modes and admired Mark Van Doren. Turning to rebellion after college he took as his model Whitman, the long line, the rhetorical sequence, and felt slightly defensive about his Whitmania with WCW. With that exception WCW was very much Ginsberg's man; Ginsberg delighted in him as both a person and an experience recorder. He wrote to WCW first from his hometown Paterson while still in his early twenties, saying to him that they both lived "in the same rusty county of the world" and then later actually passing on suggestions to WCW of places and persons in Paterson to be perhaps brought into WCW's poem. Ginsberg said he had a "flair" for WCW's style, his only complaint being,

> I seldom dig what you are doing with cadences, line length, sometimes syntax, etc.

Years later Ginsberg enlarged upon this saying that he thought there was nothing "exact" about the WCW cadences since WCW was simply trying to catch the natural rhythms of street language. Anyway WCW liked the letter so much that he put it in *Paterson* Four.

He also read the poems Ginsberg sent on, managing to admire them all down to the early rhymed ones, and a few years later wrote an introduction to Ginsberg's *Howl* in which he praised him for avoiding nothing and experiencing everything, for going through hell yet persisting in love and art, for seeing his "horrors" with "the eyes of the angels." Ginsberg was thus reinforced in putting everything down as it happened including what he called his abnormal "moments of emotional crisis — tender sighs, fuck sobs, anger raves," though he may not have needed reinforcement. He was not like Theodore Roethke to whom WCW wrote in the forties to say that the Roethke poems were good but needed to be "drunker, hotter, drippier." If not drunker Ginsberg's poems were hotter and drippier than anybody's ever had been.

The other WCW fifties disciples were equally attracted to the hot and drippy but they paid more attention to WCW's aesthetic than Ginsberg. Olson was obsessed. Olson was a very large man from Massachusetts. He was a wild theorist as well as poet and had published, at about the time of *Paterson* One, one of the most interesting and eccentric explications of *Moby Dick* ever (in it Ahab was compared with most of the characters in Shakespeare, and America was Ahab's Pacific, and both were SPACE). A few years later he produced an essay on what he called "projective verse" that was printed in the most popular paperback poetry anthology to come out of the San Francisco movement, Donald Allen's *The New American Poetry,* which became a basic alienated-student text on how verse was to be written. Olson's essay had all the marks of WCW's organic theories upon it, and WCW's incoherence about the theoretic, as well as many of the marks of Pound, of whom Olson was also a disciple, especially of Pound's capitalizations and insistent brevities, ironies, word coinings, funny spellings. The gist of the essay was what WCW's gist had been ever since he discovered what was wrong with his *Poems* (1909) : the poet must dispose of the fences around him.

The gist was in the first two or three pages of the Olson essay where Olson compared the new "open" verse that he and his peers were striving for and the old "closed" verse of bygone centuries that fenced in the poet before he began to write. Open verse had no fences to reckon with, it moved "by no other track than the one the poem under hand declare[d] for itself," it was one perception leading "immediately and directly . . . to a further perception," and it was a poetry of the head working together with the heart, the head moving the poet "by the way of the ear to the syllable" and the heart moving the poet "by the way of the breath to the line." The "sons of Pound and Williams" were, Olson said, the ones now practicing open verse, particularly himself and Creeley, and they were all indebted to Pound and Williams. He then qualified his own indebtedness by suggesting that he had gone considerably beyond Pound and Williams, and later he was easily annoyed with those who wanted to insist that he was *merely* a son of Pound and Williams; but in 1950 when he sent the essay to WCW all was peaches and cream. WCW replied enthusiastically about the essay and in his now customary manner proceeded to stuff three pages of it into one of his own works — not *Paterson* this time but his autobiography. Olson was inordinately grateful:

> My god, BILL, OF COURSE, god, how wonderful it is, your letter, to have you say to put it that way thanks thanks WOW . . . crazy good, crazy wonderful, crazy manna

As for Creeley, Creeley was a young poet with a Harvard past who also suddenly saw in the Rutherford doctor what the academies didn't have, and thereupon became with the others a WCW correspondent. Creeley was trying to start a magazine and proposed in a 1950 letter to use in the magazine what WCW had described to him as WCW's own writing program, a summary of it "for those who had managed to miss it, these past forty years." The WCW program was excerpted as follows:

> "My own (moral) program can be briefly stated: to write badly is an offense to the state since the government can never be more than the government of the words . . .
> "There is in each age a specific criterion which is the objective of the artist in that age. Not to attack that objective is morally reprehensible . . .
> "Bad art is then that which does not serve in . . . cleansing the language of all fixations upon the dead, the stinking dead, usages of the past."

These were the old WCW violences about the past and the new violent young poets liked them. And they shared not only WCW's violence but also — when they started out — the withdrawn, out-of-it, island sense of the artist, the sense of powerlessness to do anything except write statements like these. They were in the position WCW and McAlmon had been in in 1920 with *Contact*. They had a couple of tiny magazines to write for and the tiny campus of Black Mountain College in the North Carolina mountains to foment the world art revolution at, but otherwise only great expectations.

Creeley and Olson were involved in the early fifties in starting *The Black Mountain Review* as they watched Black Mountain College itself slowly disintegrate. And in Boston a poet named Cid Corman began at the same time a magazine called *Origin* to which also the revolution could be directed. But these two magazines were little more than staging areas for what was to come in 1956 in San Francisco. It was in San Francisco rather than on the East Coast that the hot and drippy, and the verse lines of the natural breath, suddenly began to be read and listened to — and published in significant quantities. It was in San Francisco, about 1956, that the revolution began to take hold and when it came it was a revolution much bigger than WCW had known in his little magazine lifetime. Yet *Paterson,* and WCW himself, played a primary early role.

The new revolution was not only bigger, it was also nastier and tougher, though it had warmth and joy in it too. Ginsberg especially had a joyousness about him that made the revolution seem, as WCW had said of him, angelic. In 1956 he wrote WCW from San Francisco that it was not a revolution but a revival, the kind of revival that WCW would "dig taking place." He added that Richard Eberhart, who was a poet twelve years older than Ginsberg and a benign unrevolutionary friend of all poets, had been there and had "understood at once." So of course had Creeley wandering in from the east. Ginsberg said the revival was "mainly magnanimity, no more tight ass . . . a spontaneous method of writing about real images." As he wrote he said that he was serving on a naval ship that was about to sail for the "north pole" to do something "paranoid" about U.S. radar defenses, and that he would write polar rhapsodies there but would not forget Paterson, dear Paterson, Paterson which was only a "big sad poppa" needing compassion. He would return to Paterson "to splash in the Passaic again only with a body so naked and happy City Hall [would] have to call out the Riot Squad." But Ginsberg's notion that the revolution was "mainly magnanimity" was not everybody's notion; the revolution was also an angry-man revolution, and the anger was sometimes of a quality and intensity of anger that WCW, though he had been an angry man too, was not familiar with except on the printed page. WCW had been a correspondence angry man, noted for his intensities by letter and his kindness and affability in the flesh and on platforms. These new angry men were earnest in trying to carry their protestations into what was beginning to be called "life-style." Next to them WCW was a model of middle-class gentility and it is to his great credit that he was able to keep their allegiance, persuade them that he was "serious" (one of their favorite words) without being hypocritical. He proved that he could go to school to youth simply by admiring their purposeful indiscretions.

The indiscretions of Ginsberg were of the life-style variety and WCW admired him for his frank self-exposures, the kind that WCW had himself worked toward in *Kora* and the later journals but had always felt forces around him resisting, keeping him from Ginsberg's directness. The indiscretions of Olson and Creeley — and of Denise Levertov, whose own poetry was closer to WCW's than any of the others' — were indiscretions of art and he admired those too. Olson's projective verse was a latter-day version of the *Kora* automatism, and Creeley's theories of measure seemed to coincide with WCW's own developing variable foot fetish as well as with Olson's pronouncement that a line was a breath. What WCW, Olson and Creeley particularly had in common — and Ginsberg did not share — was a conviction that the intuited forms and cadences of verse that they reached for could be talked about most learnedly, elevated to a science. If the three of them had been born in the Middle Ages they would all have been astrologers, and if in the modern world they had not been in poetry but over where science was supposed to be, they would have been the inventors of perpetual-motion machines or devices to extract soybeans from sea water. To read any of their aesthetic pronouncements is to be bewildered by them and yet also occasionally impressed at the prescience lurking behind the fuzz.

The pronouncements were truly pronouncements in the realm of aesthetics and not just soul. Though the San Francisco poets did want to revamp the soul, not to mention human consciousness and the nature of human relations, they wanted also to begin the revamping by changing the verse line. One of the most intellectual of the San Francisco poets, Robert Duncan, said he wanted "to make poetry as other men make war or make love" and that such a making involved exercising his "faculties at large"; but having said this he went about his business of poetry with craftsmanly persistence. Duncan's statement appeared with Olson's projective verse statement in *The New American Poetry,* and probably half the other contributors to the volume demonstrated an interest equal to Duncan's in being thought artists, not emitters of yawps. They talked like technicians, their job was with words and with word music, they were fascinated with what it was that constituted Americanness of speech right down to the syllable. The soul, yes, that was important but the soul was to be located in the energies of language. Levertov remarked for instance that "every space and comma" was "a living part of the poem"; Ginsberg described *Howl* and other of his recent works as "experiments with formal organization of the long line"; Gary Snyder's line (said Snyder) had been "influenced by the five- and seven-character line Chinese poems" that he had been reading and that worked "like sharp blows on the mind"; LeRoi Jones said that the poet's "voice" was the whole thing — "You have to start and finish there . . . your own voice . . . how you sound"; and Charles Olson, the big aesthetic spokesman of the group, talked for pages of his projective verse in terms of sounds and syllables, insisting that if the qualities of projective verse were recognized and cultivated the very content of verse would change. For Olson particularly, but for the others too, the revolution did indeed begin with the syllable and the barricades in the city squares came much later. WCW had been thinking such thoughts for years but now he had a whole movement behind him to help him think them. He could utter extravagances like, "From the beginning Whitman realized that the matter was largely technical" and know that he would have an audience that would understand. The aesthetic talk of the fifties was wild and woolly and sometimes full of the flavor of mad scientism, but it was at the center a rather sharply focused wildness with the aestheticians reaching for their peyote but also meditating solemnly on ways of changing the verse line.

It was these young aestheticians who for better or worse kept alive in him his old preoccupation with how to mix art and spontaneity, helping perhaps to produce some excessive focusing upon verbal and literary issues in the late *Paterson* books but provoking fine statements therein too, such as:

It is dangerous to leave written that which is badly written. A chance word, upon paper, may destroy the world. Watch carefully and erase, while the power is still yours, I say to myself, for all that is put down, once it escapes, may rot its way into a thousand minds, the corn become a black smut, and all libraries, of necessity, be burned to the ground as a consequence.

Only one answer: write carelessly so that nothing that is not green will survive.

4

After all WCW was at home with the poetic wild men, having had them around him ever since World War I. He had even had a genuine eccentric scientist on his hands in the thirties in the form of a radio technician who worked in a Paterson factory and wrote him interminable single-spaced random jottings describing how human consciousness was molded by language, especially by the technician's specialty Morse code. One of WCW's critics has suggested that the random unchronological juxtaposings of *Paterson* were derived from the radio technician's ideas but this seems unlikely: WCW had his own private sources of the random and unchronological and was his own breed of eccentric scientist when he wanted to be. Luckily he also had his down-to-earth side, and it was that that kept him from Zen and the rest. The down-to-earth side in the end was Rutherford, Rutherford and the doctoring; the down-to-earth side was the daily local middle-class life that he professed to rebel against but never abandoned. Ginsberg and Olson and the others had had their innings with the daily and local but as revolutionaries they gave up their Gloucesters and Patersons in favor of what the communists have aptly if tiresomely stigmatized as rootless cosmopolitanism. In the fifties Olson took on the Mayan culture, in the sixties Ginsberg "faded out" into

Calcutta, others sat on mountaintops, and it seemed for the revolution not important where they were so long as they were not where they began. They took on the occult to get away from the here and now, thereby contributing to modernism's long tradition of obscurantism. From the very beginning of the San Francisco movement the occult was in, with the believers believing with varying degrees of earnestness that there was nothing in the world but the mind itself. WCW was not without his obscurantist moments but living at 9 Ridge Road and believing in the things of 9 Ridge Road drove him to watching baseball games on TV as antidote. *Paterson* was ultimately his most obscurantist work — and partly because it was it has been accorded unusual critical attention in recent years — but his was such a wide-ranging talent that he would not be fairly represented by *Paterson* even if that work were more successful than it is. *Paterson* is not the local poem that its title suggests but WCW was a local boy despite it.

Perhaps it will be best for the long-term reputation of WCW if some of his literary enthusiasms be ignored in favor of his social honesties. Robert Coles has pointed the way in a series of lectures that he delivered about WCW at Rutgers in 1974. Coles described WCW as a superior social observer, the kind Coles wished more sociologists and psychologists should aspire to be. Coles said that he had encouraged "inner city youths" to read WCW, "young men and women who [had] never gone to college [and] who struggled hard to get by," and that their responses to reading him were "frank, pointed, insistent," because they shared the difficulties of survival of "the people Dr. Williams treated and watched so closely," shared the "moral dilemmas perhaps best summarized by, of all people, Sören Kierkegaard: 'How do I live a life?'" The WCW that Coles had the inner city youth reading was the WCW of the stories in *Life Along the Passaic River.*

Meanwhile though the variable foot, and some of the attendant mystification plaguing the poetry trade in the seventies, will continue to be attended to by English teachers if not by Coles and inner city youth; and perhaps if they do not worry about it as a great technical advance but look at it naively on the page with the white space around the lines, the words floating rather than marching, they will catch something about it that is not technical but nonetheless revealing, revealing of a good and happy change in the character of WCW in the fifties. The change was in the appearance of his poems as well as the sound, and reflected a change in the poet's spirit. His early poems had been in the mode of a man walking casually along a street and pausing irregularly to look in store windows, but the late poems with the variable foot put the man on his toes, made him hop back and forth, kept him in a high state of balance as well as making him seem lighter, more a creature of air. In the fifties WCW needed that psychologically; he needed to dance, needed to be the poet rather than the anti-poet, needed to affirm his own creations rather than deny others. The variable foot helped here.

Wallace Stevens had after all been right in 1931, though WCW didn't think so, when he described WCW's poetry as antipoetry, and a good deal of the antipoetic feel of it was in its rhythm — or nonrhythm. "The Widow's Lament" that Winters selected as an instance of WCW in his free-verse years was, though barely scannable, much more regular in cadence than most WCW. Most WCW was close to being without cadence; it was deliberately flat musically and therefore less poetic, more prosaic in the conventional meaning of those terms. With the variable foot triad he switched; he went heavily into a kind of regularity that, while not mathematically regular, shifted his central poetic focus from image and common speech to musical phrasing. It was perhaps a switch into the arty and it won him no new prole readers but it was also a switch to affirmation, making him truly at last an advocate of the qualities in poetry that he thought he had always backed but that Stevens had detected him denying.

In other words the variable foot represented a change in mood more than measure. The mood change came in the mid and late fifties and was a move out of anger, combativeness, dark inwardness, a move toward serenity, calm. It was a move remarkable because there was so much in his life in the fifties not to be serene about: the bad health, the Library of Congress disaster. The variable foot helped his poems dance but it did so because he now wanted them dancing. Though he was not possessed of death's certainty he now also had love, attention, respect, being no longer a neglected scribbler in an attic. The romance of writing was upon him with new force because reality had at last in some measure caught up with romance. He was now in the public eye as the tough-talking but kindly doctor-poet who had retired with honors from doctoring (and been given by his fellow medicos at Passaic General an early model electric typewriter that shook the house when the carriage lurched left), and had read his poems at the best places, and had written what certain highbrows had alleged was America's greatest epic. Sometimes the popular picture of him was sentimental, as in the case of a *Time* spread on him in the early fifties when he was actually pictured in a white coat earnestly stethoscoping a baby (for the picture he had to borrow the white coat as well as the baby — it was son Bill's baby) but for the most part his success was of the best possible quiet kind, success among poets themselves, all the poets, all paying homage to the good and kind (and belligerent) old doc by lining up at his door or writing to him as Ginsberg had written to him, to tell him that he was good and in turn to thank him for telling them that they were good — for he was never scanty with praise. Denise Levertov wrote him that when she read what he had said of her poems she felt "a great rushing wind that blew me off the ground, sent my cap sailing into the trees." Galway Kinnell, offended at the response to a WCW reading at Breadloaf, observed bitterly, "the lovers of literature paid you the real tribute of their almost total inattention . . . But you didn't even care . . . In an hour of talking your honesty built you a tower." James Dickey wrote to praise WCW for solving the chief writing problem in *all* poetry, that of "letting the world have its own say instead of serving as 'material' for a 'work of art.' " And Robert Lowell, the most complimentary of all, attributed to WCW the change in his own work that became manifest in his book *Life Studies* (1958):

> I like to think that often I have crossed the river into your world. It meant throwing away a lot of heavy symbolic armor, and at times I felt frightened of the journey.

In sum, there were now so many crossings of the river into WCW's world that even with the ill health it was possible at last for him to be content and to affirm the life of poetry without the old revolutionary negations.

And if it was good for WCW to receive so much outside reinforcement it was in turn good for the outside to be witness to WCW's serenity. The San Francisco movement had the happily naked Ginsberg in it and a good many other life forcers but it was also a movement full of bitterness and intolerance, vices that WCW might have shared when young and isolated but now could be above, preaching love. Charles Olson was a characteristically angry figure among the new affirmers, needing WCW's sun to shine down. Olson had his projective verse revolution on his hands and believed it could be made to happen, and believed it so hard that when Cid Corman started up *Origin* Olson wrote him the most kindly encouragement but then added the real message: "PLAY IT STRONG." Playing it strong was the San Francisco poets' way to play, and that meant blasting away at professors and poets of the wrong dispensation. They did. In the biographical notes of the Donald Allen anthology at least half the contributors took time to be unhappy or sarcastic about some aspect of their education, or to be pleased with themselves for having had no education at all since they wished it to be understood that they were beholden to no one but their own kind and that no one else should be either. There was hardly an Eliot lover in the crowd and they all loved WCW. He was the one who could at last afford to be not angry and to sit up on high asserting that the writing romance could come true if one fought the establishments hard enough, and wrote long enough.

And he could be a model too in his old age for others than poets. The base of his sudden fifties reputation was broader than poetry and was to grow in the sixties after his death. He was to be received by the young as a happy antiestablishment genius of the kind that anarchists of the sixties like Paul Goodman promoted. Goodman had greater intellecutal pretensions than WCW; his theory of learning for example was much more fully developed than anything to be found in WCW's *Embodiment of Knowledge;* yet his words about the academies echoed WCW steadily. Goodman, like a whole army of new antiacademic highbrows, was contemptuous of school curricula (any school that was "divided into compartments, using texts, lessons [and] scheduled periods marked by bells" was for Goodman simply "a sociological invention of some Irish monks in the 17th century to bring a bit of Rome to wild shepherds") and Goodman regarded what he called "incidental education" as "the chief means of learning and teaching." Diplomas were "irrelevant," pedagogues were largely exploiters who made "a special effort to awe, confuse and mystify," and though knowledge of the past was indispensable (a point WCW might not have agreed to) the past simply could not be learned, Goodman felt, in the ways that the learneries prescribed; hence he regarded the learneries as just as useless as WCW had found them in his most antiintellectual moments.

The Goodman educational gospel was preached with many variations throughout the late sixties, became part of the social-cultural stance of thousands of Americans opposed to the Vietnam war, and served to remind anyone who happened to run into the works of WCW that here was a man who had been wise before his time. WCW's poetry was important, yes, but WCW himself was more important, he who had lived on the industrial front, worked with the poor and accommodated himself to Rutherford, yet had also fought the bourgeoisie, the government and the professors — in short kept his integrity — and had done so while remaining an optimist, an affirmer, an idealist, a praiser of life and love — all that *plus* writing in his attic.

CHAPTER NINE

The Cures

Way back in 1935 when Fred Miller of the magazine *Blast* was having trouble with his wife and drinking too much WCW let the Miller family have one of the two Williams West Haven cottages on Long Island Sound for a month, and when Miller continued to have his troubles there WCW wrote him, "For the love of Mike go to bed and forget Betty and every other Jane in the world. You have work to do. I know what you must feel but . . . you're trying to be too good, that's all. Write for Chrisake, write, write drivel, write crap but write lots and lots, as fast as you can, string it out. Open the hatch and put a firecracker into it. Something will come out." WCW had had his own family troubles in his time and had made his attic his writing refuge where he did not have to be good; he had also, especially in the twenties, had his days with the bottle, though the bottle seems not to have been finally serious with him; he managed to use it rather than letting it use him; it served him as an experimental release-mechanism for uninhibited writing. But when he did escape he was convinced that the release helped, that it was therapeutic; and so with his troubled friend Miller as well as with others he was full of the gospel of release. The *Man Orchid* experiment with Miller in 1946 was another occasion when he counseled Miller to let himself go, telling Miller to get it down no matter what it was and to make it "simple" because life ultimately was simple and they were "in this for fun"; and though he would frequently append a remark to the effect that the *art* of the writing might be the better if the writer were free the health of the writer did seem to take precedence over art. He was somewhat baffled when Miller's release efforts went into drinking more than writing, and wrote him with uncharacteristic smugness that because he personally had never had "the yen for drinking" he guessed he could never thoroughly understand those who had.

The mix of freedom and discipline that he wished he could impose upon Miller he had in good measure in himself, having always been afraid of too much freedom, afraid that the male curse would be upon him and he would end up "either hunting, fighting, loafing or drunk." Flossie had kept the curse from him mostly but he continued to be afraid of it even in the fifties when he was sick and the freedom options were slight. To David McDowell, who moved to Rutherford in the period when WCW was writing for Random House and who saw him frequently and read to him when his eyes betrayed him, he remarked many times that he feared the "lure of the gutter." He wanted the gutter just as he wanted the ugly; he was attracted to the hell that Allen Ginsberg wrote about in *Howl,* and thought that the failure to face the reality of hell's presence was a prime puritan failing; but he feared that presence too, feared that if he descended to the gutter he would not "get back up." He was in other words possessed, despite many protestations, by an old-fashioned work ethic, an ethic contaminated by the usual confusions but always present in him so that he felt that to be healthy he needed to be both gloriously freed and sensibly jailed.

He seems especially to have admired freedoms when they were not too close to him, feeling that he needed to keep himself in check but that others would be better off liberated. He was for example perfectly conventional in his views of Negro jazz and literature, being convinced that blacks were best off when they were not inhibited by the white restraints, as in poetry ("when the negro turns to poetry he usually writes like Countee Cullen — just bellywash. No guts. No invention") but allowed to do their own thing as in jazz where they were "at home." He surely would have praised in theory what Allen Ginsberg said in an interview in 1964, that the important thing was to write "the same way that you . . . are!" but he might not have been as pleased with the principle in practice. The cure was writing but whether the writing was to be a loosener or a tightener he never resolved.

In the sixties writing as therapy became a big thing in the schools, and the new freewheeling creative writing programs (some of which took names like "liberated expression") became testing grounds for WCW's write-for-Chrisake notion. But the notion was strained then through a younger generation of writers like Ginsberg, writers who not only scuttled the work ethic but reassessed the meaning of the writing cure so that it was no longer a simple trip to the attic to dispose of the day's frustrations. It became instead a much bigger trip, sometimes a drug trip, usually a trip away from home bases like Rutherford (note the striking difference between Ginsberg's "Sunflower Sutra" in the remoteness of a San Francisco railroad yard and WCW's homebodiness in *The Wanderer*) and always very much an inward trip, a trip into the depths of the mind. The new liberations were much more subjective, much less tied to the integrity of *things* than with WCW, with the result that writing came to be construed as not merely a liberating from social and cultural restraints but also an exercise in fantasizing, dreaming on the page according to such new models as Ashbery and Koch in poetry, and Hesse, Vonnegut, and a bushel of others in prose. Ginsberg put it that the great thing about Cézanne was that he "reconstituted the whole fucking universe in his canvases," and that became the idea on paper too. WCW might have liked the idea because it was a strong idea, a radical idea, but he wouldn't have practiced it, wouldn't at least have been able personally to go about reconstituting the things of the universe because at heart he did believe in the integrity of things, believed that they were present with a presence that was always in some measure unreconstitutable. He could not write by pulling the blinds down on the world; he had to have the world, he even had to copy down exactly what he heard and saw in the world, feeling that anything less than a copying would be a violation of the here and now. In other words he was at heart something of an old-fashioned materialist and thus destined *not* to be wholly liberated, not at least in the new sixties mode, though the sixties came to think that he was.

But of writing as cure he was fully prophet and saint, and with those who succeeded him in such therapy he was thoroughly persuaded that the confusion between therapy and art should be allowed to persist. If the writing was good for the writer (and it was, it was; each writing therapist had to keep writing and writing that it was) then it might or might not be good art and yet, damn it, it *would* be good art if the therapy really took hold and the release was effected. Or so WCW felt. He was most insistent about the need to be serious about art, yet in practice his seriousness became not a craft-seriousness, such as an attentiveness to the actual measuring of the variable foot, but a seriousness of intent and feeling, of commitment to the truths of the senses. The art thus merged insensibly with each self's therapy-struggle and became a highly subjective enterprise despite hopes that it be more.

His rebellion against Eliot and the academics was, among all the other things, a manifestation of his therapeutic writing notions, and most of the young writer-therapists who followed after him shared his doubled-up conviction that the academicians (a) inhibited true writing therapy and (b) encouraged bad art. He and the new sixties therapists were, in other words, in agreement that the old writing standards brought on inhibitions, yet not many were prepared to say — and certainly WCW was not — that there should be *no* standards. Most of them wanted instead their own standards as they went along, but as each artist finally insisted upon his own right to establish standards it was a standardizing procedure hard to explain even to sympathizers — and to traditionalists became merely a standards-fraud. WCW had been indoctrinated by Pound too long to deny standards but everything that came to him as part of therapy-gospel did encourage him to deny standards that were not privately staked out. He therefore liked to muddle through with the paradox that the way to standards was to forget them. Was he deluded? If so, his was one of the commonest delusions of the sixties and seventies.

It was not just art that came to play second fiddle to therapy but art's dear handmaiden truth. Though the therapists liked to think that they liked truth they liked it so exclusively as private truth, truth of the senses and soul, that they promoted it as that and became thereby specialists in the truths of babes, primitives, and furious 3:00 A.M. gin-or-mescaline scribblers; and became also thereby, though psychologically oriented, poor Freudians. Freudian therapy had been committed to the use in analysis of private truths but not to the final positing of those as Truth with a capital T. Materialist Freud, graybeard of the reality principle, had sought a bedrock truth behind the subjective visions but the new writing therapists did not, being content with visions only.

Theirs was in other words a therapy in which doing rather than understanding was the key, and though they would have insisted (WCW as loudly as the rest) that doing produced knowing they would not have been informative on how the resultant knowing could be analyzed, tested, judged by others than the knower.

None of these truth-and-art problems were new to WCW even in the forties when his works and opinions were just beginning to be widely disseminated; and by the fifties they were his daily fare. He had been full of much hard-to-test knowledge back in the twenties (recorded in chapter five). He had had knowledge then for example of an army of puritans who were unlike him and were working to destroy him, as well as of a (smaller) army of writer-explorer-heroes who *were* like him and were on his side, were working with him to preserve the freedoms, save the world. The word "delusion" might be too strong to describe what he knew then, yet the evidence of delusion was sometimes strong too, evidence tending to demonstrate that what he knew could not be sustained as truth in the thingy world outside him. The same was true of some of his convictions of the fifties following his strokes, and there was the further difficulty then that because he was partly invalided he could no longer readily move out and away from his thoughts into the solid world beyond the self, but was constantly driven back and in, especially to his memories. If he mostly avoided delusion then it was not because Rutherford was preserving him but because, unlike some of his latter-day disciples, he remained strong in the service of the nonself; he knew a man's capacity for delusion, knew it and feared it, in fact wanted his ideas rooted in things *because* he feared it.

2

One of the late works in which he let his conservatism surface in a respect for things and laws outside his own organic writing machine was a play that was partly about writing as a cure — it was called *The Cure* — but did not allow writing to be everything. Plays were where he had always been most conservative anyway, and *The Cure* was no exception. As soon as stage thoughts were upon him he had normal stage impulses, thought in terms of character and situation, reached for clarity of statement, story and theme lest somebody in the last row not "get it." *The Cure* was conventional, even hammy, but it had the merit of dealing with the conventional theme of love triumphant, love the cure, that was to preoccupy him in his last years, and help keep him from delusion dangers.

He came upon the story for *The Cure* as he himself needed cure, lying in bed partly paralyzed and partly blinded from his first major stroke, the one at the home of the Gratwicks in 1952. It was the story of a young poet, not an old, and the poet had been disabled not by a heart but by a gimmicky motorcycle accident — but there remained biographical connections, chiefly in the fact of the disablement and in the victim's steady lust for a *nuevo mundo* female, namely his nurse.

The motorcycle accident of the play was such as to throw the victim unconscious but alive (the driver of the motorcycle was

killed) into the nurse-heroine's cellar, where he remained un-
noticed until the investigating police had left. The victim proved
to be not only a poet but also a bank robber who had gone to
Princeton (WCW's stroke had perhaps driven him briefly into
dada?) and the police did want him; but the nurse-heroine and
her husband kept his presence in their house secret as the cure
proceeded. The nurse's excellent ministrations were predictably
those of a more-than-nurse, another primal female, but she was not
modeled after Flossie. No, though Flossie was on the scene during
WCW's recovery an efficient nurse like the one in the play was
present too, and what the young poet in the play did with her —
that is, struggle steadily to bring her down into bed with
him — must have been WCW's own aged dream. Yet the bedding-
down did not finally occur for the odd reason that though the
nurse flirted with the victim, tempted him, and helped cure him
by stirring his young vital juices, she then turned him down flat.
He was thereupon enraged at her hypocrisy and puritanism and
she was no longer the heroine:

> You were yellow, through and through and through. I could tell
> you about some married women I've known, you'd be surprised.
> Right around you, wherever you come from — good girls with kids
> in the grades, good looking, the best. It's nothing against them —
> just the opposite — that they enjoy a little free screwing once in a
> while . . . But I thought you were wise to all that. Was I mis-
> taken! You're a hick, a real hick . . . I gave you your chance but
> you ran out on me.

The play pretty much ended with this complaint (though before
the end she slapped him for saying what he said and he then hit
her), leaving the reader looking at an inhibited female who had
been chastised for her prudery. Why WCW deprived her of her
chance to remain a heroine is not clear but the true heroine of the
play may be surmised: Flossie. For it was Flossie who was not only
present while WCW was constructing the play but taking the play
down for him as he dictated it. It was Flossie then who had not
run out, Flossie who had made the full necessary love commit-

ment? Perhaps. At any rate the play's moral would seem to have been one of which Flossie might have approved, that true cures are not effected by nurses who are nurses merely.

For over the long pull it was Flossie who played nurse to WCW and knew the depths of nursing. The nursing commitment for WCW's last decade was enormous and could have destroyed them both if the love commitment had not been as great. If in the twenties they had been "thrown violently together" by a flu epidemic, now at the end there was this other kind of necessary closeness, not violent but always potentially cruel, the cruelness of day after day of curing and caring, cruel in its demands on the marriage with the sick partner helpless and guilty about his helplessness, and the healthy partner burdened with steady servantry. *The Cure* as a play was not clearly resolved but the resolution was implicitly there at the bedside as he composed it, not a resolution with a "stolen" nurse but with the faithful (though of course now dominant) wife. He had once similarly put the writing and the loving together as cure in a short poem called "The Cure" that may have been a source of his play's direction and title:

The Cure

Sometimes I envy others, fear them
a little too, if they write well.
For when I cannot write I'm a sick man
and want to die. The cause is plain.

But they have no access to my sources.
Let them write as they may and
perfect it as they can they will never
come to the secret of that form

interknit with the unfathomable ground
where we walk daily and from which
among the rest you have sprung
and opened flowerlike to my hand.

Flossie had to be the "you" in that poem, she being the only person who walked with him daily, their arms interknit with each

other. Yet in the days of *Kora* and *Spring and All* the writing cure
had been separate. Similarly in the play *Many Loves* (1939) writing had been set forth as an alternative to love, something the
writer was obsessed by beyond all that. In old age on the other
hand coexistence set in, maybe of necessity, and Flossie was in on
his writing acts with him.

Particularly she was in the poem, "Asphodel, That Greeny
Flower," a poem to her and about her that also was a product of
the midfifties and mixed writing and love totally. With "Asphodel" there was no more stealing.

W. H. Auden and a good many others have pegged "Asphodel"
high, and Flossie herself once described it as her favorite. She had
good reason, she being the asphodel in it, the flower from whom
he forever drew inspiration. If anything WCW was too beholden
to her in the poem for the poem's good, since in places the poem
showed an uncharacteristic docility. But it still had the old WCW
in it, if subdued and softened, and it was all in all a noble exercise
in the best of sentiment, a poem full of the "love of love," drip-
ping and why not? — he was writing it as if he would die the next
day. In fact he would live another eight years and be occasionally
renewed in toughness, but in "Asphodel" he was writing "with
fear in [his] heart," hence he kept on talking, daring not to stop.
Again and again he asked Flossie's forgiveness but confessed no
new faults, having already, he assured her, confessed all. Again
and again he wandered nostalgically into the past, to days in
Switzerland, to old books and conversations, to vacations at the
shore. And again and again he searched in that past for the living
forces of love and beauty that in better days he had found in the
present. The poem was a long, benign memory trip. One of the
benignest of memories, was, oddly, of his puritan father.

WCW had been on the subway, the poem said, a day or so
before he wrote the father passage, and noticed a man on the
subway who reminded him of his father from briefcase to beard.
A detailed description of the man followed, with WCW observing
that he had almost spoken to him, being sure that the man would

know "the secret." The secret? The secret of life perhaps, the secret of cures, the sort of secret that had been answered for him years before in *The Wanderer* — but then it had been the grandmother with the secret. Now it was the father's turn to be a primal force.

But the figure on the subway did not have the look of a primal force. He was marked chiefly by his plainness, which was set forth at length in a description outdoing the description of the asphodel itself, a second plainness, or of Flossie, a third. It was a fine description, the kind WCW had been working on all his writing life and was master of, with the plain puritan salesman-soul of the man being caught in details of the face, the physique and clothes down to the brown socks. And seeing that man on the subway, recognizing him as the father image, becoming convinced that he bore "the secret," WCW found in the experience itself the curative essence. The cure was partly in the discovery of this plain man as a vital source and partly in the simple act of putting the discovery down; the old basic writing act that began with the perceiving then moved to the recording. WCW was not to have many more subway rides but he knew well how to use them.

3

Following the 1952 attack he never again regained the full use of his right arm but set about trying to learn to write with his left hand. He would send little scribbled messages downstairs to Flossie for practice that were almost illegible, and then he would go to his typewriter and pound seriously on it with his left hand, becoming busy again with his correspondence life while working on *Paterson* Five and shorter poems. Merrill Moore wrote encouragingly to Flossie after the big stroke that it was "a remarkable thing" that his condition "didn't interfere much with the creative act of his mind," and indeed the evidence of what he created in the midfifties was remarkable. The book of poems that finally emerged, *Pictures from Brueghel* (a volume containing three smaller books but all products of the fifties) may be put with *Collected Earlier Poems* as the core of WCW as short-poem poet. "Asphodel" is the longest poem of the book, but though it has been much praised there are many shorter poems surrounding it — notably the Brueghel sequence itself — that are not only more typical of WCW but also perhaps more successful. The particular kind of short poem that he concentrated on, the poem of the single occasion or observation, was in the end despite his long-poem industries the form truest to his virtu. In *Pictures from Brueghel* that virtu thrived; even the variable foot thrived upon shortness, as in "The Sparrow":

> . . . Even the Japanese
> know him
>
> and have painted him
> sympathetically
> with profound insight
>
> into his minor
> characteristics.
> Nothing even remotely
> subtle
> about his lovemaking.
> He crouches
>
> before the females,
> drags his wings,
> waltzing,
>
> throws back his head
> and simply
> yells! . . .

Then aside from the writing itself he had in the fifties several years of good literary busyness that belied his physical condition and showed him actively, determinedly serene. A poetry reading he gave on Staten Island, described in print by Charles Angoff, was typical. It was Angoff who had called him about the reading, and having done so only because he had forgotten WCW's sickness he was embarrassed and full of apologies when WCW finally reached the phone — but WCW brushed the apologies off, said he would be glad to come. Then he laughed, asked Angoff if he was sitting down, and said there were two conditions to his coming: first, that a chauffeur pick him up and afterward return him; second, that a bottle of Wilson's whiskey be provided. The first condition was easy, the second harder because the school inviting him had a no-drinking rule; but the bottle was provided, and just before going on stage WCW drank off a "half tumbler" straight. He became flushed (worrying Angoff), then resolute, saying, "Now let me get at your students" and went before them to speak "cogently, poetically, brilliantly," at the end receiving a long ovation. After the reading Angoff gave him the rest of the bottle and he accepted it gratefully as he was driven off, muttering, "You're a sweetheart, Charlie, just a sweetheart."

Beyond the occasional poetry readings there were other, less trying public appearances as well as a good deal of at-home fiddling with his own works. In 1955 he made an hourlong tape about Pound at a New Haven radio studio, his voice an old man's voice but resonant still and cheery, and his mind full of nostalgia for the old days when Pound wore his hair "wildly around his head as a halo" and once almost put WCW's eye out with his cane. In 1956 he labored with a neighbor scholar, Edith Heal, in the putting together of *I Wanted to Write a Poem,* another voyage into the past but lively and good-natured, being his own recollections of the circumstances surrounding the writing of each of his books. In 1957 he entered the pages of at least ten little magazines with essays and reviews, and he was interviewed on TV by Mike Wallace on the subject "Is Poetry A Dead Duck?" (in WCW's opinion it was not but he admitted having trouble understanding a Cummings poem). He also traveled to California with Flossie and sat in on a "psychological-philosophical conference" where he and four other writers had "their heads examined to try to find out why they had become writers" (he remarked on the conference's success, "Hope the profs got something out of it . . . I got nothing"). And to cap the year off he completed a story he had been working on for years, his last story, "The Farmers' Daughters" and he also began to put into final shape his book about his mother, *Yes, Mrs. Williams,* which would be published a year or so later. He was not idle in 1957.

And 1958 was another big year, the year of *Paterson* Five, and there was a fete in New York for him at which Zukofsky spoke mysterious but gentle words and Laughlin had a party afterward that WCW attended with Flossie and wrote his friend Abbott about:

> Laughlin borrowed his new wife's [mother's] home for the party in the fashionable east 70s where the usual literary gang drifted in for drinks and Flossie accompanied me off my feet for three or four hours.

But the signature on that letter was barely legible. In June when the great moment came of the visit, the final visit, of Pound, who had at last been released from St. Elizabeth's the two old men, each sick in his own way, had little to say to each other. Flossie reported that "Bill couldn't talk to him but sat around looking unhappy" while Ezra was "definitely a mental case" and "jittery as an eel." In October WCW had another small stroke so that his right arm was not only useless but his right leg dragged, and the doctors told him he should attempt no more public appearances. He planned more appearances anyway, according to Flossie, planned to go against the doctors after a six-month rest (that being, she said, the longest period he could stay still) ; but he was no longer his own man, could make no more plans. The cures, all the cures, were now failing.

Yet right up to the end his rare drive to live and his affability stayed with him, interrupted only infrequently by depressions. The drive could be seen in his correspondence, which kept being filled with future literary plans and with excited pleasure in current successes (Julian Beck for instance of New York's Living Theatre put on *Many Loves* in the summer of 1959, and delighted WCW with praise of the play and reviewer's comments and, best of all, a few small royalty checks) ; and the affability was in his greetings to young visiting poets, always welcome at 9 Ridge Road, and his manner at occasional public appearances. The tape about Pound that he made at Yale in 1955 is a fine still alive transcription of the manner, catching the magnanimous unpretentious tone behind his abrupt manner and his lifelong habit of overstatement as he sought to be emphatic and sometimes to shock. The tape is full of mild expletives ("Jesus," "Hell") and it is full too of characteristically extravagant assertions, many thoroughly negative, about Pound's character and work — that Pound's *Cantos* enjoyed a "tremendously inflated renown," that Pound was "tone deaf, which was why he had to pose as a great musician," that Pound had gone "to the Chinese because nobody knows any Chinese" — but underlying the assertiveness can be heard WCW's equally characteristic modesty. After declaring some of Pound's *Cantos* unreadable for instance he added, "at least by me," and while damning the poor man up and down he displayed at the same time his everlasting admiration for him, recollecting for the student interviewer loving details of his still bright visit to Pound in London in 1910, Pound being then annoyed by WCW's tourism and asking, "Did you come to see the sheep in Hyde Park or me?" and both of them being entranced by Edmund Gosse as Gosse tried to cut off Yeats at a poetry reading by going "bang bang bang" with a gavel. WCW put a lot into that "bang bang bang" on the tape, and was boyish to the last syllable in the full hour's session, being interviewed by youth, hence enjoying youth. Never did the authoritarian creep into his voice but only good humor and the joy of having someone young troubling to listen.

What it was that kept him going for so long should not perhaps be searched for. Pound had the right tone for the search in 1912 when he reviewed WCW's little book *The Tempers* and said, "God forbid that I should introduce Mr. Williams as a cosmic force." He must have meant that what he knew then of his already old friend had persuaded him that he was an ordinary unassuming human and his ordinariness was his strength. It was the ordinariness certainly that Pound found warm and congenial, an ordinariness that Pound may have wished for in himself and could therefore admire in his friend, an ordinariness that enabled WCW to do with the ordinary in his writing what Pound could not do, and in fact what few writers have ever done. And yet if WCW had been *merely* ordinary — if he had been for example of the order of plainness of the man on the subway whom he saw only in a moment and made into a prototype of the ordinary — he would not then have written a half, a tenth, of what WCW wrote, and would not have stayed up late in the attic or answered all those letters. For true plainness must be a plainness of spirit too that keeps the possessor from distinguishing himself from his companions by working harder than they do, or sleeping less, or thinking more. WCW's spirit was not plain; it was not cosmic either, but it was something special, something whose "secret" was to be revealed sooner by his fierce old English grandmother than the man who looked like his father on the subway. The father was not the strange-energy source, the grandmother was. It was appropriate that WCW should end the last of the finished books of *Paterson* by reinvoking the grandmother in her fierceness, and also by coming out at last with grandmother's secret about the first Williams:

> She did not want to live to be
>
> an old woman to wear a china doorknob
> in her vagina to hold her womb up — but
>
> she came to that, resourceful, what?
> He was the first to turn her up
>
> and never left her till he left her
> with child, as any soldier would

WCW must have known that he was special, not just a dog sniffing the trees like the other dogs. His pieties about commonness as the great art font do not ring true though he never abandoned them. He would not have written *Paterson* if he had not had a sense of high mission; he would not have been so offended at those like

Winters and Jarrell who thought him a first-rate small poet but second-rate thinker if he had not thought he was finally better than they thought he was. There was modesty in WCW's manner but not in his literary ambitions, not in his designs upon the future. Underneath the common man, the kindly tough-guy doctor, he was one of the most determined of that American species, the self-made man, knowing that he had begun as nothing, as an outsider with his nose pressed against the window, but believing in his inexhaustible Americanness that he could *be* something, in fact anything that he wanted if he just kept at it.

That sort of determination has been the source of great sadness in American letters, since there is more to literature than the doing it; and to the extent that WCW was indiscriminate in encouraging young writers to believe that they could make a life, a whole life, of writing he may be found at fault, along with dozens and dozens of teachers of creative writing, for breeding false expectations. Yet his own writing determination was mixed with a good sense of the difficulty of writing and the toughness of the reality that the writing had to search out.

4

In late 1959 he was operated on for cancer of the sigmoid. Flossie reported that though he lost twenty pounds he made a "good recovery." By this time his eyes were so bad that he could not read at all but he was still at his typewriter and would peck at it and have Flossie read back to him what he wrote and correct it. She also read to him out of books, sometimes three or four hours a day, the very last book being Marjorie Kinnan Rawlings' *The Yearling*. She found the reading exhausting but couldn't "bear to see him just sitting."

This misery lasted more than two years. Not long before the end he was interviewed by Stanley Koehler for *The Paris Review*, part of that magazine's series of literary interviews that was going strong at the time. The interview was conducted for an hour or two a day over several days, with Flossie constantly in attendance while WCW struggled "to find and pronounce words" but had to let many of his sentences end "in no more than a wave of the hand." Koehler reported that WCW approved the printing of the interview and that he had been "much entertained" by Flossie's part in it when she reported on her own feelings about his poetic career — that his early verse was "pretty bad," that the city of Rutherford never really knew he was a poet, that both Flossie and WCW's mother sometimes tried to make him write more "conventionally." But the sections with WCW struggling for words were so pitiful that the public press might well have been spared them. The interview ended with a tapering off into nonsequiturs and WCW muttering, "I'm alive," then saying it more firmly: "I'm still alive!"

That was in April of 1962. By June it was hopeless, the cures were over and Flossie said,

> Bill fades slowly and steadily. He can't read — can't talk distinctly — and his memory is just nonexistent. It's sad to witness the collapse of a personality that was so vital, energetic and humane. Such is life.

He died on March 4, 1963. His death was attributed to cerebral thrombosis. Until near the end he had said that he wished to be cremated, but when two Rutherford friends of his were buried in Hillside Cemetery within a year or so of his own death he decided, as Flossie put it, that he wanted to be with them. The family went ahead with a conventional funeral and burial, except that a Unitarian minister who was an anthropologist presided and nothing from the Bible was read and the casket remained closed.

In the funeral parlor where the main service was conducted the minister made a good deal of the incapacity of ordinary Americans — such as the Rutherford citizens sitting uncomfortably in front of him — to recognize and appreciate great artistic talent when it appeared among them, and he brought in "the Harvard philosopher and poet" George Santayana as an instance, noting that "in 1914 Santayana retired to Rome and turned his back on America as hopeless." Following that he tried to comfort his listeners by observing that WCW had, despite local indifference or resistance, tried to "look at poetry from a local viewpoint." The minister concluded by reading a not very representative example of WCW's localness, a passage from *Paterson* Five about the qualities of the imagination, and everyone then drove in the rain to the graveyard where a tent had been set up and a more local WCW poem was intoned, "Tract," one of his most anthologized pieces but one not designed to comfort those who had just ridden out in their well-upholstered machines.

> *Tract*
>
> I will teach you my townspeople
> how to perform a funeral
> for you have it over a troop
> of artists —
> unless one should scour the world —
> you have the ground sense necessary.
>
> See! the hearse leads.
> I begin with a design for a hearse.
> For Christ's sake not black —
> nor white either — and not polished!
> Let it be weathered — like a farm wagon —
> with gilt wheels (this could be
> applied fresh at small expense)
> or no wheels at all:
> a rough dray to drag over the ground.
>
> Knock the glass out!
> My God — glass, my townspeople!
> For what purpose? Is it for the dead
> to look out or for us to see
> how well he is housed or to see
> the flowers or the lack of them —
> or what?
> To keep the rain and snow from him?
> He will have a heavier rain soon:

pebbles and dirt and what not.
Let there be no glass —
and no upholstery, phew!
and no little brass rollers
and small easy wheels on the bottom —
my townspeople what are you thinking of?
A rough plain hearse then
with gilt wheels and no top at all.
On this the coffin lies
by its own weight.

            No wreaths please —
especially no hot house flowers.
Some common memento is better,
something he prized and is known by:
his old clothes — a few books perhaps —
God knows what! You realize
how we are about these things
my townspeople —
something will be found — anything
even flowers if he had to come to that.
So much for the hearse.

For heaven's sake though see to the driver!
Take off the silk hat! In fact
that's no place at all for him —
up there unceremoniously
dragging our friend out to his own dignity!
Bring him down — bring him down!
Low and inconspicuous! I'd not have him ride
on the wagon at all — damn him —
the undertaker's understrapper!
Let him hold the reins
and walk at the side
and inconspicuously too!

Then briefly as to yourselves:
Walk behind — as they do in France,
seventh class, or if you ride
Hell take curtains! Go with some show
of inconvenience; sit openly —

to the weather as to grief.
Or do you think you can shut grief in?
What — from us? We who have perhaps
nothing to lose? Share with us
share with us — it will be money
in your pockets.
                              Go now
I think you are ready.

Later, son Bill observed that maybe a few of the mourners
should have walked to the cemetery in honor of the poem but
Flossie said no, WCW would have liked the funeral the way it was,
meaning presumably that in the days of Cadillac hearses and pro-
cessions of sleek closed cars the prescriptions of the poem would
have seemed, if followed, pretentious and out of date. In any
event, during the brief tent service an ancient car that was not
sleek at all arrived from New York loaded with poets who had
been misinformed about the time of the funeral, and the poets
now in amazing numbers and dressed in black suits (ill-fitting,
their "show of inconvenience") poured from their near equivalent to a wagon and joined the other mourners. And at that time
also, after a day of rain and gloom, the skies opened and bright-
ened and gained depth making it seem, as son Bill put it, that
though the ceremony had not been conducted according to
"Tract" somebody "up there" had liked it anyway.

A few days after WCW's death a cousin of WCW's, William
Wellcome, who had lived in the fierce English grandmother's
house on the shore in West Haven for many years, was interviewed
by the *New Haven Register* about WCW. Wellcome was a guitar-
ist but otherwise not artistically inclined, and he reported to the
Register that WCW had always been most friendly, kind and respectful of familial ties but that his verse remained incomprehen-
sible to him. It was like cubism, said Wellcome; or better, it was
like modern jazz (Wellcome did not like modern jazz, playing
only Dixieland). So at least Wellcome reported, eleven years
later, to this biographer — and then he waved in the summer air a

yellow copy of the *Register* piece, being most proud of WCW but still baffled by him.

There were those, though, who did understand. Soon after his death WCW won two more big prizes, the Pulitzer and the Gold Medal for Poetry of the National Institute of Arts and Letters, and it became slowly evident, in all the places where poetry is read, that WCW had at last won his long fight for his kind of Americanness, localness and modernity in poetry, and that Rutherford with his name attached to it could no longer be regarded as, in Pound's phrase, a hole in the wall.

Bibliography

Chronology

Index

Notes

The works by WCW most frequently referred to are abbreviated as indicated below. For the dates of these works and a listing of other WCW works, see Bibliography.

Kora	*Kora in Hell*
SA	*Spring and All*
TGAN	*The Great American Novel*
IAG	*In the American Grain*
VP	*Voyage to Pagany*
LPR	*Life Along the Passaic River*
WM	*White Mule*
ADOL	*A Dream of Love*
CLP	*Collected Later Poems*
Au	*Autobiography*
CEP	*Collected Earlier Poems*
BU	*The Build-Up*
SL	*The Selected Letters*
IWWP	*I Wanted to Write a Poem*
YMW	*Yes, Mrs. Williams*
FD	*The Farmers' Daughters*
ML	*Many Loves*
PB	*Pictures from Brueghel*
Pat	*Paterson*
Imag	*Imaginations*

Chronology

(Major Events and Publications in the Life of WCW)

1883 *(September 17)*. Born in Rutherford, New Jersey

1897–8. Year in Switzerland with brother Ed. Schooled at the Château de Lancy, near Geneva

1899–1901. Horace Mann School, NYC

1902–6. Medical School, University of Pennsylvania. Meets Pound, H.D., Charles Demuth

1906–8. Interns in New York hospitals

1909. *Poems*. Proposes to Florence Herman

1909–10. Year in Leipzig. Visits Pound in London

1910. Begins Rutherford medical practice

1912. Marries Florence Herman

1913. *The Tempers*

1914. First child, William Eric Williams

1915. Meetings in Grantwood, New Jersey, with Alfred Kreymborg and the *Others* group

1916. Second child, Paul

1917. *Al Que Quiere!*

1918. Death of father, William George Williams

1920. Death of grandmother, Emily Dickinson Wellcome. Edits *Contact* with Robert McAlmon. *Kora in Hell*

1923. *Spring and All* and *The Great American Novel*

1924. Trip to Europe. "Sabbatical" from medicine

1925. *In the American Grain*

1926. Wins *Dial* Award

1927–8. Mrs. Williams and two children abroad. *Voyage to Pagany. Descent of Winter* (in Pound's *Exile*)

1930–2. *Pagany* with Richard Johns

1931. Zukofsky's "objectivist" issue of *Poetry*. Summer trip to Newfoundland

1932. *Knife of the Times*. Edits *Contact* again

1934. *Collected Poems (1921–31)*

1937. *White Mule*, James Laughlin's first publishing venture with WCW

1938. *Life Along the Passaic River* and *The Complete Collected Poems*

1938. Formation of "The Friends of William Carlos Williams"

1940. *In the Money*

1946. *Paterson I.* Honorary Degree from University of Buffalo

1948. *Paterson II* and *A Dream of Love.* Russell Loines Award. First heart attack

1949. *Selected Poems*

1950. *Paterson III.* National Book Award. *Collected Later Poems* and *Make Light of It*

1951. *Paterson IV, Autobiography* and *Collected Earlier Poems*

1952. *The Build-Up.* Appointment as Consultant in Poetry at Library of Congress, delayed first by WCW's health, then held up and finally abandoned by Library of Congress

1953. Bollingen Award

1958. *I Wanted to Write A Poem. Paterson V*

1959. *Yes, Mrs. Williams. Many Loves*

1962. *Pictures from Brueghel*

1963 *(March 4).* Death in Rutherford. Pulitzer Prize. Gold Medal for Poetry of National Institute of Arts and Letters

Notes

Chapter One *(Pages 1–56)*

3 Jones poem. "The Black Man Is Making New Gods," *Black Magic* (Indianapolis: Bobbs-Merrill, 1969), p. 205.

4 "The acanthus is." Ms., Beinecke Library, Yale University.

6 "Stray dogs," "feminism, futurism and free love." Introduction, Kilmer's *Poems, Essays and Letters,* Robert C. Holliday, ed. (Port Washington, N.Y.: Kennikat Press, 1946), 2 vols. Vol. I, p. 74.

"Incomprehensibilism." Holliday, I, p. 235.

"Celebration of the queer and nasty," "when we soldiers get back." Holliday, I, pp. 110-11.

8 "The True Contemporary." Karl Shapiro in *In Defense of Ignorance* (New York: Random House, 1960), p. 155.

9 "Yelling to be taken in again." *Au,* p. 3.

10 "Burn up fifty growing boys." *Au,* p. 5.

"Don't touch me!" *Au,* p. 24.

"A woman does not need to be a prude." *Yes, Mrs. Williams: A Personal Record of My Mother,* File 270, ms., Beinecke. The document is undated but handwritten in a firm hand — probably as late as the early 1930s.

"Dedication for a Plot of Ground." *CEP,* p. 171. The ground in question was in West Haven, Connecticut, right on the edge of Long Island Sound, where Grandmother Wellcome lived in her latter years. The other poem about her — "Last Words of My English Grandmother" — describes how she was taken by ambulance from her home in West Haven to the New Haven hospital, with grandson WCW riding along with her. The five-year-old who came over with her on the boat was WCW's father, William George Williams. The Brooklyn man she married was named Wellcome. The daughter she lost was Juanita, victim of epilepsy. Her oldest son was WCW's Uncle Irving, and it was his children that she mothered in her old age in West Haven.

12   "Her labor and delivery." File 275, *YMW* ms., Beinecke.

"The son of an Episcopal minister." *Au*, p. 167.

"Half English and half Danish." From "Dr. Williams' Position," *Literary Essays of Ezra Pound* (New York: New Directions, 1968), p. 390.

"The legend is." File 275, *YMW* ms., Beinecke.

"Now the Godwins." *YMW*, p. 6.

13   "Dropped her aiches." *Au*, p. 4.

"Dear Willy." File 274, *YMW* ms., Beinecke.

"Or tried to," "laid her out." *Au*, p. 5.

"Delightful talk." Restricted WCW file, possession of Mrs. Williams.

14   "French out of Martinique." *YMW*, p. 3.

"An obscure art student." *YMW*, p. 5.

"She returned from Paris unscathed." File 275, *YMW* ms., Beinecke.

15   "Williams is a fine young man." *YMW*, p. 10.

"On the rebound." Flossie Williams' words.

"The rum trade." EP's words. WCW described him as a "rum-taster," *YMW*, p. 9.

"Ended it." File 275, *YMW* ms., Beinecke.

"Inscribed with the legend," "She became pregnant." File 275, *YMW* ms., Beinecke.

16   "God help us all." File 275, *YMW* ms., Beinecke.

"*Allez, allez! ma petite!*" *YMW*, p. 17.

"You heard about." *YMW*, p. 47.

17   "Sometimes." *YMW*, p. 82.

"What are you doing there." *YMW*, p. 26–27.

"I took him up." *Au*, p. 15.

"Pâtés," "tidal wave," "curiously mild," detestable tomato, liberal, socialist, Unitarian Society. *YMW*, p. 7.

"Determined women." *YMW*, p. 3.

18   "At heart," "a stickler." *Au*, p. 91.

Pop's death. *Au*, p. 166.

"We must have been." *YMW*, p. 14.

19   "Forbidden works," "I remember hearing, as much as I could stay awake for, Du Maurier's *Trilby*." *YMW*, p. 9.

"What the h — l," "My dear boy." EP letter quoted by WCW, prologue to *Kora in Hell,* in *Imaginations,* Webster Schott, ed. (New York: New Directions, 1970), p. 12.

"To call." Typescript 18 of *Au*, Beinecke.

"None of his." From "Dr. Williams' Position," *Literary Essays of Ezra Pound*, p. 391.

"Where a European." *Literary Essays of Ezra Pound*, p. 392.

20   A plane over Wyoming. Introduction, *Criterion Book of Modern American Verse*, ed. W. H. Auden (New York: Criterion, 1956).

22   Bagellon House. *Au*, pp. 6–8.

"If she painted," "The restless and resistless Emily," "under the pretext." File 275, *YMW* ms., Beinecke.

23   "She enjoyed," "a house built," "what of the love." File 275, *YMW* ms., Beinecke.

"It was a good." Typescript #18 of *Au*, Beinecke.

"Lizzie, Lilah," "Charlie and Fred." From a two-page document, typed, entitled "School Stuff," in the miscellaneous pages surrounding the mss. for *Au*, Beinecke.

24   "The lust." *Au*, p. 47.

25   The man had been through hell. WCW's introduction to *Howl* (San Francisco: City Lights Books, 1956), p. 7.

26   "The young William Carlos." From "Dr. Williams' Position," *Literary Essays of Ezra Pound*.

Servant girls. *Au*, p. 12.

Dostoevskian attacks. *Au*, pp. 16–17.

28   "Circumcision." *Au*, p. 22.

"That at least." *Au*, p. 28.

"General deviltry." *Au*, p. 30.

Switzerland. *Au*, pp. 28–34.

29   The "feudle castle" essay, signed Willie Williams, is uncorrected and ungraded. It is part of the Beinecke holdings connected with the autobiography mss.

Horace Mann. The sour grapes are to be found in a ms. at Beinecke, "My Years as a Student at Horace Mann," dated 1935. In the later autobiography he is more mellow, praises Miss Butler and other teachers, and says that at Horace Mann he learned to work hard.

29–
30   "Simply enough," "lounging way." From "My Years as a Student at Horace Mann."

30   Spencer. Ezra Pound, *Guide to Kulchur* (New York: New Directions, 1968), p. 31.

"At one point the canoe had upset." *Au*, p. 45.

"A black, black cloud." *Au*, p. 47.

Notebooks. *Au*, p. 53.

page

31   White legs, *Au,* pp. 47–48.

"Adolescent heart strain." *Au,* p. 46.

32   "Wanted to tell people." *Au,* p. 48.

"Instinctively knew." *Au,* p. 49.

33   "Before he had finished." "I never went to college. I didn't have to, for at the University of Pennsylvania they admitted selected men to medical school in those days from certain high schools and I had been to Horace Mann in New York, one of the best." *Au,* p. 50. WCW later got an honorary degree from Horace Mann.

Edgar went off. WCW does not say whether Edgar completed the requirements.

"A better writer," "formal instruction." From "My Years as a Student at Horace Mann."

34   "I was going to work." *Au,* p. 49.

"There are lots." The story was told me by poet Roderick Jellema.

35 -   "Of literary differences." From "Obit: A. R. Orage," *Literary Essays of Ezra Pound.*

Forty-seven saloons. Patricia Hutchins, *Ezra Pound's Kensington: An Exploration, 1885–1913* (Chicago: Regnery, 1965), p. 29.

"They were horse thieves." Hutchins, p. 26.

36   "Publishing executives." Hugh Kenner, *The Pound Era* (Berkeley: University of California Press, 1971), p. 265.

Aldington, in *The Egoist,* 1914. Quoted by Hugh Witemeyer in *The Poetry of Ezra Pound: Forms and Renewal, 1908–1920* (Berkeley: University of California Press, 1969), p. 198.

37   "Were both too refined." *IWWP,* p. 6.

One critic. George P. Elliott in "Poet of Many Voices," *The Carleton Miscellany,* Vol. II, 3, 1961, p. 79.

"No! there is nothing!" *"Portrait d'une Femme."* Ezra Pound, *Personae* (New York: New Directions, 1950).

"All his early work." Kenner, p. 268.

"21 units." In "Penn's Poet Friends," Emily Mitchell Wallace, *Pennsylvania Gazette,* February 1973.

38   Unnecessary obscurity. " 'The jewels I speak of [said Ezra] are the backs of the books in a bookcase.' 'Oh,' said Pop. 'Of course . . . But . . . if it's books you're talking about, why don't you say so then?' Ezra appears never to have forgotten the lesson." *Au,* p. 92.

39   "Don't think I don't realize." Wallace.

"Crackerjack team," "all to the mustard," "talk about Philadelphia," "there is nothing." From letters to Edgar in college years (copies at Beinecke).

page

".. . quite a swell affair," "both puritanical," "isn't that fierce?" Letters to Edgar.

40 "You must be more merry." Letter to Mother Elena, probably 1906, Beinecke.

41 Nearly flunked. Wallace.

42 Demuth painting. "I Saw the Figure 5 in Gold," with the word "Carlos" in it. The poem is "The Great Figure," *CEP*, p. 230. The painting is described in *Au*, p. 152.

"Used to paint." *Au*, p. 61.

"Where hepaticas grew." *SL*, p. 9.

43 "Oh but she is a fine girl." Letter to Edgar, 1907, in *SL*, p. 9.

"Hark Hilda," "It was an ode." Typescript 18, Beinecke.

"Wonderfully in love," "a good guy." *Au*, p. 68.

"Beyond all others." H.D. letter to WCW, 1907, in Folder F, restricted WCW collection, Lockwood Library, Buffalo.

"Nothing but a nomad." Hutchins, p. 36.

"All great love." H.D. letter in Folder F, Lockwood.

44 "Ezra and I are not going to marry." Letter in Folder F, March 7, 1908.

"Sitalkas." *The New Freewoman*, September 1, 1913.

"Bah!" *Others*, 1919, the final issue.

45 "This would cost." From a 1907 letter in the possession of William Eric Williams.

"Remember you are going." Letter to Edgar, 1907, copy at Beinecke.

"WCW was about five feet nine." Unprinted reminiscence written by William Eric Williams. Copy in possession of biographer.

"Did not walk." Letter to Patricia Hutchins, 1957. Quoted in *Ezra Pound's Kensington*, p. 44.

46 "Nothing like it." *The Letters of Ezra Pound*, D. D. Paige, ed., (New York: Harcourt Brace, 1950), p. 41.

"Left the house." *Letters of Wallace Stevens*, Holly Stevens, ed., (New York: Knopf, 1966), p. 58.

"This morning." *Letters of Wallace Stevens*, p. 60.

47 "Tonight there was." *Letters of Wallace Stevens*, p. 81.

"I have just received." Letter to Edgar, undated, copy at Beinecke.

48 "Sewage makes gardens grow." Letter to Kenneth Burke, 1921, copy at Beinecke.

"Thou ask'st me all." From ms. of long poem entitled "A Tragedy" that was sent with letter to Edgar in 1906. 115 lines copied in Thirlwall file, Beinecke.

"Poor whore." *Au*, p. 81.

page

49   BABIES FRESH. *Au,* p. 94.

"In love with." *Au,* p. 55.

"People's guts." *Au,* p. 77.

52   Out of touch. EP letter to WCW, 1908, Paige, p. 8.

"Show the world," "Isadora when I saw." Letter to Edgar, 1908, copy at Beinecke.

54   "Is a painter's heart crooked." Paige, p. 4.

Chapter Two   *(Pages 57–91)*

61   "Like bean-stalks." *BU,* p. 255.

62   "Ground his teeth," "fought back." *BU,* p. 258.

Proposal to Flossie. *BU,* p. 261.

Mike Weaver. Weaver's book is simply called *William Carlos Williams* (London: Oxford, 1971). WCW refers to Weininger in a letter written to *The New Freewoman* in 1914. The willing-to-love theme is present in WCW's play *Dream of Love.*

"Half kiss." In the letters and the autobiography it is simply joked about as a half kiss, but in *The Build-Up* it is built up: he tried to kiss her but she was "scared at her own temerity and half turned away her face so that he touched only half her mouth with his lips." *BU,* p. 264.

63   "And oh Florence." Folder No. 1, restricted letter file, in possession of Mrs. William Carlos Williams.

"Anyhow Bo." Letter to Edgar, 1908, copy at Beinecke.

"Kindly speak." Flossie to WCW, July 12, 1909, Beinecke.

64   "Pretend." Flossie to WCW, July 12, 1909, Beinecke.

"Cattle boat," "Gee!" Folder No. 1, restricted letter file, Mrs. WCW.

"I miss you terribly." Restricted file, Mrs. WCW.

65   "As if." *BU,* p. 264.

"If I only had a car, a boat." Restricted file, Mrs. WCW.

"It would break." Paige, pp. 17–18.

66   "Didn't have much fun." *Au,* p. 111.

4 x 7 cards. His son Bill still has the file. Sample entry: *"Typhoid, Walking. Very light and no bacillae in blood. Much more frequent in men because* (?) *men keep 'walking.' Pains in the region of the spleen is often a sign. Headaches, low fever at night (39.6). After fall of fever as long as splenic humor persists there is danger of relapse."*

Chopping away. He could remember all the details much later: "When he saw the awkward, young-girl's curve of her neck had been retouched, her shoulders smoothed over by the 'skill' of that God-damned photographer

... he took the blade of a knife and ... restored the normal, the actual, not beautiful contours of the neckline." *BU*, p. 266.

67 "To teach." Restricted file, Mrs. WCW.

Constantinople letter. Restricted file, Mrs. WCW.

"Silly infatuation." *BU*, p. 265.

Vassar, nursing. *BU*, p. 265.

How-could-you. Flossie's letters to Leipzig are not in the available collections, but this one can be reconstructed in detail from WCW's methodical reply.

The letter of his life. Dated November 24, 1909. Restricted file, Mrs. WCW.

69 "Shining." *BU*, p. 262.

"That boy." *BU*, p. 260.

"He'd never amount." *BU*, p. 266.

"It stank." *BU*, p. 238.

"Highest honors." *BU*, p. 258.

73 "A poor little idle word." Letter to Viola Baxter, 1908, copy at Beinecke.

74 "An old worn out," "find some real man," "there's nothing," "forget." Restricted file, Mrs. WCW.

London with EP. *Au*, pp. 113–17.

75 WCW had *learned* something. EP letter to Mrs. Pound, 1910. Beinecke.

"The best thing." Restricted file, Mrs. WCW.

"You should have." Restricted file, Mrs. WCW.

"Landing in Hoboken." *BU*, p. 265.

76 Three-year engagement. "Three years is too long to wait to be married." *Au*, p. 127.

"Degree of blessedness." Restricted file, Mrs. WCW.

77 "Despised morality." Restricted file, Mrs. WCW.

Wished the patient. Restricted file, Mrs. WCW.

78 "Leading physician." Restricted file, Mrs. WCW.

High-minded list. Restricted file, Mrs. WCW.

79 "Would have to do," "hot times." Restricted file, Mrs. WCW.

Four short plays. The other two were *A September Afternoon* — about a seventeen-year-old boy who fights for the American cause in the Revolution while his sister sits around saying it doesn't matter who runs the country — and *Plums* — about certain soldiers in the Revolution who, like the sister above, are not much interested in the Revolutionary cause. I have not seen these two manuscripts, which are described by Vivienne Koch in her book on Williams. The other two manuscripts are at Beinecke and are both typed with the same typewriter ribbon and have on the title page WCW's parents' address for WCW: 131 Passaic Ave.

84   "I feel the glory." August 2, 1912. Restricted file, Mrs. WCW.

85   "It is a story." *IWWP*, p. 26.

87   "Delightful talk." Letter to Flossie, August 10, 1911. Restricted file, Mrs. WCW.

89   Sherwood Anderson, "The Egg," *The Triumph of the Egg* (New York: Huebsch, 1921), p. 51.

"Comment about *A Lume Spento.*" Introduction to the reprint (New York: New Directions, 1965).

90   "Kitsch." *A Clerk of Oxenford* (London: Oxford University Press, 1954). Reprinted in *Problems in Prose,* Paul Haines, ed., (New York: Harper & Row, 1957).

91   "Would you have had." EP letter to WCW, 1912, Beinecke.

"Your prose style." EP letter to WCW, November 29, 1912, Beinecke.

"Dear Bill." Accompanying letter of November 29, 1912.

Chapter Three   *(Pages 92–136)*

92   "The drab and the gross." From Theodore Dreiser's memoirs as reported by Malcolm Cowley in *A Many-Windowed House: Collected Essays on American Writers and American Writing* (Carbondale: Southern Illinois University Press, 1970), p. 121.

93   "Unassailable dogma." *Stravinsky: An Autobiography* (New York: Simon & Schuster, 1936), p. 15.

"Voyant." In *La Lettre du Voyant* (English translation in *Rimbaud's Poetic Practice,* W. M. Fruhock, Cambridge: Harvard University Press, 1963).

"All smashed." D. H. Lawrence, *Selected Literary Criticism,* Anthony Beal, ed. (New York: Viking Compass Edition, 1967), pp. 72, 74.

94   Futurists' pronouncements. From *Artists on Art: From the XIV to the XX Century,* Robert Goldwater, ed. (New York: Pantheon, 1945). The manifesto's author was Umberto Boccione.

97   Irving Babbitt. *The New Laokoon: An Essay on the Confusion of the Arts* (Houghton Mifflin: Boston, 1910). Earlier connections between painting and poetry are dealt with in a recent book, *Encounters,* John Dixon Hunt, ed. (New York: Norton, 1972), which also includes a comparison of the uses of painting in Stevens and WCW, by Bram Dijkstra.

"Has at its command," "attempts to paint." Babbitt, p. 50.

"Necessarily follow." Babbitt, p. 49.

98   "The volume." *Selected Prose 1909–65* (New York: New Directions, 1973).

"I've had a fight." Margaret Anderson, *My Thirty Years' War* (New York: Hermitage House, 1953), p. 61.

page

99   EP's "imagist gospel" has been printed widely, but perhaps the earliest printing was in *Poetry,* 1913, "A Few Don'ts by an Imagiste," p. 200.

"No ideas but in things." In a WCW poem, "Paterson," that won the *Dial* award, 1927. Later used in many contexts.

"The method of Luminous Detail." *Selected Prose 1909–65,* p. 21.

100   "An intellectual." Also in "A Few Dont's by an Imagiste."

The soul. *Selected Prose 1909–65,* p. 29.

101   "Possessed, beyond role." Kenner, *The Pound Era,* p. 268.

"Spare us the beauty." From the first stanza of "Priapus, Keeper of Orchards," which appeared in Vol. I, No. 1, of *Poetry.*

102   "A wild moment." H.D., *Hermetic Definition* (New York: New Directions, 1972), p. 112.

105   *Snobisme.* Reported by F. S. Flint in *Poetry,* 1913.

106   "Love in country lanes." *Poetry,* 1913.

"Cyclists." *Poetry,* 1914.

107   WCW poems in *Poetry.* In addition to "Sicilian Emigrants Song," the other three were "Postlude," "Peace on Earth," and "Immortal."

108   "I snort defiance." A 1901 statement of Shaw's, reprinted in *Camera Work,* 1906.

Maeterlinck on photography. *Camera Work,* No. 1, 1903.

112   Joseph Addison on Virgil. *Eighteenth Century Critical Essays,* Scott Elledge, ed. (New York: Cornell University Press, 1961), Vol. II, p. 6.

113   "The Young Housewife." The poem did not actually appear in the original *Al Que Quiere!,* though the *CEP* includes it there. It did, however, appear in *Others* in 1916, a year before *Al Que Quiere!*

114   "I could have sunk." *Au,* p. 137.

115   "They tied in." Wylie Sypher's extended historical summary, in *Rococo to Cubism in Art and Literature* (New York: Random House, 1960).

116   "Scientists studying fossils." The first chapter of Ruthven Todd's *Tracks in the Snow: Studies in English, Science and Art* (New York: Scribners, 1947) has a fine discussion of this.

119   WCW on Duchamps. Prologue to *Kora in Hell.* Appears pp. 8–10, *Imaginations,* Webster Schott, ed. (New York: New Directions, 1970).

120   "Roughly classed." WCW's phrase. *Imag,* p. 8.

"Broken style." *Imag,* p. 7.

121   "The coining of similes." *Imag,* p. 18.

123   "Essentially comic," "clarified the sleeping eye." In "The Importance of Being Dada," *Adventures in the Arts: Informed Chapters on Painters, Vaudeville, and Poets,* Marsden Hartley, ed. (New York: Boni & Liveright, 1921), p. 30.

page

Kandinsky. Kandinsky put his findings musically: "The terms 'rhythmic' and 'unrhythmic' are conventional, as are 'harmony' and 'discord,' which have no actuality." He then said that he had himself tried three kinds of painting (of which the second kind is relevant here): "(1) a direct impression of nature, expressed in purely pictorial form. This I call an 'Impression'. (2) A largely unconscious, spontaneous expression of inner character, non-material nature. This I call an 'Improvisation'. (3) An expression of a slowly formed inner feeling, tested and worked over repeatedly and almost pedantically. This I call a 'Composition.'" From *Uber das Gestige in der Kunst*, portions of which appeared in the first issue of *Blast*, 1914. WCW refers to the piece in the preface to *Kora*, in *Imag*, p. 26.

131   T. E. Hulme. "On Modern Art," *Speculations: Essays on Humanism and the Philosophy of Art*, Herbert Read, ed. (New York: The Humanities Press, 1936). Worringer's views are set forth in *Abstraction and Empathy: A Contribution to the Psychology of Style* (New York: International University Press, 1953).

133   That they simply *were*. *SA*, p. 89.

Destroy them all. *SA*, p. 90.

135   "Pure products." The poem was No. 18 in *SA*.

Chapter Four   *(Pages 137–185)*

137   "Stealing." *TGAN*, p. 161.

138   Quotations on surgery and his role in Rutherford. From WCW, "Three Professional Studies," appearing originally in *The Little Review* and reprinted in *The Little Review Anthology*, Margaret Anderson, ed. (New York: Horizon, 1970), p. 240.

Doctors who handled the poor. See WCW's story "Old Doc Rivers" in *FD*.

139   "A new chapter," "truly a great man." *TGAN*, p. 167.

141   "A white thought." From "Le Médecin Malgré Lui," first published in *Poetry*, 1918.

WCW letter to his mother. April 27, 1916, in the possession of William Eric Williams.

142   Grew orchids and entered flower competitions. See WCW's poem "A Celebration" in *CEP*.

147   Marriage remains prose, and infidelity poetry. For recent versions, see Howard Nemerov's volume *A Journal of the Fictive Life* and also the "swerve" theory of poetry enunciated by Harold Bloom in *The Anxiety of Influence*.

"My dear Miss Word." *TGAN*, p. 166.

148   Stealing moments. Ouspensky suggested thinking of one's own name and of being simply "here" for two minutes as a starter, but added that two minutes might be all one would ever get, that being the limit of consciousness.

150 "Biographies of writers." W. H. Auden, *A Certain World* (New York: Viking, 1970), p. vii.

151 Auden letter to WCW, Beinecke.

"Happy or unhappy." *A Certain World*, p. 248.

"Why should we spit." *A Certain World*, p. 225.

"Even the purest poem." *A Certain World*, p. 424.

152 "Words." *TGAN*, p. 160.

153 "Get him to swallow." *A Novelette*, in *Imag*, p. 278.

155 "Beloved likeness." WCW letters to Viola Baxter are in Beinecke file.

"Wonders today," "good party," playhouse. *Au*, pp. 152–53.

156 The town against WCW. *Au*, p. 155.

"A European politeness." Lewis Adams in an obituary for Edgar Williams in *The Century Association Year Book*, 1974, p. 280.

157 "How smoothly." *Kora*, p. 37.

"Three bullets." *Kora*, p. 38.

158 "The time never was." *Kora*, p. 47.

"Filthiness." Jordan letters, Beinecke.

159 Came to his friends. Robert McAlmon in *Post-Adolescence*, an autobiographical novel included in *McAlmon and the Lost Generation*, Robert Knoll, ed. (Lincoln, Nebraska: University of Nebraska Press, 1962). His presex period. *IWWP*, p. 23.

"Lighthouse." From the poem "Great Mullen," *CEP*.

"Create a woman." *ADOL*, p. 200.

160 "Alternate caresses." *Kora*, p. 48.

161 "Big Boy." *The Autobiography of Emanuel Carnevali.*

"A girl who had happened." *Au*, p. 266.

Description of Carnevali. Last issue of *Others*, 1919.

162 "An enormous commonplace." Carnevali, p. 148.

"My friends." Carnevali, pp. 143, 147.

163 "Group" to help Carnevali, "dearest Bill." Letters from Harriet Monroe and Carnevali to WCW, Beinecke.

"He was straight." *Au*, p. 266.

A "black" writer. Last issue of *Others*, 1919.

164 "The instructor." Knoll, *Post-Adolescence*, p. 67.

165 "One does not become." Knoll, p. 89.

"A coldly intense young man," "an ideal youth's figure." *Au*, pp. 175–76. The latter remark is unusually pretentious for WCW.

page

"Sort of father-son relationship." *SL*, p. 56.

How he felt toward McAlmon. These comments are from *VP*, pp. 22–24. The complete paragraph about connotations runs: "he was disturbed, avowedly. The connotations of his affections for Jack with nothing he could do about it — nothing to do — the slipping, slipping way the world has of getting out from under a difficulty and presenting the wrong face of an object, while it gives you, yes, perhaps what you ask, distressed him heavily."

166 "Love." *VP*, p. 25.

167 "Posing in the nude." *Au*, p. 175.

"The one thing." *Au*, p. 172.

"Yup, they give." *Post-Adolescence*, Ch. 4.

168 Lady poetess, "Swaying and spouting." *Post-Adolescence*, Ch. 4.

171 "Wiped out." *Au*, p. 174.

172 "He did not move in." The possible exception is his Stecher trilogy — but that was not, or so it will be argued later, in its main thrust naturalistic either.

173 "A prisoner." Journal of 1927–1928, Lockwood.

"Through the obscurity." *ML*, pp. 101–2.

174 Spokesman of social protest. *Au*, p. 155.

"A plump, good-natured guy." *Au*, p. 142.

176 "And what has anything." *TGAN*, p. 172.

Wells and Henry James. From *Henry James and H. G. Wells: A Record of Their Friendship*, Leon Edel and Gordon N. Ray, ed. (Carbondale: University of Illinois, 1958), p. 264.

"Cannot, must not." *TGAN*, p. 172.

178 Kept saying. Letter from *PR* to H. H. Lewis, February 4, 1936, Beinecke. See also Ch. six.

180 "In a city." Ginsberg quoted in *About Paterson* by Christopher Norwood (New York: Saturday Review Press, 1974), p. 90. The other information about Paterson in the preceding paragraph is from the same book.

"Right guy." Letter from Allen Ginsberg to WCW, June 6, 1949, Beinecke.

181 "The realism of WCW." J. Hillis Miller's thesis about WCW is contained in *Poets of Reality: Six Twentieth-Century Writers* (Cambridge: Belknap Press of Harvard University Press, 1965).

183 "Literally felt." *Au*, p. 176.

McAlmon comments on EP, Joyce. Undated letter, probably 1922, from McAlmon to WCW, in hands of WEW.

184 "Florence and the youngsters." RM letter to WCW, 1922.

"*All* the reading." *Au*, p. 183.

"I'm writing a thesis." *Au*, p. 183.

Chapter Five *(Pages 186–226)*

186 "Rushed perhaps in places." Beinecke.

"I suppose." *Au*, p. 170.

WCW's Lawrentian pronouncements. See discussion of WCW's essay on Poe, p. 204 of this book.

"All my lief." Typescript 18, Beinecke.

188 Protestations about drinking. One such protestation is in the bathtub gin passage. "[The gin] didn't bother me much aside from brief moments of asinine behavior, for I was never a drinker." *Au*, p. 170.

"Profound discussion." Kay Boyle's version of *Being Geniuses Together*, p. 187.

189 Hitting a neighbor child. According to son Bill.

"Rome" ms. Lockwood.

Anger had also moved out. WCW singled out Malcolm Cowley for attack, for example: if art were really to get out it would "kill nearly the whole world, Malcolm Cowley bitten by a copperhead." The Cowley annoyance is not wholly explicable, though Cowley scarcely mentions WCW in his mountainous writings and the neglect may have been the chief thing. WCW contributed frequently to *The New Republic* when Cowley was there. In the thirties WCW asked Cowley for a job for his son Paul but Cowley did not (maybe he could not) find one.

Anger about the academy. "The woman who throws herself from the rocks into the sea has more force than the sum of every college." Rome ms., Lockwood.

190 "Moved by." Boyle's *McAlmon*, p. 186.

191 WCW's Sacco-Vanzetti protest poem. "Why didn't they choose at least one decent / Jew or some fair minded Negro or anybody but such a triumvirate of inversion. the / New England aristocracy bent on working off / a grudge." From "Impromptu: The Suckers."

"America, made of the Puritan." Enny Veronica Sanders writing in *Broom*, Vol. I, No. 1, and editorializing on America's need to broaden itself. WCW himself did not appear in *Broom* until the fifth issue.

"You know." Lockwood, Notebook B.

192 A different ethic. *Au*, p. 224.

"You have pissed." *CEP*, p. 461.

193 Edgar vita. *Century Association Year Book*, 1974, p. 280.

Edgar's letters. August 1951. Copies on file, Beinecke.

195 "I'll tell you." *YMW*, p. 98.

"Very fine." *YMW*, p. 87.

"All sex." Letter from Elena at the shore to WCW, 1938, Beinecke.

page

196   Falling in love with a beautiful green and red truck. *Imag*, p. 173.

197   "No venom." Boyle's *McAlmon*, p. 191.

Prose was fragmented. EP had described *The Great American Novel* as "the application of the Joycean method to the American circumjacence" and the description is transferable to parts of *In the American Grain*. See EP's "Dr. Williams' Position."

198   A new suit. Letter, Flossie to WCW, July 18, 1921, Beinecke. "It really ought to be a vacation for you as well — with no kids and no wife to think about or disturb you — tell Emma to make you buy a light weight summer suit. Go on and do it."

Letter to *The Egoist. The Egoist*, August 1917.

199   "Whole" again. *IAG*, p. 3.

"Floated with luck." *IAG*, p. 16.

200   "I am beautiful." *IAG*, p. 45.

"Orchidean beauty," "conqueror." *IAG*, p. 27.

"Did one expect." *IAG*, p. 127.

"The lives," "with the sense." *IAG*, p. 137.

"So they strangled." *IAG*, p. 73.

201   "A marked man." *IAG*, p. 2.

"The pursuit," "plunging." *IAG*, p. 59.

"Each shrank." *IAG*, p. 65.

Bad spellers. *IAG*, p. 66.

202   "Force," "sly." *IAG*, p. 194.

"Harness." *IAG*, p. 195.

203   Jacataqua. *IAG*, p. 187.

204   "Admired by women." *IAG*, p. 188.

"A subversive," "they nearly," "to torture." *IAG*, p. 195.

"Frightful danger," "with shrewd dog," "locking." *IAG*, p. 197.

"Clarity," *IAG*, p. 200.

"Not tractable." *IAG*, p. 201.

"Immoral." *IAG*, p. 205.

"Delicious," "careless." *IAG*, p. 206.

"Formless." *IAG*, p. 232.

"A genius." *IAG*, p. 216.

205   Laura Riding. *transition*, October 1927. WCW replied to the review in January 1928.

"Either the New World." *IAG*, p. 219.

"A morose dead world." *IAG*, p. 231.

"The place itself." *IAG*, p. 232.

page

206   The publisher's fault, *Au*, p. 236.

Scuttled. *Au*, p. 237.

"By a young person." *Au*, p. 242.

"Writing will save." WCW's 1927 journal, Lockwood.

207   "America! ho ho." B38, Lockwood.

"Floss, of course." *Au*, p. 242.

Accomplishments appreciated. WCW and Flossie kept some of the drawings and scribblings on file and wrote on the bottom of some of them what the children were trying to do. Beinecke.

208   "Monday morning," "we busted." Beinecke.

"We invested moderately." *Au*, p. 243.

209   Flossie was the one. Mrs. WCW's letters from Geneva, 1927–1928, to WCW, in possession of Williams Eric Williams. Flossie's role is also made evident in WCW's letters to her from shipboard returning to the U.S., 1927. Beinecke.

"The stronger." Beinecke.

210   "The golden boy." January 15, 1927, Beinecke.

211   Gould's theory on the actual. From an article about Joe Gould in Vol. V, No. 3, of *Broom,* by Slater Brown and Edward Nagle. In the same issue appeared WCW's "De Soto and the New World," a part of *In the American Grain.* Joseph Mitchell later wrote a book on Gould demonstrating that Gould never really wrote down his history at all.

1927 journal. D2a, Lockwood.

213   "You're a brilliant physician, sir, and a drunkard." Paterson ms. B17, Lockwood.

214   "It grows." "An Elegy for D. H. Lawrence," *CEP.*

215   Opposed to the usual literary ways. "Poetry should strive for ... vividness alone, per se, for itself. The realization of this has its own fire that is 'like' nothing. Therefore the bastardy of the simile. That thing, the vividness which is poetry by itself, makes the poem. There is no need to explain or compare. Make it and it is a poem." *The Descent of Winter,* p. 258.

"A black flag." From "The Clouds."

"Red cold world." In "A Morning Imagination of Russia," *CEP,* p. 305.

WCW on Shakespeare, 1927 journal, D2b, Lockwood.

"Took the print." *The Descent of Winter,* p. 258

216   [*VP*] didn't make money. "It was published by a man from Passaic, N.J., operating under the title of the Macauley Publishing Company" and "it didn't sell either." *Au*, p. 237.

"More romantic." *IWWP,* p. 46.

"He ... lay" *VP,* p. 128.

page

217 "Industrious night schools." *Innocents Abroad,* Vol. 1, Harpers 1911 edition, p. 26.

"Copyright secured." *Innocents Abroad,* p. 84.

"Write one." *Au,* p. 237.

218 "Women the American." *IWWP,* p. 45.

"Few teeth." *VP,* p. 73.

"Perfect bitch." *Au,* p. 221.

A Fräulein. *VP,* pp. 220–21.

"Venus on the half shell." *VP,* p. 111.

Venus Anadyomene of Cyrene. *VP,* p. 118.

Iris Tree. *Au,* p. 220.

"A character." *IWWP,* p. 46.

219 Flint arrowhead. *VP,* pp. 265–66. The Fräulein episode is printed as an appendix to *VP,* having been omitted from the original edition and then used by WCW as a separate short story. But he had it as an integral part of the original ms.

"Fine people." *VP,* p. 213.

Clotilda and Lawrence Vail. *Au,* p. 219.

220 "Wonder of abandon." *VP,* p. 155.

221 Memories of Leipzig. *VP,* p. xvii.

1924 Vienna episode. *Au,* p. 208.

"The apex of his tour." *VP,* p. 143.

"There was no feeling." *VP,* p. 155.

"The great science." *VP,* p. 157.

222 "A smoking," "blatant ignoramuses." *VP,* p. 148.

"What, not a member?" *VP,* p. 149.

"A person." *VP,* p. xiii.

223 His own wild poem. John Riordan letter to WCW, March 31, 1926, Lockwood.

224 Old hat. EP said so in several letters to WCW about *Kora* in 1920, Paige, pp. 156–61. In the last he said that the improvisations were déjà vu — he had seen them in Rimbaud. Seven years later WCW was still smarting about the complaint and said, in his 1927 journal, that EP was all wet.

"From the seed." Yeats, *Autobiography* (New York: Collier edition, 1966), parerback, p. 296.

"To write." File B123, Lockwood.

225 "Obliged to carry." Wylie Sypher, *Loss of the Self in Modern Literature and Art* (New York: Random House, 1962), p. 57.

Lowell on WCW. *Hudson Review,* winter 1962. Hugh Kenner has picked up Lowell's image of the homemade and written an excellent book tracing its course through the major American modernists of the century: *A Homemade World* (New York: Knopf, 1975).

Chapter Six   *(Pages 227–265)*

227 "Thrown violently." WCW letter to Louis Zukofsky, quoted by Webster Schott in *Imag,* p. 269.

She made the gin. From conversation with William Eric Williams.

"Rather good French," "I've already done it." Letter to Marianne Moore, 1928, *SL,* p. 106.

228 Felt guilty. 1942, *SL,* p. 201.

"Poor brats." "A Face of Stone," in *Make Light of It.*

"Give it an enema." "Jean Beicke," *Make Light of It.*

"The sleepy doctor." "A Night in June," *Make Light of It.*

"Every distortion." In "Dance Pseudomacabre," *Make Light of It.*

229 "Under the guise." Letter to EP, November 26, 1928, *SL,* p. 108.

"Smal ferns." From ms. "The North Shore," File B50, Lockwood. (This has been filed under "In Northern Waters," a short story having no connection with the Newfoundland trip.)

230 "To the last spool." *YMW,* p. 24.

"Bestial in a man," "with the title." *YMW,* p. 36.

"Too mixed up." *YMW,* p. 27.

"The inside near the skin." *YMW,* p. 66.

"Cut their heads." *YMW,* p. 47.

231 "Realistic novels of stupid people." 1927–1928 journal, Lockwood. See p. 212 of this book.

"It began to expand greatly." The best evidence is in the increase in quantity of letters to him in the thirties and forties, visible in Beinecke letter files.

232 See a human being. EP letter to WCW, 1922, Lockwood.

233 "Do you think me a fool?" 1921, *SL,* p. 55.

"It's a damned good book." Of *The Hasty Bunch* by McAlmon, 1923, *SL,* p. 56.

"You are a genius." 1919, *SL,* p. 45.

"The most distinguished," "Why should I not." 1928, *SL,* p. 45.

"We had a gang." 1939, *SL,* p. 182.

234 "Hang it onto." 1928, *SL,* p. 100.

"Nothing will ever." 1928, *SL,* p. 108.

235 "The print shop." KB to WCW, 1946, Beinecke.

A circulation of 80. EP to Margaret Anderson, 1917, Paige, p. 121.

"My Dear Old Sawbuck." 1919, Paige, p. 145.

236 "A vile scum." 1917, Paige, p. 116.

"Fundamentally trivial." 1922, Paige, p. 181.

"I really can't." 1920, Paige, p. 159.

237 "Entre nooz." 1917, Paige, p. 168.

"By about every editor," "vengeance." 1919, Paige, p. 151.

"Leading the world's future." Paige, p. 325.

WCW a loser. See p. 224 of this book.

No Alexander Pope. Eliot's introduction to EP's *Selected Poems*, 1928. See also note to the manuscript *The Waste Land*, Valerie Eliot, ed. (New York: Harcourt Brace, 1971), p. 127.

"You needn't feel." 1926, Paige, p. 202.

238 "Ole dopo." KB to WCW, 1957, Beinecke.

"So much depends." The student was Mary Duval, date unknown, Beinecke. She reported to WCW that her teacher had said the poem was simply a word picture with no metaphor, but she didn't believe that. WCW's reply is not on file.

239 "Something called Aesthetic Realism." In 1951 WCW praised the poetry of Eli Siegel, founder of "Aesthetic Realism," but soon discovered that Eli Siegel was a persistent friend. WCW stopped answering Siegel's letters. Siegel kept writing, and Siegel's wife kept writing. A characteristic remark from Mrs. Siegel: "There is something you want to know; he [Eli] can teach you how." These events are recorded in *The Williams-Siegel Documentary*, Martha Baird and Ellen Reiss, eds. (New York: Definition Press, 1970) that was summarized and reviewed by Hugh Kenner in *The New Republic* (December 12, 1970). In 1974 boosters for Aesthetic Realism were still active, sending broadsides through the mails proclaiming "the right of Aesthetic Realism to be heard."

Objectivism: Only its enthusiasts. Hugh Kenner is an enthusiast, and in his wise and witty book *A Homemade World,* he asserts that Objectivism and Zukofsky truly caught the spirit of modernism. The difficulty with Zukofsky that Kenner perhaps underrates is that Zukofsky's examples of Objectivism, from his own work and others', seem not nearly as Objectivist in practice as the examples Kenner himself gives from writers like Hemingway who had nothing to do with the Objectivist group.

"Human values," "good cook." WCW to LZ, 1928, *SL,* p. 93.

"Yes, yes." 1928, *SL,* p. 94.

240 "The lens." Zukofsky introduction to Objectivist issue of *Poetry,* February 1931.

241 "Of the eccentric." Monroe in *Poetry,* March 1931.

"Objectivist poetry equals poetry." LZ to WCW, February 27, 1956, Beinecke.

"Isn't it a shitting crime?" WCW to LZ, August 27, 1931, Beinecke.

242 Cooperative Publishers. WCW to LZ, June 1933, Beinecke.

Pagany. Its beginnings are discussed in the Introduction to *A Return to Pagany: The History, Correspondence, and Selections from a Little Magazine, 1929–1932,* an anthology edited by Stephen Halpert and Richard Johns (Boston: Beacon Press, 1969).

"Williams gives me an inelegant." *Pagany,* p. 150.

"Crazy bug." Letter dated October 20, 1930, in *Return to Pagany,* p. 164. The story referred to is probably "The Red Head" though in that the redhead is a boy by whom the girl fears she has been made pregnant. The story was not published in book until 1950, in *Make Light of It.*

243 "Clean, stripped." JCR to WCW, June 3, 1941, Beinecke.

"What in heck." WCW to Johns, 1932, *A Return to Pagany,* p. 378.

"Unduly complicate." EP to Johns, 1932, *A Return to Pagany,* p. 380.

244 Night letters. Yvor Winters, receiving one, was flattered but surprised, praised *White Mule* but did not contribute to *Contact.* He also took a slam at Zukofsky, WCW's "pet bull pup," and said, "if I were you — or Pound — I think I'd try to tie him up." November 2, 1931, Beinecke.

Being taken for a regionalist. "Good God, is there no intelligence left on earth? Shall we never differentiate the regional in letters from the objective immediacy of our hand to mouth, eye to brain existence?" Of Eliot and academic poetry: "There is a heresy, regarding the general character of poetry, which has become widely prevalent today and may shortly become more so; it is that poetry increases in virtue as it is removed from contact with the vulgar world. I cannot swallow the half alive poetry which knows nothing of totality. It is one of the reasons to welcome communism ..." (*Contact,* 1932). In a footnote to the above remarks he gave as an example of the "academic fostering" of poetry "T. S. Eliot's recent appointment to Harvard."

"Under the editorship." WCW to LZ, December 12, 1932, Beinecke.

"The young writers today." *Blues,* Vol. I, No. 2, 1929.

245 "There isn't enough." WCW to T. C. Wilson, undated, presumably 1933, Beinecke.

"Eliot's valet." WCW to EP, December 30, 1931, Beinecke.

246 "The ceaseless weaving." LZ himself in the Objectivist issue of *Poetry.*

Details of *New Masses.* From *New Masses Anthology,* Joseph North, ed. (New York: International Publishers, 1969).

247 "Who shot down the man." North, p. 39.

248 Albert Maltz story. 1934, North, p. 284.

page

249 Thomas Wolfe story. 1938, North, p. 114.

250 Union shop argument in *WM*, pp. 264–67.

"Face smeared." *WM*, p. 291.

"Confined to special roads." *New York Times,* December 11, 1938.

251 Prohibition. Henry Ford proposed to go out of business if prohibition was repealed and WCW's response was "fine!" Lockwood ms. entitled "A Democratic Party Platform."

"Why in beer." From the story "Four Bottles of Beer" in *LPR.*

252 WCW's review of Lewis. In *Poetry,* February 1936.

"By crossbreeding." March 1937, North, p. 59.

253 "Jean Beicke." *Blast,* Vol. I, No. 1, 1933.

254 Fitch story. *Blast,* Vol. I, No. 2, 1933.

PR advertisement. Blast, Vol. I, No. 3 (January-February 1934).

255 "Seemed unaware." Blast, Vol. I, No. 5 (October-November 1934).

Anvil. The *PR Anvil* symposium was in the issue for April 1936.

WCW's comments to the symposium. Reprinted in *SL,* p. 157.

256 "Sanctions Against Williams." *PR Anvil,* May 1936.

257 "Demonstrably false." Sydney Hook to WCW, November 25, 1939, Beinecke.

258 Hot headlines. From *The New Leader* issues of January 21, February 28, April 29, and May 20, 1939.

Sinclair Lewis. *New Leader* headlines, July 8, 1939.

Lillian Hellman, Mumford, etc. *New Leader,* July 29, 1939.

259 "No creative intelligence." WCW to Macdonald, December 11, 1942, Lockwood.

"Caution." The woman was Myra Marini Goddard, with whom WCW had a long correspondence, Lockwood.

260 "Rugged ole lady's." EP to WCW, 1931, Lockwood.

"In yewth." EP to WCW, 1932, Lockwood. The one-column summary of Social Credit that EP wrote for the *New English Weekly* and sent WCW a copy of read as follows (it was entitled "Volitionist Economics"):

WHICH of the following statements do you agree with?

1) It is an outrage that the state shd run into debt to individuals by the act and in the act of creating real wealth.

2) Several nations recognize the necessity of distributing purchasing power. They do actually distribute it. The question is whether it shd be distributed as favour to corporations; as reward for not having a job; or impartially and per capita.

3) A country CAN have one currency for internal use, and another good for both home and foreign use.

4) If money is regarded as certificate of work done, taxes are no longer necessary.

5) It is possible to concentrate all taxation onto the actual paper money of a country (or onto one sort of its money).

6) You can issue valid paper money against any commodity UP TO the amount of that commodity that people WANT.

7) Some of the commonest failures of clarity among economists are due to using one word to signify two or more different concepts: such as, DEMAND, meaning sometimes WANT and sometimes power to buy; authoritative, meaning also responsible.

8) It is an outrage that the owner of one commodity cannot exchange it with someone possessing another, without being impeded or taxed by a third party holding a monopoly over some third substance or controlling some convention, regardless of what it is called.

Answer to E. Pound
Via Marsala 12/5 Rapallo, Italy

"Money cancer." In WCW's Social Credit lecture. The lecture, drawing from EP, was printed as an article in the magazine *New Democracy,* April 1936.

261 Alfred Venison. I am indebted to Ruthven Todd for introducing me to Venison. A copy of the original Venison pamphlet is in the Lockwood poetry collection, but the Venison poems are now in general circulation in Pound's *Pavannes and Divagations* (New York: New Directions, 1958).

262 "No, doc." EP to Felix Schelling, April 1934, Paige, p. 256.

"The American political upheaval." WCW to EP, November 6, 1935, *SL,* p. 163.

Lecture in Charlottesville. The lecture was arranged, according to James Laughlin, by Gorham Munson and Paul Hampden.

263 Rabbitt Britches. 1936, Paige, p. 280.

"Waal." 1936, Paige, p. 283. Presumably the WAR was the Spanish Civil War. Hemingway had just been there.

264 "I found." WCW to James Laughlin, June 7, 1939, *SL,* p. 184.

265 "More than usually." WCW to McAlmon, December 26, 1938, Beinecke.

"Having turned their backs." WCW to Horace Gregory, May 8, 1944, Beinecke.

"Bastard and a son of a bitch." WCW to Gregory, February 1, 1946, Beinecke.

"I feel ashamed." WCW to EP, July 1, 1946, Beinecke.

Chapter Seven *(Pages 266-298)*

266 A swell gang. Letter from WEW to WCW, October 17, 1937, Beinecke.

The hurricane. Told to the biographer by Mrs. Williams and WEW and also reported in part in *Au,* pp. 303–04.

380 *Notes*

page

267 Sixty cents. Letter from WCW to McAlmon, July 18, 1939, Beinecke.

"My God!" October 27, 1936, *SL*, p. 161.

Macy's had none. Letter from WCW to Miss Dermarest of ND, July 26, 1937, Beinecke.

Lost the big sales moment. "I was heartbroken but there it was I had to take it," *IWWP*, p. 62.

268 "The one publisher." WCW to JL, January 1939, Beinecke.

"Enough time." WCW to JL, September 3, 1941.

Poetry section. The magazine was Gorham Munson's *New Democracy*. See Emily Wallace's bibliography, p. 40. According to Laughlin the magazine was a Social Credit monthly that had been stimulated by Pound. Laughlin had two pages for poetry in it each issue.

Wanted it served. Laughlin reports that this was not quite so. "EP was always annoyed because I didn't publish many historical and economic texts he wanted done. There is a letter somewhere where EP complains that I *never* followed his suggestions." From a letter, Laughlin to biographer, March 1975.

271 "I can't take." WCW to John Riordan, October 13, 1926, University of Virginia ms. collection.

273 Eliot. One of his better anti-Eliot outbursts was a letter to Allen Tate in the forties when Tate was editing *The Sewanee Review:* "Dear Mr. Tate, Your magazine will never amount to much until you, its editor, have learned to print your Eliot at the back in small type." Beinecke. There is no indication that the letter was actually sent.

'The lunatic fringe." *Au*, p. 312.

"I watched them closely." Letter to Charles Keppel, 1940, Lockwood. As for the slippers, WCW had written a poem about them, "The Thinkers" (*CEP*), that he presumably read on that occasion.

274 "I am in demand." From Arthur Mizener, *The Saddest Story* (New York: World, 1971), p. 444.

275 Nothing a man. EP, *Canto 84*.

"The Friends of William Carlos Williams." Mizener, pp. 444, 447, and 455.

"Horribly embarrassed." *Au*, p. 300.

Prix Goncourt. January 31, 1939, Paige, p. 321. Also in Mizener, p. 455. The French writer Edmund de Goncourt "left his estate for the endowment of an academy ... to consist of ten members, each of whom would receive an annuity of 6000 francs, and a yearly prize of 5000 francs was to be awarded to the author of some work of fiction ... On the 19th of January, 1903, after much litigation, the academy was constituted." *Encyclopædia Britannica*, 11th ed.

"A 'sort.' " 1939, Paige, p. 321.

Big names. There's a printed list of the members of the organization in the Beinecke file under the name Paul Lecke.

276 "That night." *Au*, p. 300.

Too anti-Russian. "Though I'm no Communist as you know I couldn't stand for the Committee's covert attack on Communism so I resigned from their God damned committee." WCW to McAlmon, July 18, 1939, Beinecke.

"Implacable opposition." *PR*, July-August 1941.

277 "Irresponsible." MacLeish had written a lecture called "The Irresponsibles" that was in wide circulation at the time.

Not quite ready. He met MacLeish at a high-powered writers' conference in Puerto Rico in 1941. He and Flossie made their first plane trip for it and WCW was so fatalistic about it that he asked two friends in separate letters to be his literary executors if he did not survive. They were Horace Gregory and Louis Zukofsky (Beinecke), and he reported to Horace Gregory that "a group of local communists" had characterized the conference as "a conspiracy by MacLeish and others." He was angry at the accusation but still sided with Macdonald.

"Attacking MacLeish and Brooks." Dwight Macdonald, *Memoirs of a Revolutionary* (New York: Meridian, 1958), pp. 203-14.

"Exultation." *PR*, July-August 1941.

278 "You say." September 25, 1942, *SL*, p. 202.

"The first and only." Introduction to *The Wedge*, published in 1944 by the Cummington Press (Massachusetts) after Laughlin had said he couldn't get paper for it and Macmillan had rejected it. The piece is reprinted in *Selected Essays*, WCW, New Directions paperback, 1969, p. 255.

279 "Assault." Letter to Laughlin, January 24, 1943, *SL*, p. 214.

"Our greatest leader." *PR*, September-October 1943.

"Discovered." Letter to JL, *SL*, p. 214.

280 "As one." Letter from Schwartz to WCW, August 10, 1943, Beinecke.

"Writer like Williams." *PR*, September-October 1943.

283 Early version of *Paterson* with Doc and Willie. The ms. is part of a collection of fragments called "Detail and Parody," File D4, Lockwood.

"Comparing in his own mind." Another "Detail and Parody" ms., E17, Lockwood: "a design on the general structure of *The Canterbury Tales* at least in parts: such as The Dream of Beautiful Women — to be the dreams of N. F. Paterson — stirred by Mrs. Paterson — but not to be (unless desired) stated as dreams. They are not 'dreams' but more than ever the actuality."

284 Yvor Winters. From a review of WCW's *Complete Collected Poems* in *The Kenyon Review*, Vol. I, No. 1, 1939, reprinted in *The Uncollected Essays and Reviews of Yvor Winters* (Chicago: Swallow Press, 1973).

286 Rome radio. *Au*, p. 317.

page

287 "Cracking up." WCW's review of EP's first 30 cantos, *The Symposium,* 1931, reprinted in *Selected Essays,* WCW, p. 105.

288 "Meaning." *Pat,* p. 111.

"Disease." *Pat,* p. 145.

289 Paraphrased Mencken's position. From WCW's review of the fourth edition of *The American Language,* printed in *The North American Review,* 1946, and reprinted in *Selected Essays,* WCW, p. 170.

"The great majority." Mencken to WCW, 1934, Beinecke.

291 She herself wrote up. This is the passage about Jackson's Whites and Cromwell.

"It had no flow." WCW to Miller, September 14, 1945, University of Virginia.

"I'll do them." WCW to Miller, December 21, 1945, University of Virginia.

292 *Man Orchid.* All the materials about *Man Orchid* are taken from *The Massachusetts Review,* winter 1973, in which *Man Orchid* was printed together with an introduction by Paul Mariani containing the relevant quotes from Miller-WCW letters.

293 Poet Laureate of the Tree Peonies. *Au,* p. 326.

Jarrell complaints. *Partisan Review,* Vol. VII, No. 2, 1940.

"I for one." *Partisan Review,* Vol. VII, No. 3, 1940.

"Far and away." *Partisan Review,* Vol XIII, No. 4, 1946.

Moss review. *Kenyon Review,* winter 1947.

Lowell review. *Sewanee Review,* summer 1947.

294 "Let 'em flounder." July or August 1946, though letter is undated, University of Virginia.

"You should wear." Letter from Stevens to WCW, April 29, 1948, Beinecke.

"Faded vine leaves." Letter from Tate to WCW, April 28, 1948, Beinecke.

295 "Part One introduced." *Pat* in the preliminary "Author's Note."

296 Burning library. George Zabriskie has a thorough account of the fire the passage is based on, in *Perspective,* Vol. VI, No. 4, autumn-winter 1953, p. 214.

"What is more clear." *Pat,* III, p. 116.

Analogies between the uranium atom. In his notes for Book IV he even compared the splitting of the atom to the splitting of a verse foot.

297 "I have come." Author's note at the beginning of the paperback, *Pat.*

298 "One of the best." Jarrell, *Poetry and the Age,* p. 236.

"The poetry, the pure poem." *Pat,* IV, p. 171.

"A very good." *Poetry and the Age,* p. 236.

TLS review. February 1, 1952.

Chapter Eight *(Pages 299-333)*

299 Letter to Flossie. 1940, Lockwood.

"I suppose." WCW to Kitty Hoaglund, August 29, 1939, University of Virginia.

300 A painfully intimate letter. Undated letter, presumably from the early forties, under "O," Beinecke.

301 "Very shoulders." Letter to Norman Macleod, January 5, 1942, Beinecke.

"Terrifying." Letter to KH, June 14, 1946, University of Virginia.

'Thrilled me." Letter to KH, July 1949, University of Virginia.

"I won't go far." Letter to KH, July 1949, University of Virginia.

"If the mind." WCW to Charles Abbott, 1942, Lockwood.

"We've gotten." 1940, Lockwood.

302 "Nothing about." Letter to KH, December 18, 1946, University of Virginia.

"They tell me." Letter to Charles Abbott, about mid–1948, Lockwood.

A Dream of Love. Laughlin printed it in September 1948.

303 "Oh, come out of it." *ADOL,* p. 212.

304 Dialogue from *ADOL.* Early draft, B18, Lockwood, written on a number of prescription blanks.

Letter to Flossie. 1948, Lockwood.

"Straight and clear." Letter from Daphne Williams, 1948, Beinecke.

305 "To sit here." Draft of 1948 letter, Beinecke.

Brendan Gill's interview. Described by Gill in *Here at the New Yorker* (New York: Random House, 1975), pp. 332–33.

"Women! with their small heads." *ML,* p. 84.

A falling out with Laughlin. Letter to Charles Abbott, 1950, Lockwood. "I hadn't realized how badly Laughlin had managed. I was close to being entirely at his mercy. I have had to employ legal advice."

306 *The Desert Music* appears in *PB.*

307 "I had the respect," "rapidly and carelessly." *IWWP,* pp. 86–87.

Stroke. Letter to Charles Abbott, May 1951, Lockwood. "It was the writing of the autobiography for Random House that laid me low."

Recovered, and went on. *IWWP,* p. 87: "I had a very devoted friend and patient, an educated woman, who took the manuscript as I wrote it at tremendous speed and transposed my sometimes illegible writing to the neatly typed page ... very possibly the results were sometimes distorted because of illegible writing transcribed by a third party."

Bollingen Prize to EP. WCW had wanted EP to get it, however — "give him the prize and hang him if you like but give him the prize." *Imagi,* spring 1949.

page

308 "Had [Evans] not stood." Letter to CA, January 1950, Lockwood.

"Good gang." Letter to CA, January 1950, Lockwood.

"Something's come." Letter to CA, April 29, 1952, Lockwood.

309 Flossie's description of his severe stroke and temporary loss of speech. Letter to Oscar Silverman, May 12, 1963, Lockwood.

Moore recommendations. Merrill Moore to Mrs. WCW, September 1952, in possession of Mrs. WCW.

Lyric editor's letter. Reported in the Washington *Times Herald,* October 20, 1952. The woman was Mrs. Virginia Kent Cummins. *Lyric* was published by The Lyric Foundation, which was her Foundation.

310 "Nixon Declares." Washington *Post,* October 26, 1952.

"McCarthy Makes." Washington *Post,* October 28, 1952.

"Much misunderstood." Roy Basler, *The Muse and the Librarian* (Westport, Conn.: Greenwood Press, 1974), pp. 19, 20.

311 Clapp letter, paraphrased by Basler, p. 19.

312 Evans letter revoking appointment. As quoted in Mary McGrory's summary account of the whole episode in the Washington *Evening Star,* September 26, 1954, The McGrory story is the most complete source of information about the episode by a person outside the Library. Persons inside the Library claim it is inaccurate.

"Library's view." Basler, p. 20.

David McDowell pleading with FBI. In McGrory. McDowell now denies this version of his action, however, saying that he went at the problem through Nixon himself but without success (in conversation with biographer).

313 "Or as soon thereafter." Quoted by McGrory.

"Evaluated." Basler, p. 26.

WCW was not told. McGrory.

WCW complaint in the *Times.* October 12, 1954.

Shock treatment. MM to Mrs. WCW, March 1953, in possession of Mrs. WCW.

"A full report." Basler, p. 21.

315 "The whole school." *PR Anvil,* May 1936.

Time story. February 13, 1950. See also p. 331 of this book.

316 Winters' essay. From Winters' *In Defense of Reason* (New York: Morrow, 1947), p. 112.

318 Relativity Theory. Essay printed in *Origin,* 1953, reprinted in *Selected Essays,* WCW, p. 337.

Sandburg not as good. A student at UCLA, Theodore Clark, wrote WCW in 1961 to describe an interview with Sandburg in which Sandburg was asked about Williams. Sandburg replied (1) "if you want to know about that ask Williams," (2) "I've reached the stage where I won't discuss differences with other poets anymore," and (3) "He ain't as good as he thinks he is." Beinecke, under "Clark."

319 "Worthy and courageous." *Leaves of Grass One Hundred Years After,* Milton Hindus, ed. (California: Stanford University Press, 1955), p. 31. Other quotations in this paragraph and the next appear on pp. 22, 23, and 27 of Hindus' volume.

321 WCW on Van Wyck Brooks. Letter to Dwight Macdonald, February 1942, Beinecke.

322 "In the same," "I seldom dig." *Pat,* pp. 173–74.

"Horrors." WCW's introduction to Ginsberg's *Howl,* p. 8.

"Moments of emotional crisis." Ginsberg letter to WCW, 1949, Beinecke.

"Drunker." WCW to Roethke, November 14, 1944, Beinecke.

Olson on *Moby Dick.* In *Call Me Ishmael* (New York: Reynal & Hitchcock, 1947).

323 Olson's "protective verse" essay is now printed in *Human Universe and Other Essays* (New York: Grove Press, 1967).

"Merely a son." Marjorie Perloff investigates at length Olson's tendency to qualify his indebtedness to EP and WCW, once, for example, calling them his "two inferior predecessors" in a letter to Cid Corman — see *Letters for Origin 1950–1955,* Albert Glover, ed. (Cape Goliard: Grossman, 1969) and "Charles Olson and the 'Interior Predecessors': 'Projective Verse' Revisited," by Marjorie G. Perloff, *Journal of English Literary History,* Vol. 40, No. 2, summer 1973.

"My god, BILL." Letter from Olson to WCW, updated, probably 1950, Beinecke.

324 "My own (moral)." Letter from Creeley to WCW, quoting WCW, Beinecke.

"Disintegrate." What Martin Duberman calls "the final desperate illustrious years" of the college are described in a chapter on Olson in *Black Mountain: An Exploration in Community* (New York: Dutton, 1972), pp. 367, 368–84.

325 "Dig taking." Ginsberg letter to WCW, May 20, 1956, Beinecke. Partially reprinted in *Pat,* p. 212.

326 "Serious." This biographer for example met Creeley at an academic gathering once and was immediately asked, out of the blue, if he was serious.

Duncan's statement. *The New American Poetry,* Donald M. Allen, ed. (New York: Grove Press, 1960) p. 407.

327 Levertov. Allen, p. 412.

Ginsberg. Allen, p. 416.

Snyder. Allen, p. 421.

Jones. Allen, p. 425.

Olson. Allen, p. 394.

"From the beginning." WCW in Hindus, p. 27.

page

328 Radio technician's ideas. Jerome Mazzaro, *WCW: The Later Poems* (Ithaca, New York: Cornell University Press, 1973), pp. 62–63. The technician's name was David Lyle and his letters are to be seen at Beinecke and Lockwood. Another source for *Pat's* structure has been suggested in Skipwith Cannell's volume of poetry, *By the Rivers of Babylon,* which WCW read and wrote an introduction for in the late thirties, saying that it was time the poets took over the journalists' work and that they could do so by writing an epic like Cannell's every year, letting the poet's eye and sensibility report on the world rather than the journalist's. Milne Holton of the University of Maryland has described the Cannell connection in an as yet unpublished article.

"Nothing in the world." Jack Kerouac's phrasing in *The Dharma Bums,* which is perhaps the best account of the San Francisco poetry scene around 1956.

Coles lectures. Quotations from p. 12 of the ms. of Coles, *WCW: The Knack of Survival in America* (New Brunswick, N.J.: Rutgers University Press, 1975).

331 *Time* story. February 13, 1950.

Letters from Levertov, Kinnell, and Dickey. Undated, Beinecke.

332 Letter from Lowell. 1958, Beinecke.

333 Goodman. *The New Reformation* (New York: Random House, 1970), pp. 73, 81, 91, 70.

Chapter Nine *(Pages 334–354)*

334 "For the love." May 14, 1935, University of Virginia.

"In this for fun." January 30, 1946, University of Virginia.

335 "The yen." May 11, 1954, University of Virginia.

"Either hunting." Letter to *The Egoist,* August 1917.

"Lure of the gutter." McDowell in conversation with biographer, November 1974.

"When the negro." WCW letter to Fred Miller, November 5, 1946, University of Virginia.

336 Cézanne. In *Writers at Work,* Malcolm Cowley, ed. (New York: Viking, 1967), third series. *Paris Review* interview with AG conducted first in 1965 (by Thomas Clark), p. 295.

340 An efficient nurse. Recorded in John Thirlwall's "Notes" to *ML,* p. 436.

"You were yellow." *The Cure,* in *ML,* p. 424.

341 "Thrown violently together." See p. 227 of this book.

342 "Asphodel" Flossie's favorite. To the biographer in conversation, 1974.

"Love of love." "Asphodel," *PB,* p. 160.

page

"With fear in [his] heart." "Asphodel," *PB,* p. 154.

343   "A remarkable thing." Moore to Mrs. WCW, September 1952, Lockwood. As short-poem poet. An interim book, *Collected Later Poems,* was published in 1950 and contains his short poems of the forties, but as a whole it is surprisingly inferior to that which came before and after it. Perhaps *Pat* occupied his mind then to a degree that left little energy for short poems.

344   Angoff description of WCW Staten Island reading. "A Williams Memoir," in *Prairie Schooner,* winter 1964–1965. Reprinted in Jerome Mazzaro's *Profile of WCW* (Columbus, Ohio: Merrill, 1971).

345   "Wildly around." 1955 tape, Beinecke.

A Cummings poem. Part of the interview is included in *Pat* V. This may have been the same interview of which he told Miller that it had stirred up trouble for him. "They tricked me into making some damaging statements against the Jews and Senator Kennedy. I fell for it and now have to pacify my friends. Too damned bad about those thin-skinned bastards. But maybe I'm more prejudiced than I realize but I don't think so." September 24, 1957, University of Virginia.

"Hope the profs." WCW to Fred Miller, November 21, 1957, University of Virginia.

346   Letter to Abbott. 1958, Lockwood.

"Definitely a mental case." Mrs. WCW to Abbott, July 17, 1958, Lockwood.

Right arm. Mrs. WCW to Abbott, October 1958.

Julian Beck. Several 1959 letters, Beck to WCW, Beinecke.

347   "Terribly inflated." 1955 tape, Beinecke.

"God forbid." *Poetry Review I,* Vol. X, October 1912, pp. 481–82.

349   "Bear to see." Mrs. WCW to the Abbotts, August 1960, Lockwood.

350   Interview with Koehler. The interview was printed in *The Paris Review* in 1964, then reprinted in *Writers at Work,* third series.

"Bill fades." Mrs. WCW to Oscar Silverman, July 3, 1962.

The funeral. The funeral account was derived from conversations with Mrs. WCW and son Bill as well as the minister Don Curry, now of Columbia University, who kindly supplied the text of his service. James Laughlin also recalled, in conversation, a number of details of the event.

351   "Tract." *CEP.*

Bibliography

The Works of William Carlos Williams
(All the paperbacks listed are published by New Directions and are in print).

Poems, 1909. Rutherford, New Jersey (not reprinted).

The Tempers, 1913. London: Elkin Mathews (most poems included in *CEP*).

Al Que Quieri!, 1917. Boston: Four Seas Company (most poems included in *CEP*).

Kora In Hell: Improvisations, 1920. Boston: Four Seas Company (included in *Imaginations*).

Sour Grapes, 1921. Boston: Four Seas Company (included in *CEP*).

The Great American Novel, 1923. Paris: Contact Editions (included in *Imaginations*).

Spring and all, 1923. Paris: Contact Publishing Co. (included *in Imaginations,* and the poems of it included in *CEP*).

Go Go, 1923. New York: Monroe Wheeler (included in *CEP*).

In the American Grain, 1925. New York: Albert & Charles Boni (paperback, 1956).

A Voyage to Pagany, 1928. New York: The Macaulay Company (paperback, 1970).

A Novelette and Other Prose, 1932. Toulon (included in *Imaginations*).

The Knife of the Times, 1932. New York: The Dragon Press (included in *The Farmers' Daughters*).

Collected Poems 1921–31, 1934. New York: The Objectivist Press (included in *CEP*).

An Early Martyr and Other Poems, 1935. New York: The Alcestis Press (most poems in *CEP*).

Adam and Eve and The City, 1936. Peru, Vermont: The Alcestis Press (most poems in *CEP*).

White Mule, 1937. Norfolk, Connecticut: New Directions (paperback, 1967).

Life Along the Passaic River, 1938. Norfolk, Connecticut: New Directions (included in *The Farmers' Daughters*).

The Complete Collected Poems, 1938. Norfolk, Connecticut: New Directions (included in *CEP*).

In the Money, 1940. Norfolk, Connecticut: New Directions (paperback, 1967).

The Broken Span, 1941. Norfolk, Connecticut: New Directions (poems in *CEP, CLP,* or *Pat*).

The Wedge, 1944. Cummington, Massachusetts: The Cummington Press (most poems in *CLP*).

Paterson I, 1946. Norfolk, Connecticut: New Directions (paperback, 1963).

Paterson II, 1948. Norfolk, Connecticut: New Directions (paperback, 1963).

The Clouds, 1948. Cummington, Massachusetts: The Cummington Press and The Wells College Press (included in *CLP*).

A Dream of Love, 1948. Norfolk, Connecticut: New Directions (included in *Many Loves*).

Selected Poems, 1949. Norfolk, Connecticut: New Directions (paperback, 1963).

The Pink Church, 1949. Columbus, Ohio: Golden Goose Press (included in *CLP*).

Paterson III, 1949. Norfolk, Connecticut: New Directions (paperback, 1963).

The Collected Later Poems, 1950. Norfolk, Connecticut: New Directions (revised, 1963).

Make Light of It, 1950. New York: Random House (included in *The Farmers' Daughters*).

Paterson IV, 1951. Norfolk, Connecticut: New Directions (paperback, 1963).

Autobiography, 1951. New York: Random House (paperback, 1967).

The Collected Earlier Poems, 1951. Norfolk, Connecticut: New Directions.

The Build-Up, 1952. New York: Random House (paperback, 1972).

The Desert Music, 1954. New York: Random House (included in *Pictures from Brueghel*).

Selected Essays, 1954. New York: Random House (paperback, 1969).

Journey to Love, 1955. New York: Random House (included in *Pictures from Brueghel*).

The Selected Letters, edited by John C. Thirlwall, 1957. New York: McDowell, Obolensky.

I Wanted To Write A Poem, reported and edited by Edith Heal, 1958. Boston: Beacon Press.

Paterson V, 1958. Norfolk, Connecticut: New Directions (paperback, 1963).

Yes, Mrs. Williams: A Personal Record of My Mother. 1959. New York: McDowell, Obolensky.

The Farmers' Daughters, 1961. Norfolk, Connecticut: New Directions (also in paperback).

Many Loves, edited by John C. Thirlwall, 1961. Norfolk, Connecticut: New Directions (paperback, 1965).

Pictures from Brueghel, 1962. Norfolk, Connecticut: New Directions (also in paperback).

Paterson (collected), 1963. Norfolk, Connecticut: New Directions (also in paperback).

The William Carlos Williams Reader, edited by M. L. Rosenthal, 1966. New York: New Directions paperback.

Imaginations, edited by Webster Schott, 1970. New York: New Directions (also in paperback).

The Embodiment of Knowledge, edited by Ron Loewinsohn, 1974. New York: New Directions.

Selected Literary Criticism about Williams

Angoff, Charles, editor. *William Carlos Williams* (several contributors). Rutherford, New Jersey: Fairleigh Dickinson University Press, 1974.
Breslin, James E. *William Carlos Williams: An American Artist.* New York: Oxford, 1970.
Coles, Robert. *William Carlos Williams: The Knack of Survival in America.* New Brunswick, N.J.: Rutgers University Press, 1975.
Levertov, Denise. *The Poet in the World.* New York: New Directions, 1973.
Mazzaro, Jerome. *Profile of William Carlos Williams* (several contributors). Columbus, Ohio: Charles Merrill Publishers, 1971.
———. *William Carlos Williams: The Late Poems.* Ithaca, New York: Cornell University Press, 1973.
Miller, J. Hillis. *Poets of Reality.* Cambridge, Massachusetts: Harvard University Press, 1965.
Wagner, Linda Welshimer. *The Poems of William Carlos Williams.* Middletown, Connecticut: Wesleyan University Press, 1963.
———. *The Prose of William Carlos Williams.* Middletown, Connecticut: Wesleyan University Press, 1970.
Wallace, Emily Mitchell. *A Bibliography of William Carlos Williams.* Middletown, Connecticut: Wesleyan University Press, 1968.
Weaver, Mike. *William Carlos Williams.* New York: Oxford, 1972.

Selected General Readings

Anderson, Margaret. *My Thirty Years' War.* New York: Hermitage House, 1953.
Babbitt, Irving. *The New Laokoon: An Essay on the Confusion of the Arts.* Boston: Houghton Mifflin, 1910.
Basler, Roy. *The Muse and The Librarian.* Westport, Conn.: Greenwood Press, 1974.
Bloom, Harold. *The Anxiety of Influence.* New York: Norton, 1972.
Carnevali, Emanuel. *Autobiography,* edited by Kay Boyle. New York: Horizon Press, 1966.
Cowley, Malcolm. *A Many-Windowed House: Collected Essays on American Writers and American Writing,* edited by Henry Dan Piper. Carbondale, Illinois: Southern Illinois University Press, 1970.
Dahlberg, Edward. *Alms for Oblivion.* Minneapolis, Minnesota: University of Minnesota Press, 1964.
Dijkstra, Bram. *The Hieroglyphs of a New Speech.* Princeton, New Jersey: Princeton University Press, 1969.
Duberman, Martin. *Black Mountain: An Exploration in Community.* New York: Dutton, 1972.
Eliot, T. S. *The Waste Land,* Manuscript Edition, edited by Valerie Eliot. New York, Harcourt Brace Jovanovich, 1971.
Frank, Joseph. *The Widening Gyre.* New Brunswick, N.J.: Rutgers University Press, 1963.
Fruhock, W. H. *Rimbaud's Poetic Practice.* Cambridge, Mass.: Harvard, 1963.

Hutchins, Patricia. *Ezra Pound's Kensington*. Chicago: Regnery, 1965.
Ginsberg, Allen. *Howl*, with an introduction by William Carlos Williams. San Francisco: City Lights, 1956.
Goodman, Paul. *The New Reformation*. New York: Random House, 1970.
Hartley, Marsden. *Adventures in the Arts: Informed Chapters on Painters, Vaudeville, and Poets*. New York: Boni & Liveright, 1921.
Jarrell, Randall. *Poetry and the Age*. New York: Knopf, 1955.
Jones, Leroi. *Black Magic*. Indianapolis: Bobbs-Merrill, 1969.
Kenner, Hugh. *A Homemade World*. New York: Knopf, 1975.
‑‑‑‑‑‑. *The Pound Era*. Berkeley: University of California Press, 1971.
Kilmer, Joyce. *Poems, Essays & Letters*, edited by Robert C. Holliday. Port Washington, New York: Kennikat Press, 1946.
Kreymborg, Alfred. *Mushrooms*. New York, 1914.
‑‑‑‑‑‑. *Troubador*. New York: Liveright, 1914.
Lawrence, D. H. *Selected Literary Criticism*. New York: Viking, 1967.
McAlmon, Robert. *Being Geniuses Together*, edited and enlarged upon by Kay Boyle. New York: Doubleday, 1968.
‑‑‑‑‑‑. *Post-Adolescence* (printed in *McAlmon and the Lost Generation*), edited by Robert Knoll. Lincoln, Nebraska: University of Nebraska Press, 1962.
Macdonald, Dwight. *Memoirs of a Revolutionary*. New York: Farrar, Strauss, 1957.
Mizener, Arthur. *The Saddest Story*. Cleveland, Ohio: World, 1971.
Nemerov, Howard. *A Journal of the Fictive Life*. New Brunswick, N.J.: Rutgers, 1965.
Norwood, Christopher. *About Paterson*. New York: Saturday Review Press, 1974.
Olson, Charles. *Call Me Ishmael*. New York: Reynal & Hitchcock, 1947.
‑‑‑‑‑‑. *Human Universe and other Essays*. New York: Grove, 1967.
‑‑‑‑‑‑. *Letters to Origin*, edited by Albert Glover. New York: Grossman, 1969.
Pound, Ezra. *A Lume Spento*. Venice, 1908. Reissued by New Directions, 1965.
‑‑‑‑‑‑. *Guide to Kulchur*. Norfolk, Connecticut: New Directions, 1938.
‑‑‑‑‑‑. *Letters to Ezra Pound, 1907–1941*, edited by D. D. Paige. New York: Harcourt Brace, 1950.
‑‑‑‑‑‑. *Literary Essays*. New York: New Directions, 1968.
‑‑‑‑‑‑. *Selected Prose 1909–1965*, edited by William Cookson. New York: New Directions, 1973.
Ray, Gordon, and Edel, Leon, editors. *Henry James & H. G. Wells* (letters). Urbana, Illinois: University of Illinois Press, 1958.
Shapiro, Karl. *In Defense of Ignorance*. New York: Random House, 1960.
Stevens, Wallace. *Letters of Wallace Stevens*, edited by Holly Stevens. New York: Knopf, 1968.
Stravinsky, Igor. *Stravinsky: An Autobiography*. New York: Norton, 1936.
Sypher, Wylie. *Loss of Self in Modern Literature and Art*. New York: Random House, 1962.
‑‑‑‑‑‑. *Rococo to Cubism in Art and Literature*. New York: Random House, 1960.
Todd, Ruthven. *Tracks in the Snow: Studies in English, Science and Art*. New York: Scribners, 1947.

Winters, Yvor. *In Defense of Reason*. Chicago: Swallow, 1947.
———. *Uncollected Essays & Reviews*. Chicago: Swallow, 1973.
Witemeyer, Hugh. *The Poetry of Ezra Pound: Forms and Renewal, 1908–1920*. Berkeley: University of California Press, 1969.

Anthologies with Relevant Biographical or Critical Material

Allen, Donald, ed. *The New American Poetry*. New York: Grove, 1960.
Anderson, Margaret, ed. *Little Review Anthology*. New York: Hermitage House, 1953.
Cowley, Malcolm, ed. *Writers at Work, 3rd Series*. New York: Viking, 1967.
Elledge, Scott, ed. *Eighteenth Century Critical Essays*. Ithaca: Cornell, 1961.
Halpert, Stephen and Johns, Richard, eds. *A Return to Pagany: The History, Correspondence, and Selections from a Little Magazine*. Boston: Beacon Press, 1969.
Hindus, Milton, ed. *Leaves of Grass One Hundred Years After*. Stanford: Stanford University Press, 1955.
Hunt, John Dixon, ed. *Artists on Art*. New York: Norton, 1971.
North, Joseph, ed. *New Masses Anthology*. New York: International Publishers, 1969.
Read, Herbert, ed. *Speculations: Essays on Humanism and the Philosophy of Art*. New York: Humanities Press, 1936.

Chief Periodicals Dealt with

(WCW's chief editorial contact in parentheses when applicable)

Blast (London, Pound), *Blast* (New York, Fred Miller), *Blues* (Parker Tyler), *Broom* (Alfred Kreymborg), *Camera Work* (Alfred Stieglitz), *Dial* (Marianne Moore), *Egoist* (Pound), *Little Review* (Margaret Anderson), *Kenyon Review* (John Crowe Ransom), *Massachusetts Review, New English Weekly* (Orage), *New Freewoman* (Pound and Dora Marsden), *New Masses* (Jack Conroy), *Origin* (Cid Corman), *Pagany* (Richard Johns), *Poetry* (Harriet Monroe), *Poetry Review* (Pound), *Partisan Review, New Leader, transition* (Pound), *Sewanee Review* (Allen Tate), *Others* (Alfred Kreymborg), *Contact* (Robert McAlmon).

Index